Anti-social Behaviour in Britain

Anti-social Behaviour in Britain

Victorian and Contemporary Perspectives

Edited by

Sarah Pickard
Senior Lecturer, Université Sorbonne Nouvelle, France

First published 2014 by
PALGRAVE MACMILLAN

Palgrave Macmillan in the UK is an imprint of Macmillan Publishers Limited,
registered in England, company number 785998, of Houndmills, Basingstoke,
Hampshire RG21 6XS.

Palgrave Macmillan in the US is a division of St Martin's Press LLC,
175 Fifth Avenue, New York, NY 10010.

Palgrave Macmillan is the global academic imprint of the above companies
and has companies and representatives throughout the world.

Palgrave® and Macmillan® are registered trademarks in the United States,
the United Kingdom, Europe and other countries.

ISBN 978–1–137–39930–4

This book is printed on paper suitable for recycling and made from fully
managed and sustained forest sources. Logging, pulping and manufacturing
processes are expected to conform to the environmental regulations of the
country of origin.

A catalogue record for this book is available from the British Library.

Library of Congress Cataloging-in-Publication Data
Anti-social behaviour in Britain : Victorian and contemporary perspectives /
    edited by Sarah Pickard, Senior Lecturer, Université Sorbonne
    Nouvelle, France.
        pages   cm
    ISBN 978–1–137–39930–4 (hardback)
    1. Disorderly conduct—Great Britain—History.   2. Disorderly
    conduct—Law and legislation—Great Britain—History.   3. Juvenile
    delinquency—Great Britain—History.   4. Juvenile delinquency—
    Prevention—Great Britain—History.   I. Pickard, Sarah,
    editor of compilation.
    HV6491.G7A58 2014
    364.1′430941—dc23   2014021121

Contents

Part III   Anti-social Behaviour, Recreation and Leisure

Acknowledgements

I would like to thank all the contributors for being so accommodating and enthusiastic.

I am indebted to Aurélie Baudry-Palmer, Emma Bell, David Fée and John Mullen who participated in a workshop on anti-social behaviour I organized in Paris some time ago – their inspiring involvement triggered the idea for this book.

Thanks also go to Julia Willan and Harriet Barker at Palgrave Macmillan for giving me valuable help and advice, along with the anonymous peer reviewers.

Christopher Cavey, Lee Phillips and Sebastian Lopez deserve special thanks for their helpful comments during the preparation process.

Lastly, I am grateful to students on my Youth Policy in Britain course at the Sorbonne Nouvelle University whose imagination and zeal provided me with vital food for thought.

Sarah Pickard

Contributors

Constance Bantman is a Lecturer at the University of Surrey. Her research focuses on the history of the anarchist movement and trade unions in France and Britain up to 1914, as well as transnational history and international networks.

Aurélie Baudry-Palmer is a researcher with a PhD thesis on class and social relations in Victorian Bristol. Her research interests include nineteenth-century history, philanthropy, labour history, popular culture, friendly societies, and religious history.

Anne Beauvallet is a Senior Lecturer in British Studies at the Université Toulouse-Le Mirail and she belongs to its research group (Cultures Anglo-Saxonnes). She has published several papers on British education policies.

Emma Bell is a Senior Lecturer at the Université de Savoie where she teaches British History and Politics. She is the author of *Criminal Justice and Neoliberalism* and current coordinator of the European Group for the Study of Deviance and Social Control.

Shane Blackman is Professor of Cultural Studies at Canterbury Christchurch University; he has conducted research into sociological and ethnographic aspects of young people's culture. His most recent book is *Chilling Out: The Cultural Politics of Substance Consumption, Youth and Drug Policy*.

Sue Bond-Taylor is a Senior Lecturer in Criminology in the School of Social and Political Sciences at the University of Lincoln. Her research focuses on youth crime prevention, anti-social behaviour, family interventions and 'troubled' families.

Colin Clark is Professor of Sociology and Social Policy at the University of the West of Scotland (UWS). His principle research interests lie within the broad field of ethnic and racial studies, with a particular concern for migration, Romani Studies, multiculturalism and intersectionality.

Neil Davie is Professor of British History at the Université Lumière Lyon 2. He has published widely on penal policy and criminology in the Victorian and Edwardian periods. He is the author of *Tracing the Criminal: The Rise of Scientific Criminology in Britain, 1860–1918*.

John Flint is Professor and Head of the Town and Regional Planning Department at the University of Sheffield. The common theme to all his research is urban governance, citizenship and social justice, especially in relation to housing.

Sinéad Gormally is a Lecturer in Community and Youth Work at the University of Hull. Her research and practice interests are varied, but broadly centre on community development, youth work, youth justice, social justice, equality and rights-based work.

Jamie Harding is a Senior Lecturer in Research Methods in the Department of Social Sciences and Languages at Northumbria University. His research interests are primarily in housing and homelessness, higher education, criminal justice and racial inequality.

Trevor Harris is Professor of British Studies at the Université d'Amiens. His areas of research are the political and intellectual history of nineteenth- and twentieth-century Britain, especially the interaction between external policy and the evolution of national self-image.

Adele Irving is a Research Fellow in the Department of Social Sciences and Languages at Northumbria University. Her areas of research interest and experience include social exclusion, homelessness, welfare reform and youth offending.

Mark James is Professor of Laws at Northumbria University School of Law. He has published extensively on sports law issues, in particular football-related disorder and Olympic Law.

Craig Johnstone is Principal Lecturer in Criminology at the University of Brighton. His research is predominantly concerned with exclusion and social control in urban space.

Didier Lassalle is Professor of Contemporary British Studies at the Université de Paris-Est-Créteil (UPEC). His research is centred on social, economic and cultural integration of ethnic minorities.

Andrew Millie is Professor of Criminology and Director of the Criminology Research Group at Edge Hill University. His current research spans criminology, philosophy and human geography. He is author of *Anti-Social Behaviour*.

Christian Morgner is a Lecturer in International Communication at the University of Leicester. He has published on the process of global meaning-making, violence, and political communication, as well as global media and the globalization of arts and culture.

John Mullen is a Senior Lecturer at the Université de Paris-Est-Créteil (UPEC). His book on popular song in Britain during the Great War was published in Paris in 2012, and will be published in the UK in 2015.

David Nash is Professor of History at Oxford Brookes University. He has researched the issue of blasphemy for over 20 years and has written a number of articles and two monographs on the subject including *Blasphemy in the Christian World: A History*.

Geoff Pearson is the Director of the MBA (Football Industries) at the University of Liverpool Management School. He is an expert in social, legal and ethnographic analyses of football-related disorder.

Sarah Pickard is a Senior Lecturer in British Politics and Society at the Université Sorbonne Nouvelle. Her research area is contemporary Youth Studies focusing on the interaction between youth policy and youth politics.

Ryan Powell is Principal Research Fellow in the Centre for Regional Economic and Social Research at Sheffield Hallam University. He has diverse research interests across the broad areas of geographies of exclusion and urban sociology.

Emmanuel Roudaut is a Senior Lecturer in British Studies at the Institut d'Études Politiques (IEP) in Lille, France. His main field of research is the social and cultural history of late Victorian and twentieth-century Britain.

Peter Squires is Professor of Criminology and Public Policy at the University of Brighton. He has written extensively on the criminalization of marginality (via ASB, youth justice and gang strategy), he edited *ASBO Nation* and his most recent book is *Gun Crime in Global Contexts*.

Deborah Talbot is a Lecturer of Criminology at the Open University. She has two broad fields of research, the night-time economy and urban parenting. She is author of *Regulating the Night: Race, Culture and Exclusion in the Making of the Night-time Economy*.

Becky Taylor is a Lecturer in History at Birkbeck College, University of London. She specializes in twentieth-century social history, using archives and oral histories, examining the impact of state expansion and the welfare state on minority and marginal groups.

Stuart Waiton is a Lecturer in Sociology and Criminology at Abertay University and writer for a variety of newspapers. Author of *The Politics of Anti-social Behaviour: Amoral Panics*, his latest book is *Snobs' Law: Criminalising Football Fans in an Age of Intolerance*.

Andrew Wilson is a Senior Lecturer in Criminology, at Nottingham Trent University. He has researched anti-social behaviour and drug use for several projects. His most recent book is *Northern Soul: Music, Drugs and Subcultural Identity*.

An Vleugels teaches the History of Medicine at Birkbeck College, London. She is interested in the history of cultural meanings of medicine in Europe. Her book *Narratives of Drunkenness* explores the meanings of drunkenness in Belgium in the nineteenth century.

Abbreviations and Acronyms

ABC	Acceptable Behaviour Contract
ACPO	Association of Chief Police Officers
ADZ	Alcohol Disorder Zone
ASB	Anti-social Behaviour
ASBO	Anti-social Behaviour Order
BBC	British Broadcasting Corporation
BIBIC	British Institute for Brain-Injured Children
BIS	Department for Business, Innovation and Skills
BME	Black Minority Ethnic
BMJ	British Medical Journal
BRO	Bristol Record Office
CASE	Centre for Analysis of Social Exclusion
CBO	Criminal Behaviour Order
CCHQ	Conservative Party Campaign Headquarters
CCJS	Centre for Crime and Justice Studies
COS	Charity Organization Society
CPI	Crime Prevention Injunction
CRASBO	Criminal ASBO
CRB	Criminal Records Bureau
CRJ	Community Restorative Justice
CSJ	Centre for Social Justice
CSO	Community Safety Order
DCLG	Department for Communities and Local Government
DCMS	Department of Culture, Media and Sport
DCSF	Department for Children, Schools and Families
DfEE	Department for Education and Employment
DOE	Department of the Environment
EAN	Education Activist Network
EMA	Educational Maintenance Allowance
EU	European Union
EWS	Education Welfare Services
FBO	Football Banning Order
FIFA	Fédération Internationale de Football Association
FIP	Family Intervention Project
FIT	Forward Intelligence Team
GCSE	General Certificate of Secondary Education
HMIC	Her Majesty's Inspectorate of Constabulary
IPCC	Independent Police Complaints Commission
IPNA	Injunction to Prevent Nuisance or Annoyance

IRA	Irish Republican Army
ISO	Individual Support Order
ITMB	Irish Traveller Movement in Britain
LCC	London County Council
LEA	Local Education Authority
LSE	London School of Economics and Political Science
MJ	Ministry of Justice
MPS	Metropolitan Police Service
MUD	Moral Underclass Discourse
NAGL	National Anti-Gambling League
NAO	National Audit Office
NCAFC	National Campaign Against Fees and Cuts
NCIS	National Criminal Intelligence Service
NEET	Not in Education, Employment or Training
NPIA	National Policing Improvement Agency
NSIR	National Standard for Incident Recording
NUS	National Union of Students
NUT	National Union of Teachers
OBJT	Offences Brought to Justice Target
ODPM	Office of the Deputy Prime Minister
Offa	Office For Fair Access
Ofsted	Office for Standards in Education
ONS	Office for National Statistics
PbR	Payment by Results
PCSO	Police Community Support Officer
PND	Penalty Notice for Disorder
PP	Parliamentary Paper
PSNI	Police Service of Northern Ireland
RED	Redistributionist Discourse
RSPCA	Royal Society for the Protection of Animals
RTF	Respect Task Force
SEU	Social Exclusion Unit
SID	Social Integrationist Discourse
TES	*Times Educational Supplement*
TFP	Troubled Families Programme
TUC	Trades Union Congress
UCU	University and College Union
UEFA	Union of European Football Associations
UKDPC	UK Drug Policy Commission
ULU	University of London Union
UNODC	United Nations Office on Drugs and Crime
YJB	Youth Justice Board
YJS	Youth Justice System
YJT	Youth Justice Team

Introduction

Sarah Pickard

The Anti-social Behaviour, Crime and Policing Act 2014, introduced by the Conservative–Liberal Democrat coalition government, clearly demonstrates sustained political concern about anti-social behaviour (ASB) in Britain. This piece of legislation builds on the Anti-social Behaviour Act 2003 and the Crime and Disorder Act 1998, both passed by the Labour government led by Tony Blair. Over the past 20 years, anti-social behaviour has garnered considerable interest from all three main political parties and the legislative landscape pertaining to the control of it has been transformed. At the same time, anti-social behaviour has attracted substantial attention from the general public, practitioners and academics, as well as the media, particularly the tabloid press with its recent emphasis on 'Broken Britain'.

Yet anti-social behaviour is not a new phenomenon; in previous generations individuals and groups behaved anti-socially, but their behaviour was labelled differently: it was vulgar, immoral, or not respectable. Similarly, previous generations of governments legislated on deviancy and deviants in order to promote respectability and public order. The nineteenth century stands out regarding interest afforded by authorities on the control of the conduct of the population. Indeed, the Metropolitan Police Act 1829, introduced by the Conservative Prime Minister Robert Peel, created the first modern police force. Furthermore, the English criminal justice system was transformed during the Victorian era, and copious legislation, especially the Prison Act 1865 and the Prison Act 1877, increased state control and centralized management of the incarceration of the 'criminal class'.

A nebulous and tenuous term

Anti-social behaviour is a nebulous and some would say tenuous term. According to the Anti-social Behaviour, Crime and Policing Act 2014, it means:

(a) conduct that has caused, or is likely to cause, harassment, alarm or distress to any person,
(b) conduct capable of causing nuisance or annoyance to a person in relation to that person's occupation of residential premises, or

(c) conduct capable of causing housing-related nuisance or annoyance to any person (Anti-social Behaviour, Crime and Policing Act, 2014: 2).

The terms harassment, alarm and distress concerning ASB also featured in the Police Reform and Social Responsibility Act 2011, the Anti-social Behaviour Act 2003, the Crime and Disorder Act 1998 and the Public Disorder Act 1986. In these pieces of legislation, anti-social behaviour is defined in relation to its *impact*. Nonetheless, there was a key shift after the arrival of New Labour in government because the Crime and Disorder Act 1998 removed 'intent' from the meaning of anti-social that had featured in the Public Disorder Act 1986.[1] Thus, the legislative focal point shifted from a focus on *intent* to one on the *impact* of the behaviour. The Crime and Disorder Act 1998 also marked the advent of the term 'anti-social behaviour' in British legislation with the launch of Anti-social Behaviour Orders (ASBOs).

The National Standard for Incident Recording (NSIR) was introduced by the Home Office in 2007 for use by police forces. The 2011 version classified ASB into three new types. The first category is 'Personal': behaviour that is perceived to be deliberately targeted at an individual or group, or having an impact on an individual or group, rather than the community at large. It includes 'incidents that cause concern, stress, disquiet and/or irritation through to incidents which have a serious adverse impact on people's quality of life. At one extreme of the spectrum it includes minor annoyance; at the other end it could result in risk of harm, deterioration of health and disruption of mental or emotional well-being, resulting in an inability to carry out normal day to day activities through fear and intimidation' (Home Office, 2011a: 14). The second category is 'Nuisance': an act, condition, thing or person causing trouble, annoyance, inconvenience, offence or suffering to the local community in general, rather than to individual victims. It includes 'incidents where behaviour goes beyond the conventional bounds of acceptability and interferes with public interests including health, safety and quality of life' (Home Office, 2011a: 14). The third category is 'Environmental': behaviour that is not aimed at an individual or group, but targets the wider environment, for example public spaces and buildings. It thus deals with the interface between people and places. It includes 'incidents where individuals and groups have an impact on their surroundings including natural, built and social environments. This category is about encouraging reasonable behaviour whilst managing and protecting the various environments so that people can enjoy their own private spaces as well as shared or public spaces' (Home Office, 2011a: 15).

These broad impact categories are generalist in their language and do not specify concrete examples. For apparent clarity, the Metropolitan Police currently uses 13 qualifiers within these three categories: rowdy or inconsiderate behaviour, street drinking, noise, begging and vagrancy, prostitution-related activity, rowdy and nuisance neighbours, trespassing, littering and drugs paraphernalia, animal problems, vehicle abandonment (not stolen), vehicle nuisance and inappropriate use, nuisance calls and fireworks. Clearly, a number of these kinds of behaviour existed in the nineteenth century and would also have qualified as immoral or inappropriate behaviour. Indeed, in his lively description of late Victorian London, Geoffrey Pearson examines the public panic caused by 'disorderly behaviour, drunkenness, assaults on police, street robberies and fighting' (Pearson, 1983: 74).

A cross-disciplinary dialogue

This edited volume examines anti-social behaviour in Victorian and contemporary Britain in its diverse settings and populations, in order to establish whether there are parallels regarding anti-social behaviour and governmental responses. The chapters address two key debates. First, what constitutes anti-social behaviour among individuals or groups. Second, how and why governments attempted or attempt to deal with anti-social behaviour.

This volume aims for coherence and comprehensiveness in addressing these two key debates. The book brings together 30 academics in History, Criminology, Sociology, Politics, Social Policy and Law whose 25 chapters complement and build on each other to provide a multi-disciplinary and wide-ranging treatment of the subject of anti-social behaviour. Special attention has been given to enable a comparison of similar subjects from the Victorian era and the contemporary period. This is achieved by including either a comparative chapter or more than one chapter dealing with a similar subject but in different periods. Thus, some chapters focus on the Victorian period, others on the contemporary period, while many chapters are comparative. In this way, this book seeks to provide a robust historical contextualization of contemporary anti-social behaviour and social control, by putting into perspective anti-social behaviour and reversing the academic tendency to narrow down. Its wide scope creates a useful cross-disciplinary dialogue providing 'the long view' for historians and the genealogy for scholars of the current period.

A comprehensive comparison of anti-social behaviour

The first part of the book is titled 'Anti-social Behaviour, the Urban Environment and Public Spaces'. The initial chapters explore behaviour in towns and cities during the Victorian era. Neil Davie examines debates on public 'incivility' and 'rowdyism', considering reactions on the ground from local elites and the police regarding the surveillance and control of public spaces. Trevor Harris then analyses how intellectuals and politicians in the late Victorian period grappled with the problem of anti-social behaviour, seeing it as a symptom of Britain's faltering rank in the world. Next, Craig Johnstone compares the increasing intolerance and tighter regulation of public and street activities during the mid-nineteenth century with the more recent attempts of New Labour to curb anti-social behaviour. The conceptualization and governance of anti-social behaviour in cities during the Victorian and contemporary periods are then explored by John Flint and Ryan Powell, using the sociology of Norbert Elias and his theory of the civilizing process. The following three chapters observe the policing of incivility during the two periods under scrutiny. David Nash studies the evolution of policing and blasphemy with the control of public blasphemy through the 'long nineteenth century' in relation to its contemporary manifestations. Constance Bantman presents the political and economic context from which the Anarchist movement emerged, and the modalities of anti-social behaviour in urban areas with which anarchists came to be associated in public opinion. Then Sarah Pickard continues with a discussion of the subjectivity of anti-social behaviour and public disorder in relation to protestors and the police during recent student protests. Afterwards, Christian Morgner continues with a theoretical analysis of social meaning-making of the anti-social as regards the 2011 London 'riots'. The last chapter draws on philosophical, criminological and other writings to unpick how influences on aesthetic taste in the urban environment shape what is perceived to be anti-social and it is written by Andrew Millie.

Part II is entitled 'Anti-social Behaviour, the Vulnerable and the Marginalized'. It examines how the social control of anti-social behaviour has been centred on certain types of people, especially the young who have frequently been accused of being the main protagonists of anti-social behaviour and they have been the focus of governmental attempts to control it. First, Aurélie Baudry-Palmer discusses the efforts to address juvenile anti-social behaviour in Victorian England by Mary Carpenter and her Reformatory schools. The theme of schooling continues in Anne Beauvallet's comparative chapter on truancy in the late Victorian era and under New Labour. Sue Bond-Taylor then analyses the politics of 'anti-social' behaviour within the Conservative–Liberal Democrat Coalition's new Troubled Families Programme. Next Jamie Harding and Adele Irving discuss the vulnerable homeless in relation to anti-social behaviour. Afterwards Colin Clark and Becky Taylor compare the social construction of Gypsies and Travellers as perpetrators of 'anti-social' behaviour in Britain during Victorian and contemporary Britain. Analysis next moves to the specific complexities, contradictions and consequences of being young in Northern Ireland in the chapter by Sinéad Gormally. Next Didier Lassalle clarifies the relationship between anti-social behaviour and 'underclass' discourse in contemporary Britain. This is followed by an analysis by Stuart Waiton discussing the transformation of the liberal subject into a newly conceptualized vulnerable individual held responsible for crime by an insecure elite. Peter Squires then explores how anti-social behaviour management forms part of a wider project of neo-liberal 'cultural governance' targeting the poorest and most marginal, that is to say the young, by dismantling 'welfare' and discrediting those most reliant upon it. Emma Bell's chapter closes Part II by considering the anti-sociality of anti-social behaviour policy.

The last part of the book is 'Anti-social Behaviour, Recreation and Leisure'. It deals with how Victorian governments tried to reduce the 'unrespectable' and 'immoral' pleasures of the working class in various settings, and how recent governments have attempted to control activities associated with the British 'Broken Society'. Conflicting representations of 'disreputable behaviour' on the Victorian racecourse and the interaction of moral panics with class demarcation and commercial interests are first discussed by Emmanuel Roudaut. Then John Mullen analyses the Music Hall in relation to the social effect of the concern for respectability and he debates how Victorian authorities attempted to ensure it triumphed over the 'vulgar' and the 'common'. An Vleugels explores Victorian drunkenness and how an understanding of anti-social drinking as a vice that mostly affected the working classes was complemented by a new interpretation of anti-social drinking as a disease, which led to the Habitual Drunkards Act. The relationship between the regulation of alcohol and 'alcohol-related disorder' in the past and today to the broader impact of economic, social and cultural influences on nightlife is then studied by Deborah Talbot. Shane Blackman and Andrew Wilson analyse how the conception of anti-social behaviour is merged with recreational drug use in order to signify a social problem group. The final chapter, by Mark James and Geoff Pearson, is on changing government priorities visible in the evolutionary regulation of anti-social behaviour and disorder among football spectators.

Each of the three parts of this volume focus thematically on a specific aspect of anti-social behaviour. By doing so, they address common tropes of anti-social behaviour among individuals and groups and governmental responses. The 25 chapters work together to coherently draw out answers through historical contextualization and an exploration of the relationship between the state and its peoples. The conclusion at the end of the book attempts to draw all the main themes and revelations together. It discusses whether there are clear parallels (and differences) in anti-social behaviour and policy responses. Thus, as a whole, this volume is more than simply the sum of its parts. By bringing together scholars from diverse fields with useful and up-to-date analyses of anti-social behaviour, it offers complementary and contrasting perspectives on something that was and remains a key sociological and political issue in Britain.

Note

1. Anti-social Behaviour Act 2003 (c. 38), Part 4 – Dispersal of groups.

    36 Interpretation

    'In this Part –

    "anti-social behaviour" means behaviour by a person which causes or is likely to cause harassment, alarm or distress to one or more other persons not of the same household as the person.'

    http://www.legislation.gov.uk/ukpga/2003/38/part/4/enacted

    Crime and Disorder Act 1998 (c. 37), Part 1 – Prevention of crime and disorder

    Chapter I England and Wales

    1. Anti-social behaviour orders.

    '(1) An application for an order under this section may be made by a relevant authority if it appears to the authority that the following conditions are fulfilled with respect to any person aged 10 or over, namely –

    (a) that the person has acted, since the commencement date, in an anti-social manner, that is to say, in a manner that caused or was likely to cause harassment, alarm or distress to one or more persons not of the same household as himself; and

    (b) that such an order is necessary to protect persons in the local government area in which the harassment, alarm or distress was caused or was likely to be caused from further anti-social acts by him;

    and in this section "relevant authority" means the council for the local government area or any chief officer of police any part of whose police area lies within that area.'

    http://www.legislation.gov.uk/ukpga/1998/37/selection/1/enacted

    Public Order Act 1986 (c. 64), Part 1 – New offenses

    5. Harassment, alarm or distress.

    '(1) A person is guilty of an offence if he –

    (a) uses threatening, abusive or insulting words or behaviour, or disorderly behaviour, or

    (b) displays any writing, sign or other visible representation which is threatening, abusive or insulting, within the hearing or sight of a person likely to be caused harrassment, alarm or distress thereby.'

    http://www.legislation.gov.uk/ukpga/1986/64/enacted

Part I

Anti-social Behaviour, the Urban Environment and Public Spaces

1
A Less than Polite People? Incivility, Ruffianism and Anti-Social Behaviour in Urban England, 1830–1900

Neil Davie

Introduction

During the period from the late eighteenth century to the middle of the nineteenth century, a wide range of behaviours, hitherto sanctioned or at least tolerated in British society, attracted widespread scrutiny, and in some cases, criticism. Some would subsequently become the targets of official intervention at the national or local levels. New laws were passed and bye-laws voted; existing legislation was resurrected or revised, while certain older statutes, no longer considered suited to the exigencies of the new century, were repealed or allowed to fall into abeyance. The reasons for these changes are complex. Earlier studies tended to highlight the key role played by a tight-knit group of London-based modernizers, reforming politicians, philanthropists and jurists, fired by that particularly British cocktail of Enlightenment philosophy and evangelical Christianity (Spierenburg, 2013: 281). More recent work has emphasized rather how new concepts of 'sensibility', 'humanity' and 'politeness', together with new attitudes to pain and suffering, mobilized a much broader swathe of elite opinion. In this context, successive campaigns to impose these new ideas have been seen as part of an attempt on the part of the emerging middle classes to recast the world in their image (Sharpe, 2000; McGowen, 2007).

In particular, it is suggested, vigorous efforts were made to 'civilize' the lower orders. A series of reform campaigns mounted by MPs, charities and moralists, and egged on by certain sections of the press, aimed at tackling previously tolerated forms of behaviour that might not be illegal as such (though something could perhaps be done about that, it was often pointed out), but which were now considered as socially corrosive and/or immoral. Thus, particular practices linked, for example, to popular sports and entertainments, sexual mores or street vending were widely blamed for being the direct or indirect cause of public disorder and immorality. Or, as modern parlance would have it, of *anti-social behaviour*.

3

By the end of the 1980s, a consensus had emerged among social historians, as Rosalind Crone has pointed out (2012: 2), that:

> a more disciplined and restrained society emerged during the early decades of the nineteenth century as change was imposed from the top downwards. New values and behaviour adopted by the higher classes slowly trickled down, influencing the lifestyles of those below. In addition, public order necessary for economic progress was enforced by new structures of authority and the extension of the law. Thus, by the Victorian period, society had been largely 'tamed'.

This paradigm, drawing on Michel Foucault's pioneering work from the late 1960s and 1970s, as well as a parallel interest in the concept of social control, has tended to present efforts to regulate plebeian behaviour as part of a more or less hidden agenda (though not of course hidden to historians) on the part of the country's ruling elite to create an obedient, subservient workforce of the kind needed for the emerging capitalist economy, with the 'new' police given a pivotal role (Forsythe, 1995; Spierenburg, 2004; Lawrence, 2004: 210–11). It would be naïve to suggest that the discipline and control of the lower orders did not enter into the equation, but as Martin Wiener has noted, there is a danger here of replacing a one-dimensional, Whiggish account of criminal justice reform (disinterested, forward-thinking humanists leading their reluctant countrymen into the modern age) with an equally simplistic one invoking the inexorable forward march of top-down surveillance and control, masterminded by an omniscient 'policeman-state' (Wiener, 1990: 8; Gatrell, 1990). In this latter account, the only possible outcome seems to be a society rendered ever more 'docile' in Foucault's terms by the unchallenged – and indeed unchallengeable – disciplinary machinery put in place in the Victorian period via such institutions as the police, the prison and the workhouse (Foucault, 1977; 1980).

This chapter argues that the assault on disorderly and immoral behaviour in Victorian England was real enough, but less pervasive, less effective and, crucially, less socially exclusive, than the foregoing account may imply. In order to impose new standards of public order and civility, the efforts of reformers, whether in Parliament, the press or among those self-appointed guardians of the nation's morals who gathered in the country's charities and pressure groups, were aimed not only at 'disorderly' elements within the working class, but also at insufficiently zealous public servants and more generally at those within the middle and upper ranks of society felt not to be setting a good example. Indeed, in certain contexts and at certain periods, such elite wrongdoers were singled out for particularly vehement condemnation and vigorous action.

Attention will be focused principally on the regulation of disorderly public conduct in England's larger towns and cities during the 70-year period from 1830 to 1900. It is important to be clear exactly what kinds of behaviour

I am talking about here. There is a danger that the 'anti-social behaviour' tag with its modern legislative manifestations and media-fed associations with working-class loutism (what the Victorians would have called 'ruffianism' or 'rowdyism'), may function to restrict attention to certain kinds of public behaviour in the past, while leaving others largely unexplored. It is not just a question of recognizing that loutish behaviour then as now was not the prerogative of the working class – the mid-Victorian radical press gleefully hunted down examples of 'aristocratic rowdyism' and provided readers with a (sometimes literally) blow-by-blow account of blue-blooded misdemeanours – but of broadening our focus to encompass a category of other attitudes and behaviours which prompted moral censure for reasons which do not relate to violent crime in the sense the law understood the term (see Sindall, 1990: 9–10).

The foregoing remarks are not intended to minimize the impact of socially discriminatory official intervention in this area. On the ground, the Victorian police customarily interpreted flexible legal terms like 'disorderly conduct', 'obstruction', 'breach of the peace' or the marvellously imprecise 'loitering with intent' in ways which meant that surveillance and intervention fell disproportionately on working-class commercial and leisure activities, as well as crime (Storch, 1976). Indeed, as Victor Gatrell (1990: 271) points out, 'Poorer law-breakers were the only ones the [Victorian] policeman could usually see, or was inclined to see'. The reasons for this tunnel vision are various, and cannot be explored in detail here, but the important point for us is that while the Victorian policeman's eyes may have been 'usually' blind to infractions committed by anyone other than those he associated with the 'criminal class', there were other eyes abroad. Moreover, the gaze of those other eyes was not confined, or at least not entirely confined, to the inhabitants of the rookeries, the back-alleys and low courts of the Victorian city. Usual suspects there might have been, but suspicion evidently did not stop there.

To understand the range of passions unleashed by 'inappropriate' public behaviour in urban England in the nineteenth century, it will be argued in this chapter that it is crucial to have a clear idea about just how respectable Victorians were expected to behave on the city streets. This means drawing on a body of historical research which has hitherto been little concerned with crime, and at the same time drawing on sources that have generally been of little interest to historians of crime. In short, to understand attitudes to incivility, we need to know about civility, which means knowing about manners, and even about etiquette.

Reading the face in the crowd

The history of elite attitudes to violence and disorder in the last two centuries has been described by Geoffrey Pearson, an early researcher in the field, as 'a seamless tapestry of fears and complaints about the deteriorated present';

and 'each era has been sure of the truthfulness of its claim that things were getting steadily worse and equally confident in the tranquillity of the past' (Pearson, 1983: 207, 209–10). However, to observe the perennity of hand-wringing appeals to a golden age of public order and harmonious social relations, though a valid enough point, can only take us so far. It does not explain why particular forms of behaviour came under scrutiny at particular historical moments, nor why certain solutions among the range on offer were put forward, rather than others. To explore such issues, what is needed, as John Carter Wood has argued (2004: 15), is a recognition that 'attitudes towards violence are inextricably connected to issues of identity, class hierarchy, institutional development, codes of behaviour, views of recreation, the nature of public and private spaces, and societal arrangements'. Once we begin to examine such factors, Pearson's 'seamless tapestry' begins to unravel somewhat.

It is no accident that a veritable deluge of books and articles on etiquette and manners accompanied the emergence of a self-conscious and self-confident urban middle class in Britain in the first third of the nineteenth century. As historian John Kasson observes, much more was at stake here than how best to eat asparagus. It was about establishing and maintaining standards of order and authority in a restless, highly mobile, rapidly urbanizing society (Kasson, 1990: 62). Apart from the sheer scale of production in these years – an indication of a flourishing market among middle-class readers – what is also striking is the broadening scope of the advice on offer (Morgan, 1994; Nead, 2000: 72–3). Guidance on entertaining and visiting continued to take centre stage, but chapters on 'street manners' began to make their appearance, offering readers advice on how to behave in the new public spaces of the industrial town. With the small-scale, face-to-face society a thing of the past, at least for inhabitants of the larger Victorian towns and cities, there arose the question of how, as it were, to manage anonymity; what rules to observe with strangers whose precise social position, not to mention their intentions, were often frustratingly opaque (Sennett, 1977).

Some turned to phrenology in these years, reassured by the apparent ability of this 'infallible oracle' as one enthusiast called it, to take the risk out of vetting a servant, a tradesman or a future son-in-law (Lundie, 1844; see Cooter, 1984). Others pored over conduct books, which purported to explain how the minutest detail of a stranger's appearance – a polished coat button perhaps, or an untrimmed moustache – was sufficient to 'read the illegible man of the crowd' (Kasson, 1990: ch.3; Sennett, 1977: 161–8). But would this social radar be sufficient? Should it, for example, have alerted William Corder's new metropolitan wife to her husband's sinister provincial past in the months leading up to his arrest in 1828? Much was made at the time of the scene of bourgeois domestic bliss which greeted the arresting officers when they arrived at the Corder home, with the dressing-gown-clad Red Barn murderer busy boiling an egg for his newly pregnant wife

(Pedley, 2004: 35). Could there be other William Corders leading apparently respectable lives, hidden in plain sight amid the teeming millions of the Victorian city? The question did not bear thinking about.

Civility and incivility

Whatever their efficacy for the identification of potential murderers, street manners were considered of vital importance for those unaccompanied, respectable women who were now a 'routine presence' on the streets of the Victorian city (Nead, 2000: 62–7). Women were warned that they would inevitably be exposed, as one 1884 article put it, 'to the observation and coarser comments of a mixed crowd of spectators' when out of doors (Caulfield, 1884). Another authority warned its female readership to 'avoid contact in trams and omnibuses as far as possible with her neighbours, and not lean up against them or behave with disagreeable familiarity'. However, it was made clear that any olfactory 'aversion' which readers might feel towards their neighbours and surroundings while travelling should be tactfully concealed, so as not to cause offence (*Hearth and Home*, 1897).

The emphasis, then, was on self-restraint, tact and discretion, even self-effacement, in public, and not just for women (Davetian, 2009: 169–74; Kasson, 1990: ch.4). Men were regularly advised to 'cultivate the glorious power of Bearing in Silence' and reminded that 'politeness is the art of disguising our feelings and passions' (*Chambers'*, 1853: 290; *London Society*, 1864: 397). Spontaneous outbursts of emotion and passion were to be regarded with the utmost suspicion and avoided at all costs (Wiener, 1990: 11; Wood, 2004: 31). As if to ram the point home, frequent references were made to the unbridled 'sensuality' and 'savagery' of 'the lowest portion of the labouring classes', that 'race of barbarians, ignorant alike of their duty to God and man, and stimulating the most ferocious passions by the most brutal excesses' (*Leicester Chronicle*, 1852). For those considered by birth or education to be free of such base instincts, 'civility' was vaunted as the key to meaningful social relationships, including that between man and wife. It promised, moreover, to oil the wheels of business and held out the prospect of prosperity, even conquest and power, to those who embraced it (*Manchester Times*, 1893; *Reynold's Miscellany*, 1855: 359). While some accepted the need for artifice in one's public dealings with others, many were at pains to point out that, on the contrary, the 'mere politesse' of earlier etiquette manuals was insufficient (Nichols, 1873: 68; *Eclectic Review*, 1860: 293. See Morgan, 1994: 120–31). Conduct was increasingly expected to 'proceed from an inner fount of humanity and honour' (*Blackwood's*, 1861: 164). Indeed, to behave otherwise was a sign of barbarism. As an 1866 article from the penny weekly *Bow Bells*, entitled 'Etiquette for Gentlemen', put it, 'No man has a right to consider himself entitled, as a unit in the millions which constitute a society, to act entirely for himself and by himself.

[... T]here must be certain laws and regulations to keep us in order and promote our civilization' (*Bow Bells*, 1866: 330). In this way, the public space of the Victorian city could be rendered more harmonious and predictable, and thereby less threatening (Morgan, 1994: 97).

It was clear to many observers, however, that the 'laws and regulations' intended to promote such harmonious co-existence were being honoured more in the breach than the observance on the streets of Britain's towns and cities; a state of affairs which called into question the 'civilized' status of Victorian urban existence (Croll, 1999: 252). The following extract from an 1890 article by Cornish Congregational minister J.F. Hooper reveals the kind of petty incivilities which attracted repeated comment, and is worth quoting at some length:

> Street Etiquette.– Some people would narrow it down to the graceful lifting of the hat and the cordial handshake and the sang froid greeting to the passing acquaintance, but it is much more comprehensive than this. To-day in my walk to Malpas I overtook a group of young misses, well-dressed and of comely appearance, but they talked loud, and as I passed them they broke into a silly gigle [*sic*]. There was a suggestion of rudeness and loudness, unbecoming in girls who evidently came from the respectable homes of Truro. Again, the side-walks of our small city are narrow and it is often necessary for groups to spring out and proceed tandem fashion. We cannot always walk four abreast without shoving some people in the gutter. I have felt rude thrusts of men's elbows several times since I have been in Truro and my lady friends have been subject to similar jostling. This needless dash is not confined to men alone [...] Not long ago, a young man well-dressed and wearing a tidy moustache, met a young lady and with becoming ease and grace, he raised his hat and beamed a most gracious and expansive smile, – adjusting the muscles of his face, he leaned forward and expectorated on the side-walk. Ah! well, I thought, you have pretty wings, but you are a foul bird nevertheless. (Hooper, 1890)

Giggling, jostling, elbowing and spitting. Clearly, 'respectable' young women – a favourite target of the anonymous 'disciplinary gaze' in the letter pages of Victorian newspapers (Croll, 1999: 263) – could not be relied upon to behave with decorum on the sidewalk. Neither was the possession of a 'tidy moustache' a guarantee of refined conduct, whatever the etiquette manuals might say. This was a deeply troubling state of affairs, for it confounded a firmly-held Victorian belief in behavioural consistency; that the roughs were always rough, and the respectables always respectable (Croll and Johnes, 2004: 154). This helps explain why wrongdoing, which might appear trivial to the modern eye, could provoke such ire in certain sections of the Victorian middle class; whether it be monopolizing the pavement with a 'perambulator' for example, wearing a wide-brimmed 'tea-tray' hat or simply 'standing on the footpath gossiping'. In each of these cases, it was made clear that culprits included those from the refined classes, who, it was implied, should have known better (*Morning Post*, 1856; *Cheshire Observer*, 1860). Clearly, what Wood terms the 'shadow of middle-class refinement' (2004: 21) was not limited to the 'savagery' and 'brutality' of certain sections of the working class (Davetian, 2009: 206–7).

'Social rowdyism'

Unsurprisingly perhaps, particular opprobrium was heaped on the actions of those above the middle class in the social hierarchy, and on those struggling to join it from below. This took many forms. It included, as I have noted, often politically-charged criticism of aristocratic 'rowdyism' or 'ruffianism'; of that class's alleged penchant for pugilism and gambling, together with disapproving reports of the exploits of rowdy students, drunken lords and boorish army officers (*Reynold's Newspaper*, 1851a, 1851b, 1859, 1869; *Bradford Observer*, 1871; *Sheffield & Rotherham Independent*, 1878; *Pall Mall Gazette*, 1882; *The Era*, 1884; *Daily News*, 1887). There were also concerns expressed from the 1870s onwards about lower-middle-class encroachment on traditional middle-class preserves, notably in the field of leisure; part of a broader concern with a perceived 'moral vulnerability' among those aspiring to respectability from below (Bailey, 1998: 26–9; Roberts, 2004: 148).

An episode on Folkestone Pier in 1877 provides a case in point. According to a report in the *Saturday Review*, a crowd composed of 'a certain class of well-to-do' took to jeering at a group of sea-sick passengers disembarking from a cross-Channel steamer; the former 'amus[ing] themselves in a very low and disreputable manner'. The article went on to list other manifestations of what it called 'social rowdyism', including river-hogging steam-launches and punts, together with 'reckless' cyclists, accused of 'coming along in the dark without a light or bells' or riding several abreast, 'frightening and scattering everybody before them' (*Saturday Review*, 1877; *The Times*, 1877). Lower-middle-class rowdyism was also the subject of a letter addressed to *Reynold's Newspaper* in 1900 following celebrations in the capital to mark the relief of Mafeking. Those at fault, described significantly as 'London clerks and counterjumpers', were clearly not felt to have respected middle-class standards of public refinement. Their unacceptable behaviour reportedly included 'embracing', 'squealing' and 'staring with a vacant expression of incipient idiocy' (*Reynold's Newspaper*, 1900).

Only rarely was it openly admitted that representatives of mainstream middle-class culture were capable of such disorderly behaviour. One such case, studied by historian John Pinfold, was that of James Maybrick, a prominent Liverpool cotton merchant, who died in suspicious circumstances in 1889. Poisoning was suspected, and his American wife Florence was charged with, and subsequently convicted of, his murder. In the trial, the unorthodox lifestyle of the couple, which included lovers, drugs and racecourse gambling, came under the microscope, and was widely reported in both the local and national press (Pinfold, 2004: 74–8. See also Knelman, 1998: 118–20). In reality, certain elements at least of that lifestyle were relatively commonplace in Liverpool's business community in the late Victorian period. Indeed, as far as horse racing is concerned, Pinfold argues that many, perhaps a majority, of Liverpool's middle class were involved as owners, spectators and, especially, as punters. In fact, the city's racecourses enjoyed a *de facto* special status in this period. By common consent, normal rules of middle-class respectability were effectively suspended, and drunkenness, prostitution, pugilism, cock-fighting and, most controversially of all, gambling, were tolerated. Pinfold notes that Liverpool's close-knit business community generally made sure that any misdemeanours that did occur on or around the racecourse did not become public knowledge. In Maybrick's case, such damage control was of course out of the question (64–6).

What the Maybrick case reveals is something that was sometimes lost in the early work on policing and the reform of popular culture, namely the heterogeneous character of middle-class culture in nineteenth-century England. My earlier point about the tendency of many Victorians to divide their compatriots into two hermetic categories of the 'respectable' and 'rough' should not blind us to the fact that not everyone drew the boundaries in quite the same way. The result was that there was consensus among middling groups neither on the nature of the problem of street disorder, nor on the solutions to be adopted. I shall examine this heterogeneity in more detail presently, but first of all it needs to be emphasized that for all the variation there seem to have been certain constants. Throughout the Victorian period and throughout urban Britain, there was what has been termed a 'feverish' level of interest in news relating to crime and violence (Wood, 2004: 18, 30). Indeed, as Croll and Johnes argue, an obsession with viciousness and barbarism was in fact crucial to the construction of middle-class identity in Victorian England:

> The diligent study of the degraded and the demoralised became a necessary activity in a world in which maintenance of character and reputation was everything. After all, only by regularly confronting the vicious in all its terrible glory could self-confessed respectables remind themselves that they were indeed located on the right side of the sometimes wafer-thin line. (Croll and Johnes, 2004: 162)

This made Britain, or at least large swathes of its middling sort, into 'connoisseurs of the disreputable [...] endlessly on the look-out for viciousness and barbarism' (170–1). For the most part, that search took them to the pages of the growing number of local and regional newspapers, and to the 'police court' pages in particular. A minority also contributed directly to that discourse via the medium of the letters page. Contributions were usually anonymous, or signed with a Latin nom de plume or other assumed name, which left readers in no doubt that the correspondent stood squarely on the respectable side of the cultural divide (Croll, 1999: 262). In this respect, newspapers were both the principal source of information about crime for most middle-class Victorians (Sindall, 1990: ch.3), and a powerful means of applying pressure on local officials and police to react in particular ways to a perceived threat to law and order. The press was thus what Croll calls a 'piece of civilising technology [... whereby] all urbanites were placed under its watchful eye whether they were holders of public office or the lowliest of public drunks' (Croll, 1997: 3–4).

Policing incivility

Theirs were not the only eyes on the Victorian street of course. Pioneering research by historian Robert D. Storch (1975; 1976) established the idea of the Victorian police as 'domestic missionaries', working in tandem with local politicians, religious and charity groups to push for the moral improvement of the working class. As the state gave the police new statutory powers over such morally-sensitive activities as drinking, gambling and prostitution, the neighbourhood bobby acquired the potential to become 'the eyes and ears of ruling elites at the very centers of working-class daily life'; his truncheon (even when sheathed) 'the other side of the coin of middle-class voluntaristic moral and social reform' (Storch, 1976: 496, 481; Taylor, 1997: 91). While more recent research has tended to confirm Storch's basic thesis, adding detail and nuance from a series of local studies (for example, Philips and Storch, 1999; Taylor, 2002), the picture emerging with regard to urban disorder is complicated by two factors. First, as we have seen, censure was by no means reserved for working-class rowdyism. The other point is that while historians of policing understandably focus on those aspects of violent and disorderly conduct which incurred legal sanction, there existed a whole range of behaviours that were either unambiguously beyond police control – like 'the irregular manner in which people walk along the streets and rows; some going on one side, and some on the other; some going fast and others slow' (*Cheshire Observer*, 1860) – or belonged to that grey area where everything depended on how councils, magistrates and police chiefs, as well as the beat officer, chose to interpret the law.

A good example of such a grey area was a staple of press coverage and complaint from the 1840s onwards: the rowdyism associated with the presence of groups of youths and young adults of both sexes congregating in the streets, notably on Sundays. Many of the reports follow the same pattern: respectable passers-by (perhaps on their way to or from church or chapel in the case of Sunday incidents) jostled and insulted, and forced off the pavement in order to continue on their way. Sometimes things would stop at that; sometimes clothes would be torn and hats knocked off or 'bonneted'; sometimes stones, snowballs, footballs or other projectiles would be thrown or kicked. Occasionally, as might be expected, things would degenerate still further, with blows exchanged or pockets picked, in which case police intervention often followed, perhaps with further violence.

Of particular interest in the context of this chapter are reactions to the less serious of the various scenarios indicated. I shall examine more closely a few cases, starting with one from the early part of the period. In October 1843, the *Sheffield & Rotherham Independent* printed a letter from 'A Burgess', addressed to his colleagues on Sheffield Borough Council. The letter, written a few months before the city's new police force was to pass under council control, began by referring to the fact that:

> It is notorious that the peaceable inhabitants of the town, particularly those resident in the northern and western portions thereof, have long been extremely annoyed, from six to nine o'clock every evening, by groups of youths of both sexes, who issuing from the numerous courts and yards, assemble in the streets, and by their noise, rudeness, profaneness, and obscenity, disturb whole neighbourhoods.

The anonymous correspondent goes on to urge his fellow burgesses to withhold their vote in the upcoming council elections from any candidate who will not 'distinctly pledge himself' to prevent the recurrence of such 'demoralising and disgraceful' behaviour on the streets of Sheffield; a clear indication of divisions within the council on the issue. Interestingly, the newspaper editor clearly sides with those council members favouring a less muscular policing policy, for he appended the following note to the foot of the letter: 'This is simply a matter of police which the more effective force that the Town Council will have the power to provide, may fully meet. Of course, we must not have police regulations so strict as to interfere needlessly with personal freedom' (*Sheffield & Rotherham Independent*, 1843).

The divisions in Sheffield in 1843 reflect a common situation in this period of embryonic professional law enforcement in Britain, where concerns about the consequences of both under- and over-zealous policing combined with political conflict over issues such as democratic control and cost. By the late nineteenth century, however, in middle-class circles at least, those early concerns had largely faded into the background (Taylor, 2002: 179–81). It is not surprising in this context that boosting police numbers (including by the recruitment of special constables) was a popular remedy in the late Victorian period among seemingly beleaguered middle-class communities when faced with street disorder, and that frustration was the result when evidence of apparent police impotence presented itself (Emsley, 1996: 70–1). Presumably statements like that of the Metropolitan Police Commissioner in 1869 that 'at best the Police can only make clean the outside of the platter; the improvement of the morals and manners of the people must be left to higher authorities' (cited in Lawrence, 2004: 221) did not help matters. There were always those of course who placed greater confidence in the dissuasive effect of the cat and a dose of hard labour than in the police (magistrates were regularly castigated for their 'squeamishness' and 'leniency' in this respect). For those disorder 'offences' where police intervention could not be relied on, there was also the possibility of bye-laws, or failing that, of patrols by vigilante committees. One such body was put in place in Islington's Upper Street in 1870 to deal with an 'intolerable' outbreak of rowdyism in the borough. While some marvelled ironically that private individuals were taking on tasks which the police were paid to do (*Punch*, 1870), there was clearly support in some quarters for seeing 'respectable inhabitants of the vicinity' administering 'a sound thrashing here and there with a stout cane' to the borough's roughs (*John Bull*, 1870).

An article from the *Saturday Review*, published some six months before the Islington initiative, gives a sense of the bleak mood in conservative circles at the time regarding law enforcement in the capital. It came hard on the heels of the Habitual Criminals Act 1869, itself a reflection of a growing conviction in official circles that existing police powers were proving inadequate for tackling the country's 'criminal class' of dangerous, often incorrigible, offenders (Davie, 2005). The author begins by noting police impotence in the face of street disorder in the capital, taking the example of recurring scenes of disorder on the recently constructed Embankment. Noting that 'the London rough is irrepressible by any methods which modern refinement suffers to be employed against him', the author proceeds to make an unfavourable comparison between the state of law and order in the capital and the situation in the provinces:

It is only in the centre of civilization, and amid a dense population of three millions, that society has almost returned to its primitive condition, in which men can find safety only in their own strength and women can find safety nowhere. It is only by the forbearance of the roughs that other open places in and near London have not become as inaccessible to respectable people as the Thames Embankment. Unless the police can catch these roughs, and the magistrates will punish them, it will begin to be truly said that the two most lawless places in Europe are Attica and the metropolis of London. (*Saturday Review*, 1870: 575)

However, while there was frequently a near consensus on the gravity of the crime problem, middle-class opinion was never confined to urging more punitive penal remedies or more muscular policing as the only solution to urban disorder. Different currents of opinion and a variety of moral reform movements jockeyed for position, each aiming to set agendas, and mobilize resources and supporters (Roberts, 2004: 281). While middle-class reformers were likely to share the same broad objectives as the police, they did not necessarily give priority to policing solutions. In the 1830s and 1840s, for example, a movement was launched to provide 'innocent and rational' – that is say, middle-class-approved – recreation for the working classes, a means of avoiding the perceived excesses of the pub and rowdy street-based sports and entertainments (*Liverpool Mercury*, 1843. See Bailey, 1978). The penny gaff was one of the popular forms of leisure under the spotlight, widely condemned in middle-class circles, as one Liverpool correspondent put it, for providing a 'rendezvous of wretched town arab[s], prostitutes and thieves, whose blasphemous and disgusting language is a disgrace to civilised society' (*Liverpool Mercury*, 1869).

The 'rational recreation' movement petered out in the face of widespread elite apathy and working-class suspicion. However, that did not stop certain sectors of liberal opinion from continuing to argue that the expansion of leisure amenities, along with wider social and educational reforms, were the best way of dealing with rowdyism. Universal elementary education was widely vaunted as offering a major opportunity, as one source put it, to 'soften and humanize the manners of the young' (Bridge, 1898: 314). Others remained sceptical. An 1890 editorial in the *Huddersfield Chronicle* began by noting the fact that:

> We have had our very expensive School Board for 20 years. We have had numberless other institutions – homes, reformatories, night schools, Christian institutes, and so forth – for all sorts of periods, longer and shorter. With all these, the Englishman has fair reason to expect that the youth of his country – the youth that is of the lower and lower middle classes – shall have improved in something more than in knowledge of practical geometry and the use of globes.

Had that been the case? Clearly not, in the opinion of the Huddersfield editorialist:

> nobody who has attempted to pass along a fairly well-frequented suburban street on Sunday evening can fail to be struck with what is certainly no improvement in either manners or the morals of the rising generation of our masters, the people. (*Huddersfield Chronicle*, 1890)

'The torment of street music'

However, middle-class peace and tranquillity were not only threatened by abuse and jostling at the hands of loutish roughs in the suburban street, worrying though such behaviour might be. A major concern was the level of street noise. Here too was an area where the precise boundary between crime and mere nuisance was hotly contested, and despite vigorous efforts in Parliament (including a law on the subject in 1864) and by a variety of pressure groups and press-based campaigns, the controversy rumbled on for over 50 years (Winter, 1993: 71–9). Middle-class sensibilities were increasingly intolerant of what one editorialist writing in 1880 described as 'the martyrdom of the senses through sights, smells, tastes, noises and crowding', associated with modern urban life (*Saturday Review*, 1880: 786). Certain of those assaults on the senses – like the 'unseemly' spectacle of 'bleeding and lacerated flesh' on public display in butchers and fishmongers, referred to by one anonymous correspondent (*Morning Post*, 1870) – were transient and could perhaps be avoided altogether with the right planning. This was not the case, however, with the music (though some contested that appellation) produced by barrel-organs, hurdy-gurdies, bagpipes and brass bands, or the shouts and cries of street vendors and hawkers. Here were noises capable of penetrating right into the sacrosanct domestic interior of the middle-class home.

I have noted the emphasis placed in middle-class culture of the period on self-reliance, discretion and mutual respect; the conviction that 'Life would not be tolerable in a city [...] if personal freedom were not tempered by a regard for the feelings of others' (*Saturday Review*, 1880: 786). This was the ideal of Richard Sennett's silent spectator, 'shielded by his right to be left alone'; only entering into social intercourse on terms of his own choosing (Sennett, 1977: 217). The aural overload emanating from London's streets seemed to drive a coach and horses through such worthy principles, and neither the solid brick walls nor the heavy drapes of the typical Victorian middle-class home seemed able to provide an effective barrier to 'the torment of street-music' with its 'combination of many abominable sounds striving for ascendancy' (*The Examiner*, 1858: 276).

A correspondent to *The Times*, signing herself 'A Suffering Woman', described how this 'external torture' could undermine the fundamentals of domestic life: family prayers were disrupted, children's lessons interrupted, and women's nerves shot to pieces. It was evidently to be expected that the 'small back streets and lanes' where the poor lived would be subject to high levels of noise. What was intolerable was that this ragtail army of 'Italian organ boys, German bands, bones, harpists, ballad singers, and Scotch fiddlers' was plying the streets of respectable suburbs. Not to mention those 'street loiterers, idle maid and men servants, waiters, and shopboys who profit[ed] by and encourage[d] this vagabond race' (*The Times*, 1857).

Conclusion: contested space

Two diametrically opposing conceptions of public space can be seen to confront each other here, a reflection of the fact that the urban physical environment then as now was perceived in culturally-structured ways, creating '"imagined spaces": notions of what being in particular spaces means, the actions that are appropriate within them and the ways the people make use of built space' (Wood, 2004: 105). Both sides agreed that 'the streets must be free for all legitimate purposes', as an 1863 article in *The Examiner* put it; the problem of course was defining just what those purposes should be. Street music was not without its champions within the upper and middle classes, convinced that it was the one of the few aspects of urban life that could be enjoyed by all. There was also considerable reluctance to interfere with what were regarded as the long-established rights of 'free-born Englishmen' to do what they pleased on the public highway (Winter, 1993: 9–11; 77).

However, such arguments cut no ice with supporters of regulation. As *The Examiner* put it bluntly, 'the streets are for traffic and communication [...] not for orchestras, or stages' (*The Examiner*, 1863: 466; Bass, 1864). Nor, it might be added, did reformers consider the streets the right place for commercial transactions – particularly when vendors interfered with the 'legitimate' operations of tradesmen and shopkeepers. In this sense, as Andy Croll points out, there was a 'hierarchy of space' in the Victorian town:

> There was general agreement among many 'civilized' urbanites that the 'main' streets of the town should be the safest of all. Indeed, the distinction between 'main', 'front' or 'principal' streets on the one hand, and the 'back' streets on the other, appears to have been one of the most significant of the imaginary spatial divisions invoked by inhabitants. (Croll, 1999: 256)

The imagined geography of Croll's 'civilized' urbanites came into conflict with an alternative, primarily working-class, conception of public space; one which saw 'the street' as the legitimate site for a variety of activities linked to work, consumption, leisure and sociability (Wood, 2007: 32). It was this perception that was likely to bring poorer street-users into conflict both with the alternative middle-class conceptions I have described and with the official machinery of law enforcement. The result was that the public lives of working-class districts were increasingly 'circumscribed, criminalised and subject to regular surveillance' (Taylor, 2002: 95). One of the chief causes of resentment was the way in which police disrupted what were regarded as legitimate street-traders, with its statutory power to 'move on' vendors like costermongers who were held to be causing an obstruction (Inwood, 1990: 134; Winter, 1993: 107–9). Street sports, games and fairs also came in for persistent attention from the 'blue locusts', as did working-class drinking and gambling, though the balance of political forces and the resources available, together with the priorities set by local magistrates and police chiefs, meant that the pace and reach of intervention varied considerably from place to place (Storch, 1976: 487–9; Taylor, 1997: 103–5, 115–18; Lawrence, 2004: 221–3).

Clearly though, a common factor was an important *geographical* component in the way in which anti-social behaviour – like crime – was perceived and interpreted (Williams, 2003: 106). Certain districts were considered 'naturally' rowdy and disorderly, and as noted earlier, likely to be the principal focus of police resources and surveillance. Up to a point, both police and many middle-class reformers were prepared to turn a blind eye to low-level disorder in working-class districts providing it did not lead to major disturbances or threats to property (Inwood, 1990; Emsley, 1996: 74–5). There were of course those prepared to go the extra mile both figuratively and literally in their eagerness to bring what they considered to be order and decorum to the Victorian town, and attempted to tackle this apparently endemic working-class rowdyism head-on. However, whether undertaken by moral reform groups or the police, the results of such initiatives were uneven. Apart from the logistical difficulties involved in policing activities like prostitution, illegal gambling and cock- and dog-fighting, which could easily change location or go underground, there were also, as we have seen, frequent divisions within elite opinion about just where public conduct stopped being merely 'social' and became 'anti-social': when a drunkard became a 'disorderly' drunkard, when legitimate street vending became 'obstruction' and when youthful high spirits became 'rowdyism'.

There is some evidence that public disorder was on the decline in late Victorian England, and that the police had won grudging toleration from those social groups who had borne the brunt of official surveillance and regulation (Gatrell, 1990: 290–1; Taylor, 1997: 124–7). This did not mean, however, that the issue of anti-social behaviour faded from view as the century drew to an end: on the contrary. Indeed, it has been argued that with overall levels of crime falling from the 1880s, those groups that appeared stubbornly resistant to the downward national trend consequently attracted increased attention from government, criminologists and public opinion (Wiener, 1990: 300). The 'street ruffians', 'rowdies' or 'roughs' were thus in some respects an even more visible feature of England's urban landscape in 1900 than they had been in 1830.

2
Anti-social City: Science and Crime in late Victorian Britain

Trevor Harris

Introduction

In an age of Anti-social Personality Disorders (ASPDs) and Anti-social Behaviour Orders (ASBOs), when anti-social behaviour is often presented as the consequence of a quintessentially contemporary 'breakdown of authority', it is easy to forget that the question is far older than early twentieth-century promoters of moral declinism would have us believe. It is what the criminologist Geoffrey Pearson has identified as one of the 'disturbing continuities' of British society: 'what is wrong with government and media responses to youth crime and anti-social behaviour', he points out, 'is its emphasis on the unprecedented nature of the problem, while losing its grip on the actual social and historical background' (Pearson, 2006: 7).

Accordingly, it is the aim of this chapter less to describe the phenomenon, than to link the question of 'anti-social' behaviour to the history and the wider intellectual framework of Britain between, roughly, 1880 and the end of Victoria's reign. It is clear, looking at this period, that in attempting to make sense of criminal activity of all kinds, politicians and intellectuals found themselves increasingly polarized between explanations motivated by heredity, and those motivated by environmental factors: the nature–nurture debate which is still such a familiar part of arguments in this area was coming much more clearly into view. It was a dichotomy, moreover, which took its place within a context of scientific and pseudo-scientific accounts of what was perceived as Britain's threatened fall from the grace of unstoppable progress to that of ignominious decline. The ultimate fate of the nation, indeed of the English 'race', was coming to occupy a key role in political discussion and in political re-alignment, both within and outside Parliament.

The problem

There seemed to be little doubt that a fundamental behavioural problem existed within late Victorian British society, a climate of regular and casual violence which was all too visible when 'Gangs of boys and young men assemble, and for sport assail any respectable person passing' (*The Spectator*, 11 March 1882: 3). Though the term 'anti-social' was not as widely used then as today, the behaviour of numerous groups had for some time been identified as a social fact which ran contrary to the collective interest. True, the people in question were not always those one might spontaneously think of as anti-social: *Hansard*, for example, records the readiness of MPs to criticize the 'ruffianism' of the government (HC Deb, 14 April 1887, vol. 313, col. 895), the 'wanton ruffianism on the part of the police' (HC Deb, 3 March 1887, vol. 311, col. 1148), or the 'ruffianism of landlordism' in Ireland (HC Deb, 27 January 1887, vol. 310, col. 140).

Far more often, of course, the ruffians, the 'hooligan boys' and the 'young roughs' who plagued and even terrorized British society were drawn from the working classes. In addition to the 'street Arabs' or abandoned children whose plight had been the object of government interest as early as the 1840s, or the 'juvenile delinquents' first studied by Mary Carpenter in 1852, other groups in late Victorian Britain increasingly attracted public attention. The 'Rochdale Road War' of 1870, in Manchester, inaugurated a period of sustained gang violence in the city, which lasted until the end of the century. Numerous groups of delinquents, or 'scuttlers' as they were known, divided Manchester into territories each of which was ruled by a particular gang – the 'Bengal Tigers' from Ancoats; Buffalo Bill's gang from Salford; the Clock Alley Lads from the streets around Victoria Station; the Meadow Lads from nearby Angel Meadow; the Frenchmen, the Germans, the Russians (see Davies, 2008). For 30 years these gangs – immediately identifiable thanks to their distinctive mode of dress – defended their own space and attacked that of rival gangs, while routinely laying waste (beating the victim with belt buckles was a favourite method) to unfortunates who, by chance or by necessity, had ventured into one of the city's many forbidden districts. Such issues of public order, policing, crime detection, penal policy and the prison system had, during the course of the nineteenth century, increasingly become the responsibility of local and national government, and come to colonize the public imagination, journalism and fiction: the publication in 1887 of the first Sherlock Holmes story, *A Study in Scarlet*, was quickly followed by a peak in violence, public agitation and anxiety, as the 'Jack the Ripper' murders made headline news.

The causes

Discovering the causes of anti-social behaviour – indeed, the causes of the whole process of criminalization – in the late Victorian period, as now, was a public priority. The massification of the ability to read and the easy availability of reading material of dubious quality were both objects of suspicion. Popular access to lowbrow literature or 'penny dreadfuls', as well as the popular illustrated press, generated considerable anxiety among politicians and intellectuals insofar as this aspect of the problem combined both hereditary and environmental threats, placing as it did those held to be morally weak at the mercy of an emerging and, as yet, poorly understood, mass medium. What Deana Heath (2010) has called the 'politics of moral regulation', was pressed into service through the judicial system – as in the high-profile prosecutions in 1888 and 1889 of Henry Vizetelly for the publication of 'obscene' literature (his translations of *La Terre* and other works by Émile Zola). In Parliament, MPs found themselves discussing the effects of 'pernicious reading' (see Springhall, 1994) and 'poisonous books' (see Brantlinger, 1994): for example, the Liberal, Anthony Mundella, lamented 'the pernicious effects of the poisonous stuff' and the 'moral poison' of inappropriate literature (HC Deb, 8 May 1888, vol. 325, col. 1722), while Sir George Trevelyan, Liberal Chief Secretary for Ireland, pointed the finger at those 'newspapers which absolutely poison the minds of the people with exhortations to crime and outrage' (HC Deb, 18 May 1882, vol. 269, col. 1014).

The reforms of the mid-Victorian period and the extended remit of central and local government, particularly, which emerged from these, were producing a political system and a society in which mid-Victorian values – embodied by the middle classes, propelled by the adoption of free trade from 1846, and projected in, notably, the Great Exhibition of 1851 – were now themselves coming under scrutiny and pressure. What W.L. Burn called 'the age of equipoise', the self-confident, even self-satisfied, mid-Victorian age of progress, had shaded – imperceptibly, perhaps, but very definitely – into an 'age of anxiety'. The Labour question, a series of violent public order disturbances – 'Black Monday', 8 February 1886 (when a demonstration against unemployment led to a riot in Pall Mall), 'Bloody Sunday', 13 November 1887 (when a pitched battle took place between police/soldiers and the Social Democratic Federation and the Irish National League), the London matchgirls strike of July 1888, the London dock strike of August–September 1889, and so on – as well as clear moves through the 1880s towards a political culture of 'rights' as opposed to privileges or duties, were now raising the prospect or, for some, the spectre, of moral management not as the responsibility of the individual, but as that of the state. This was more unsettling even than the prospect of democracy, since irresponsible individuals would, many thought, be unable to appreciate or make such a system work. The combination of bigger government and smaller consciences was, in effect, tantamount to a moral revolution.

The economic downturn that affected Britain from the later 1870s onwards; the 'new Unionism' which increasingly controlled industrial relations into the 1880s and which saw the emergence of a number of figures who quickly became prominent in the Labour movement; the impact of anarchism and anarcho-socialism on the public imagination: these and other factors came together to create not only a sense of 'moral panic' among the middle and upper classes, but also, within the broader political culture, led many observers to posit the existence of a logical relationship between poverty, politics and crime. The working classes shaded ineluctably into a 'criminal class'. William Gladstone was moved, during a Commons debate in 1887, to stress the seriousness of 'offences that are not only in a high degree criminal, but are anti-social and almost unnatural, going beyond the lines of human nature and beyond the lines of human crime' (HC Deb, 10 May 1887, vol. 314, col. 1497): here was a type of behaviour, implied the Grand Old Man, which was not merely against the law, but which was against society and against nature, making the offender, as it were, into the representative of a different species. Another bemused observer noted ('Our "Larrikins" ', *The Spectator*, 2 June 1888: 11) how young men 'fight one another with a fierceness and continuousness such as we attribute to Irish factions'.

The English criminal class, in other words, was not English. The anti-social were a race apart, as were the 'race of paupers', or 'race of beggars' who were regularly mentioned in Commons exchanges during the 1880s and 1890s: and this in the context of a struggle between, on the one hand, the 'Latin and Teutonic races' (HC Deb, 1 July 1881, vol. 262 col. 1762) and, on the other, 'half-civilised and savage races' (HC Deb, 24 April 1888, vol. 325 col. 406). 'Race' was indeed a prominent theme in late Victorian science. John Beddoe's *The Races of Britain: A Contribution to the Anthropology of Western Europe* (1885) was typical of the work then being published. Beddoe dedicated his book to the French craniologist, Paul Broca, and produced a mass of 'evidence' in the form of skull measurements, column upon column of statistics on eye and hair colour, and so on, asserting that his aim was to 'test directly whether, through natural selection or any other process, the colour type has altered among our upper classes' (Beddoe, 1885: 225). His unruffled conclusion was that 'the Gaelic and Iberian races of the west, mostly dark-haired, are tending to swamp the blond Teutons of England' (Beddoe, 1885: 270). Small wonder, in such a context, that where gypsies were concerned, for example, 'their presence in England struck some reformers as an intolerable affront to the values of modern civilization' (Behlmer, 1985: 231).

Poverty, of course, was not a new theme in late Victorian Britain – the investigative journalism of Henry Mayhew, for example, had famously burrowed deep into the detail of *London Labour and the London Poor* (1851–61) to explore the low life of the capital – though the social conditions of the depressed 1880s had revived the subject, and the new popular press had publicized it very successfully: the Reverend Andrew Mearns' pamphlet, for example, *The Bitter Cry of Outcast London: An Inquiry into the Condition of the Abject Poor* (1883), caused a major sensation when it appeared. Nor was the state of the English nation an entirely new subject of enquiry: the same Henry Mayhew, in the preface to his *German Life and Manners as seen in Saxony at the Present Day* (1864), had reeled off a set of typically smug, mid-Victorian platitudes on the superiority of the English when compared to the drab lowliness of the Continent, and beyond:

> travelling southward from England is like going backward in time – every ten degrees of latitude corresponding to about a hundred years in our own history; [...] in Germany we find the people, at the very least, a century behind us; [...] whilst, in Central Africa, we reach the primitive condition of nature – the very zero of the civilized scale – absolute barbarism itself. (viii–ix)

Mayhew's pseudo-scientific calibration is striking for the matter-of-fact, and to us rather ridiculous, way it posits geography as the main factor in establishing differential evolution among peoples. But Mayhew had certainly been fascinated by the link between environment and social development. By the 1880s, Charles Booth was investigating similar social phenomena using a much more rigorous methodology. His *Life and Labour of the People*, publication of which began in 1889, was an intricate, street-by-street survey of the East End of London, from which Booth and his collaborators produced equally intricate, colour-coded poverty maps, quantifying the living conditions in each district.

What Mayhew, Mearns and Charles Booth progressively establish, as they each reformulate the 'social question', is the link between ongoing urbanization and the existence of large-scale poverty. The collection of data using an increasingly meticulous scientific approach provides growing evidence of a causal relationship between city, poverty and criminal behaviour. The moral and metaphysical consequences of this were not lost on the philanthropist and Methodist preacher, William Booth, the founder of the Salvation Army. *In Darkest England and the Way Out* (1890) is 'General' Booth's account of his work among what he calls in his preface the 'outcast' or 'sinking classes', 'the submerged tenth' of the city. He establishes a deliberate parallel between London and Africa; but instead of primitive tribes, he encounters a 'race of drunkards' (Booth, 1890: 192), a 'festering mass of vice and crime' (Booth, 1890: 256), which it is his Christian mission to combat. In proceeding in this way, William Booth explores the same territory as his namesake, Charles, but collapses Mayhew's entire evolutionist geography into the limited space of the city. The latter, for William Booth, equates to a new wilderness and clearly for him, and others, the eighteenth-century city, from being a centre of culture and gentility, a space in which 'enlightenment' could come about, had now become an over-developed place of darkness where the poor material conditions led unavoidably to poor moral ones, to illness and crime of all sorts, a situation which gave rise to:

> the increasingly pervasive belief in the 1880s and 1890s that the rapid growth of the towns and the transformation of Britain from a rural to an urban society was having a profound, deleterious effect upon the

physical, and, perhaps, heritable characteristics of the populace. (Soloway, 1982: 138)

The city, in short, was becoming an essentially anti-social space. The concentration of such a large population in such a reduced physical space was not compatible with public health or public order.

In a lecture delivered in January 1885 at London's Parkes Museum of Hygiene (which had opened in 1879 as part of a developing campaign to raise awareness of public health issues), James Cantlie, a doctor working at Charing Cross hospital, pointed out – on the basis of a somewhat convoluted calculation concerning air movements over the capital – that 'the air breathed within a given area, centred around, for instance Charing Cross, or the Bank, has not had fresh air supplied to it for, say, 50 or 100 years' (Cantlie, 1885: 12). It was not that the pollution was simply uncomfortable or inconvenient, it was symptomatic of the city as a pathological space, ruining the health of those who lived and worked there:

> It is sad to contemplate that nowadays honest labour brings with it of necessity illness and misery, instead of health and comfort – that the close confinement and the foul air of our cities are shortening the life of the individual, and raising up a puny and ill-developed race. (Cantlie, 1885: 32–3)

Indeed, the entire population was succumbing to an ' "*urbomorbus*" or "city disease" ' (Cantlie, 1885: 24) and running the risk of collective atrophy: 'In place of our hands and arms we use machines nowadays, and in place of our legs we have railways, omnibuses, cabs, etc., to supplant the necessity for their use' (Cantlie, 1885: 30–1).

The slums which Mayhew, Mearns and Charles Booth had studied in such detail were, indeed, the logical consequence of the Industrial Revolution, of that vast transformation when carried through to its logical conclusion. The city now came to express, as it were, the negative stage of positivism, and was beginning to reveal itself as the 'integral accident' – to use an expression coined by Paul Virilio – of modern capitalism, a 'city of panic', whose environmental action on its population was even threatening to undo the work of evolution which had placed Britain in a position of pre-eminence: hence the title of Cantlie's lecture, 'Degeneration amongst Londoners'. Cantlie's title, 'calculated to excite surprise' (Virilio, 2004: 13), introduces the theme of degeneration which was to become such an important part of the public health and public order debate – and does so ten years before the publication in Britain of Max Nordau's *Entartung* (1892) as *Degeneration* (1895).

In 1886, Arnold White, a member of the Liberal Party and, hitherto, a supporter of Gladstone, having engaged in his own survey of London (*The Problems of a Great City*), was now sufficiently convinced of the reality of 'mental and physical deterioration' (White, 1886: 28) to realign with those

Liberal Unionists and Conservatives who advocated a much stronger state: a political move highlighting a cultural pessimism which was to appeal to a large number of erstwhile Liberals and, over the next 20 years, to exercise intellectuals on all sides of the political debate. For White, 'criminals and paupers' (White, 1886: 49) were, self-evidently, to be taken together. Further, and far more serious, White insists that 'dynasties of criminals and paupers hand down from generation to generation hereditary unfitness for the arts of progress and all that brings greatness to a nation' (White, 1886: 49). White's anxieties in respect of London's problems were extreme. His attitudes only continued to harden, as he proceeded to promote imperial federation and protectionism abroad, and opposition to immigration at home, taking advantage of the growing tensions – especially in the East End – around the question of 'alien' (principally Russian and Jewish) immigration into the capital.

Most reactions, true, were less strident. But the theme of degeneration was now part of the national agenda. In a well-crafted and well-documented speech, quoting leading authorities on statistics, economics and English history, Liberal MP Charles Conybeare, for example, provided the Commons with a thorough account of the income and precarious living conditions endured by the working classes. He was not about to miss the opportunity, in a Commons adjournment debate, to generate a small frisson of Conservative anxiety on the benches opposite:

> no one can contemplate the present condition of the masses without desiring something like a revolution for the better. We are anxious to see a revolution for the better, and we are anxious to see it take the form of a peaceable and Constitutional revolution. [...] We fortunately, in this country, have never seen revolutions of the worst type, nor do we wish to; but human nature is human nature all the world over. We shall soon be celebrating the centenary of the French Revolution of 1789; is it not, then, a season when our minds may be usefully turned to the consideration of the causes of the distress of the people? (HC Deb, 6 March 1889, vol. 333, col. 1071)

But even a radical like Conybeare – already a strong supporter of women's suffrage, for example – found himself drawn to acknowledge the new orthodoxy and express his own fear that 'the congestion of our working population in great cities is tending greatly to the moral as well as physical deterioration of our race' (HC Deb, 6 March 1889, vol. 333, col. 1079).

Solutions

Solutions to this social question, however, were not easy to find. 'What is to be done to discipline the hobbledehoys of the working classes?' asked *The*

Spectator (2 June 1888: 11): 'In all our great cities', it continued, 'more espe-cially in London, there are now thousands [...] of lads between fifteen and twenty who, the moment hard work is over, have, in practice, no possible mode of recreation except wandering through the streets in gangs.' Science and technology were thought to hold the answers. Natural science in its social Darwinist phase shaded increasingly towards minute statistical classi-fication as the preferred method of collating reliable evidence on which to offer promising avenues of action for public policy. The prospect was held out, notably, of using such detailed measurements as a basis for intervening to buck the damaging statistical trends which had been documented, and to halt the observed deterioration by weeding out those of a weak or crimi-nal character from the population. Sir Francis Galton's eugenicist approach, as well as working on hereditary human traits, retained a debt to the 'sci-ences' of physiognomy and phrenology, and continued to hunt for ways in which facial and physical characteristics might be used to define, predict and alter criminal types in the population. Much of this mass of 'biometric' data, acquired through such techniques as 'composite portraiture', was brought together in *Inquiries into Human Faculty and its Development* (1883). Galton takes degeneration as a given of human development, and he presents 'the coarse and low types of face found among the criminal classes', the crim-inal classes whose breeding, Galton adds, constitutes 'one of the saddest disfigurements of modern civilisation' (Galton, 1883: 15).

The torch of statistical inquiry and of eugenicist ideas was taken up by Galton's protégé, Carl Pearson, for whom the conduct of 'society to its anti-social members can never be placed on a sound and permanent basis without regard to what science has to tell us on the fundamental problems of inher-itance'. Pearson maintained the utmost confidence in his method, and was categorical where any hope of regenerating the deteriorated parts of the nation was concerned: 'No degenerate and feeble stock will ever be con-verted into healthy and sound stock by the accumulated effects of education, good laws, and sanitary surroundings' (Pearson, 1892: 33–4). Such dogmatic views in respect of social and welfare reform were shared by many – Arnold White, for example, went on to become a leading member of the Eugenics Education Society and argued strongly in favour of 'Sterilisation of the Unfit' (White, 1909: 107).

Such drastic cultural pessimism was not, mercifully, shared by every-one, and a number of more practicable, even pleasant solutions were put forward to help the less fortunate elements of the population. Not surpris-ingly, some form of military service was often seen as a way to reduce the impact of criminal and anti-social behaviour, notably among the young. The Conservative MP, naval officer Admiral Bedford Pim, for example, dur-ing a Commons debate on 'the State of the Navy', affirmed to the House that 'there are hundreds of thousands of British boys who would gladly devote themselves to a sea life, and who would become useful, very useful citizens, instead of, as is only too often the case, adding to the criminal and pauper class' (HC Deb, 8 March 1880, vol. 251, col. 576). The University Settlement movement gathered momentum from the mid-1880s, especially with the opening of Toynbee Hall in 1884 in Whitechapel, at the heart of London's infamous East End. Here was, ostensibly, a less regimented, but none the less serious proposition to (re-)build bridges between the Establishment and the lower reaches of society, through social work and education: as one settlement worker put it, 'a hundred years have done much to divorce masters and men' (Paterson, 1915: 177). It was an attempt, in a sense, to re-socialize the working-class population, to re-create, artificially, an 'organic' community where 'a union based on sympathy and mutual understanding' (Paterson, 1915: 177) between classes could be rekindled. It was an initiative which effectively trained an entire cohort of Liberal and Labour intellectuals – William Beveridge and Clement Attlee among them – and, arguably, set the agenda for British social policy until well into the twentieth century.

While Pim's suggestion smacked of Victorian 'manliness', and the Toynbee Hall endeavour still derived from a philanthropic, even paternalistic view of the working classes, the 1880s also saw policy changes which reflected the growing professionalization and sophistication of 'social science' (later consolidated by the establishment, for example, of the London School of Economics in 1895), and its political corollary: the emergence of the 'expert' bureaucrat/technocrat. The new London County Council (LCC), established by the Local Government Act 1888, was a key example of this evolution: it replaced the Metropolitan Board of Works, an archaic and far more fragmented system of provision. The legislation gave the LCC much wider powers in a number of areas – education (especially technical education), housing, town-planning and so on. It was, in addition, an elected body, returned by London's ratepayers. Moreover, a majority of those elected to the first LCC in 1889 were radical Liberals, or 'Progressives' as they preferred to call themselves in this context. The LCC was to be prominent, for example, in the preparation and passage of the Housing of the Working Classes Act 1890, the text of the legislation – perceived at the time as a landmark (amended and its provisions extended in 1884, 1900, 1903 and 1909) – making it clear that the LCC and the other county councils were now to be right at the centre of provision for public health and planning. This was the beginning, in earnest, of a period of 'municipal enterprise', putting an end to or severely restricting the influence of many private vested interests. Put differently, this meant an acceptance that the state, through national and local government intervention – as opposed to private, charitable or voluntary initiatives – could and should attack root causes and take responsibility for questions which were chronic social ills, not crimes or the moral failings of individual 'character' curable via simple 'self-help'.

It was, in short, 'the start of a pattern of social legislation that quickly overwhelmed the last barriers of nineteenth-century laissez-faire liberalism' (Soloway, 1982: 151).

True, the debate would continue to take considerable account of the position and role of the individual in their responsibility for behaviour, and for its correction or improvement: 'Progressives' and promoters of the state's responsibility would, notably, gravitate to one of two poles – that involving a measure of selection and coercion (a route which appealed to many Fabians, for example), and that which favoured the unconditionality/universality of measures designed and adopted to deal with poverty and 'deterioration'. If the Elementary Education Act 1870, also called the 'Forster Act', was the first in a series of acts in this area, its main provisions still aroused very considerable opposition: the economic arguments (improving British competitiveness relative to European rivals) tended to outweigh any educational or social dimension, and for this and other reasons school attendance was not in fact made compulsory until 1880. But it was clear that arguments based on socialization, on the perception of childhood and youth, and their importance in terms of the development and formation of the adult were now gaining ground and being translated into public policy: adolescence and the behaviours associated with it, rather than deriving from a view of the individual as determined by social station and capable only of behaving in accordance with that (a form of moral degeneracy), was increasingly seen as dictated by a stage in physical and psychiatric/psychological development with its own particular needs and rights.

The 'Children's Charter', for example, of 1889 (or the Prevention of Cruelty to, and Better Protection of, Children Act) – amended and extended in 1894 (to include mental cruelty, for example, and forcing parents to care for sick children) – allowed state intervention for the first time into the relations between parents and children, giving police the authority to enter homes if it was thought children were in danger. This effectively implied that the family itself was dysfunctional and anti-social and sought to neutralize negative adult influence, as well as tackling anti-social behaviour head-on by, for example, outlawing begging. The establishment of a Child Study Movement in 1893 by British psychologist James Sully, underlined the extent to which childhood and youth required separate investigation and specific measures and policies. Indeed, the whole penal framework for children and young people came under scrutiny. From 1899, children were not to be sent to adult prisons, which had hitherto been the case; and a long campaign to change the workings of the court system bore fruit in 1900 with the institution of the first British juvenile court. The relationship between parliamentary and extra-parliamentary – not least municipal – action in this area would continue to evolve, with the Liberal government elected in 1906, particularly, bringing a non-conformist zeal to social and humane welfare reform: the Children and Young Persons Act 1908, notably, strengthened the powers of local authorities further and made provision for the introduction of school meals and regular medical examination, as well as creating a distinct judicial system for young offenders by generalizing the establishment of juvenile courts.

More conservative approaches to these questions were nothing if not resistant, however. The anxieties unleashed by the Boer War (1899–1902), especially, when many potential recruits were deemed unfit for service, revitalized the 'degeneration' debate and prompted calls for a campaign to improve 'national efficiency'. The very diverse political provenance of the members of the 'Coefficients' dining club, formed to further this cause, emphasizes the extent to which the socialization of Britain's working classes was a theme which could institute what today would be deemed a highly incongruous alliance for reform. Among those joining Sidney and Beatrice Webb, who founded the club in 1902, were such disparate figures as Leo Amery (a future Conservative Colonial Secretary); the future Liberal Foreign Secretary, Sir Edward Grey; the budding Germanophobe and editor of the *National Review*, Leopold Maxse; the author and poet Henry Newbolt; the philosopher Bertrand Russell; and the novelist and Fabian, H.G. Wells. The composition of the group shows how the methods and the policies of social reform remained negotiable and could still be positioned on a scale of state involvement anywhere between traditional Liberal philanthropic voluntarism, through Fabian gradualism, to a quasi-militaristic, centralized bureaucracy. Above all, the cross-section of intellectuals involved shows both the essentially conservative assumption, running through the late Victorian (and Edwardian) attitudes of the members, of a necessary deference to a form of benign statism (whether aristocratic, technocratic or meritocratic).

Conclusion

British intellectuals in the late Victorian period were grappling with the anxieties engendered by what many of them saw as Britain's faltering rank in the world. If imperial pre-eminence seemed, from the 1880s to the end of Victoria's reign, to be a fragile thing, some of the symptoms of the downward national trend often converted anxiety into something resembling panic. Diagnosing and treating problems raised by economically deprived, yet politically empowered sections of the working classes in British cities proved especially unsettling. The cultural pessimists attributed criminal and anti-social behaviour to a form of quasi-genetic national deterioration: this had to be halted, or it would lead to decadence, and thence – applying an implacable evolutionist logic – to national extinction itself. The 'Progressives', by contrast, put their faith in 'social' science, and the developing insights into the impact of the environment and cognitive or emotional motivations for individual and collective behaviours. For many intellectuals, whatever their precise political affiliation, however, a strong moral character continued to colour informed opinion of the individual's relationship with national purpose and national self-image: values which, arguably, have remained firmly entrenched within British political culture ever since.

3
Greater Expectations: Intolerance and Control of Public Space Anti-social Behaviour in the Nineteenth and Twenty-first Centuries

Craig Johnstone

Introduction

One hundred years and very considerable social, economic and cultural change separated the end of the Victorian era and the opening decade of the twenty-first century. Nevertheless, this chapter argues that there are clear parallels between the concerns that fuelled the intense focus on anti-social behaviour (ASB) which characterized Tony Blair's premiership and those that existed throughout much of the nineteenth century, most notably during its middle decades. It is contended that New Labour did not so much 'invent' anti-social behaviour as to draw fresh attention to long-standing concerns by fusing them together under the anti-social behaviour banner or, to borrow Vic Gatrell's (1990: 254) observation on another period, 'Old issues still worried people. Only the language got fancier.' This chapter argues that what particularly links the Victorian and Blair eras was the concern with the use and perceived abuse of public space. The policy solutions to this problem were era-specific, but the outcome was the same: a concerted effort to manage the usage of public space by the removal of signs and symbols of disorder through exclusion or enforcing a modification of proscribed behaviour. Both periods under consideration were noteworthy for the reframing of what constituted acceptable conduct, both in public space and everyday life. Indeed, the chapter views the attention given by policy to what we now know as anti-social behaviour as part of broader disciplinary projects concerned with maintaining order, upholding new definitions of 'normal' behaviour and correcting the faulty morals of what New Labour called the 'hard to reach',[1] but which the Victorians more commonly condemned as the 'residuum' or 'undeserving poor'.

Despite the potentially far-reaching consequences of the wholesale reform and rebranding of anti-social behaviour controls in England and Wales set in train by the Conservative–Liberal Democrat Coalition government through its Anti-social Behaviour, Crime and Policing Act 2014, it is New Labour, and particularly the governments of Tony Blair, that is most closely associated with this social phenomenon. The Crime and Disorder Act 1998 fired the legislative starting gun on anti-social behaviour intervention, but the profile of anti-social behaviour peaked in the period between New Labour's second election victory in 2001 and Blair's resignation as Prime Minister in 2007, which saw the passing into law of the Anti-Social Behaviour Act 2003, the introduction of the Anti-social Behaviour Order (ASBO) 'on conviction' or CRASBO and the launch of the Respect Agenda. Post-Blair, the rhetoric on anti-social behaviour has become markedly less shrill (Burney, 2009). Moreover, Labour's flagship anti-social behaviour intervention, the ASBO, has been deployed more and more sparingly with each passing year (Ministry of Justice, 2013), concerns about disorderly conduct were overtaken after the 2011 riots by worries about youth gangs (Centre for Social Justice, 2012) and more pressing political matters such as the scale of the national debt. The picture could not have been more different during Blair's premiership. New Labour largely constructed the concept of anti-social behaviour as we understand it today, introducing it to the political lexicon. Blair (2010) argues that addressing anti-social behaviour was central to New Labour's vision for society and he, along with his first two Home Secretaries, Jack Straw and David Blunkett, were proactive in developing a narrative about the causes and consequences of anti-social behaviour and the most appropriate methods for tackling it. This was backed up by legislation creating a smorgasbord of new sanctions and criminal justice powers targeted at anti-social acts and individuals (see Squires, 2008c; Crawford, 2009a and 2009b; Millie, 2009a for discussion). New Labour's approach to anti-social behaviour, and the legal instruments it created to convince the irresponsible and disrespectful to change their ways, have received extensive coverage in academic and policy literature during the last 15 years. It is my intention here, therefore, to cover more recent developments relatively sparingly, enabling the chapter to draw out Victorian parallels more fully. The selection of nineteenth- and twenty-first-century developments for comparison should not be read as a suggestion that disorder in public space was of no concern during the intervening century: it simply had particular salience during the two time frames under consideration.

New Labour and anti-social behaviour: concerns and motivations

Anti-social behaviour was very imprecisely defined by the Crime and Disorder Act 1998 making it a rather 'catch all' concept. This was intentional, allowing the measures put in place to curb it to be used against all forms of behaviour with the potential to cause 'harassment, alarm and distress', from minor law breaking, which typically only attracted small penalties in the Magistrates' Courts (Squires, 2008c), through to activities that some might consider inconsequential, but to the victim had a significant impact on well-being and quality of life. Much of this behaviour could be characterized as persistent nuisance; the sort of acts that might not attract criminal sanction, but were fear-inducing and troubling in their own right (Blair, 2010). Significantly, the Labour government was able to present the concept of anti-social behaviour as new because the activities it defined as problematic had been progressively marginalized within policy and policing over a number of decades, particularly as crime rates accelerated after the 1970s. As David Garland (1996) has noted, 'high crime societies', among which he included Britain, had tended to 'define deviance down' as crime rates rose in order to enable resources to be concentrated on addressing what was considered more serious crime. This translated into less and less attention being paid to everyday disorderly-but-not-strictly-criminal behaviour.

While some anti-social behaviour cases have involved disputes between neighbours or the victimization of particular people, the Fiona Pilkington case being an especially tragic example,[2] the main target of the mechanisms developed for clamping down on anti-social behaviour was public space disorder. This is evident in legislative solutions. The ASBO, as well as requiring desistance from specified behaviour could also require recipients to stay out of certain geographic areas. The Dispersal Order was specifically designed to remove groups of people, typically the young, from designated places (Crawford, 2009b), while the Local Child Curfew Scheme was concerned with the presence of unaccompanied children in public places at night. A suite of orders and the expansion in the use of the fixed penalty fine were also designed to combat the disorder associated with public drunkenness in the night-time economy (Hadfield, 2006). The measures implemented were not limited to anti-social acts, with the Clean Neighbourhoods and Environment Act 2005 targeting other forms of public space 'abuse' such as the abandoning of vehicles, littering in open spaces and leaflet distribution. To aid in the enforcement of these new rules the role of Police Community Support Officer (PCSO) was created by the Police Reform Act 2002 with many thousands of them employed to work with regular police officers in new neighbourhood policing teams, walking the beat to offer reassurance, collect information and enhance surveillance of 'problem' communities. The police and PCSOs were helped in building cases against the anti-social, and enforcing the penalties imposed, by local authority staff and housing officers, who had been empowered by the Crime and Disorder Act 1998, and by the public, who were encouraged by the Together campaign and by the naming and shaming of ASBO recipients to be proactive in ridding their communities of threats to their quality of life (Home Office, 2003; Squires, 2008c; Crawford, 2009a).

New Labour's commitment to doing something about anti-social behaviour was driven by a number of interlocking factors. First, it offered a practical remedy to the very real problems that constituents, particularly in poorer inner city communities, were reporting to their Labour MPs (Blair, 2010). Secondly, Blair and other senior ministers had bought into the argument about the importance of order maintenance set out in J.Q. Wilson and George Kelling's (1982) 'Broken Windows' article. Blair captures the crux of their argument in his memoir: 'The concept is this: if you tolerate the small stuff, you pretty soon find the lawbreakers graduate to the high-level stuff. So cut it out at source; tolerate nothing, not even painting a street wall or dropping litter' (2010: 493). The primacy afforded the broken windows perspective by New Labour is evident particularly in the Respect and Responsibility White Paper (Home Office, 2003), which rehearses Wilson and Kelling's arguments almost verbatim. Thirdly, it reinforced the narrative about Labour's tough and serious approach to crime and disorder that Blair started to develop as Shadow Home Affairs spokesman and captured in the now-familiar slogan 'Tough on crime, tough on the cause of crime',[3] which went on to become a New Labour mantra. Fourthly, it was also part of a more fundamental reform of a criminal justice system which, Blair argued, was still using nineteenth-century means to tackle twenty-first-century problems (Squires, 2008c; Burney, 2009).

From fear and disorder to 'mastering the masterless' in early Victorian Britain

On first impressions, the problems confronting the political elite in early Victorian Britain appear to be of an entirely different register to those occupying Blair's Labour Party. However, controlling street behaviour was central to the imposition of order in a rapidly urbanizing society and played an important role in shaping the industrial working class of popular imaginary. The first decades of the Victorian era were characterized by concerns arising from the mass migration of labourers from the countryside to the newly industrializing towns and cities. The speed of change was striking (see Lawless and Brown, 1986; Harrison, 1971 for details) but the laissez-faire state, unwilling to interfere with the free market, was slow to respond to the multiple implications of such fundamental transformation. Of greatest concern to the early Victorian elite was what the urban 'masses' might get up to if new means to govern them were not found and 'a stable pattern of civil and moral order' preserved (Storch, 1977: 138). Their unease peaked in the 1830s and 1840s, when it was feared that Chartist protests would spiral into more general insurrection. According to Robert Storch:

> both the actions and the 'language' spoken by urban masses were, if intelligible at all, deeply frightening. The notion that the movements of the lower orders had comprehensible or 'legitimate' objectives [...] was

replaced by the feeling that they aimed at the utter unravelling of society. By the 1830s and 1840s dread of the 'dangerous classes' could be transformed into near hysteria at times of great social and political tension. (Storch, 1975, 62)

The system of social control that had operated for generations in traditional rural communities, where the population had been fairly stable and outsiders were noticed, had blended formal policing with intense scrutiny of the lives of the poor by employers, neighbours and the Church (Neocleous, 2000). In the expanding industrial towns and cities, increasingly characterized by the relocation of those with money to new suburbs away from the overcrowding and stench of old urban cores, the close supervision of the labouring classes by their social superiors and, crucially, the Church (Briggs, 1968), whose ecclesiastical courts had served as a mechanism for imposing discipline over everyday behaviour in previous centuries (Neocleous, 2000), was almost totally absent. Although the factory, with its fixed hours of employment and the wage, provided a new form of discipline, many traditional working practices and non-factory forms of employment persisted until mid-century (Storch, 1977; Cohen, 1979). Moreover, 'the unparalleled discipline [...] of the mill was accompanied by the appearance of free and untrammelled a recreational life as has probably ever existed in England' (Storch, 1977: 142). Such were the fears of the age that there 'was no question of the poor being left to themselves in a state of social laissez-faire' (Donajgrodzki, 1977: 55), so the central conundrum for early Victorian reformers was how best to 'master the masterless' (Neocleous, 2000: 65): to make them work for a living, convince them to accept their position in the social hierarchy, discourage them from law breaking and stop their pastimes and traditions from disrupting the smooth operation of the evolving capitalist system – and upsetting the middle-class sense of decorum.

Given this situation, it is perhaps no surprise that the first significant intervention finally squeezed by reformers from the laissez-faire state was the creation of the new police, first in London in 1829 and then piecemeal across the country until the establishment of county police forces was mandated by Parliament in 1856. The new police became the main vehicle for imposing a semblance of control during this early period over a population which had 'not fully experienced industrial discipline' (Cohen, 1979: 129) or compulsory schooling. While rising crime had been mobilized as a justification for police reform in London (Reiner, 2010; Taylor, 1997), policing was orientated around preventative beat patrolling which meant officers were arguably better placed to confront challenges to public order and 'inappropriate' uses of public space than they were criminality. Indeed, Mark Neocleous (2000: 4) observes that police concentrated on 'activities potentially damaging to communal good order' rather than the purely criminal, which in any case tended to be a greater source of public concern at the time than crime as we conceive of it today (Gatrell, 1990; Weinberger, 1981). This chimes strongly with the argument of revisionist social historians, such as Storch (1975; 1977; 1993) and Phil Cohen (1979), that the police played a crucial mid-century role in disciplining the working classes by clamping down on their street activities, particularly their leisure pursuits, to the point that many communities saw officers as little more than the repressive arm of the bourgeois state; 'an all-purpose lever of urban discipline' (Storch, 1993: 282) both loathed and resisted.

Ordering public space, disciplining the working classes

Maintaining order and shaping a working class both suited to the urban industrial economy and whose behaviour was acceptable to the bourgeoisie, who had greater expectations as regards decorum than previous generations (Taylor, 1997), meant curbing two 'inappropriate' uses of public space: informal economic activity and as an all-purpose leisure space. In his work on pre-1850s Portsmouth, Miles Ogborn (1993: 517) argues:

> No longer were [the streets] to be a market place for farm animals, a theatre for public entertainments, a shop counter or an impromptu abattoir. Pavements and roads were to be kept clear of all obstruction and dangers, from crowds and cattle to furniture and ferocious dogs. They were to be become arteries whose orderly flows of people and goods involved the rationalisation and regulation of the moral behaviour of the streets users.

Not only did costermongers and hawkers, for example, disrupt the smooth flow of traffic in the streets, they were also viewed as something of a throwback to an earlier time when pilfering goods from the workplace to use or sell as a way of supplementing income was considered the norm. According to Neocleous (2000: 76):

> The attack on the non-monetary form of the wage and its transformation into a fully-fledged money form meant criminalizing a range of traditional working class activities, bringing them into the orbit of police power and thus legitimising their oppression, a project designed to stamp the authority of private property over the living conditions of the majority of the population and confirm the power of capital as the new master.

The suppression of street trading was the cause of many violent confrontations with the police. Costermongers gained a reputation for being especially resistant to attempts to move them on and took pride in assaulting officers for interfering in their livelihood (Storch, 1975).

While some leisure pursuits, particularly fairs and fêtes, were econom-ically troublesome because they precipitated mass absenteeism from the workplace, mid-Victorian reformers were equally worried by the threat to decorum and what they considered acceptable standards of behaviour posed by street-based leisure. There was also the potential for events causing the working classes to gather in numbers to spill over into protest and violence (Storch, 1977). The police played a significant role in disciplining public working-class leisure, but this should not be overstated; some traditional pas-times were abandoned as new indoor leisure opportunities arose and many street cultures faded later in the century as the unskilled and semi-skilled sought respectability and material advancement through the opportunities provided via education, trade unionism and early Labour politics (Cohen, 1979). This notwithstanding, in the middle decades of the nineteenth cen-tury, the police were given a wide remit to target 'popular activities and recreations considered conducive to immorality, disorder or crime' (Storch, 1993: 286).

Storch's (1993) research into the police as 'domestic missionaries' offers considerable insight into police efforts to suppress working-class leisure pur-suits, from animal fights through to the singing of profane songs on the streets and gatherings associated with popular fêtes and festivals. A challenge was also posed to the long-standing freedom of assembly on the streets, with men, who had traditionally occupied periods of leisure time hanging around in groups, made to 'move on'. Direct suppression of problem activities often just drove them underground or moved them elsewhere, although this was often considered a successful outcome if thoroughfares were cleared. Fêtes and fairs, held in public and not easily relocated, gave the police oppor-tunities for high-profile direct action in a way that activities hidden away behind the closed doors of the public house did not; 'The police proved to be a weapon well-tuned to the task of terminating the popular fête with all its connotations of disorder, drunkenness, sexual license, and property damage' (Storch, 1993: 295). If these, sometimes brutal, confrontations were quite rare the use of physical force by the police to clear the unwelcome from the streets was commonplace (Cohen, 1979). Although middle-class tolerance of violence was waning (Taylor, 1997), it remained a feature of everyday life at this time (Gatrell, 1990) and police officers had few qualms in cuffing boys round the head to convince them to 'move on' (Cohen, 1979).

The Victorian police were aided in their task of curbing acts that had been reconstructed as disruptive or out of place by both new and existing legislation. This 'concerted attempt on the part of the state to crimi-nalize traditional activities which were either recreational or rooted in an alternative economic mode of life and which centred on the street' (Neocleous, 2000: 75) could mean that those who attracted the attention of the police, much like those branded anti-social today, could be behav-ing in a manner which they considered both reasonable and normal and may, indeed, have previously been legal. A good early example of the nar-rowing of acceptable street behaviour in London is the Metropolitan Police Act 1839 which encompassed, among other things, the permitted hours and licensing of fairs, the outlawing of animal fights for entertainment, restrictions on the driving of cattle on the streets and otherwise obstruct-ing thoroughfares, penalties for what we might call carriage 'joyriding', discharging a cannon in residential areas, using a dog for drawing a cart, and dumping waste in the streets. Section LIV proscribes various forms of nuisance in thoroughfares, its 17 sub-clauses spanning street entertainment, ferocious dogs, 'furious' carriage driving, riding (a horse) on the pavement, bill posting, hoop rolling, selling of profane or obscene material, soliciting by prostitutes, the throwing of missiles, kite flying and unwarranted door bell ringing.

Just as concerns about street behaviour in Victorian Britain mirrored those of more recent times, so did apprehension about who occupied pub-lic space. In the Blair era, it was young people whose mere presence or 'hanging around' became discursively associated with anti-social behaviour (Squires, 2006; Crawford, 2009b; Bannister and Kearns, 2012). Although the Victorians had their own hang ups about loitering groups, their *bête noir* was the vagrant. An apparent unwillingness to work, lack of fixed abode and popular association with petty criminality, ensured the vagrant's place as a folk devil in the Victorian imaginary; the 'epitome of uncivilised self-indulgence' (Jones, 1982: 178). As Caroline Steedman (1984: 56) points out, in addition to being a potential criminal, the vagrant 'represented a mobile anomaly in the structure of social control' that was symbolic of disorder (Neocleous, 2000: 20). Discouraging vagrants from lingering or imposing on them the discipline of the workhouse were favoured solutions made possible by the Vagrancy Act 1824 and later legislation that widened the definition of 'vagrant' and thus 'conferred a statutory and universal power on all police-men in the surveillance of poor people mobile on the roads' (Steedman, 1984: 56).

There was a limit to the ability of the police to suppress unwanted street behaviour due both to manpower availability and the resistance of those being policed. Both Cohen (1979) and Storch (1993) argue that the police quickly learnt to pick their battles carefully and would tolerate cer-tain types of behaviour in some urban spaces, which would be suppressed elsewhere. In the longer term, what became much more important to imposing discipline on the streets than the high-profile crackdown was the promise of intervention arising from the 'constant surveillance of all the key institutions of working-class neighbourhoods and recreational life' (Storch, 1993: 292). Indeed, Ogborn (1993: 516) argues that the prime objective of police reform in the nineteenth century was to institute 'a police programme which organized authority and information across space to produce a new and systematic surveillance of the city'. The impact of surveillance on street activities may not have been as dramatic as that of direct confrontation but, in Storch's (1993) opinion, it could cause problem behaviour to dwindle over time while securing a degree of decorum in the short term. The importance of surveillance and information gathering to the maintenance of order is one of the main refrains of the broken windows argument. Drawing on observations made in the United States, Wilson and Kelling (1982) lament the demise of beat policing precipitated by the switch to patrolling by car. In addition to officers no longer being physically present to deal with disorderly behaviour on the streets, they were also less well informed about what was going on in a neighbourhood. In many respects, British responses to these concerns in the 2000s – neighbourhood policing, neighbourhood wardens, PCSOs – have sought to reinstitute street surveillance and knowledge gathering akin to that of the Victorian age.

Beyond disorder: moral failings and disrespect

Much as the disciplining of the masses in the early Victorian period discussed in this chapter so far reflected middle-class instincts of self-preservation in turbulent times and the demand of emerging industrial capitalism for a compliant pool of labour, another crucial motive force was a shift in middle-class values and a concomitant recalibration of what constituted suitable behaviour in the modern urban age. The Victorian era was notable for the stark social and physical separation of the classes not seen previously (Briggs, 1968; Harrison, 1971). As Friedrich Engels (1999) noted in his famous description of mid-century Manchester, the different classes lived in their own urban enclaves and unless the prosperous needed to enter the city centre for business or entertainment their interactions with the working classes were infrequent and they rarely had need to enter the poorest communities. Indeed, bourgeois concerns about the bankruptcy of working-class culture and leisure pursuits seldom arose out of first-hand experience (Harrison, 1971), but were a reaction to what was read in pamphlets and newspapers written by those who had entered the 'terra incognita' of the slums, either to investigate or to evangelize (Walkowitz, 1992). Such physical distance led to the establishment of different social worlds; fêtes and festivals that had once been communal events were recast as boorish and troublesome working-class pastimes that were no longer welcome (Storch, 1993). Even the public hanging, for so long a showpiece demonstration of justice in action, was moved behind closed doors in 1868, in part at least over concerns about the inappropriate behaviour of the crowds which came to watch and the challenge to Victorian claims of civility posed by death-as-spectacle (Gatrell, 1994).

The Victorian middle class, characterized by piety, sobriety, self-control, thrift and hard work, was generally horrified by the apparent immorality of the working classes (Storch, 1977). Once Chartism had faded and fear of the masses gave way to a more nuanced, if still rudimentary, distinction between the respectable poor and the criminal classes (Gatrell, 1990), considerable efforts were made by reformers, often driven by a sense of Christian duty, to take on a tutelary role, providing moral guidance to the working classes (Donajgrodzki, 1977; Storch, 1977). While the state played a role with legislation on, for example, education, child labour and housing, this was the age of the philanthropist, the paternalist and the evangelist. They moved on many fronts, seeking to challenge troubling working-class mores by showing them a better way or, to put it less charitably, seeking to impose upon them a 'cultural lobotomy' (Storch, 1977: 139).

The desire of Victorians to remedy not only the behavioural failings of the poor, but also their moral shortcomings might appear to be what differentiates this period from the Blair years, yet this is not the case. Although many of the measures introduced by New Labour to target anti-social behaviour were officially to deter further or more serious deviation from the (locally defined) norm through the threat of criminal sanction, they were also 'designed to signal the unacceptability of ASB' (Bannister and Kearns, 2012: 382) within contemporary society. Furthermore, they fitted into a much wider agenda centred on social values and, essentially, morals. Throughout his time as leader of the Labour Party, Tony Blair continually returned to the Communitarian refrain that with rights come responsibilities to society; 'Respect for others – responsibility to them – is an essential prerequisite of a strong and active community' (Blair, 1996: 237–8; see also Blair, 2010: 78). These twin concerns with respect and responsibility and, most crucially, how to reconstruct them in communities where they were lacking, were to become central to the anti-social behaviour agenda in the 2000s. Anti-social behaviour was emblematic of the decline of respect and, Peter Squires (2006: 151) observes, 'became virtually a metaphor for the condition of contemporary Britain'. Reflecting on this period, Blair (2010: 274) writes that he 'felt we had gone really badly wrong as a society and had to correct it'. The Respect and Responsibility White Paper (Home Office, 2003), which formed the basis for the Anti-Social Behaviour Act 2003, and the Respect Action Plan (Respect Task Force, 2006) discursively aligned renewed action against anti-social behaviour with a project to rebuild respect for others, enforce responsibility and make people behave (Burney, 2005; 2009). Whereas the 'tough on crime, tough on the causes of crime' slogan promised a marriage of the punitive and an attack on the broader structural causes of crime and disorder, the Respect Agenda was geared around enforcement (Squires, 2006; Burney, 2009) and fell back on a number of tropes – the dysfunctional family, the flawed individual and inappropriate behaviour as a lifestyle choice (Squires, 2008c) – popular in right-wing discourse and undoubtedly familiar to Victorians, even if the language used had changed with the passage of time.

From police to 'social police'?

The urge to discipline and re-moralize the poor that is evident in the two eras was based on a central unifying factor: a conviction that the state has a crucial role to play in shaping the working class. The laissez-faire state was in many respects an unwilling participant for much of the nineteenth century, quite content to leave moral reform to industrial paternalists, housing chari-ties, evangelical Christians, the temperance movement and anti-prostitution campaigners. But many influential thinkers persistently argued that the masses needed direction and it was the duty of their social betters to pro-vide it. Writing at the time of the Chartist protests, Thomas Carlyle (1998: 161) observed:

> Bellowings, inarticulate cries as of a dumb creature in rage and pain; to the ear of wisdom they are inarticulate prayers: 'Guide me, govern me! I am mad, and miserable, and cannot guide myself!' Surely of all 'rights of man', this right of the ignorant man to be guided by the wiser, to be gently or forcibly, held in the true course by him, is the indisputablest.

Whereas Carlyle favoured leadership by an authoritarian figurehead, others sought to mould the working classes through an all-encompassing system of what Donajgrodzki terms 'social police', characterized 'by a belief that a strong tutelary grasp should be maintained over the poor' (1977: 52). Today the domain of the police is limited to crime control and order main-tenance but, early in the nineteenth century, reformers such as Patrick Colquhoun and Edwin Chadwick conceived of the system of police as being a far-reaching disciplinary apparatus, combining what we now view as polic-ing with many aspects of what today would be classified as social policy. To their mind, to police meant the 'good ordering of society' (Neocleous, 2000: 41; see also Ogborn, 1993: 507) and this entailed addressing the per-ceived failings of the working classes in totality, rather than simply focusing on their disorderly conduct. Indeed, Donajgrodzki (1977: 71) asserts that Chadwick proposed a system of tutelary control so comprehensive that it would entail a 'merciless assault on a very widely defined range of deviant activities' including, much as a Criminal Behaviour Oder might impose today, limitations on the movements of ex-offenders through public space. Early reformers were convinced that 'the preservation of order must include not only consideration of legal systems, police forces and prisons, but of religion and morality, and of those factors which supported or propagated them – education, socially constructive leisure, even housing and public health' (Donajgrodzki, 1977: 52). But such a monolithic system of police was far too anti-libertarian ever to be realized at that time and instead state intervention proceeded piecemeal with the definition and role of police greatly narrowed (Neocleous, 2000), the workhouse tasked with reinforcing the discipline of labour, and moral reform relying on a mixed economy of the state, motivated individuals, charitable groups and the non-conformist churches.

Conclusion

Early Victorian reformers and New Labour were motivated by context-specific social problems and developed their own equally high-profile and controversial solutions to remedy them. Nevertheless, what echoes across the ages is the desire to regulate public behaviour, maintain order and enforce moral improvement on the most worrisome elements of the working class. As such, the Blair government's attempts to curb anti-social behaviour, enforce responsibility and rebuild respect can be read as part of an ongoing disciplinary project, rather than a wholly new departure. However, New Labour's willingness to impose strict controls over behaviour that was nuisance rather than criminal and to mobilize the power of the state against those who refused to desist from anti-social behaviour or accept their responsibilities to wider society, signalled a transition to an arrangement more akin to 'social police' than the laissez-faire Victorian state could countenance; one in which the criminal justice system was afforded a greatly enhanced tutelary role at the expense of other branches of social policy (see Wacquant, 2001; Rodger, 2008 for a discussion of this inversion). Although the heat has gone from the rhetoric surrounding anti-social behaviour and the Respect Agenda was short lived, the enhanced powers to confront these phenomena the state acquired during the 2000s remain, and their reform in 2014 through the Anti-social Behaviour, Crime and Policing Act 2014 has the potential to give new life to the disciplinary project.

Notes

1. See Squires, 2006; Minton, 2009; Crawford, 2009a for discussion of the concentration of New Labour's ASB policy on the behaviour of the socio-economically marginalized.
2. In 2007, Fiona Pilkington killed herself and her severely disabled daughter following a long period during which they had been the targets of constant verbal harassment and abuse and had objects thrown at their home by local youths. Despite 30 reports about their victimization to the authorities over a 10-year period, including 13 in the year prior to their deaths, no significant steps were taken to deal with the situation, as either a case of anti-social behaviour or disability hate crime.
3. Blair (2010) credits Gordon Brown as having coined this phrase during one of their policy discussions in the USA, in the early 1990s.

4

Anti-social Behaviour and 'Civilizing' Regulation in the British City: Comparing Victorian and Contemporary Eras

John Flint and Ryan Powell

Introduction

Urban history has always been concerned with the governance of 'unruly spaces, marginal subjects and deviant practices' (Crook, 2008: 414). Precedents for the governance of anti-social behaviour in the Victorian and our contemporary period may be found in preceding eras, including the annoyance juries of the mid-eighteenth century regulating minor neighbour disputes and the Disorderly Houses Act 1752 responding to concerns about alcohol and drug misuse, riotous conduct and sexual promiscuity and commercialization (Cockayne, 2007; Cruickshank, 2009). The end of the Georgian era and early Victorian period were characterized by a reframed consciousness about urban improvement with new forms of civic morality and new models of urban management to address the challenges of urban and commercial expansion; symbolized by the emergence of police as a broad mechanism of urban governance, rooted in concerns with criminality, anti-social behaviour and the urban poor (Barrie, 2010).

The chapter begins by summarizing the contemporary governmental architecture and apparatus to address anti-social behaviour that was constructed in the New Labour period and has continued under the Conservative–Liberal Democrat Coalition government which came to power in 2010. It then explores the historical problem figuration of anti-social behaviour, drawing on the work of the German sociologist Norbert Elias and other theorists. Both the precedents and key differences of Victorian and contemporary periods are examined in turn. The chapter concludes that the wider contemporary urban context increasingly resembles the landscape and circumstances of Victorian British cities and that a sociological focus on longer-term historical figurations can illuminate our understanding of the continuities and discontinuities of these two eras.

The contemporary governance of anti-social behaviour

Tackling anti-social behaviour was a major priority of the New Labour governments between 1997 and 2010 (see Flint, 2006; Squires, 2008a; Millie, 2009a and 2009b), operationalized by a range of new governmental mechanisms. These included Anti-social Behaviour Orders (ASBOs), Dispersal Orders, Parenting Orders, Acceptable Behaviour Contracts and strengthened powers of housing management, including enhanced eviction and tighter tenancy eligibility, surveillance and controls. There was also an expansion in the use of intensive Family Intervention Projects, using key workers to investigate all elements of a household's circumstances and offer holistic packages of support and sanction (Flint, 2012).

The Conservative–Liberal Democrat Coalition government that came to power in 2010 has maintained a governmental focus on anti-social behaviour and the Anti-social Behaviour, Crime and Policing Act 2014 received Royal Assent in March 2014 (House of Commons Library, 2013a). This Act streamlines 19 existing legislative powers into six: Injunctions to Prevent Nuisance and Annoyance; Criminal Behaviour Orders; Community Protection Orders; Public Space Protection Orders; Closure Notices/Closure Orders; and Dispersal Powers. The Coalition government critiqued New Labour's enforcement approach, arguing that it failed to address the underlying causes of anti-social behaviour, emphasizing the need to prioritize prevention and 'a second chance society' and making the economic case for intensive intervention. The Coalition has also sought to facilitate an enhanced role for the community, voluntary and private sectors in addressing anti-social behaviour (Home Office, 2012b). Similar to New Labour, housing remains a central element of governmental intervention; with a new emphasis on rogue landlords and anti-social behaviour in the private rented sector (Communities and Local Government, 2011; DCLG, 2012a; House of Commons Library, 2013b).

In combination with the new Anti-social Behaviour, Crime and Policing Act 2014, the Coalition's flagship initiative is the £448m Troubled Families Programme (TFP), coordinated by the Troubled Families Unit which aims to 'turn around the lives' of 120,000 families during the 2010–15 Parliament (CLG, 2012). Every local authority in England is required to identify their most troubled families, appoint a coordinator, and design and deliver services and interventions. There is a new payment by results mechanism that proportionately funds local authorities depending on (self-verified) reductions in anti-social behaviour, school exclusions and truancy, engagement in work programmes, and/or movement off out of work benefits (CLG, 2011; DCLG, 2012b). The Scottish Government (2009) has also prioritized prevention and engagement in its framework for tackling anti-social behaviour 'Promoting Positive Outcomes'.

Despite the Coalition government's rhetorical differentiation from New Labour, the rationalities and techniques being deployed retain key elements of the previous regime, including an emphasis on early intervention, intensive whole-family projects and a belief in 'non-negotiable' support and the deterrence powers of sanctions (Home Office, 2012b). In contrast to the Coalition's rhetorical critique of the punitive elements of existing powers, the new powers being introduced actually broaden the range of behaviours that may be defined as 'anti-social', lower thresholds and burdens of proof, and extend the geographical reach of intervention. These techniques of governance reflect the broader figuration of the nature of anti-social behaviour as a problem, to which the chapter now turns.

Problem figuration

Figuration is the term used by Elias to refer to 'the modes of living together of humans' (Elias in Kilminster, 2014: 6). It emphasizes the dynamic nature of human relations with figurations in a state of flux as power relations shift, altering the nature of the social interdependencies between individuals and groups (see Elias, 1978; 2000). There are many similarities in the Victorian and contemporary 'problem figuration' (Van Wel, 1992: 148) of 'anti-social' families requiring intervention: that is, the socially constructed nature of the images of problematic households and the nature, causes and implications of the problem to be addressed, which as Fritz Van Wel (1992) argues, have always comprised both rational and fictional elements. First, in both eras, the efforts of the police, courts, local authorities and philanthropic organizations were and are primarily focused on regulating the 'rougher' or 'outsider' elements of working-class culture; seeking to exert control over public spaces and streets by clamping down on vagrancy, begging, disorderly behaviour, prostitution and illegal drinking practices (Barrie, 2010). For example, Andy Croll emphasizes the importance of public space to the Victorian sensibility and understandings of the social order. Prostitutes, corner gangs and public drunks were characters who could 'invert the norms of civilised street behaviour' and challenge the assumptions informing 'respectable street etiquette' (Croll, 1999: 257).

Secondly, both Victorian and contemporary governmentalities were and are underpinned by a 'civilizational perspective' (Mandler, 2000) in which anti-social behaviour is juxtaposed against wider progress in a self-consciously civilizing society (Crook, 2008). New Labour's Respect Agenda, which framed its governance of anti-social behaviour, was premised on a belief that 'values necessary to support respect are becoming less widely held' and that there is 'an increase in disrespectful behaviour' (Respect Task Force, 2006; Millie, 2009a). Similarly, current Prime Minister David Cameron, in defining the need for a 'Big Society' as a solution to social problems in Britain (2010) and in his immediate rhetorical response to the riots and disorder in English cities and towns in the summer of 2011 (Cameron, 2011b), has described a 'Broken Britain' characterized by 'a complete absence of self-restraint' and 'a slow motion moral collapse' (see Flint and Powell, 2012). For Victorian observers, high levels of self-control and conformity were demanded of 'respectable' males (Wise, 2012), but the city could turn the 'civilized man back almost into a savage' (de Tocqueville, quoted in Hall, 1998), and addressing the housing conditions of the working class was a response to 'homes being the cause of moral degradation' (Smith, 1980). In both eras, thresholds of decency were believed to have changed, linked to nostalgia for previous times of civility and the need for a polite ethos (Pearson, 1983; Sweet, 2002).

Thirdly, the primary understanding of the causes of anti-social behaviour is the 'character' of individuals (Crook, 2008; Riots Communities and Victims Panel, 2012), with a focus on domestic and family orientations and practices. The recent report by Louise Casey, Head of the Troubled Families Unit (DCLG, 2012c) identified the troubles of families 'arising from their home life', with an emphasis on individuals 'not being very good at relationships' and 'dysfunctional peers' and references to incest. This mirrors very long-standing tropes of deviant sexuality and domesticity (see Wise, 2009 on Victorian London) and the 'chaotic lives' of families in contemporary policy discourse have their precedents in Victorian concerns about the inability of 'anti-social' individuals to plan for the future (Crook, 2008). Such a problem figuration frames the 'disciplinary individualism' (Poovey, 1995) underpinning the techniques for regulating conduct deployed in both eras.

Precedents and parallels

Urban conditions in contemporary British cities increasingly resemble some aspects of Victorian cities, including the precarious labour market circumstances for growing sections of the population (Standing, 2011) and a housing crisis in which the private rented sector again becomes increasingly prominent in providing accommodation to the poorest households. The growth of the private rented sector has increased the visibility of significant problems of exploitative rent levels and tenancies, overcrowded and poor quality accommodation, illegal migration and benefit fraud. The New Labour administrations and the current Coalition government have responded by introducing legislative powers including mandatory and additional licensing of Houses in Multiple Occupation and Special Interim Management Orders. The government now explicitly identifies rogue landlords as a source of anti-social behaviour (DCLG, 2012a; House Commons Library, 2013b; Minton, 2012), as well as seeking to enhance the responsibilities and capacities of private landlords to regulate and manage anti-social behaviour. This expansion in the private rented sector and the growing reliance on private and voluntary provision for housing the most vulnerable families is combined with the growth of gated communities, Common Interest Developments and the privatization of urban space, including privately managed residential complexes (Minton, 2012). Such an urban landscape is reminiscent of the Victorian period of slum landlordism, refuge shelters provided by philanthropic organizations and private and commercial 'common lodging houses' (Crook, 2008; Wise, 2009; Wohl, 1977). The growing use of private security and management instruments illustrates the limitations of state power, which were apparent in the Victorian era. For example, the power of the University of Cambridge to regulate conduct in the town in the nineteenth century included appointing special constables, identifying and regulating suspected houses of ill fame and brothels and operating 'the Spinning House' a university-run prison for prostitutes (Oswald, 2012).

The Victorian and contemporary periods are further characterized by the limited sovereignty of state authorities to regulate conduct (Stenson, 2005) and the resistance of different sections of the population to governmental interventions. Figures of public authority including police officers and park wardens were regularly subjected to ridicule and on occasion assault. Mechanisms such as bye-laws and naming and shaming techniques used in Victorian local newspapers were subverted (Croll, 1999; Marne, 2001) and Metropolitan Police officers were frequently outnumbered by crowds when attempting to apprehend suspects and these suspects were often 'rescued' by these crowds (Wise, 2012). This challenge to the power and legitimacy of policing processes in the Victorian era provides a precedent for the contemporary concerns about dwindling 'respect' for authority figures that characterizes discourse about anti-social behaviour and the responses to the riots in urban England in 2011. But in the Victorian period there was also resistance from the middle and upper classes to forms of state intervention that could open up private and domestic lives to the scrutiny of bureaucratic strangers (Wise, 2012: xx; Flint, 2012). This state role in family life, for example to protect women and children from violence and in sexual matters or lunacy inquisitions, challenged what a *Medical Times* 1848 Editorial described as humanity's desire to 'draw a veil over domestic calamity' (Wise, 2012: 87).

The parallels in the techniques utilized to regulate conduct are also often striking (see Powell and Flint, 2009; Flint and Powell, 2012 for further accounts). Police courts in the 1880s regularly dealt with minor disputes between neighbours, indicating that conflicting life-styles and orientations to neighbourliness are not confined to our own era (Cockayne, 2012). Indeed, the Coalition government's new Community Trigger mechanism requiring authorities to take action where complaints about the same source of anti-social behaviour have been received from five households, has its precedent in the Nuisance Removal Act 1855, which required the complaints of two neighbours for nuisance inspectors to follow up a report. Similarly, female district visitors and Octavia Hill's housing officers in the Victorian era (see Cockayne, 2012; Flint, 2012) preceded the role of key workers in Family Intervention Projects today.

Underpinning these similarities in governance techniques between the two eras is a common assumption of moral and social decline, or of decivilizing tendencies in society, which draws upon exaggerated fears about the depacification of public space and the loss of self-restraint among sections of the population (see below for a discussion of socialization processes). Both periods exhibit a heightened level of fear related to gang violence on British streets. As Andrew Davies (1998: 351) notes, 'scuttling gangs were neighbourhood-based youth gangs which were formed in working class districts across the Manchester conurbation' in the late nineteenth century. Indeed, there is a clear resonance with twenty-first-century anti-social behaviour discourses in Davies's account of the way in which the respectable are clearly distinguished from the anti-social or morally unsound minority. Davies also acknowledges the way in which Victorian perceptions were informed by gendered constructions of 'problem' behaviour and parenting discourses – both of which are central to debates about anti-social behaviour and street violence today. Indeed, in a 2007 speech the Conservative Party MP Alan Duncan argued for the 'need to re-civilize the nation' implying that Britain is in the midst of a decivilizing process (or what he termed 'a real life Lord of the Flies'); a reversal in the overall direction that British society was heading. Thus, each era understands 'itself as standing at a point of radical discontinuity with the past' (Pearson, 1983: 210).

Yet there is more than enough existing evidence to refute the claim that western society is becoming more violent and less civilized. Two extensive, wide-ranging and meticulously researched accounts of the long-term decline of violence, written over 70 years apart, provide ample evidence of the long-term trajectory of western societies towards a more peaceful co-existence of citizens (Elias, 2000; Pinker, 2011). At the same time, Geoffrey Pearson's wonderfully detailed history of respectable anxieties from the Victorian period onwards skilfully articulates 'a seamless tapestry of fears and complaints about the deteriorated present' from the Victorian era to the contemporary period (Pearson, 1983: 207; 2009). So, if the 'decline of the present' is a stable and ubiquitous, albeit mythical, aspect of the British way of life, what is different about the 'current crisis' and in what respect does the post-1997 period diverge from the familiar and repetitious complaints of the Victorian era? For, 'it is one thing to wriggle free of the ageless mythologies of historical decline. It is quite another to leap into the arms of the equally pernicious social doctrine that nothing ever changes' (Pearson, 1983: 223). With Pearson's warning in mind, we now turn to the differences between the two periods.

Differences between Victorian and contemporary eras

A significant difference between the Victorian and contemporary period is the direction of societal and governmental shifts. While above we have identified striking similarities in the governmentality of regulating conduct and the techniques deployed to do so, these commonalities and parallels, taken as a snapshot of two specific periods, mask directly contrasting shifts. The Victorian period was characterized by the precarious and transient existence of the urban poor, a housing crisis fuelled by laissez-faire economics and rogue landlordism, and a deliberate distancing (through the moralization of poverty) of state and government from the causes of, and responsibility for responding to, the urban crisis. However, it was partly the recognition that local mercantile philanthropy and self-regulation were limited and inadequate to respond to the scale of crisis, which instigated the process of first local municipalization and, subsequently, national state intervention, including policing, public housing and the welfare state (see Hunt, 2004). So, for example, in the context of episodic rioting in Manchester in the first half of the nineteenth century, the traditional 'civic force of the town' became viewed as being 'totally inadequate to defend property from the attacks of lawless depredators' and unable to construct 'good order' (Briggs, 1963: 92). Such an understanding influenced the subsequent Borough Police Act 1844 and the Sanitary Improvement Act 1845, which sought to provide a municipal framework for regulating conduct in Manchester (Briggs, 1963).

The Victorian era was also characterized by a constant exploration of the boundaries and limitations of urban governance and the role of the state, with particular incursions into domestic residential spheres. These included growing state authority in regulating mental health, including in middle-class households (see Wise, 2012); and the housing and incarceration of the poor through by-laws, mechanisms of surveillance, a prison, asylum and sanitation inspectorate, registration and certification schemes, and the building of 'model' and municipal lodging houses (Crook, 2008; Foucault, 1977), supported by an expanding legislative framework such as the Common Lodging Houses Act 1853 and the later Public Health Act 1875. There was also increasing scrutiny by the Home Office and the development of uniform national regulations and a centralized inspectorate for lunacy asylums. The Victorian age of incarceration (Foucault, 1977) was equally a project of inspection and the move towards national standardization. This rise in municipalization and state power may be symbolized by the demolition of the University of Cambridge's 'Spinning House' in 1901 and its replacement by a police station (Oswald, 2012).

In contrast, we are now witnessing a period of active de-municipalization, in which, through the tropes of the Big Society and localism, the governance of anti-social behaviour, and accommodating the poor and vulnerable, is increasingly returned to private and charitable organizations and local residents. For some urban scholars this is seen as a key and distinctive characteristic of the neoliberal period and calls for 'linking changing forms of urban marginality with emerging modalities of state-crafting' (Wacquant, 2013: 9). It is also illustrative of the problematic nature of state intrusion upon private property and domestic realms (see Wise, 2012), which was as prominent a site of contestation in Victorian times as our own era.

As well as these governmental shifts, it is also crucial to consider changes in wider social processes and it is here that Elias's theoretical work is instructive. Elias's figurational sociology provides a useful framework for understanding the differences between the two eras; a framework which places power relations and the changing nature of social interdependencies at the centre of any understanding of behavioural and societal change (Elias, 2000). Here we use the example of *informalization* and the changing nature of socialization processes in illustrating the merits of Elias's approach, and particularly the way in which wider social changes are inextricably linked to changes in behavioural standards and human orientation.

It is clear from the preceding discussion that claims over moral decline are closely linked to nostalgia, emotions and their relationship to group relations and conflict: territorial, inter-generational, class, etc. So addressing the question of why people behave or act 'anti-socially' requires an understanding of how codes of conduct are defined and when these codes are challenged and transgressed by groups. Regardless of the timeframe, in Elias's terminology, the views of the complainants are invariably those of the 'established' (middle classes) and the targets are the lower classes, or 'outsiders'. In Elias's detailed analysis of the *Civilizing Process* (2000) he illustrates how the dominant long-term trend within western European societies is towards a stricter and more rigid control over emotions and behaviour linked to the increasing complexity, differentiation and interdependence within society. 'Put briefly, in the course of a civilizing process the self-restraint apparatus becomes stronger relative to external constraints. In addition, it becomes more even and all-embracing' (Elias, 1996: 34). However, Elias also detailed the related process of *functional democratization*, whereby the relative power balances between different groups in society are lessened as society becomes increasingly differentiated. This process is accompanied by a corresponding shift in the relations between generations and sexes and an emancipation of emotions (Wouters, 2007). For example, young women are less bound by the strict rules and etiquette of previous generations as they experience a relative increase in power, undergo an 'individualization boost' and consequently face greater demands and responsibilities in negotiating their own decision-making processes.

The Dutch sociologist Cas Wouters has developed Elias's notion further through his theory of informalization, which refers to 'the trend towards diminishing formality and rigidity in the regimes of manners and emotions and towards increasing behavioural and emotional alternatives' (Wouters,

2007: 8). These social processes are beset by tensions however as: 'people can frequently see nothing in these changes other than degeneration into disorder. It appears merely as an expression of a loosening of the code of behaviour and feeling, without which a society must fall into destruction' (Elias quoted in Mennell and Goudsblom, 1998: 245).

Historical accounts drawing on documentary evidence from the Victorian era are littered with references to the 'unrestrained liberty' and 'irresponsible freedom' of the nation's youth facilitated by a growing economic independence and the opportunities of factory employment for young women (Pearson, 1983; Croll, 1999). Similar accusations are also levelled against the youth of today with a lack of self-restraint and consideration for others (often linked to deficient parenting) being dominant themes within contemporary discourses (Respect Task Force, 2006; DCLG, 2012c; Riots Communities and Victims Panel, 2012). The empirically and historically informed work of Elias and Wouters however, highlights the changing nature of the social interdependencies between groups as a key consideration in understanding the perceived 'relaxation' in social standards. As Alexis de Tocqueville noted 'manners are softened as social conditions become equal' (quoted in Kilminster, 1998: 149). Similarly, during waves of informalization:

> the upwardly mobile strata have risen in social strength and self-awareness to such a clear degree that their members orient themselves more to each other and toward their own life-styles and modes of conduct, and reject attempts from above to colonize or discipline them as being overly patronizing or imperialistic. Members of the higher strata are forced to adopt an attitude of greater restraint, and withdraw in joint defence. In this phase the tensions in society become stronger. (Wouters, 1986: 6)

Wouters identifies waves of informalization which correspond to a heightening of fears and anxieties expressed by 'established' groups whose behavioural standards are being challenged and who face pressures to accommodate other behaviours (Wouters, 2007). Victorian respectable fears related to the working classes were often based on the idea 'that they were getting above their station in life, or that they were encroaching upon previously reserved territories of the middle class' (Pearson, 1983: 65). At the same time, the automatic identification with the standards of the established on the part of the lower strata of society, as detailed by George Orwell (1970: 411–12), is broken:

> I did not question the prevailing standards, because so far as I could see there were no others. How could the rich, the strong, the elegant, the fashionable, the powerful, be in the wrong? It was their world, and the rules they made for it must be the right ones.[1]

The 1890s and the 1920s, as well as the 1960s and 1970s, are all earmarked by Wouters as specific waves of informalization where the challenges to prevailing standards and tensions between generations and groups are more discernible, but which are ultimately part of a longer-term, gradual process of social levelling. In this sense, an appreciation of long-term social processes helps to explain the remarkably similar rationalities and governance projects of different governments across the two eras and points to the dangers of short-term (and often ideologically driven) social misdiagnosis (Kilminster, 2008), while also illuminating the discontinuities between the two periods. While we can only scratch the surface within the confines of this chapter, we would suggest that Elias's sociology offers huge potential to the longer-term study of anti-social behaviour and the social construction of deviance more broadly.

Conclusions

The history of the governmental construction of and response to anti-social behaviour is not one of cumulative acquisition of knowledge and insight about families with problems (Van Wel, 1992). Rather it reflects the particular 'structure of bias' or 'rational fiction' of the problem figuration in particular historical periods. As John Welshman (2012) argues, conceptualizations and rhetorical accounts of anti-social behaviour have always been linked to notions of a social residuum or 'underclass', perceived as being distinct from a broader working class. Though he identifies at least eight major reconstructions of the underclass debate since the later Victorian period of the 1880s, with continuities and discontinuities with previous formulations, the alleged behavioural inadequacies of the poor and the belief in intergenerational continuities have been consistently dominant themes. Both Van Wel and Welshman also powerfully argue that anti-social behaviour has often primarily served as a symbol and metaphor for urban fears and anxieties without empirical reality being established and with a failure both to fully investigate and understand the complex lives of marginalized groups, and to link these lives to wider structural societal change, and the role of government within them. It is through a focus on figurations – how wider societal change is related to individual human orientation and conduct – that the sociology of Elias and others influenced by his ideas offers a framework for such understanding.

The precedents and parallels in the framing and governance of anti-social behaviour in Victorian and contemporary periods are striking and we have sought to illustrate these. However, there are also important differences. Perhaps the central distinction is that, despite aspects of urban contexts in our own time increasingly resembling those of Victorian cities, the late Victorian response to urban crisis, including anti-social behaviour, was to construct an enhanced role for the state, at local and national levels. In contrast, current governmentalities are framed within a problematization of government itself and a promotion of non-state actors, including private and charitable (third sector) organizations, to govern conduct. This specifically includes governing anti-social behaviour as evidenced in the government's policy and good practice papers (Home Office, 2012b; DCLG, 2012b, House of Common Library, 2013b) and the new Anti-social Behaviour, Crime and Policing Act 2014 (House of Commons Library, 2013a). The new powers established in the Act broaden the range of behaviours that may be defined as 'anti-social', lower thresholds and burdens of proof, increase requirements for conditional positive behaviours and extend the geographical reach of intervention. A new discretionary ground for possession will be created where a tenant or person living with them has been convicted of an offence committed at the scene of a riot anywhere in the United Kingdom – a response to the riots in urban England in 2011. The Coalition government has also recently focused on rogue private landlords as a causal element of criminality and anti-social behaviour and emphasized enhancing the responsibilities and capacities of private landlords to regulate conduct and manage anti-social behaviour, once again illustrating the parallels with the urban housing circumstances and regulation of conduct in the Victorian era.

Note

1. We would like to thank Cas Wouters for bringing this George Orwell quote to our attention.

5
From Scurrilous Periodical to the Public Platform. Policing Blasphemers and Anti-social Behaviour: Constructing the Public Peace Then and Now

David Nash

Introduction: The modern origins of blasphemy policing

Policing blasphemy and blasphemers has caused problems for various forms of authority since time immemorial. It combines the conflicting imperatives of controlling anti-social behaviour, public order, protection of the peace and the lasting concerns of individuals having rights to freedom of expression. While the imperatives of the first two conceptions have been fundamentally important in Europe since medieval times, the issues associated with the second two have only emerged with any serious and lasting impact since the Enlightenment. Although the Reformation heightened the urge and aspiration among authority to establish behavioural conformity around the subject of religion, it was later developments that cemented the significance of this. Thus, this chapter is an assessment of how the uneasy balancing act between anti-social behaviour/public order and freedom of expression has been managed by policing authorities over the 'long nineteenth century' (1790–1920). When we turn to the recent contemporary history of blasphemy public order concerns remained paramount in the considerations of this issue by the House of Lords Select Committee of 2003. Thereafter, the arrival of incitement to religious hatred laws confirmed, more firmly than ever before, the primacy of public order approaches to the policing of blasphemy's anti-social potential. From this it emerges that, not altogether surprisingly, policing regimes understand public order imperatives and appreciate their importance to a much greater extent than more abstract concerns around freedom of expression. Moreover, during this period, whether they were overseeing events, or whether they were giving evidence in court, or advising higher authority, or interacting with the media and the public sphere, policing authorities always asserted the primacy of public order over conceptions of public freedom.

With the arrival of Enlightenment views of the universe and the individual, a more obviously ideological content crept into blasphemous utterances, and various forms of policing authority throughout Europe certainly began to theorize about the offence in this way. In England, the turn of the eighteenth century witnessed the fear of Jacobin ideas infecting English life as particularly through the writings of Thomas Paine. His work the *Age of Reason* was especially singled out for attention as indicative of challenges to Christianity, both as a philosophical belief, but also as a moral and social underpinning of government. Its populist tone as well as a cutting and damaging exposition of Christianity were perceived as a profound and proliferating danger to the government.

This frightened society little understood how to police the actions of those who seemed to be such implacable enemies of British civilization. One response was to find ways of displacing, overwriting or 'shouting down' such views with whatever means were considered appropriate. One such method was the distribution of Christian inspired tracts which preached an alternative message of forbearance and the virtues of a tried and adaptable system – in short, a method of offering the conservative message of Edmund Burke wrapped in quasi-religious language. In the years after the Napoleonic Wars, Paine's works were numerically swamped by a range and volume of these competing pamphlets, which sought to drown out the clamour for liberty from the tyranny of Christian dominated society.

Policing blasphemy in the long nineteenth century

Many of the government's fearful declarations portrayed Jacobin tendencies as held and espoused by dangerous individuals. In the 1820s, however, the government authorities found themselves faced by a much more organized political opposition. During the following decade and a half, Richard Carlile and his compatriots represented a serious, literate, and organized challenge to government and the Christianity which underpinned it. The backdrop to Carlile's radicalism was the government repression that followed the 'Six Acts', which limited the rights of individuals to publish, meet and campaign in the years after 1819. Carlile had himself published Paine's *Age of Reason*, which galvanized government opposition action against him. Once again, both government strategy and tactics were severely limited by the tools at its disposal. Precisely because these tools were limited, and the government also wanted to demonstrate a modicum of consent, it chose during this period to work with the Society for the Suppression of Vice.

This Society produced volumes of carefully worded advice for the constables of the metropolis about the nature of the especially pernicious evils within their midst. Among a host of dangerous moral evils, assaults upon religion (in the shape of both Sabbath breaking and outright blasphemy) constables were urged to apprehend and take action against those who perpetrated these offences. By focusing upon street profanation of the Sabbath and blasphemous or lewd utterance, the Society indicated that tradesmen, butchers, carters, fish carriers and soldiers were those most likely to be encountered by the constables as potential miscreants. However, the trading of lewd or blasphemous publications was also most likely to be the preserve of 'foreigners' (Society for the Suppression of Vice, 1818, *The Constable's Assistant*: 1–8).

One aspect of policing ideology this advice clearly demonstrates is a belief in a fragile moral order, potentially undermined by the smallest of unpunished moral infractions that would invite trouble leading to chaos and the collapse of civilized society. This envisaged a sort of domino theory in which, as each infraction went unpunished, it established the likelihood that a subsequent, still greater, offence would take its place. Nonetheless, there was also a specific role for religion closely related to the definition of the offence of blasphemy. As the Society's advice to its constables noted, the English common law of blasphemy defined in a 1675 case, suggested that religion was 'part and parcel of the law of the land' with the clear implication that to attack one of these bricks of the Constitution was to attack the whole edifice – this construction thus meant preventing blasphemy and defending the peace would always remain linked together in policing mentalities during the nineteenth century. Although this policing must have been effective against ignorant, wilful or negligent tradesmen, it was scarcely prepared for action against the ideologically committed. This was especially the case when the part and parcel argument also made both the law and religion targets for attack. In this respect, attacks upon religion were more readily spotted than attacks upon the fundamental and inviolable nature of the law (Carlile *et al.*, 1825: 15, 17 and 56).

By 1824, the folly, ineffectiveness and unpopularity of this hybrid public and private action against blasphemers became obvious when the government under Sir Robert Peel was forced to abandon cooperating with the Vice Society. This is an important point at which to consider whether the policing of blasphemy in the first third of the nineteenth century was in any sense effective. As with any 'dark figure' in criminal and legal history, it is impossible to know how many incidents of blasphemy were prevented by the law's agencies and their function as an active deterrent. Nonetheless, the record of these agencies was scarcely exemplary or effective. The 'shouting down' of radical views may conceivably have displaced them from some eyes and ears, but they did not dissuade the committed – or even the half-committed. Prosecutions were not always effective and the management of these and courtroom procedure could be so obviously partial as to be counter-productive. Such actions, included the denial of prosecuting evidence to the defence alongside the sometimes perilously short periods of time allowed to prepare defences, and these were regularly exposed by energetic and determined defendants who had access to avidly consumed organs of publicity (Harling, 2001). Yet arguably, the situation also should have been easier for the government authorities and private agencies of this period. They did not face, in the fullest sense, the problematic balancing act felt by later social democratic societies. While they clearly had a manifesto to root out anti-social behaviour and protect people from the chaos threatening society, they obviously had rather less in the way of constraints upon free speech to consider. In this period, it was clear that preserving the social peace trumped individual rights. However, such decisions were less easy to make as the century progressed.

Nonetheless, by the middle of the nineteenth century the Home Office and policing agencies had begun to learn important lessons. One particular piece of legislation, the Town Police Clauses Act 1847 (51 & 52 Vict. c. 47), regulated profanity in an especially flexible manner. In the early 1850s, action against publications was avoided through the use of the refrain that it was 'impolitic to call attention to this by the prosecution' (Home Office file HO45 3017). However, one individual scrutinized in this manner was John Stuart Mill who gave a lecture in Newcastle, in January 1851. Mill's lecture was the culmination of a number of philosophically discursive meetings that had occurred in Newcastle. This had meant that the local authorities were prepared for Mill's arrival because plainclothes policemen and reporters were stationed in the audience. Mill did not disappoint either section of his audience since he questioned the veracity of the Bible because its various translations could not agree on the meaning of certain passages, and in the end pronounced it 'of no service to mankind, the book of revelation "was destitute of everything that was useful" '. The local authorities in Newcastle wanted a lead from London, but the Home Office was adamant that it would leave the responsibility within the locality declaring:

> We are of opinion that John Mill is liable to prosecution and that it may be either by indictment or by information but we think it proper to add that we should in this case consider it highly inexpedient for the government to institute any such proceedings but that it may be properly left to the magistrate to take such cause in this matter as they may consider to be most advisable. (HO45 3537)

This attitude effectively sums up the growing gulf between the attitudes of central government and local policing administration. Central government would not lend support to beleaguered local authorities, nor take action on its own account. Local agencies might take action themselves, but it was clear they would do so on their own initiative and without central government support; this had also happened when George Jacob Holyoake had been prosecuted in Cheltenham in 1842 at the behest of individuals who had persuaded him to utter blasphemous and injudicious remarks (Nash, 1999: 93–5). While this safeguarded the Home Office from criticism, local authorities felt themselves bereft of help and the support of central agencies. This would re-emerge as a theme later on in the history of blasphemy in England. Moreover, this tension between demands to protect local standards of morality against central (federal) indifference would become a standard of the American history of censorship and the control of morality (Heins, 1993). In many nineteenth-century and early twentieth-century incidents, the initiative of local authorities seeking to protect communal standards of morality saw their crusades quashed by federal action, which regularly declared such initiatives unconstitutional.

Thus, another element was becoming important in the philosophy of policing blasphemy. The Home Office could afford to be relaxed about passing incidents, such as the one that had occurred in Newcastle in 1851, since whatever action had been deemed necessary at the time had clearly been taken by the local policing authority. This meant their immediate concerns had now firmly focused upon the rather more precise issue of public order: an easier equation for any individual policeman or police authority to calculate. The precise offensiveness of material became a matter for debate while the preservation of public order and breaches of it through blasphemy were evidently a matter for the police to take immediate and decisive action. The police themselves were also actively asked to behave in this way, especially when such things occurred where they did not have an obvious presence. An example which demonstrates this happened in a London open space (Regent's Park) in 1884, where the local Constabulary did not have clear jurisdiction. A man from the Protestant Evangelical Mission and Electoral Union, a Mr William Browne had been accused of inflammatory pronouncements about the Catholic Church and Faith. During the course of this, he had been attacked several times by several members of the Catholic Church. One of those accosting Browne declared, when speaking to a police inspector, 'how would you like to have your religion run down and ridiculed like that; what would you do if you heard me, or anyone else, preaching that the Queen was a whore and that sort of thing' (HO45 9645A3). The plea here was a request to take action, but also an acknowledgement that the police had a fundamental role in protecting public order.

Blasphemy in the 1880s

The nature of this approach to policing – whereby local agencies empowered themselves – was arguably emphasized by the action of one particular Home Secretary, Sir William Harcourt. Harcourt operated a version of this policing phenomenon in London in the early 1880s. In this he appeared sometimes to act like a local magistrate since frequently he was advised against action – opinions which he often disregarded. As the 1880s dawned, Sir William Harcourt found London colonized by an effective and popular secularist movement led by the ideology's leading advocate of the latter part of the century, Charles Bradlaugh. Attempts to discredit Bradlaugh and prevent him from entering Parliament after he had been duly elected persuaded one secularist journalist, George William Foote, to make a concerted attempt to break the blasphemy laws. This he did through a newspaper entitled the *Freethinker*, which ran the gamut of biblical jokes, serious assaults upon aspects of Christian doctrine, anti-religious cartoons and a great variety of anti-clericalism. With each issue, Foote pushed further at the boundaries of what was acceptable and many contemporary commentators wondered why the government waited so long before taking action. Initially Harcourt held to the standard policing line, namely that to take action against such publications would be counter-productive and court unnecessary publicity for them. However, by May 1882, Harcourt changed his mind and wanted Foote pursued with every means available to the law and was only prevented from a reckless mistake by the stern advice of the Attorney General, Sir Henry James.

However, the action of Foote and the *Freethinker* was to escalate the depth of the offence. The *Freethinker*'s Christmas number of 1882 included a comic strip life of Christ, pirated from the French anti-clerical Leo Taxil, alongside other articles undermining Christian doctrine. It is ironic that this seemed to be a reversal of the philosophy that underpinned policing in the first years of the nineteenth century. The very failure to take action in this instance provoked blasphemers to stronger and deeper levels of offence – the growing menace that would have been stamped out by prompt action in an earlier epoch. Harcourt wanted to take action despite the belief among his more junior civil servants that the Home Office should remain aloof from such actions. Once a privately initiated court case had commenced, both Harcourt and the Home Office could step into the shadows until the matter was concluded. Eventually this is what transpired.

When the result of a private prosecution went against Foote and his fellow defendants (Ramsey and Kemp) all three were convicted and imprisoned. This provoked considerable outcry from the literary world and wider liberal England. The Home Office was faced with a veritable deluge of petitions claiming that blasphemy laws were against 'the spirit of the age' – a phrase George William Foote was particularly fond of using. For the first time, all of this starkly demonstrated the dilemma of policing a free society which still had usable and potent blasphemy laws. Foote's work promoted free speech imperatives, but the logical consequence of these also produced offence on a considerable scale. Although many signed petitions against his incarceration, there were also letters regularly arriving at the Home Office declaring his writings and publications to be deplorable and unacceptable. This policing dilemma was perhaps behind many subsequent occasions when the

Freethinker and its potentially blasphemous contents were brought to the attention of subsequent Home Secretaries. In these instances, the Home Office agreed to shelve the matter and not pursue prosecution by ensuring it would not gain unnecessary publicity and would merely circulate among those that would not find its message injurious or offensive (HO45 10406 A46794). Again this reflected a marked preference for, wherever possible, seeing blasphemy as a public order issue – a situation which policing philosophies were more comfortable dealing with. Indeed even Foote used this to his advantage in his accusation that if he were a dangerous and vulgar challenge to Christian England, then the Salvation Army posed an equally dangerous and vulgar challenge to his own personal atheism. This particularly hit home since the Salvation Army had been a considerable public order headache to the Home Office in the years leading up to the Foote case (HO45 9613A9).

Public order had also been enshrined in the change in the law that had occurred as a result of one of the cases against Foote. The so-called Coleridge judgment effectively admitted that it was no longer blasphemous to attack Christianity. In seeking to weave its way between the imperatives of protection and free speech this reached for a public order solution. It stated categorically that the 'manner' in which anti-religious words were spoken was the test of its offensiveness. Thus this brought to mind real-life situations where the views of one were actively (face-to-face) encountered by the opposing views of another individual. Though some senior judges such as James Fitz James Stephen saw this as prolonging a bad and unworkable law, those lower down the policing hierarchy tended to welcome it as providing a workable measure of offensiveness and a set of tools for taking action only when it was absolutely necessary.

Policing blasphemy in Edwardian England

Public order was once again at the forefront of police concerns as the twentieth century dawned. Ideological challenges and the importance of the public sphere had been heightened by the spread of anarchism at the end of the nineteenth century. With such international and far-reaching challenges to the social order, it is no surprise that some blasphemers in this period had associations with individuals of an anarchist bent. This association, and to an extent some of the nihilism that went with it, shaped the manner and tone of blasphemous rhetoric during these years. One individual against whom the police took action was the street preacher Harry Boulter who regularly launched inflammatory attacks upon the Bible and numerous Christian doctrines. What appeared uppermost in many of the reports of Boulter's activities was a suggestion that his views were anti-social, scurrilous and uncouth. This reawoke many of the criticisms of the Coleridge judgment since some argued that it was opinions being prosecuted. However, policing philosophy which concentrated upon public order as its imperative would be duty-bound to say that it was precisely such people that posed a profound and potentially dangerous public order threat. As such, they cut through rhetoric about opinions to focus on much more precise issues. Harry Boulter indeed had gone beyond denying the existence of Christ and had raised the stakes considerably with a genuinely threatening promise to kill anyone he found to be a Christian. This clearly echoed the Coleridge judgment and its assessment of the 'manner' in which words were spoken and how these still constituted an issue strongly related to public order.

Although Boulter was a genuine hothead whose potential threat was relatively easily neutralized, there was greater difficulty taking action against three more sophisticated individuals: Thomas William Stewart, Ernest Pack and John William Gott. In their lectures, biblical doctrines were attacked and Stewart (lecturing with his stage name of Dr Nikola) offered family limitation advice and literature promoting this. Although many chief constables were content merely to take notes of what occurred at their meetings, their regularity and persistence eventually meant that the authorities somewhere would be drawn into action. In December 1911, the Chief Constable of Leeds showed how his hand had been forced:

> For some years past, certain individuals have periodically visited Leeds and addressed meetings in the street on religious matters. Their discourse although of a very vulgar character and to a great extent blasphemous, have not hitherto been made the subject of police proceedings, although the speakers have been a cause of great trouble to the police. The man Gott has been a frequent offender in this respect. In July last, however, the man Stewart (also known as Nikola) first appeared upon the scene, and the violent character of his language attracted a large concourse of people, as many as 1000 persons being reported to be present. (HO 144 871 160552)

When Stewart's case came to court, the inexperience of policemen not regularly called upon to regulate blasphemy laws came to the surface. One of the indictments contained wording which had been lifted from the original blasphemy statute of 1698. This lent real confusion to proceedings since it was unclear under which law (statute or common law) individuals were being prosecuted. This allowed Stewart, and his fellow defendant Gott, to claim they had the 'manner' protection extended by the Coleridge judgment. For philosophies of policing blasphemy, this was something of a very tense moment since it threatened to remove the entire public order justification for police action. If this had been allowed to stand, it would conceivably have provided something of a free speech charter, not dissimilar to that enjoyed by the First Amendment provisions of the American Constitution. The eventual opinion of the judge reimposed limits, regaining possession of the 'manner' issue around blasphemy and its expression. Justice Horridge once again focused upon language and that the test of offensiveness was its capacity to irritate or occasion breach of the peace among religious people. Indeed this section of the Horridge judgment was particularly underlined in Home Office papers indicating its assent to its contents and considerable relief that the issue had been resolved in this way (Nash, 1999: 185).

In the years after the First World War, stretching through to the years leading up to the Second World War, there were regular attempts to repeal the blasphemy laws in England. The records of these are particularly useful in demonstrating the attitude of government to how these laws should be regulated. Generally speaking, those who were socially and politically progressive argued for the repeal of these laws, although the British Labour Party would always fight shy of offering party political support for such a measure. Home Office commentaries on attempts to repeal the laws once again betray an enduring obsession with public order. Rejecting a proposal to repeal the Town Police Clauses Act of 1847 (51 & 52 Vict. c. 64) a civil servant at the Home Office noted that protecting the blasphemer would create a legal anomaly since this behaviour on public streets was as likely to be as offensive as indecent or obscene language. Thus, why should the blasphemer receive protection while the other forms of expression would continue to be prosecuted (Nash, 1999: 195)? Nonetheless, the same civil servant was prepared to consider repealing the blasphemy laws *provided* that the public order elements of the Town Police Clauses Act would remain intact and could convincingly do the job.

Policing blasphemy: the contemporary history in Britain

When the House of Lords Select Committee on Religious Offences met in 2003, it found itself pitched into the centre of the classical liberal dilemma faced by modern social democratic societies. From the first, it was torn in a number of directions. It felt compelled to state that Britain was still a Christian country, yet was also anxious to enshrine the benefits of free speech in its approach to what was potentially anachronistic thinking and law-making. It had also to think its way through the consequences of Christianity now comprising merely a section of the wider religious community within Britain. As if these three concerns were not enough, it was also coming to realize that the partiality of blasphemy laws were under threat from supranational jurisdictions and law-making bodies – in this case emanating from the European Union. The Committee felt relatively certain that the existing common law of blasphemous libel was probably unfit for purpose (the statute law had been repealed in the early 1960s), but had other important and pressing issues to consider. It listened patiently to representatives from the contemporary secularist and humanist movements who argued the law should be repealed. The Committee's members exhibited considerable sympathy with this view, but in turn suggested there were real public order concerns that they had to address. In showing inflammatory leaflets, which racist right-wing organizations had placed through the letterboxes of individuals in the north of England, this House of Lords Select Committee was showing the very latest dimension of the public order imperative.

Thus, one aspect of its deliberations was to establish that blasphemy laws perhaps could be consigned to the dustbin of history, but they would need to be replaced by laws against incitement to religious hatred. These would equalize religions, perhaps quite neatly, but would not address the lingering concerns of the earlier century civil servants (who had approved of the Horridge judgment) who were concerned that the blasphemer would otherwise escape justice. In this instance, the blasphemer was argued to be the object of justice allowing other forms of offensiveness to escape. This prompted the suggestion that wider forms of legislation against incitement to hate should be enacted and some subsequent, if limited, legislation has followed this path.

Although the Select Committee had appeared to offer the removal of remaining blasphemy laws in return for incitement laws, this was not eventually the course of action that was followed. The blasphemy law remained intact, while a law against incitement to religious hatred joined it as a central part of the law in this area. Governments tried to incorporate religious hatred into the Serious Organised Crime and Police Bill 2004, but it was sacrificed in the run up to the 2005 General Election. This anomalous situation did not last for long and the law of blasphemous libel fell one evening in 2008 following the persistence of a private member, the Liberal Democrat MP Evan Harris, who placed it into an amendment to the Criminal Justice and Immigration Bill (2007–08).

Two years before this, the play *Behzti* (its actors and its audience) had been besieged in a Birmingham theatre by members of the local Sikh community who argued the play brought discredit to a sacred text by having it on stage, while acts that could defile it were part of the play's action. For the police, this was again a public order issue turning around anti-social behaviour, rather than any need to recognize the multicultural nature of religious offence and legislate. Indeed, according to press reports, the management of the theatre had been advised that the policing of this issue was a considerable drain upon the public purse (Nash, 2010: 34–5). This incident led to police activity arguably demonstrating how public order considerations had been further enshrined in legislation. The Racial and Religious Hatred Act 2006, which amended the Public Order Act 1986, also reflected this since the original conceptions of 'abuse' and 'insult' were removed from the eventual legislation by the House of Lords which, potentially mindful of its ambivalence earlier in the decade, came down in favour of making 'Religious Hatred' a public order question. Trying to assess the abusiveness or insulting tone of material was shelved in favour of whether it could be considered 'threatening' to peace or order.

Despite this, the history of blasphemy and its policing does not end here. There are indications that its status may follow the American model after blasphemy prosecutions became unconstitutional there in 1952 (Burstyn v Wilson, 343, U.S. 495 1952). In the United States, this had driven organizations and individuals seeking to protect religion to starve suspect forms of free expression of taxpayer's dollars, or to the claim that they were species of obscenity – the one form of expression not protected by First Amendment rights. In England, this led to the exploration of this area in a case which followed soon after. This concerned an arts display at the Baltic Centre for Contemporary Art Gateshead, Newcastle upon Tyne, at which a statue of Christ with an erect penis had caused offence. While it was not altogether clear what the precise blasphemy was (mocking a religious figure or indeed even suggesting that he had a wholly human existence) it was clear that a blasphemy prosecution was no longer possible. Nonetheless, motivated Christian legal opinion looked closely at section 5 of the Public Decency Act 1986 to see if action could be taken. The case collapsed when the individual bringing the prosecution was shown never to have attended the exhibition. From this point onwards, the Crown Prosecution Service stepped in and took charge of this particular incident. Removing this from the hands of individuals was something that many had argued for since the start of the twentieth century and the fear of the arbitrariness this provoked seemingly stretched right the way back to the Vice Society and the cloak and dagger atmosphere that surrounded its activities. Once the Crown Prosecution Service intervened in this particular case, it decided that the individuals at the art exhibition had no case to answer. This was because there had been no public disorder at the exhibition and, importantly, significant provisos had been put in place to ensure such offence or public disorder did not occur. In this instance, the obvious visibility of warnings about the possible offensiveness individuals might encounter at the exhibition proved decisive.

Truly, this very last factor brought Britain into line with many European countries whose blasphemy laws had fallen at a much earlier stage. In these countries, individuals were required to realize and demonstrate much higher levels of individual personal responsibility in their journey through the cultures of their respective countries. Thus, the existence and provision of warning signs prevented anti-social behaviour and offence. Moreover the fundamental principle that individuals have the responsibility to accept the cultures of others and regulate their own strong feelings had long governed how countries like Germany and, to a lesser extent France, would be dismissive of the individual claiming damage to their religious feelings. In this respect, almost by accident, the policing of blasphemy in Britain, if not the policing of incitement to religious hatred and the anti-social behaviour that went with this, at last caught up with its European siblings.

Conclusion

Thus, as we have seen, there is a persistent strand of policy and attitude that runs through the policing of blasphemy from the end of early modern times until the twenty-first century. This is perhaps surprising given the far-reaching developments in most other aspects of policing technology and philosophies. Nonetheless, forms of authority, whether in the medieval world or Victorian England, displayed a surprisingly enduring perception of how to approach the crime and the policing of it. Throughout policing was expected to prevent the consequences of anti-social behaviour in the form of blasphemy. In its initial phases this protected religion as the ideology of early modern society. Especially in England this equated religion with the law and thus guaranteed prosperity and stability. In the seventeenth and eighteenth centuries, the policing of this anti-social behaviour aimed to prevent its escalation into something more dangerous and threatening to society. This policing of minor infractions to prevent major ones was arguably the only strategy available to a society that scarcely understood what policing could mean. The Victorian experience was perhaps partially successful. Although policing authorities and their interventions were spectacularly noticed when they went wrong, they were quietly successful when they stayed their hand and allowed issues to dissipate or blow over. By the end of the twentieth century, they arguably felt on much surer ground with the recasting of blasphemy laws into versions of incitement to religious hatred laws. Unlike their predecessors, these all had direct application to issues of public order and were thereafter generally easier to regulate and operate. Thus, we can see that throughout the period investigated by this chapter, philosophies of policing, as well as its agents and policing mechanism, frequently clung on to the concept of preserving public order because it was practical and easily understood. Moreover, it dictated the action that beleaguered individuals in these institutions could take when faced by the much more opaque concepts of freedom and free speech. The final arrival of laws against incitement to religious hatred actively enshrine these principles by making real public order transcend abstract ideals of freedom of expression – thus enabling policing agencies to go about their business with greater levels of confidence and professionalism.

6
Anarchists, Authorities and the Battle for Public Space, 1880–1914: Recasting Political Protest as Anti-social Behaviour

Constance Bantman

Introduction

Victorian anarchists in Britain were a marginal group whose political significance far outweighed their actual powers and scope for action. As a catalyst for discourses and debates, their history provides many insights into the values and fears of their contemporaries regarding immigration, crime, urbanization, the rise of the labour movement and the meaning of British liberalism (Shpayer, 1981: 23; Shpayer-Makov, 1988; Bantman, 2013). The anarchist groups who burst onto the public stage in the late 1880s and remained there until the First World War brought together native militants and immigrants from all over Europe, notably Eastern Europe, France and Italy. At the end of the nineteenth century, London became the main refuge for those individuals who sought to escape repression in their own countries, as anarchist-inspired terrorist attacks brought a great deal of police attention and repression to the movement. For many contemporary observers and politicians – especially those with Conservative leanings – anarchists were therefore suspect on the triple count of their status as immigrants, potential terrorists and socialists. As a result, they found themselves the centre of lively debates throughout the period. These resulted in formal legislation aimed at controlling their entry into Britain, alongside that of other 'undesirable' population categories, with the Aliens Act passed in 1905.

This chapter argues that the case of the anarchists provides a long-term perspective on discourses about anti-social behaviour and the ways in which they were modified by far-reaching socioeconomic changes, which came to maturity in the last decades of the century. In this light, the moral panics provoked by the 'anarchist peril', as it was then known, can be interpreted as a reinvention of the association between the labouring classes and the dangerous classes established earlier in the nineteenth century. The end-of-century variation on this now-familiar motive incorporated new emphases on degeneracy, the risks of immigration, transnational conspiracies and a different view of the threat posed to traditional British values by radical political protest. Equally noteworthy is the centrality of space and physical perception in constructing notions of deviancy, through the fears generated by the mere sight – actual or imagined – of anarchists in the city, as well as recurring arguments over their presence in public spaces, especially highly symbolic ones such as Trafalgar Square in London. Consequently, controlling and restricting the physical presence of anarchists in the metropolis, or, on the contrary, deciding not to impose any control over it, became key stakes in the debates. These developments illustrate Leif Jerram's claim that 'politics in this urban context [became] not just a battle for ideas, but fundamentally a battle about whose band played loudest, whose street discipline was clearest' (Jerram, 2011: 23). The dilemmas over the extent to which anarchist presence and propaganda in public should be allowed were a symptom of diverging opinions regarding the limits of liberal toleration. They also underline the role of visual elements and 'street problems' as a historical constant in debates on anti-social behaviour, as well as the role of public spaces as key symbolical stakes and agents in political debates (South Kesteven District Council, 2013).

In this chapter, the revivification of the early and mid-century equation between labouring and dangerous classes, with new connotations, in the context of anarchism, will be examined first. The subsequent redefinition of anarchism and socialism as forms of anti-social behaviour will then be charted. The perceived need to restrict manifestations of anarchism as a result, leading to a symbolic battle over the occupancy of public spaces which is characteristic of efforts to control anti-social behaviour, will be discussed in a third part.

Labouring classes, dangerous classes: the anarchists and the nineteenth-century criminal equation

The 1880s was a period of growing stigmatization but relative tolerance for anarchists in Britain, at a time when continental countries opted for a drastic repression of the movement, while only a few voices could be heard calling for similar measures to be adopted in Great Britain; consequently, in the 1880s and 1890s, anti-anarchist fears were the preoccupation of a minority over a radical group. But the anarchist stereotype was well entrenched; moreover, as the movement attracted a lot of negative publicity owing to its terrorist involvements – both actual and suspected – the stereotype underwent several evolutions. To begin with, stereotypical depictions of anarchists rehearsed the familiar themes connected with representations of crime and deviancy: 'the companions' (the term chosen by anarchists to describe themselves) were commonly depicted as an anti-society of villains conspiring against society, with a criminal subculture or a fully-fledged counter-culture. The conspiracy motive had different guises: agents spoke of an 'anarchist *Bund*' (APP BA1509, 19 June 1894) led by a London-based 'committee', of a 'cult', of 'the dynamite party' (*Le Gaulois*, 1887) and, most frequently, of the great anarchist 'conspiracy'. Whichever terminology was used, the emphasis on a secret malicious organization was the recurring feature: 'Whether it succeeds or not, the fact of the conspiracy is beyond doubt, and the international anarchists in refuge in London expect to hear, any minute, that "the universe is free from its worst tyrants"'(APP BA435, 16 September 1884). The emphasis on internal structures and hierarchies which had been an important element of this collective criminal imagination earlier in the century was not absent from representations of anarchist groupings: some journalists did not hesitate to speak of 'the adherents of the various sections' of the movement, ignoring the fact that anarchism, being a libertarian and anti-hierarchical ideology, did not condone any such formal political structure in their groups ('The Anarchist in London', *Otautau Standard and Wallace County Chronicle*, 1909). However, in the context of anarchism, the earlier obsession with internal organization tended to be replaced with an insistence on transnational tentacles – a clue to the late Victorians' increased sense of living in a global age, where crime too was organized across borders (Knepper, 2009).

Secrecy and conniving were unavoidable motives in any discussion of anarchists. The London companions famously met at the Autonomie Club (Charlotte Street and then Windmill Road), which attracted much speculation: 'The activity of the club extended also to the provinces, and its assistance was readily given to the promotion of crime and the spread of anarchism' ('The Anarchist in London', *Otautau Standard and Wallace County Chronicle*, 1909). The press relished detailing the signs of anarchist affiliations and behaviour: for instance, pointing to the supposedly tell-tale sign sported by Charles Gallau when he came to London in 1894 in order to attend the funeral of his fellow French anarchist Martial Bourdin; a portrait of Ravachol, who was one of the early French practitioners of anarchist terrorism ('Arrest of an alleged anarchist', *Daily News*, 1894). Such an obsession with signs and secret codes derived from the imagination of secret political societies and groupings was still very much alive in the nineteenth century (Girardet, 1986) and was spurred by the realities of existence in a large industrial metropolis, with its interplay of hidden and visible activities. In this sense, representations of anarchists testified to a new, urban criminal imagination.

An important new inflection to early- and mid-century discourses on anti-social behaviour was the addition of immigration as a key theme. The context in which immigration grew to be perceived as a problem in this period was that Britain became host to tens of thousands of deprived immigrants fleeing poverty and persecution in Eastern Europe (Gainer, 1972; Fishman, 2004). While anarchists were not numerous enough to be perceived as problematic owing to the size of their groups, with respect to competition for jobs and housing, several public figures conflated anti-anarchist and anti-immigration arguments – a strategy facilitated by the development of an organized Jewish anarchist and trade union movement. The campaigner Arnold White was pivotal in building a sense of threat attached to both immigration and labour, in the broad perspective of the demise of English values. In 1885, he was one of the leading exponents of state-sponsored emigration to Canada, which he saw as a solution to growing social unrest – an evil which, in his view, was chiefly embodied by H.M. Hyndman and the Social Democratic Federation, with their 'wild and sanguinary talk' ('Mr Hyndman and Distress in London', *The Times*, 25 January 1887). Come 1887, his argument had shifted and his main concern was now 'pauper immigration' as the main threat to social stability. In 1892, *The Destitute Alien in Britain*, an essay collection on these themes edited by White, drew links between immigration (with hints at cultural incompatibility), poverty and the threat of socialism:

> They come simply to swell the swollen tide of immigration into the towns, to reduce the rate of wages there, and therefore to strengthen that spirit of discontent and disorder on which the agitators live and batten, and which in time may pollute the ancient constitutional liberalism of England with the visionary violence of Continental Socialism [...] Mr. Burns, Mr. Tillett and Mr. Mann could raise a *Judenhetze* tomorrow if they liked to do it. (Jeyes, 1892: 189–91)

Like White, Sir Howard Vincent was another influential person who brought together the themes of anarchism, immigration and labour protests. On 19 February 1894, in the immediate aftermath of Martial Bourdin's death, he asked in the Commons whether 'the Government propose to place any limit upon foreign immigration or the reception in the overcrowded centres of the United Kingdom of the refuse population of Europe?' ('Foreign Anarchists in London' House of Commons Sitting, 1894). The use of the terms 'overcrowded' and 'refuse' were clear hints at Booth's residuum, threatening the country's social and political stability as well as its moral welfare. Less than a decade later, Vincent was Britain's main emissary to the International anti-anarchist conference in Rome, where an international legislation to control anarchists was agreed upon.

Most continental anarchists escaped the full stigma of such anti-immigration discourses, owing to the fact that they came from Western and Christian nations. They might be called 'political desperadoes of all nationalities', and in the aftermath of terrorist attacks initiated by French exiles, the press repeatedly noted that 'the club where these homicidal lunatics met had a French name; its members were Germans, Frenchmen, Poles, Russians – but not English' (*The Bristol Mercury and Daily Post*, 1894). However, Western European anarchists were rarely discussed as members of an inferior race because of their ethnic origin ('Aliens Bill. Second Reading', House of Lords Sitting, 1894). The emphasis on their foreign origins was constant, and their Latin characteristics were often underlined, but this was most likely due to the association between Latin nations and revolutionary tendencies, which were considered very 'un-English'. For instance, for the influential Italian criminal anthropologist Cesare Lombroso, hot temperatures were conducive to insurrections, and 'the number of seditions' grew as one travelled southwards from the North (Lombroso, 1896: 165–7). But while racial discourses about the anarchists were less stigmatizing, like Eastern European Jewish immigrants, they were commonly described as degenerates, which was another recent addition to the criminal stereotype at the end of the century, under the influence of phrenology and Lombroso's criminal anthropology. Lombroso himself completed a full-length study of anarchists as an example of 'congenial criminality' (Lombroso, 1896: 59) – a theme and a keyword, which brought together fears of individual and collective decay. The progress of criminal anthropology as one of the main lenses filtering public perceptions of anarchism, as well as the sharp rise in Jewish immigration into Britain meant that anarchists and immigrants were jointly subsumed under a new racial discourse which served to exclude them. The conflation was helped by the existence of a significant immigrant Jewish and trade union movement, and manifested itself very clearly in the Aliens Act 1905, which considered as 'an undesirable immigrant [...] the insane, the diseased, the criminal, the putative public charge' (Gainer, 1972: 200).

Socialism as anti-social behaviour

While these traits were fairly generic in discussions of crime, the most powerful association in fanning the panic triggered by anarchism was socialism. At a time when the 'socialist revival' increasingly materialized into an organized, militant labour movement, with parliamentary counterparts, the tenets of mid-Victorian stability seemed to come under increased pressure. The opponents of anarchism conflated it with terrorism in an attempt to tarnish the entire anarchist movement, but also all socialist organizations. This process transpired in writings by eminent Victorian writers, which may be described as a late resurgence of the old theme of the 'dangerous and labouring classes' (Arnett Melchiori, 1985). However, it remains to be established to what extent this fear was felt by the population, and spread by politicians and the media. Such interpretations have been debated by historians, resulting in the suggestion that the political fears inspired by radicals and the poor were a minority phenomenon. Bernard Porter, for instance, has spoken of 'a drop in an ocean of murder, suicide, infanticide, epidemic,

accident and other "natural" horrors' to characterize the comparative importance of anarchism for the crime-obsessed Victorians (Porter, 1987: 107).
That the threats supposedly posed by anarchists were a minority concern
is confirmed by facts, and especially debates in Parliament, where calls for
anti-anarchist measures modelled on the Continent's did not prevail against
non-interventionist arguments until the Aliens Act 1905. However, there is
no doubt that the protests that occurred between 1886 and 1889, starting
with the Bryant and May Strike, through to Bloody Sunday and the Dockers'
Strike, loomed large in the mind of contemporaries and determined the perception of anarchism. As late as 1893, the connection was made between
London's unemployed and their protests and the risk of continental-style
terrorism:

> Attention has been called to a meeting, stated to have been held at Tower
> Hill, of the unemployed, when a speech was made by a Mr. Jewnes [...]
> in which he said [...] that unless the demands of the unemployed were
> satisfied before Christmas, there would be a reign of terror in London
> unprecedented in the annals of history, and deeds would be perpetrated
> which would have more effect, and cause a greater sacrifice of life, than
> those which had occurred in the French Chamber of Deputies and at
> Barcelona. ('The unemployed meetings in London', House of Commons
> Sitting, 1893)

In other words, the traditional association between labouring and dangerous
classes was revived, albeit with a new emphasis on terrorism and violence,
since 'the French Chamber of Deputies' and 'Barcelona' were references to
anarchist-inspired terrorist attacks. The same speech had already been discussed in the Commons, with direct reference to the anarchists, in the
context of a question on the asylum afforded to French anarchists in Britain
('The Anarchists', House of Commons Sitting, 1893). Similarly, some papers
juxtaposed attention-catching headlines about anarchism with reports on
labour activism, thereby associating them implicitly. Such strategies are illustrated by *The Bristol Mercury*, which ran a small paragraph entitled 'The
London unemployed – an incendiary speech' just next to a longer article on
the London anarchists, suggesting that some working-class organizers were
turning to the anarchists' direct-action methods: 'He would be sorry to prop-
agate a system of fires, but if fires did nothing else they provided a certain
amount of work and if half of London were burned down much more work
would be created' ('The London unemployed. An incendiary speech', *The
Bristol Mercury and Daily Post*, 1894).

Paradoxically, while the fear of radical politics and class fear lay at the
root of public sentiment against anarchists, a process of depoliticization
in the depiction of anarchism and anarchists was notable. Their ideas
were systematically dismissed as mad, erroneous, and only a handful of

newspapers considered them as political ideologies (Shpayer-Makov, 1988: 510). The same process prevailed at the legal level, whereby anarchism gradually stopped being seen as a political ideology (which involved granting its champions a number of rights, and especially asylum), and was reclassified as a criminal affiliation (through the Aliens Act 1905 and several extradition cases in the 1890s). The Marquess of Salisbury, one of the most vocal advocates of changes in asylum laws thus stated in the Lords that:

> Everything has changed since the days of Kossuth, Mazzini, and Garibaldi. It is no longer a case of liberty against despotism. It is no longer a question of giving a harbour of safety to those who, in the vicissitudes of politics, have failed to carry their own ideals into effect. You are now dealing with men for whom any such excuse is impossible, and would be almost disgraceful. You are dealing with men who commit crimes. ('Aliens Bill', Second Reading, House of Lords sitting, 1894)

This was the continuation of a longer trend in the treatment of potentially disruptive groups. Victor Bailey, focusing on the first half of the century, has examined 'how and why the collective construct of the "dangerous classes" was gradually reduced by social classification and by police and penal routines to the slimmer notion of the "criminal classes", no longer associated with political subversion and social breakdown' (Bailey, 1993: 222). A similar process characterized the treatment of anarchists; it started in the 1880s in most European countries, and was only completed in 1905 and 1914, but the ideological and discursive strategies of the 1890s were essential in paving the way for the redefinition of liberalism and the way the state dealt with internal revolutionary threats and the gradual recasting of a primarily political debate in terms of criminality and anti-social behaviour.

Anarchism, public space and social breakdown

The risk of social breakdown through internal subversion was repeatedly highlighted; this is a recurring feature of discourses on anti-social behaviour, as the very meaning of the term suggests. In the case of anarchism, the menace of social breakdown was often understood in its most complete sense: there was a sense that anarchists sought to pervert English liberal values, in collusion with part of the political class. These ideas were articulated in the Commons and the Conservative press (notably in *The Times*). Criticisms of Britain's asylum policy were a recurring feature of these debates, since the hospitality afforded to international anarchists was increasingly perceived as a perversion of liberal principles.

The theme of corrupted liberalism was also developed in the Commons in the context of debates over the anarchists' right to occupy public spaces in order to publicize their ideas. This seemingly anecdotal digression is especially interesting as it hinges on issues of visibility and appearances, which are key points for discourses on anti-social behaviour. On 13 November 1893, Charles Darling, Conservative MP for Deptford, raised a question in the House of Commons regarding:

> the meeting which was held [the day before] in Trafalgar Square; whether that demonstration was organised by the London Anarchist Communists to deplore the death of the Chicago Anarchist 'martyrs', yesterday being the anniversary of their execution for murder. ('The Anarchists in Trafalgar Square', House of Commons Reading, 1893)

Pending an answer, the question was repeated the following day, and answered by Asquith who clarified that 'the notice was given on October 3 by a Mr. Weiss on behalf of the members of the "Freedom" Group [one of the main anarchist groupings in the country]' ('Anarchist meeting in Trafalgar Square', House of Commons Sitting, 1893). Far from being satisfied with these clarifications, Darling called an adjournment on the same day, in order to discuss 'the inexpediency and danger to the public peace of permitting Anarchists and disorderly persons to hold public meetings in Trafalgar Square' ('Public meeting in Trafalgar Square', House of Commons Sitting, 1893). There, he clarified his objections to allowing public anarchist meetings, stating his view that:

> such persons should be allowed under the protection of the police, and with the sanction of the Government, to hold public meetings in the heart of the Metropolis, and there to excuse the acts, ask for the pardon, and celebrate the memories of those who had committed deeds which led to great destruction of life and property, and also to public disorder and crime. (*Ibid.*)

The debate was eventually narrowed down to the question of rights and compliance with 'English values', that is to say liberalism. For those who regarded anarchists as a serious threat, like Darling:

> The holding of meetings in the square was a privilege which had been much abused in the past, and would be withdrawn if it were abused in the future [...]. He hoped the result of calling attention to these matters would be that these Anarchists would be informed that they were not to be placed on the same level as Englishmen who desired to advocate reforms by means coming within the laws of England. (*Ibid.*)

Asquith's reply rehearsed familiar liberal arguments: it consisted in deriding the seriousness with which Darling took the anarchists' actions, arguing that ignoring them was the best way to defuse their potential menace. For him, Darling was simply offering 'a gratuitous advertisement to a handful of insignificant men who used, no doubt, foolish and violent language on Sunday afternoon in Trafalgar Square, but who [...] have not committed any offence against the law'. For this reason, Asquith 'entirely [declined] to exercise any censorship over the objects for which meetings are held'. For him, the anarchists were not a threat, and their meetings were in fact 'vapourings of very foolish and very ignorant people as having, at any rate, this advantage – that, to use a vulgar expression, they, "let off the steam" ' (*ibid.*). Other members concurred, such as Mr Byles, for whom 'Anarchy could only be rendered harmless by being allowed to speak out publicly and openly in such places as Trafalgar Square'. Turning the Conservatives' argument on its head, the Liberal John Burns contended that their Motion for Adjournment was an attack on 'the right of public meeting and freedom of discussion' – core liberal values of course. Restricting their right to meet would be 'a blow at freedom of expression and the right of public meeting and at the right of London citizens to meet in Trafalgar Square, even to the point of a foolish object, in order to express their opinions' (*ibid.*). The anarchists themselves were 'a few precocious youths and young men', notorious for their 'stupid, violent, criminal proceedings', but the defence of English freedoms required that they should be given the same rights of expression as more moderate groups (*ibid.*).

Things were different when, two weeks later, Darling asked Asquith about a new application to hold a meeting in Trafalgar Square, and was told that an application had been made but had been turned down. Was it because the application was made on behalf of the Commonweal Group, which was more radical than the Freedom Group, and had been known to advocate violent methods? Was it because the avowed purpose of the meeting was 'to explain the principles and aims of anarchist communism'? Most likely, it was a combination of the two, since Asquith explained that the meeting would be 'unlawful', because the group 'applaud and justify the wholesale massacre of innocent persons' ('Anarchist Meetings in Trafalgar Square', House of Commons Sitting, 1893). Another few weeks later, it was the turn of Mr Knachtbull-Kagessen, MP for Faversham, Kent, to initiate a discussion on the topic of demonstrations by French anarchists in Trafalgar Square ('The Anarchists', House of Commons Sitting, 1894). The question reappeared a few years later, in 1898, during a period of heightened anarchist activism, and Charles Vincent enquired about a meeting held by the an anarchist lobby, the Spanish Atrocities Committee, and whether they were 'required to recoup the ratepayers of London the cost of the police, deprived of their Sunday rest and prevented from attending Divine service, in order to protect them?' ('Trafalgar Square Meetings', House of Commons Sitting, 1898).

Debates on the control of anarchism in Britain encompassed a number of themes, notably the redrafting of immigration and asylum laws, as well as the need to pre-emptively raid anarchist houses and clubs in order to prevent possible terrorist outrages ('The Greenwich Explosion', House of Commons Sitting, 1894). However, discussions on the right to hold public meetings were an especially sensitive topic where the ambiguous link between the defence of liberal values and the control of the anarchists' public presence was articulated. Darling made similar cases on various occasions. In February 1894, when the French exile Martial Bourdin was killed in Greenwich Park by the accidental detonation of a bomb which he was carrying, his funeral looked set to attract a lot of attention and become another catalyst in the confrontation between the anarchists and public authorities. On this occasion, Darling intervened to make a thinly-disguised plea for Bourdin's funeral to be postponed, and his body to remain above ground as long as the investigation into the Greenwich events was under way ('The Anarchist Bourdin', House of Commons Sitting, 1894). His justification for this most unusual step was that 'the Anarchists of London propose to make it the occasion of a public funeral' – a message which had been propagated by the press too (*The Yorkshire Herald*, 1894). It was indeed common for anarchists to use any event involving them, such as funerals, commemorations or trials, as an opportunity to display and celebrate their beliefs publicly. However, there again, Darling was rebuffed by Asquith, who underlined how rare such a step would be, and denied that any anarchist demonstration was in preparation.

Once allowed, the funeral took a rather unexpected turn, which seemed to mark a turning-point in the reception of anarchists in Britain. It soon appeared that the comrades were indeed intent on turning the funeral into a platform for propaganda. However, their plans were thwarted when the police diverted the itinerary of their procession, which had initially been designed to go from Fitzroy Square (the heart of the French anarchist quarter) to St Pancras Cemetery, in East Finchley. Moreover, no sooner had Bourdin's funeral oration begun, than the speaker 'was abruptly stopped by the prompt interference of a police inspector' (*The Times*, 1894). Quite clearly, as the possibility of an actual anarchist attack became stronger, the anarchists' public presence and activities were more strictly controlled. Moreover, the companions also had to contend with public hostility initiated by the opponents of anarchism, seemingly attending in order to make their hostility to the movement known: *The Times* spoke of 'the fury of the mob' at the cemetery, and 'free fights' between 'Anarchists' and 'Anti-Anarchists' in Fitzroy Square. All in all, the event 'gave opportunity to the London mob to show the hearty detestation they felt for anarchy and for anarchists'.

There emerged, however, rumours that such confrontations were secretly engineered by British Secret Intelligence services, in an attempt to discredit the movement and give a distorted view of the public's positions. A French informer thus wrote in a report that 'On Sunday, at the Trafalgar Square meeting, Malatesta [one of the foremost Italian anarchists exiled in London] got two black eyes and Agresti [another prominent companion] had his left cheek cut. This was done by M. Melville's agents' (APP BA 1508, 12 December 1893). In other words, as the anarchist 'epidemic' peaked on the Continent and made itself felt in Britain, the street, in its function as a political theatre, had become an important stake in the battle of opinion. Anarchists tried to use it to gain political credence and publicize their ideas. Public authorities had to control this presence in order to prove that they remained in charge of the situation, and politicians were torn by disagreements over how much public visibility should be tolerated. While anarchism was primarily perceived as a political threat, its public staging was a key concern, as it is in most instances of perceived anti-social behaviour.

Conclusion

The period between 1880 and 1914 was a time of mass immigration, industrial coming of age, growing industrial and political unrest, when Britain found its international leadership increasingly challenged. These factors combined to change national self-perception, resulting in a new discourse of Liberalism (Marx, 1987; Porter, 1987). It is hardly surprising that it also resulted in redefining the figure of 'the Other' against whom national cohesion could be built and exalted. The anarchists, who were one of the many embodiments of this threatening 'Other', alongside the unemployed and immigrant paupers or other criminal figures such as Jack the Ripper, crystallized many of the fears of the age. They were a powerful instance of anti-social behaviour in the eyes of their Victorian contemporaries, and the numerous discussions and debates centring on them feature many of the characteristic tropes and themes which went hand in hand with the late nineteenth-century criminal stereotype: the emphasis on the breakdown of social values, the theme of the internal enemy, the exegesis of secret codes, the sense of a threat lurking in the metropolis. The emphasis on racial degeneracy and a renewed fear of socialist militancy were important elements, which were specific to the late Victorian period. A legacy of the street-based nineteenth-century revolutionary culture, but also possibly a sign of the increasingly public and media-influenced nature of politics at the time, debates on how to police this criminal underclass devoted great attention to the street as a key political stage.

The depiction of anarchists in the press and parliamentary debates corresponded to two understandings of what constitutes anti-social behaviour, based on a reworking of the laborious/dangerous classes stereotype, with new inflections prompted by the momentous changes, which the country had undergone in the space of a few decades. Amid the less alarmist fringes of opinion, anti-social behaviour was unthreatening, although it could be unpleasant. It was usually benign and presented only a minor form of disturbance, which was best defused through tolerance. This corresponded to the

Liberal position throughout the 1890s. On the other hand, those who were alarmed by 'the anarchist peril' saw it quite literally as a type of behaviour which threatened society in its cohesion, values, and very existence; after a ferocious battle from the late 1880s onwards, in a propitiously repressive international context, this party and their positions came to prevail in the early twentieth century.

7
Keep Them Kettled! Student Protests, Policing and Anti-social Behaviour

Sarah Pickard

Introduction

The Labour government led by Tony Blair introduced annual university tuition fees of £1,000 in 1998, following recommendations made in the Dearing Report – *Higher Education in the Learning Society* (Dearing, 1997). According to the Prime Minister, the revenue obtained through the new 'up front' payment would be used to finance the planned expansion of higher education. The Teaching and Higher Education Act 1998 withdrew maintenance grants in favour of income-contingent student loans. During Labour's next term of office, the Higher Education Act 2004 brought back grants and introduced variable tuition fees, or top-up fees as they became known. Under the terms of this act, from 2006-7 universities could charge students annual tuition fees up to the government imposed cap of £3,000. Students no longer pay tuition fees at the start of each academic year, but instead take out a student loan to be repaid following graduation, if their income reaches a certain threshold. These significant changes to the financing of higher education made by Labour met with relatively limited opposition among students and university staff.

The Conservative–Liberal Democrat Coalition government came to power in May 2010 and five months later was published the Browne Review – *Securing a Sustainable Future for Higher Education* (Browne, 2010). It recommended a higher education system, which according to Holmwood (2011: 1) was 'directed by market forces and the replacement of direct funding of undergraduate courses by students fees', with the complete removal of the cap on university tuition fees. Soon afterwards, on 20 October 2010, the Conservative Chancellor of the Exchequer, George Osborne, stated in his Comprehensive Spending Review that universities were 'jewels in our economic crown'. Then he announced that public spending on higher education was to be cut dramatically, especially the budget for teaching and non-STEM (science, technology, engineering and maths) subjects. Humanities and social sciences were to lose all state funding, and so become reliant on the income generated by tuition fees.

The Coalition unveiled further plans for the funding and organization of higher education at the start of November 2010. Contrary to Lord Browne's recommendations, it was decided to keep a cap on university tuition fees, increasing it to £9,000 per year for new undergraduates at English universities from September 2012. Institutions charging over £6,000 per annum would have to actively help and encourage potential students from low-income backgrounds via an 'access agreement' negotiated with the Office For Fair Access (Offa); maintenance grants and means-tested loans were to remain (see Pickard, 2014a; 2014b). On 9 December 2010, the House of Commons voted for the rise to £9,000 by a majority of 21 votes. Most Conservative and Liberal Democrat MPs voted for the increase, including Deputy Prime Minister and Liberal Democrat leader Nick Clegg. This was despite the fact that he and all Liberal Democrat candidates had signed in April 2009 a National Union of Students (NUS) pledge not to increase tuition fees and his party's 2010 manifesto having promised to scrap tuition fees altogether (Liberal Democrats, 2010).

Labour Party leader and Leader of the Opposition Ed Miliband wrote in *The Observer* that the planned rise in tuition fees and cuts in higher education spending were 'cultural vandalism' (Miliband, 5 December 2010). He thus implied that the Conservative–Liberal Democrat Coalition government had behaved anti-socially, although the Labour Party had introduced tuition fees and had then broken an electoral pledge by raising them to £3,000, and would most likely have increased them again had they remained in power after 2010.

Following this announcement of Coalition plans to cut higher education budgets and to raise university tuition fees, the country witnessed the largest student movement in a generation (Rees, 2011: 118). In political discourse and in the media, both the protesters and the police were condemned for anti-social behaviour, that is to say: 'Acting in a manner that caused or was likely to cause harassment, alarm or distress to one or more persons', as defined in the Crime and Disorder Act 1998.

This chapter explores the conduct of protesters and police during student-led protests during the winter of 2010, as well as more recent developments. Legislation pertaining to the policing of public protests in the urban environment, published testimonies, interviews with protesters and media reports are all examined. The chapter thus analyses anti-social behaviour during student protests from both sociological and political perspectives.

Anti-social behaviour and protesters

Students took an active role in the anti-globalization movement during the World Trade Organisation (WTO) protest of 1999 in Seattle and then the Stop the War Coalition (StWC) against the invasion of Iraq in 2003, which gathered one million protesters in London. However, the new generation of student activism during Winter 2010 was centred on higher education issues and this undoubtedly gave it broader appeal. There was also a specific set of circumstances conducive to opposition and unrest. The Labour Party was no longer in power and thus the Labour-leaning NUS was more prone to act against the government; new activist networks had been set up to react against the Conservative–Liberal Democrat Coalition government's austerity measures and public sector cuts; the country had been experiencing economic and financial crises attributed by critics to the greed of the banking and financial sectors; the poor economic climate exacerbated the fear of graduate debt and that higher tuition fees would discourage potential students especially those from low-income backgrounds; the leaders of the three main political parties had all attended university when higher education had been free; the Liberal Democrats had broken a manifesto pledge not to raise university tuition fees; there was a larger critical mass of students than ever before because of the previous decade's expansion of higher education; and the development of new social media facilitated communication. Furthermore, a long occupation had already started in Spring 2010 at Middlesex University against the planned closure of its Philosophy department and there were occupations at other universities affected by budget cuts (see Bailey, 2011: 6).

Following the announcement in the October 2010 Comprehensive Spending Review of substantial cuts to public funding of higher education as well as the plans to increase tuition fees and ending the Educational Maintenance Allowance (EMA),[1] many cities especially London, witnessed various forms of opposition. Protest focused on days of action on 10 November, 24 November, 30 November, 9 December 2010 and 29 January 2011, mostly corresponding to when the policy changes were being debated in Parliament (see Pickard, 2014a; 2014c). Protesters mainly consisted of university students (who would not be affected by the future policy changes), parents, university staff and school pupils (who would be affected by the scrapping of the EMA or the increase in tuition fees). Dissent included peaceful marching, civil disobedience in the form of occupations of university buildings and criminal damage of private property, as well as aggressive verbal and physical behaviour towards the police.

The first and biggest day of action was on 10 November 2010 when around 50,000 protesters marched in the capital. It was organized by the NUS and the University and College Union (UCU), the largest trade union for higher education staff. The unions invested time, money and resources in their organization of this first march, in stark contrast to the limited efforts deployed by the NUS when its ally Labour had been in government, which somewhat explains why protest regarding tuition fees had been so muted in the past. In Winter 2010, the NUS played no role in organizing any demonstrations after the 10 November march, which in part was due to the behaviour of certain protesters.

While most of the large demonstration in London on 10 November 2010 was peaceful, a splinter group of around 200 demonstrators headed for

30 Millbank, Westminster, the Conservative Party Campaign Headquarters (CCHQ).[2] According to testimonies, the first protestors walked in and met no resistance, then some started to shatter the glass front of the building, and broke furniture once inside (see Solomon and Palmieri, 2011). About 50 protestors gained access to the roof, including Edward Woollard, an 18-year-old further education student who hurled an empty fire extinguisher off the top of the building, which narrowly missed a police officer in the crowd below. Around 2,000 protestors gathered in the courtyard and lit fires, wrote graffiti on the walls of the Conservative headquarters before leaving late in the evening. By deviating from the route agreed between the NUS and the police, trespassing, causing criminal damage to private property and throwing an object from the roof, these protestors were criticized for their public disorder and anti-social behaviour, including by the NUS leader, Aaron Porter:

> I make no apology for condemning the mindless violence of a few that tried to undermine the case of a great many. I wish that rather than spending so much of our time talking about that reckless minority that we had more opportunity to talk about the real issues that brought so many people out on the streets. That violence by a tiny minority sought to detract from our powerful collective message and let students down. We will never defend those who took actions that put innocent people's lives at risk. (Porter, 2010)

His effort to distance himself from the 'reckless minority' was in turn slated for dividing opposition to the government's policies (for example, Kumar, 2011: 136). Prime Minister David Cameron was also highly critical of the occupation of his party's campaign headquarters and called for the 'full weight of the law' to be brought to bear on those involved.

Conversely, supporters of what happened at Millbank defended the actions by claiming that civil disobedience drew vital media and public attention to the Coalition's plans for higher education. Clare Solomon, President of the University of London Union (ULU), declared on the BBC programme *Newsnight* the same evening, that 'Peaceful protest achieves nothing [...] a few smashed windows is a small price to pay for a smashed educational system' (BBC *Newsnight*, 2010), thus public disorder is a legitimate form of protest. For her and others, the damage done to Millbank on 10 November 2010 suggested to some commentators that emboldened protestors were not scared of being radical in their behaviour: 'Here were young people who had taken their fight to the centre of power, who had shown no fear of authority and who had wrong-footed the police and, for a short moment, who had rekindled the energy of political struggle' (Bloom, 2012: 18).

In the weeks following the 10 November demonstration, a plethora of protest groups and horizontal networks in favour of direct action participated in the organization of further protests. The National Campaign Against Fees and Cuts (NCAFC) and the Education Activist Network (EAN), both formed in February 2010, coordinated local anti-cuts campaigns and they jointly called for a day of action on 24 November 2010. Other social movements included the Stop the Fees Campaign, the Campaign for Free Education, the Coalition of Resistance, the Alliance for Workers' Liberty and UKUncut. Dozens of occupations of university buildings across the country were crucial 'organizing centres for the movement' (Casserly, 201: 72), which included communicating about protests and policing. Before and during the days of action, social media was invaluable, for example, Twitter and Facebook updated protestors on where routes were blocked by police, or where there was a weaker police presence (see Aitchison and Peters, 2011).

The other protest that attracted a lot of media attention due to public disorder occurred in London on 9 December 2010 – 'Day X' – when the parliamentary vote on the increase of tuition fees took place. The Treasury, the Supreme Court, the Cenotaph and other buildings in central London were defaced and damaged. There was also significant conflict between protestors and police (Olcese and Saunders, 2014). According to the Metropolitan Police, some protestors threw missiles at police officers and riot police, including flares, sticks, snooker balls and paint balls. BBC *Newsnight* journalist, Paul Mason, reported: 'Heavy objects land among the police, amid a much larger volume of paint, fireworks and flash-bangs' (Mason, 2010; 2013: 50). Video recordings reveal taunting of the police by protestors, for example shouts of 'it will be your job next', referring to the Conservative–Liberal Democrat Coalition's public spending cuts. In the evening, an official car driving Prince Charles and the Duchess of Cornwall along Regent Street was spotted by a splinter group of protestors who had moved away from Parliament Square. They daubed the Rolls Royce with paint and pursued it chanting 'off with their heads'. The contorted faces of the royal couple featured on the front pages of most newspapers the next day with condemnation of the culprits' disrespectful and anti-social behaviour.

Prime Minister David Cameron stated that it was not possible to blame the disorder on just a small militant element, when so many in the crowd were acting in an 'absolutely feral way'. He declared:

> The scenes people saw on their TV screens were completely unacceptable. [...] There were quite a lot of people who were hell bent on violence and destroying property. [...] It is not acceptable, it is against the law to smash property, to behave in that way, to attack police officers, and I want to make sure that they feel the full force of the law. (Quoted in Batty, 2010)

Other critics of the violence complained that it deflected attention away from thousands of peaceful demonstrators who were largely ignored by the media, as were the controversial tactics used by the police. Once again, supporters of the civil disobedience defended the public disorder because it gave oxygen to the anti-cuts and fees cause and was an 'act of resistance' to the government's anti-social higher education policies.

After the parliamentary vote on the increase of tuition fees on 9 December 2010, almost all the occupations were suspended (Kumar, 2011: 139), which reduced the organizational resources and momentum of the protests. Activity wound down after the Christmas holidays and a last demonstration on the 29 January 2011. In November 2011, the NUS and the Trades Union Congress (TUC) organized a day of protest against the Coalition's austerity policies. Following the introduction of the £9,000 university tuition fees in September 2012, the NUS held a march in November 2012 with the slogan 'Education, Employment, Empowerment', which attracted around 10,000 protestors, far fewer than in 2010, signalling the apparent decline of student resistance.

Police arrested over 200 protestors during the Winter 2010 protests for breach of the peace and other public disorder offences.[3] According to Petra Davis, 'of the 58 young people charged with violent disorder from the student demonstrations, 12 have received custodial sentences' (Davis, 2013). Altogether, there were 19 unsuccessful prosecutions of protestors charged with public disorder, although the courts did not uphold many of the police's charges.

Edward Woollard the 18-year-old who threw the fire extinguisher from the roof of Conservative campaign headquarters was jailed for two years and eight months in January 2011. According to the judge, Geoffrey Rivlin QC, it was a 'deterrent sentence' (see Hall *et al.*, 1978 for analysis of the impact of deterrent sentences). Critics claimed it was repressive and disproportionate for a young man who did not act with forethought, was not wearing a hood or a mask, had no previous convictions, did not injure anyone and pleaded guilty. It would thus be an indication of the state attempting to repress and control the right to protest and freedom of expression, for example:

> The judge reckons he is protecting the right of people to take part in peaceful protest. [...] Only the sincerely peaceful are going to be discouraged by this sentence, and the scenes at Millbank which spawned it. Those of a more revolutionary frame of mind are simply going to view it as further evidence of the state's repressive tendencies, and more proof that hoods, masks, and billiard balls are absolutely necessary. Geoffrey Rivlin QC, you're as wrong here as wrong can be. (Orr, 2011)

Similarly, in what was considered by opponents to be an over-harsh sentence to set an example, Charlie Gilmour who swung on the Cenotaph Union flag during the 10 December march was sentenced to 16 months in Wandsworth prison for 'violent disorder'. This is a severe public order offence that can lead to a sentence of up to five years under Section 2 of the Public Order Act. Another student, Alfie Meadows, was charged with 'violent public disorder' for assaulting a police officer. The jury failed to reach a verdict at his first trial, but during the retrial the jury returned a unanimous not guilty verdict and he was acquitted. He had claimed he needed to defend himself and other protestors from police violence.

During Winter 2010, for some protestors, civil disobedience including criminal offences was a legitimate form of protest against anti-social austerity policies of the Coalition government, especially as it attracted media coverage. While the events at Millbank clearly inspired certain activists, they also dissuaded other young people from taking part in further demonstrations for fear of becoming embroiled in anti-social behaviour and violence. Indeed all subsequent demonstrations were smaller than the first. However, alarm among some stemmed not only from the direct action of a minority of protestors and the fear of being arrested, it also resulted from the actions of some police officers and police tactics.

Anti-social behaviour and the police

The actions of the London Metropolitan Police during the higher education protests in Winter 2010 need to be understood against the backdrop of condemnation made of their policing methods during the G20 protests in London in April 2009. Ian Tomlinson a newspaper seller who was not involved in the protest and posed no threat, collapsed and died after he was hit by a police baton and pushed to the ground by a London Metropolitan police officer. PC Simon Harwood had acted illegally, recklessly and dangerously, using 'excessive and unreasonable' force, according to the jury who found him guilty of 'unlawful killing'. *Adapting to Protest*, a report written by Her Majesty's Inspectorate of Constabulary (HMIC), analysed the policing methods used during the G20 summit protests. It made a number of immediate recommendations, including that the police should (1) Facilitate peaceful protest; (2) Improve dialogue with protest groups where possible; (3) Improve communication with the public; (4) Moderate the impact of containment when used; (5) Improve training to equip officers to deal with the full spectrum of protest activity; and (6) Wear clear identification at all times. The HMIC report also recommended that national guidance on the policing of protest needed overhauling by the Association of Chief Police Officers (ACPO). The fundamental message of the report was that the policing of public order events must be lawful, consensual and legal, not provocative and aggressive (Bloom, 2012: 3).

The London Metropolitan Police Service was criticized for a variety of reasons during the Winter 2010 protests. The first criticism made concerning its policing of the 10 November 2010 demonstration was that it was inadequate and badly planned. The Metropolitan Police underestimated the scale of the protest and was clearly understaffed with only 225 officers assigned to the protest that day (Helm *et al.*, 2010). This was put down to an 'intelligence gap'; police intelligence officers monitored politically extremist websites, but did not find evidence of any organized civil obedience being planned for that day, which raises issues about surveillance tactics. When some protestors broke from the main demonstration and moved towards Millbank, the police did not manage to prevent them from breaking into and occupying the Conservative Party campaign headquarters. Nor did the Metropolitan Police succeed in protecting the official royal car carrying Prince Charles and the Duchess of Cornwall down Regent Street. Furthermore, the Metropolitan Police Commissioner, Paul Stephenson admitted that his officers had 'lost control' with regard to the attacks on government buildings in central London the same day. He faced calls for his resignation over the breakdown of law and order during the protests, but he did not leave his job.

More significantly, regarding anti-social behaviour, the police were accused of brutality, including the charging of demonstrators by mounted police, as well as the batoning and striking with shields of demonstrators. On 24 November 2010, demonstrators in Whitehall were charged without warning by mounted police; the Metropolitan Police issued a denial, but witnesses reported the event and the charge can been seen on video footage posted on the website of *The Guardian* (Gabbatt and Lewis, 2010). During the next demonstration, Paul Mason gave the following account of police violence: 'A girl steps though a break in the police line and gets batoned. She crumples to the ground, where the police continue beating her. Afterwards she stays there, inert for a long, long time [...] she doesn't speak. Her face is screwed up, disbelief mingled with terror' (Mason, 2013: 50).

There are two particular cases of note with regard to police violence. First, on 9 December 2010, 20-year-old Alfie Meadows was allegedly struck on the head by a police officer's truncheon and had to undergo surgery due to bleeding on the brain. The incident was to be investigated by the Independent Police Complaints Commission (IPCC), but the Middlesex University student withdrew his complaint when he was accused of violent disorder during the protest (see above). It remains to be seen whether the police officer involved is prosecuted. Second, the same day, Jody McIntyre, a known activist (who had been on the roof of Millbank the week before) was removed from his wheelchair on two occasions by riot police and pulled across the road. This is his account:

Batons began to fly. One came landing straight onto my left shoulder, sending a sharp, shooting pain down my arm. Those standing around me were taking blows to the head and body; children, women, men, all being brutalized by the police. Then the horses came, horses that could easily kill people. [...] Suddenly, four policemen grabbed my shoulders and pulled me out of my wheelchair. My friends and younger brother struggled to pull me back, but were beaten away with batons. The police carried me away. [...] From the corner of my eye, I spotted one of the policemen from the earlier incident. He recognized me immediately and came charging towards me. Tipping the wheelchair to the side, he pushed me onto the concrete, before grabbing my arms and dragging me across the road. (McIntyre, 2011: 76–7)

Jody McIntyre made a complaint to the Metropolitan Police Service (MPS) about the treatment that he had received from their officers in Parliament Square. The incident was investigated by the IPPC and its ambivalent response was published in 2011:

The IPCC agreed with the Metropolitan Police Service's findings in relation to a number of aspects of Mr McIntyre's complaint. In particular the IPCC agreed that officers' initial actions in removing Mr McIntyre from his wheelchair and away from a dangerous part of the demonstration were appropriate in the circumstances. However, the IPCC has concluded that, when an officer dragged Mr McIntyre along the ground, towards the end of the incident, this did amount to excessive force.

The IPCC believes there was an indication that a criminal offence of common assault may have been committed and the matter should therefore have been referred to the Crown Prosecution Service (CPS). However, the six month time limit in which such a prosecution could be commenced had already passed by the time this appeal was lodged.

The IPCC has upheld this part of the appeal and believe that that officer's behaviour has fallen below the standards of professional behaviour and should be subject to management action.

The IPCC also found that the MPS were right to conclude that Mr McIntyre was struck by a baton but that it could not find a case to answer against any particular officer for the strike. However, the IPCC considers that Mr McIntyre does have a legitimate grievance in respect of the baton strike and therefore his complaint should have been upheld. We have suggested that an apology would be an appropriate way of dealing with this particular part of the incident. (IPCC, 2011)

The chairperson of the Metropolitan Police Federation (the staff association that represents all police officers up to and including the rank of Chief Inspector), Peter Smyth, justified police violence of 10 December 2010:

We're damned if we do and damned if we don't. We accepted that at Millbank we got it wrong, so we put out more police officers. But when they throw snooker balls and lumps of wood, as they did on Thursday, you can't be surprised when the police hit you back. If they really think we're going to stand there and take it, and let them into the Houses of Parliament, or wherever they want to go, they should be in kindergarten. (Dugan and Paige, 2010)

On 29 November, Commander Bob Broadhurst, head of the MPS Public Order Branch, legitimized the police behaviour and called for protesters to carefully consider their behaviour:

The Met will always respect the right to protest peacefully, but I would urge all those considering taking to the streets of London again this week to think carefully about the consequences of engaging in violence and disorder. This behaviour doesn't help anybody, least of all those who have a genuine and peaceful point to make. We will always work with protesters and consider their needs and aims, but we have to balance these against the needs and rights of other Londoners. While protesters should be able to march peacefully to highlight their concerns, they should not be able to seriously disrupt the lives of Londoners and prevent them going about their daily business. People have a right to go to work, go shopping or sightsee without fear of violence and disorder. (Metropolitan Police Service, 2010)

Another policing tactic stood out during the protests and it has come in for much criticism for its anti-social nature: kettling.[4] Kettling, officially known as 'containment', involves the encircling of the members of a crowd either by blocking them into a confined area, or by surrounding them with a police cordon. This thus prevents their exit from a specific area; it also controls their departure allowing the police to obtain personal data and make arrests. After the under-policing of the first demonstration, kettling was used on more than one occasion and not only in London. This police tactic was employed most conspicuously in the capital on 9 December 2010, in Parliament Square where hundreds of people were contained for hours via police lines and barriers cutting off side streets and then in the evening for several hours on Westminster Bridge (see Penny, 2010).

The police kettling during the higher education protests (and others) has been condemned for many reasons linked to anti-social behaviour: 'The police now consistently face criticism both from officially recognized bodies and from protest groups for disregarding human rights law by their incorrect or questionable actions at demonstrations, of which kettling is the most obvious' (Bloom, 2012: 40). Condemnation centres principally on three issues. First, it is inhumane: those kettled were deprived of their basic human rights in violation of Article 5 of the European Convention on Human Rights, which is the right to liberty and security. Those kettled had no access to food, or water, or toilets for sustained periods, in some cases up to ten hours. Moreover, temperatures were below zero and the kettling lasted well into the night. Those involved – including school children – complained that they were severely crushed and had respiratory problems and panic attacks during the kettling. Moreover, there was a real danger of someone falling over the waist-high walls of Westminster Bridge into the river Thames (see Hancox, 2011b). Second, it is indiscriminate: those kettled were contained as a homogenous group, whereas they were not all 'agitators', or even potential troublemakers; it is thus 'collective punishment' and against the Geneva Conventions, 1949. The third criticism levelled against kettling is that it is *de facto* open air imprisonment without a trial.

The wider use of kettling by the police is being challenged in the European Court of Human Rights (ECHR). In April 2011, the High Court (of Justice) ruled that the Metropolitan Police acted unlawfully when it kettled protestors during the G20 protests in 2009. The High Court issued a warning that kettling should only be a 'last resort catering for situations about to descend into violence'. The Metropolitan Police is appealing against the decision, because it considers kettling to be a 'vital public order policing tactic that prevents disorder and protects the public' (Metropolitan Police Service, 2011). Sir Paul Stephenson, the Commissioner of the Metropolitan Police defended the use of containment, claiming that it allowed protestors to calm down and permitted the diffusion of disruptive behaviour. By this reasoning, protesting is considered to constitute anti-social behaviour and thus allows the police to request the identity of those being released from a kettle, as stated in Section 50 of the Police Reform Act 2002:

Persons acting in an anti-social manner

(1) If a constable in uniform has reason to believe that a person has been acting, or is acting, in an anti-social manner (within the meaning of section 1 of the Crime and Disorder Act 1998 (c. 37) (anti-social behaviour orders)), he may require that person to give his name and address to the constable.

(2) Any person who—

  (a) fails to give his name and address when required to do so under subsection (1), or
  (b) gives a false or inaccurate name or address in response to a requirement under that subsection,

is guilty of an offence and shall be liable, on summary conviction, to a fine not exceeding level 3 on the standard scale. (Police Reform Act 2002, section 50)

The use of kettling in order to carry out data collection, or surveillance and the association made between protesting and anti-social behaviour has been much criticized. Netpol, a 'network for police monitoring' states the following:

> Any power which allows the police to 'round up' people engaged in polit-
> ical protest in order to demand their names and addresses under threat
> of arrest, is a serious and fundamental threat to civil rights and freedoms.
> Providing police with the ability to build personal profiles of political
> demonstrators is a dangerous step to take. Neither should protest ever
> be treated as 'anti-social behaviour'. People invariably engage in protest
> because of a sense of social responsibility. Protest should be seen as an
> important and protected right, not as an unwanted societal problem.
> (Netpol, 2013)

During the Winter 2010 protests, other covert and overt surveillance tactics were deployed, which can be considered to be anti-social, especially in a country that does not have identity cards. Forward Intelligence Teams (FITs) were employed to gather information overtly during demonstrations for example, including taking photographs and filming demonstrators. The Metropolitan Police released a gallery of protest suspects wanted in connection with committing violent disorder and criminal damage during the protests. Such surveillance and the use of CCTV footage, can be interpreted as indiscriminate and intimidatory regarding the right to protest.

Rather than soothing and subduing the emotions of those contained (Penny, 2010), in some cases, kettling enflamed them; it thus stoked agitation and made a number of protestors even more determined to cause trouble at the next protest (Hancox, 2011c). Indeed, because of kettling and other police tactics, including the excessive use of force, some young people have been radicalized (Mason, 2013: 47). For these activists, police harassment (including stop and searches), police surveillance and police brutality legitimized provocation and violence against the police at the subsequent demonstrations. The campaign group Defend the Right to Protest was set up to address this issue and it has been active in subsequent demonstrations. In this way, the anti-social behaviour of the police meant that they came to be perceived as legitimate targets for verbal and physical attacks. This hostility is exacerbated because law enforcers are seen as agents of the state and the unpopular Coalition government. In 30 semi-structured interviews I did with protestors in November 2012 when asking about policing methods, there were numerous complaints, describing it for example as 'heavy', 'a bit much', 'too much', 'over the top', 'excessive', 'intimidating' and 'harassing' (Pickard, 2012).

During the Winter 2010 protests, police tactics including surveillance, kettling and batoning were mostly appropriate to the scale and nature of the protests, according to the police who consider police methods to be legitimate as police officers were attacked verbally and physically. Nevertheless, many recommendations of the *Adapting to Protest* (HMIC, 2009) document were not respected by the Metropolitan Police and the conduct of some police officers amounted to anti-social behaviour and in some cases criminal behaviour. Moreover, these policing methods probably incited radicalization, further violence and hostility directed at the police. This led to new legislation on public protests being initiated by the Coalition government.

Conclusions

Most protestors and police officers acted peacefully and within the law during the Winter 2010 protests. However, a minority of both protestors and the police were accused of anti-social behaviour. Those involved have both justified their acts in relation to the behaviour of the other: the police behaved violently and so we had to protect other protestors and ourselves, or the protestors behaved violently and so we had to protect other protestors and ourselves. Protestors further legitimized their conduct by considering the police to be agents of the state government, which they feel is destroying higher education in England and attempting to repress the right to protest. Clearly, what constitutes anti-social behaviour: 'acting in a manner that caused or was likely to cause harassment, alarm or distress to one or more persons' (Crime and Disorder Act 1998) is highly subjective as are responses to it.

Following the student protests of 2010 the Conservative–Liberal Democrat Coalition government has made further attempts to control public assemblies. Prior to a march planned by the NUS and the TUC in November 2011, Conservative Home Secretary Theresa May answered questions from the House of Commons Home Affairs Committee on the 'preauthorized' use of baton rounds and rubber bullets by the Metropolitan Police for the first time on mainland Britain in a planned protest.[5] In February 2014, there was a consultation at London City Hall on plans by the Metropolitan Police to purchase water cannons that could be used as a 'public order tool', according to Bernard Hogan-Howe, who became the new Commissioner of Police of the Metropolis (head of London's Metropolitan Police Service) in September 2011.

Since the summer of 2013, there has been a rebirth of resistance among students, characterized by a marked increase in occupations around the country (Allegretti, 2013). This direct action has been about a number of issues including tuition fees, the privatization of university positions, staff pay, and other conditions of university workers within the new higher education environment. There has been an increasing police presence on university premises to quell student protest with the encouragement of university managers. The police have been accused of heavy-handed tactics, leading to a national social media campaign 'Cops off Campus Now!' In Summer 2013, a student was allegedly 'pinned down, handcuffed and charged' for writing slogans in chalk on the walls of a university (Denham, 2013). Michael Chessum, President of the University of London Union (ULU) was arrested in November 2013 for not announcing to the police a campus protest. The following month, the University of London obtained a High Court injunction forbidding protests on its premises.

This all happened while the Anti-social Behaviour, Crime and Policing Bill 2013–14 was debated in Parliament. The original draft would have introduced new powers to suppress protest (in addition to the Serious Organised Crime and Police Act 2005 and the control orders legislation in the Prevention of Terrorism Act 2005). Injunctions to prevent nuisance and annoyance (Ipnas) would have replaced Anti-social Behaviour Orders (ASBOs) to deal with nuisance and annoyance; they would have only required proof on the balance of probability, could have lasted for an indefinite period, could have resulted in a prison sentence if breached and could have been used on anyone over the age of ten. However, on 8 January 2014, the House of Lords voted 306 to 178 (a 128 majority) against the introduction of Ipnas. According to Lord Dear, a former chief constable of West Midlands, the Ipna would 'have put at risk fundamental freedoms' including free speech:

> It risks it being used for those who seek to protest peacefully [...]. I shall continue to be annoyed at those who [...] protest noisily outside parliament or my local bank, but none of that surely should risk an injunctive procedure on the grounds of nuisance and annoyance.

Ipnas will not be introduced; it remains to be seen whether the right to protest is controlled by further repressive anti-social behaviour legislation, and whether certain protestors and police officers are accused of anti-social behaviour.

Notes

1. The EMA was a grant for poorer 16–19 year-old students in further education. On 20 October 2010 the government announced that the scheme was to be cancelled in England as part of a programme of budget cuts.
2. The Conservative Party Campaign Headquarters (CCHQ) left Millbank and moved to 4 Matthew Parker Street, London SW1H on 10 February 2014.
3. In London on the third day of protests against plans to raise student tuition fees 153 people were arrested (Coughlan, 1 December 2010).
4. One of the first times kettling was used as a police tactic was in 1986, by the Hamburg police, in Germany, during anti-nuclear protests. The English word 'kettle' comes from the German word 'kessel' which means kettle.
5. Q81 Dr Julian Huppert MP (Liberal Democrat, Cambridge): 'There is, as you know, a protest march tomorrow happening in London and I understand that rubber bullets and baton rounds have been preauthorised for the first time on the mainland

for a planned protest march. I am very concerned about this and the messages that it sends. Would you agree that they should not be used and, if they are, it shows that the police have completely failed to keep control of the situation?'

Theresa May: 'What I am clear about is that it is appropriate that the police have the powers and resources necessary. You said that they have been authorised to use baton rounds. They are already authorised, of course, to use baton rounds should they choose to do so and the police made it clear in the riots in August that that was a consideration that they gave. So this is not something that is new. It is not that the Government has suddenly said that they can; it is that that is available to the police anyway. [...]'

Q83 Mr David Winnick MP (Labour, Walsall North): 'Would you accept that in a student demonstration that is taking place, as has already been stated this week, it would escalate the situation very much if baton rounds and water cannon were used and there seems to be the utmost reservation on the part of the most senior police officers that such weapons should not be used?'

Theresa May: 'I repeat, baton rounds are available to the police, as they have been in other circumstances. I think the police are very clear that in other circumstances robust policing has been what has dealt with the situation. It has not been necessary to use baton rounds. As I understand it, they have no plans to deploy.'

8
Anti-social Behaviour and the London 'Riots': Social Meaning-making of the Anti-social

Christian Morgner

Introduction

Politicians, the media and even social scientists unanimously reacted by using the label 'riot' for the events that took place in early August 2011 in several English cities, following the death of Mark Duggan (Gorringe and Rosie, 2011; Greenslade, 2011a and 2011b; Morrell *et al.*, 2011; *The Guardian*/LSE, 2011; Benyon, 2012; Briggs, 2012a). The Conservative–Liberal Democrat government has typically defined the events as 'riots' involving anti-social behaviour. Indeed, on 10 August 2011, David Cameron (2011a) called the London riots 'mindless selfishness', while Joe Anderson (cited in Bartlett, 2011), a member of Liverpool's city council, referred to the participants as 'mindless thugs'; and the *Daily Mirror* (2011) reported the occurrences as 'mindless rioting'. This chapter argues that the so-called rioters were not mindless. Instead, such declarations are part of a larger process of meaning-making in which rioting is only one piece of the narrative. Virtually no one questioned this process of meaning-making, discussed the inherent (political) meaning and application, or addressed the analytical and conceptual qualities of the term 'riot' with regard to its anti-social configuration.

This chapter outlines a different approach to understanding the complex formation of social meaning and suggests that the overall narrative is created in a complex network of different narratives, stories or communicative exchanges. The act of labelling the riot as anti-social behaviour is only one component. This chapter will explain that the meaning-making led to the construction of this narrative and to the focus on anti-social rioting, but it was only one part of a complex process of social meaning-making. Furthermore, this chapter will argue that the common description of the events relied on a simplistic narrative of cause and effect, particularly when addressing the triggers and explaining the participation of people.

Triggers of anti-social behaviour: social uncertainty, meaning-making and frames of antagonistic behaviour

The common description of the events that this chapter will examine critically is as follows. On the 4 August 2011, a 29-year-old man of mixed race, Mark Duggan, from Tottenham, a deprived area of north London, was killed by a special police unit. Disturbances began on 6 August 2011 and were related to a protest in Tottenham, which involved family members, friends and locals who demanded further information on the death of Mark Duggan from the local police station. The police had failed so far to inform his parents. The situation at the police station evolved into aggressive and disorderly behaviour with both sides blaming each other. The activities resulted in several violent clashes with the police, burning of police vehicles, governmental buildings and a double-decker bus. The mass media and social media picked up quickly on the events. Overnight, looting took place in the area and nearby Wood Green, then during the next few days these scenes of looting and clashes with the police spread to other parts of London. From 8 until 10 August 2011, other cities in England including Birmingham, Bristol, and Manchester experienced similar activities. On 11 August 2011, law enforcement was finally able to establish law and order. The events involved several thousand people and received considerable attention by the media and political arena. Estimated losses to businesses, of which about 48,000 had been affected in England, were indicated to be in the region of £200 million. The riots were described as the worst disturbances of their kind in the last 20 years.

Several accounts have stated that the shooting of Mark Duggan was the trigger for the riots (Briggs, 2012b: 30; Waddington, 2012). By definition, a trigger suggests a near instant reaction in the form of violent behaviour.[1] However, the rioting occurred two days later. Little research has addressed what happened during those two days, and communication regarding the events caused much confusion. The event was reported by multiple sources. The police and the media issued statements, discussions of the event took place in social media and personal networks (Briggs, 2012b). This dissemination of information had two effects: many people were informed about the event, and much uncertainty was created through inconsistent reports, different opinions or general confusion. For instance, the parents of Mark Duggan had not been informed of his death before the media (Reicher and Stott, 2011). The process of meaning-making was far from clear, as a specific cause and a particular reaction were not identified. Therefore, the social channels that people typically use to cope with uncertainty of meaning actually increased the social uncertainty instead of reduced it.

This uncertainty led to the development of the event on a Saturday (6 August 2011), a day when the majority of people do not work or are involved in other social activities. To reduce the subjective uncertainty, people related to Mark Duggan, friends and people from the neighbourhood joined a group with which they could identify (Hogg and Mullin, 1999). The presence of other people reinforced feelings of a shared identity, of having something in common, and several hundred people marched to the police station in Tottenham. However, police-group member communication did not lead to a mutually supported agreement to decrease the uncertainty; instead, the different facts, interpretations and behaviours formed a contradiction that became an antagonism. The uncertainty was reduced through a form of social regression (Slater, 1963). Multiple sources and directions or other social contingencies can be reduced to a communication between only two partners: in this case, the police against the 'protesters'. Georg Simmel (1964: 14) draws attention to this issue where both sides had something in common: working against each other in a form of shared antagonism. However, this antagonism is not anti-social, but instead initiates a process of social meaning-making where both parties are linked through negative contingency: 'I will not do what you want if you do not do what I want' (Luhmann, 1995: 389). The logic of 'us versus them' is employed by both sides.

This antagonism should not be confused with anti-social behaviour. Behaviour signifying one against the other already precedes a social regression, in which two sides seemingly face each other. In this context, another development can occur: the imputation of malevolent or anti-social behaviour. When the motives of the behaviour are inferred, the meaning-making is directed to the situation/person directly involved and not to the external circumstances (Hotaling, 1980: 138). For aggression and violence, the imputation of intention is crucial, which explains how the situation at the police station facilitated an attribution of malevolent or anti-social intent. Whether intentional or not, a number of issues facilitated an attribution of deliberate and malevolent behaviour, and the police did not react immediately. There was little communication between the two groups, and the public experienced long bouts of silence from the police. Further, the police appeared to be hiding something, as the police officer with the authority to speak openly about the case was not communicating. The public regarded this silence as intentional, and it was met with even stronger reactions. Information about the event was also spread via social media, including a considerable increase in Twitter messages (Bennett, 2011; Burn-Murdoch *et al.*, 2011; Tonkin *et al.*, 2012), which brought more people to the scene. Furthermore, the police imputed uncooperative actions or the use of non-legitimate force as likely motives. Consequently, the situation escalated, and all behaviour was framed as anti-social through which a variety of motives could appear; the behaviour was seen as violent, sparking further violence, that is to say, the dispersing of the crowd through 'normal' police tactics or the burning of police cars (Manning, 1980). In particular, activities regarded as an illegitimate and intentional use of physical violence functioned as a threshold symbol, for instance, one protester stated: 'But then it kicked off, people got angry because of the girl – police hit her or something [...] this pushed them over the top' (Morrell *et al.*, 2011: 15). Here, a logic of counter-violence unfolds that leads to more violence (riot police, police officers on horseback and the crowd throwing rocks, bottles and bricks at them). Although physical violence or violence against other people represents a minor portion of the events, the symbolic quality of an action excised only under extreme circumstances stands out and gives the entire situation meaning. As a result, the meaning constructed was not simply anti-social, but this narrative was embedded in a more complex process of meaning-making, which signalled the notion of a reversed social order.

In sum, the death of Mark Duggan did not trigger immediate violent behaviour. However, the uncertainty surrounding his death (the police issued contradicting reports), the spread of the news through social media, the increased ability of people to form a group because it was a Saturday, and the framing of the situation through antagonist and then anti-social behaviour led to a situation where the social order appeared to be in reverse, supporting motives of unrest, morally false behaviour or newsworthy actions.

Notions of the anti-social, outstanding and reversed order: the construction of media meaning

The notions of the anti-social and reversed social order are not solely authored by the police, governmental authorities or protesters. The use of social media and the mass media coverage also had a reinforcing quality. When something is widely reported, it is considered important, so more people will follow the event and attend it in person, thus making the event itself even larger and better known. Therefore, an increasing singularity of a possible major conflict develops. This outstanding quality is again enhanced by a particular logic of the media themselves, such as the focus on pictures (Internet, newspapers and television), the highlighting of a negative or deviant action as a source for news and the attraction of something big, namely large-scale conflicts (Staab, 1990). Although the role of the media has been noted as a crucial factor in spreading events and diffusing information (Singer, 1970; Myers, 2000; Russell, 2007), this research has overseen the self-referential quality in the construction of meaning or narrative with regard to these events (Morgner, 2010).

The mass media should not be seen as a neutral channel, but they give meaning to events. This meaning is then picked up by the audience, leading to subsequent reactions that work along this frame (using a language of the outstanding, surprising or singular) and thereby reinforcing the frame and enhancing the media's narrative, which leads to another narrative of reactions *ad infinitum*.

The early media reports on 6 August 2011 focused on three images: the burning of two police cars, a double-decker bus in flames and a fire that destroyed the Carpetright building in north-east London. These pictures were repeated across the different channels and media, shown from various angles and embedded in the general coverage as a peak or particular highlight. Thus, the image of all of Tottenham/London being in total chaos emerged, with a comparison to the bombings during the Second World War: 'London and the Blitz' (Reicher and Stott, 2011). A frame of the extraordinary was established, uniting the different actions under the label of a riot and as an event that deviated from the ordinary: the anti-social. Other channels interrupted their scheduled programming, reinforcing the notion of the extraordinary: 'television's most powerful gesture consists precisely in interrupting the continuous flow of its programs' (Dayan and Katz, 1998: 162). Consequently, the extraordinary circumstances attracted even more people to the area, which confirmed the narrative because an exceptionally large number of people were present (for more on large numbers and media, see Staab, 1990).

The narrative of the anti-social received further support within this framing of a deviation: most of the protesters were in fact criminals. Data from the Ministry of Justice (Home Office, 2011b) revealed that the majority of the active participants had previous offences. Thus, a picture of greedy people who steal for their own good and thereby act against society emerged. Although one cannot argue with the data, the overall explanation is flawed; according to the general crime statistics in London during the previous 12 months, the criminal histories of all offenders were virtually the same as those participating in the London Riots. Thus, nothing stands out as being different in the profile of offenders. If the event had been especially attractive to these criminals, their percentage would have been considerably higher than average. Additionally, the data does not support the luring thesis of ordinary citizens being attracted by such circumstances. The outstanding fact is that with regard to their criminal histories, the majority of people participating in the event differed quantitatively but not qualitatively. This conclusion leads to two questions: why was the situation constructed as 'normal', and why did the event vary in terms of its quantitative extent, for instance, the number of people participating?[2]

The normality of the social ruptures: anti-social versus pro-social behaviour and the semantics of reversed order

This section addresses why people joined the riots. They did not join because of a motivational logic of behaving anti-socially; instead, people 'helped' their peers or in-group members during a situation of reversed social order. In this sense, they acted pro-socially. This conclusion leads to another question: why did the situation appear normal, even though the media presented it as outstanding?

That people act upon an assumed understanding of one another as being ordinary or 'normal' receives special attention in the work of Harvey Sacks (1992: 218):

> There's a business of being an 'ordinary person', and that business includes attending the world, yourself, others, objects so as to see how it is that it is a usual scene. And when offering what transpired, you present it in its usual 'nothing much' fashion, with whatever variants of banal characterizations you might happen to use.

The analysis thus should elaborate on the issue of what kinds of normalities (including types of deviance) are produced within the accounts in the particular setting of the so-called London 'riots'?

The events in London were reported as social rupture marked by a temporary interruption of the continuous flow of social activities – something occurs that stands out. Pierre Bourdieu describes moments in which the meaning of the ordinary is turned upside down (Bourdieu, 1990: 159). This idea is also explored by Mikhail Bakhtin (1993). Carnivalism refers to a narrative of suspension and/or reversal of the rules and regulations of ordinary life. Bakhtin demonstrates that this state leads not to an anti-social chaos, but to a temporal order on which social reality is made contingent. Common ideas and truths are endlessly tested and contested, appearing in relativity to all things and claiming to voice alternatives. When the world is in an upside-down state, other norms and values will be replaced. Activities regarded as criminal, including police struggles and conflicts with others, are not extraordinary circumstances, but represent their 'normality' to a certain extent (Osvaldsson, 2004; for the normality of the locations, see Till, 2012): 'Normally the police control us. But the law was obeying us, know what I mean?' (*The Guardian*/LSE, 2011: 23).

The reversed order and its normality was crucial for three developments: the asymmetrical relationship with the police (strict policing and the possibility of reversing that order was a catalyst, which made the violence a collective phenomenon), descriptions of the events using a language of the lawless (Greenslade, 2011a; Greenslade, 2011b; O'Carroll and Davies, 2011) that redefined the notion of property, and a new 'audience' for the event, which engaged the circumstances through a highly moral language of anti-social behaviour.

A considerable amount of research has demonstrated that partisanship or frame alignment depends on the superior status of one side and the social closeness of the other (Arms and Russell, 1997; de la Roche, 2001; Snow *et al.*, 1986). This concept implies that a third party will not be neutral if the person involved in the conflict is regarded as an in-group member, a like-minded person, part of the same social web (de la Roche, 2001),[3] or someone in conflict with a group that shares an asymmetrical relationship. In such a setting, a collectivization of violence is then possible due to strong partisanship or pro-social behaviour; solidarity emerges to support one group against the other because the members are socially close and at the same time distant from the other. The adversary status of the other is thereby influenced because of its superior status (Manning, 1980; Hotaling, 1980; de la Roche, 2001). Studies published in the aftermath of the events have demonstrated that the policing practice (*The Guardian*/LSE, 2011: 18 and Klein, 2012) contributed to the notion of being socially close (the police violate the rights of the people), enlarging the distance between the police, who used their superior status to implement such a violation (*The Guardian*/LSE, 2011: 19).

The partisanship also becomes possible through the use of the BlackBerry Messenger service (*The Guardian*/LSE, 2011: 30). This violation was implemented via dense coverage by the media with information about the event, as well as through personal networks. Consequently, these structures were crucial in spreading the activities. People were part of these wider networks, socially integrated and informed, and they could be mobilized more quickly than large numbers of isolated, anti-social or excluded people (Bohstedt, 1994: 269). Further, those being informed could 'copy' the activities of other areas (Bohstedt, 1994: 281): 'few young people got involved in the riots on their own. Most went along with friends and both influenced and were influenced by their peers in terms of how far they went in their involvement' (Morrell *et al.*, 2011: 6).

Narratives of redefinition and the communication of moral judgements about anti-social behaviour

Most offenders brought to trial were not prosecuted for violence against any given person but instead for looting or looting-related activities (on looting, see Mac Ginty, 2004). As Mikhail Bakthin (1993), Pierre Bourdieu (1990) and Michael Rosenfeld (1997) have all noted, the reversal of the social, in a sort of carnival spirit, opens up new possibilities:

> The breaking with ordinary experience of time as simple re-enactment of a past or a future inscribed in the past, all things become possible (at least apparently), when future prospects appear really contingent, future events really indeterminate [...] [their] consequences unpredicted and unpredictable. (Bourdieu, 1990: 182)

This important narrative is reflected in a broad range of semantics depicting the situation of the looting: 'It was like Christmas', (Topping and Bawdon, 2011) or 'This was more of a party' (*The Guardian*/LSE, 2011: 20 and 28), or a 'feast', a 'spectacle', or a 'festival' (Morrell *et al.*, 2011: 21).

In such a setting, the narrative leads to a redefinition of property rights (Dynes and Quarantelli, 1968; Varul, 2011; *The Guardian*/LSE, 2011: 28): 'People were picking up things like it was in their homes and it was theirs already', 'Get stuff for free', 'Get anything you want, anything you ever desired', and 'It would have been like a normal shopping day [...] but with no staff in the shop.'

The issue of ownership is often questioned during conflict. This concept is strongly reflected in the selectiveness of the stores being looted. Of the targeted stores, more than 60 per cent were retail shops. Within this category, the most common were electronics and clothing stores (Home Office, 2011b). General stores selling goods of symbolic value or status were also targeted; so-called lifestyle goods, such as large, flat-screen televisions and mobile phones were the overwhelming majority of the products looted. For example, banks, utility stations, industrial plants, private residences, and schools were largely ignored. The damaged apartments and homes were in or near burned business establishments. Such selective looting can only be explained through a collective narrative in which 'good' and 'bad' businesses are defined (gangs also might have spurred this process (Harding, 2012)).

With the establishment of such a reversed and highly selective order, another party emerges in conflict that makes use of moral judgements of good and bad behaviour, highlighting the notion of anti-social behaviour. On 10 August 2011, David Cameron (2011a) called the riots 'mindless self-ishness', Joe Anderson, a member of Liverpool's city council, called the participants 'mindless thugs', while the *Daily Mirror* (2011) classified the occurrences as 'mindless rioting', describing the 'scum' who needed to be 'swept from the street' or 'the looters who should be shot' (Henley, 2011). Through such moral judgements, a new description or narrative is offered, creating a sort of sub-human person driven by greed and anger. Thus, another group emerged that rearranged the meaning-making and therefore the procession of meaning in the events. This change legitimized talk about more drastic means, sending in the army, or using rubber bullets or water cannon.

There is no doubt that some people were afraid to continue looting, but the abrupt ending to the events suggests that the narrative of the reversed order consumed itself. As Bourdieu (1990: 193) outlined, the ordering and the beginning grip of the normality of the event consume the spontaneous energy. The behaviour becomes predictable; the contingency of *the against* changes into a repetition of the same, and suddenly the potential of pumping even more negative contingency into social reality decays. The order is restored, at least temporarily.

Conclusion

The analysis in this chapter criticized the unquestioned use of the term 'riot' as anti-social behaviour. The focus of this chapter was to outline a different approach to understanding the complex formation of social meaning in which the label 'riot' as anti-social behaviour is but one part of an overall narrative created in a complex network of different narratives, stories or communicative exchanges. Therefore, the overall process of meaning-making, which informed and structured the events, was examined. The chapter suggested that the common readings of the events through a cause and effect scheme are based on a simplistic narrative, which ignored the complex and often uncertain nature of meaning-making. Furthermore, the analysis revealed that the meaning-making was not simply to be left to a particular group or author, but required a more complex approach of networked exchanges, fusion and defusion of meaning. Anti-social behaviour and riots appeared as a particular story tie, which informed the meaning-making of governmental actors and the motive complex of non-participants.

The analysis challenged common descriptions of the trigger through an investigation of similar events that had no such effect and by providing a close reading of the communication structure through which an antagonism, a conflict and collective violence evolved. The analysis of the communication could demonstrate that rule violations occur as a result of patterns of attribution, which again has serious consequences for subsequent reactions. Furthermore, such developments were not local phenomena, but were already embedded in a wider social world through social media, personal networks and the mass media. Through the inclusion of all these narratives into a wider web of communication, new links could be forged and activities could unfold through links into this meaning-making. Such important linkages and narratives were facilitated by the media, which provided a description of a world turned upside-down. In these settings, the notion of a carnival atmosphere emerged; what was considered deviant became normal. Therefore, a range of other activities could be acted out; motives that enabled such behaviour became possible. The social media, the mass media and personal networks could mobilize other people to take part, enlarging the idea of the event and making it even more attractive. In such a setting, the redefinition of property becomes possible as a sort of normality: shopping without paying at the counter. However, the looting did not occur at random. The upside-down order is not simply an alternative but provides an alternative to obtain what is considered to be of symbolic value in the everyday, which is related to questions of identity and status. The narrative of the reversed order induces a narrative of moral communication, mainly by describing the reversed order as morally bad or anti-social and thus legitimizing a language that is even more drastic.

In sum, this chapter criticized the unproblematic view of the term 'riot' as anti-social behaviour and provided different conceptual considerations to produce new viewpoints regarding the study and a better understanding of the events. These perspectives stand apart from the current account of the deviant, the criminal or the mindless.

Notes

1. The idea of the 'trigger' is, however, problematic in another way, as it does not compare the event to other similar events that did not have the same effect. A person's death is no doubt a tragic and very emotional moment for many people. Individual deaths are a recurring event for the British (England and Wales) and Metropolitan Police. Twenty-one people have died in shootings within the jurisdiction of the Metropolitan Police, which is about one person per year for the last 20 years. The highest number was in 2007, when three people were shot. But none of these deaths triggered large-scale events. It is also not possible to argue that the shooting of Mark Duggan was the straw that broke the camel's back because the overall number of people dying after contact with the police has sharply declined in the last ten years. In 2010 and 2011, these numbers were the lowest they had been in 20 years (INQUEST, 2012).

2. A typical answer to the second part of the question explains the anti-social behaviour and anti-social treatment of these people, including categories such as youth, race and educational level, through which relevant motives are imputed and very often stereotyped; for instance, David Cameron stated that a lack of morality and bad parenting are the main reasons for the anti-social behaviour. As McPhail (1971: 1069) has shown: 'There is no compelling reason to accept the inference that persons are more impetuous because of their youth, more daring because of their gender, more disenchanted because of their race, or less rational because of their educational level. An equally plausible interpretation of these data is that such persons are simply more available for participation by virtue of the large amount of unscheduled or uncommitted time which results from being young, black, male and without educational credentials in the urban ghettos of contemporary US society.' Variables such as time and access to the location are a far better explanation of behaviour than anti-social explanations. The first activities in London emerged on a Saturday evening, which further extends availability; also, London's public transport offered cheap and quick access to most locations. Most of the studies with a socio-economic orientation were unable to explain why areas sharing similar features, such as youth, ethnicity, and educational level, were untouched by the activities, in particular East London (Poplar), or why areas of relative wealth (South and West London) were part of it.

3. Forms of self-categorization are crucial here, as they highlight an important difference between those who become involved and those who remain bystanders (Levine, *et al.*, 2002).

9
The Aesthetics of Anti-social Behaviour

Andrew Millie

Introduction

From the late 1990s onwards, anti-social behaviour has been high on the political agenda in Britain. Of course, at the end of the twentieth century, anti-social behaviour was nothing new, a fact highlighted in other contributions to this volume. Yet, following pressure on MPs from constituents facing difficulties with people labelled as 'neighbours from hell' (Straw, 1996; Field, 2003) – and influenced by American zero-tolerance policing strategies (Millie, 2009b) – the 1997–2010 New Labour government made anti-social behaviour one of its key policy targets. Being anti-social was defined by New Labour as behaving 'in a manner that caused or was likely to cause harassment, alarm or distress to one or more persons not of the same household as [the perpetrator]' (Crime and Disorder Act 1998: s.1(1a)). As has been well documented (Ashworth *et al.*, 1998; Ramsay, 2004; Millie, 2009b), there were issues with such a vague definition. In the first instance, what causes me harassment, alarm or distress may be quite different for someone else. Deciding what or who 'was likely' to be anti-social was even more subjective and problematic.

This chapter considers such subjective interpretations. Specifically, the focus is on aesthetic determinants of perceived anti-social behaviour – while acknowledging that there are clearly other influences on perception (see for example Jacobson *et al.*, 2008; Mackenzie *et al.*, 2010). The discussion draws on philosophical, criminological and other writings to unpick some influences of aesthetic taste on what is perceived to be anti-social. For instance, the chapter considers aesthetic interpretations of dress (such as the hoodie) that may lead police officers to see someone as potentially anti-social. Furthermore, proponents of a particular style of graffiti may be censured, yet others may fit an agreeable aesthetic and be celebrated. As for talk of 'neighbours from hell', problems may stem from serious behavioural issues, but may also concern conflicting tastes. However, is it right to censure taste, something that is both subjective and emotive? This chapter considers the impact of aesthetic taste on others and how differences in lifestyle can lead to some being labelled as anti-social.

Like New Labour before it, the 2010 Conservative–Liberal Democrat Coalition government identified anti-social behaviour as an important policy issue (Millie, 2013). According to the Conservative Home Secretary Theresa May (2012: 3), 'No one should have to accept graffiti on their walls, public drunkenness on their streets or harassment and intimidation on their own doorstep.' At first, it is hard to argue with such logic, that everyone wants somewhere 'nice' to live. Yet each part of this statement is subjective. Harassment and intimidation are perhaps less problematic, as very few people would want to put up with these types of behaviours – although tolerances may vary. Public drunkenness is again something that at first seems uncontroversial. Yet there is an aesthetic to public drunkenness which means some drunks are more acceptable than others. For example, city workers drinking outside a pub at 5 p.m. on a Friday are usually an accepted part of city life; yet a street homeless person drinking at lunchtime may be less acceptable. As for May's statement that 'No one should have to accept graffiti on their walls', this becomes problematic when certain forms of graffiti and street art can act as attractors for tourists and part of what makes an urban district 'edgy' – and therefore an attractive place to live. Here graffiti contributes to processes of gentrification rather than decline as often assumed (Young, 2014).

In this chapter, the meaning and subjectivity of aesthetic judgement are considered. The relevance of aesthetics to assessments of anti-social behaviour is then explored and examples are given of aesthetic judgements leading to censure and 'banishment'. James Wilson and George Kelling's (1982) 'broken windows' perspective has been especially influential to British anti-social behaviour policy. Because of this influence, 'broken windows' is given particular attention. In line with Jeff Ferrell (2006), this is seen as an aesthetic theory that makes various assumptions as to what – or who – act as signals of urban decay. The chapter finishes by discussing whether it is ever right to censure aesthetic taste, before concluding that it can be a mistake to enforce subjective taste and simply banish the unsightly. Instead, it is suggested that respect for difference could alternatively be promoted. However, first it is worth unpacking what is meant by aesthetic judgement.

Aesthetic judgement

Aesthetics has for many years been a concern of philosophy and art criticism focusing mainly on questions pertaining to what makes art good and whether there is such a thing as objective beauty. William Gilpin (1786), for example, considered criteria that made a landscape beautiful or sublime. Writing around the same time Immanuel Kant concluded that beauty is subjective, that 'an objective principle of taste is impossible' (1790/2011: 12). In effect, according to Kant, there can be no objectively beautiful or sublime landscape (or objectively beautiful or sublime anything else), only our interpretations depending on taste. Thus, building on a Kantian perspective, I take the view that aesthetics is concerned with taste, with subjective and emotive values attached to sensory encounters (Millie, 2008, 2011). For an example, Kant considered the beauty of a flower:

> To say, This flower is beautiful, is tantamount to a mere repetition of the flower's own claim to everyone's liking. The agreeableness of its smell, on the one hand, gives it no claim whatsoever: its smell delights one person, it makes another dizzy [...] beauty is not a property of the flower itself. For a judgment of taste consists precisely in this, that it calls a thing beautiful only by virtue of the characteristics in which it adapts itself to the way we apprehend it. (Kant, 1790/2011: 10)

This subjectivity of aesthetic taste has direct relevance to the acceptability – or otherwise – of certain anti-social behaviours. Following Kant, there can be no agreed list of graffiti or street art styles that are always aesthetically acceptable. Groups of young people wearing hoodies may be turned away from one location because they do not adhere to a particular aesthetic being promoted, yet accepted elsewhere. A visibly homeless person may be moved on from a high end retail district, but ignored in another.

For some, aesthetic preferences are restricted to visual and aural stimuli. For Kant's flower, there was also the influence of smell. You can add to this all other senses and beyond. This chapter is concerned with what Yuriko Saito (2007) refers to as *everyday* aesthetics. Influenced by Henri Lefebvre's (1961/2008) 'everyday life', everyday aesthetics relates to everyday objects, events and encounters. For instance, *reading* a message left by a graffiti writer is an everyday aesthetic experience, and so too is *feeling* the texture of a 'guerrilla knitter's' crocheted wool that has been left without permission enveloping a tree (see Deadly Knitshade, 2011). Encountering the graffiti and guerrilla knitting may be negative aesthetic experiences – and perceived as anti-social by some – yet for others they may add something positive to the urban experience that make the city somewhere that is more pleasurable to be.

Inherent to aesthetic judgements are ideas of taste, and related notions of good taste and bad taste. In relation to graffiti, Germaine Greer once commented, 'Instead of spending a fortune getting rid of it, why don't we just give it marks out of 10?' (Greer, 2007; Millie, 2008). Presumably, those doing the scoring will have 'good taste'? Greer may have been deliberately provocative with such a statement, yet, as this chapter will demonstrate, the statement gets to the heart of the problem of mixing aesthetic judgement with assessments of what is acceptable or anti-social. A graffiti writer that scores low on Greer's scale will no doubt face prosecution, whereas a high scorer – Banksy perhaps? – will be celebrated. In relation to questions of taste and neighbourliness, according to the conservative philosopher Roger Scruton (2009: 133–4):

> In a democratic culture people are inclined to believe that it is presumptuous to claim to have better taste than your neighbour. By doing so you are implicitly denying his right to be the thing that he is. You like Bach, she likes U2 [...] she likes Jane Austen, you like Danielle Steel. Each of you exists in his own enclosed aesthetic world, and so long as neither harms the other, and each says good morning over the fence, there is nothing further to be said. [...] [But] your neighbour fills her garden with kitsch mermaids and Disneyland gnomes, polluting the view from your window. [...] Now her taste has ceased to be a private matter and inflicted itself on the public realm.

It is when someone's private taste becomes public that it may be interpreted as anti-social – be that someone's taste in graffiti or gnomes and mermaids. In the above example, having a garden full of gnomes and mermaids may be perceived as anti-social, in the same way that growing a high hedge could be anti-social, because it is inconsiderate of neighbours. According to the Anti-Social Behaviour Act 2003 (s.66), a high hedge is defined as causing:

> so much of a barrier to light or access as (a) is formed wholly or predominantly by a line of two or more evergreens; and (b) rises to a height of more than two metres above ground level.

A private taste – a liking for tall hedges and privacy – has become public by restricting the amount of sunlight reaching a neighbour or making access to a neighbour's property more difficult. Much criminological and legal theory emphasize harm and offence as determinates of criminalization (Feinberg, 1984; 1985; Hillyard *et al.*, 2004; von Hirsch and Simester, 2006). With the example of 'high hedges', it is the practical harm to quality of life that is important; but also the aesthetic offence and maybe moral offence that a neighbour would inflict their taste on you, a taste for high hedges that you do not share. This is similarly the case for the garden gnomes and mermaids; however, there may also be economic impacts by lowering the attractiveness of the street and thereby deflating property prices.

According to Carolyn Korsmeyer (2005: 275), 'Those who conceive of themselves as having good taste may condescend to those with "inferior" tastes, while the later may consider the former mere snobs [...].' It is questionable why one person's taste should take precedence over another's – even if the other's taste is for gnomes and mermaids. This was a point picked up by Pierre Bourdieu (1979/2010) in charting an aristocracy of culture from popular taste, through middle-brow to the 'legitimate' tastes of the ruling classes. There are clearly issues of power in who defines what is acceptable, or what

Ferrell (1996) has termed an aesthetics of authority. Those deemed to have poor aesthetic taste tend to be the powerless. When censured as anti-social the consequences of such assessments become more serious.

Aesthetics and banishing the anti-social

The mixing of aesthetic judgement and censure has historic precedent, especially in relation to the fashion of offenders (and those thought *likely* to offend). In the eighteenth century, the Black Act 1723 meant having your face blackened or being otherwise disguised was a capital offence (Treadwell, 2008). Determining what constitutes a disguise may not have been straight-forward. In Victorian Britain, dressing in a fashion similar to a 'Hooligan', 'Peaky Blinder' or 'Scuttler' could have landed you in all sorts of trouble (Pearson, 2009). Similar stereotypes persist today making some young people more likely to attract the attention of the police than others, as those *likely* to be anti-social and in need of dispersal. The hoodie, along with a baseball cap, 'designer' sports attire and trainers is the uniform of the 'chav'[1] (Hayward and Yar, 2006) or 'ned'[2] (Brown, 2008) – the young working class that, to use Korsmeyer's words (2005: 275), are condescended as having 'inferior tastes'. Famously, the Bluewater shopping centre in Kent was the first to ban the wearing of hoodies (Hayward and Yar, 2006; Millie, 2009a), ostensibly so that all could be seen by their CCTV systems; but also to ally the prejudicial concerns of other customers that hoodie-wearing youths were anti-social – despite hoodies being on sale within the shopping centre. According to Hayward and Yar:

> street-level attempts to mobilize cultural capital based on overt displays of designer clothing have instead inspired a whole new raft of bizarre micro social control mechanisms, including everything from town centre pubs and night clubs refusing entry to individuals wearing certain brands within their premises [...] to the recent 'zero tolerance' policy imposed on 'designer hoodies' and baseball caps [...] by major shopping cen-tres [...]. Thus the situation arises in which many of the labels and monograms valorized by young people as badges of identity serve also to function as overt signifiers of deviance. As such they become tools of clas-sification and identification by which agencies of social control construct profiles of potential criminal protagonists. (2006: 22–3)

Not only are the young stereotypically regarded as 'problem' populations, but so too the poor. To be young *and* poor amplifies the potential threat. Aesthetics is relevant to both groups as aesthetic cues – including dress codes – can influence initial assessments of what type of person someone is (although, of course, such assessments are not always accurate). Charles Baudelaire's poem 'The Eyes of the Poor' encapsulates the ruling class's aesthetic assessment of the poor. In the poem, two lovers enjoy a new café in George Haussmann's redesigned nineteenth-century Paris. As retold by Marshall Berman (1982: 149):

> As the lovers sit gazing happily into each other's eyes, suddenly they are confronted with other people's eyes. A poor family dressed in rags – a gray-bearded father, a young son, and a baby – come to stop directly in front of them and gaze raptly at the bright new world that is just inside [...]. He is 'touched by this family of eyes' [...]. 'I turned my eyes to look into yours dear love, to read *my* thoughts there' [...] she says, 'These people with their great saucer eyes are unbearable! Can't you tell the manager to get them away from here?' (Berman, 1982: 149)

The visible presence of the poor does not meet the lovers' aesthetic expectations. The sight of 'a poor family dressed in rags' jars with the romance of the situation. What the lover calls for is what, in a North American context, Katherine Beckett and Steve Herbert (2010) have called banishment. In Seattle, for example:

> Increasing swathes of urban space are delimitated as zones of exclusion from which the undesirable are banned. The uniformed police are marshaled to enforce and often delineate these boundaries; they use their powers to monitor and arrest in an attempt to clear the streets of those considered unsightly or 'disorderly'. (Beckett and Herbert, 2010: 8)

Key here is the idea of banishing the 'unsightly'. As Beckett and Herbert emphasize, the situation is not unique to Seattle. It is also a common approach in Britain, for instance with the use of Dispersal Orders[3] to move on those thought likely to be anti-social (Crawford and Lister, 2007). As already mentioned, street-drinking city workers are more acceptable than a street-drinking homeless person, with the homeless person regarded as 'unsightly' and moved on. Furthermore, the homeless person's contribution to the local economy is not on the scale of the city workers' – and if you are not making a significant contribution to the economy your presence is more likely to be criminalized (Coleman, 2004; Millie, 2011). Such aesthetic – and economic – assessments can be seen as part of revanchist processes of revitalization and gentrification (Smith, 1996). Alongside aesthetic and economic value judgements are moral and prudential/quality-of-life assessments (Millie, 2011). For instance, for the homeless person, is it morally right to be living on the street? Or, perhaps, are the viewers' morals challenged and quality-of-life affected by the sight of such visible poverty leading to calls to 'get them away from here'? (cf. Berman, 1982). All four value judgements inter-relate in determining what or who are acceptable or deemed to be anti-social and banished. An influential American perspective that incorporates these value judgements is Wilson and Kelling's (1982) 'broken windows'. Their view has had a major influence on British anti-social behaviour policy and it is to this that I now turn.

The aesthetics of breaking windows

Much has been claimed about 'broken windows', both for and against; as Kelling (2000: 12) later observed, 'it has caused considerable consternation in much sociological, legal and criminological literature'. Kelling was right in that the 'broken windows' perspective has been critiqued at length (for example Walker, 1984; Sampson and Raudenbush, 1999; Harcourt, 2001; Mitchell, 2001), as has the zero tolerance policing that it inspired in New York and Britain from the 1990s onwards (for example Bowling, 1999; Smith, 2001). It is not my job here to repeat all that has been said before. What 'broken windows' provides is a simplified story causally linking disorder (or anti-social behaviour) to crime. The broken window is read as a signal of neglect, leading 'good' citizens to withdraw from the streets resulting in less informal control, more broken windows and for crime to take root. It is the job of the police and other agents of social control to get in early before such decline can take root. Despite the prominence of 'broken windows', Wilson and Kelling were not the first to express such a view, although they were perhaps the first to link it to policing strategies. In the American states of California and New York, Philip Zimbardo (1973) had already run an experiment with abandoned cars to see how long it would be before they were vandalized and stripped for parts. In Britain, Colin Ward (1973) had also considered relationships between the environment and vandalism, according to whom:

> An atmosphere of dereliction and neglect evokes misuse and careless, if not wilful, destruction, by some users, while good maintenance and surfaces of good quality, are respected and sometimes cherished. The environment, in other words, transmits signals to which users respond. Following this theory, one architect who was conscious of the usual drab, cold, litter-strewn appearance of staircase landings in blocks of flats, persuaded his client that it was useful to carpet the landing and provide a radiator. Over the radiator he installed a shelf, and was later gratified to see that a tenant had put a bowl of flowers on the shelf. The signal read CIVILIZED. (Ward, 1973: 14)

In this regard, aesthetic signals are read as either signs of civilization or de-civilization or somewhere in-between – of something that is celebrated, merely tolerated or censured as being anti-social or criminal. A carpeted hallway is usually going to be seen as more attractive than one strewn with litter and graffiti. However, as noted, our assessments of aesthetic worth are both subjective and emotive, thus some forms of graffiti may in fact be welcomed in particular circumstances – although perhaps not the litter.

According to Ferrell (2006: 261–2), ' "broken windows" is essentially an aesthetic analysis of crime's etiology'. In effect, our interpretations of aesthetic signals lead to assessments of what is criminal, anti-social, tolerable or celebrated. It is an attractively simple idea, yet problematic for those people read as broken windows – the street homeless person, the graffiti writer, the hoodie-wearing youth – who are then banished from public view. As Wilson and Kelling suggest, 'Arresting a single drunk or a single vagrant who has harmed no identifiable person seems unjust, and in a sense it is. But failing to do anything about a score of drunks or a hundred vagrants may destroy an entire community' (1982: 35). For Wilson and Kelling the homeless person is a signal of decline that makes other crime more likely. For Don Mitchell (2001), the logic is incredible, that homeless people should be punished, not for any crimes they have done, but 'because of the potential in a particular place for other people's crimes to occur' (2001: 68). Mitchell further notes:

> [T]his defence of punitive measures against homeless people simply asserts that the *aesthetics of place* outweigh other considerations, such as the right of homeless people to find a means to live, to sleep, *to be*. (Mitchell, 2001: 68, emphasis in original)

The study of semiotics is useful in trying to interpret such aesthetic signals (for example Barthes, 1972; Eco, 1979) and the idea of signal crimes and signals of control was later elaborated by Martin Innes and colleagues (for example Innes and Fielding, 2002). Roland Barthes (1972), for example, followed a semiotic-structuralist approach where signs mean the same to all readers. An alternative perspective – adopted in this chapter – takes an interpretivist view 'where individuals are creative agents that make their own meanings' (Millie, 2012: 1094). Wilson and Kelling clearly adopted a structuralist approach assuming that we all make the same aesthetic judgements. As mentioned, there can be quite different interpretations of graffiti writing or street art, which can be censured in one situation, yet celebrated as part of urban life elsewhere. The act of breaking a window itself can have different interpretations. A year before Wilson and Kelling published 'broken windows', the Irish rock band U2 released their second album that included the track 'I threw a brick through a window' (U2, 1981). For Bono, the writer of the lyric, the broken window was not read as a signal of neighbourhood disorder or decline and something to be feared; rather, breaking a window was expressive and a metaphor for youthful frustration; as he declared elsewhere in the song:

> I was walking, I was walking into walls
> And back again
> I just keep walking
> I walk up to a window to see myself
> And my reflection, when I thought about it
> My direction, going nowhere, going nowhere.

The broken window was important for what it signified to the one breaking the window, it was a positive thing. Similarly, for the street artist or graffiti writer, their uncommissioned images and words (cf. Young, 2014) are part of who they are, even if this is not read the same by all of their audience. As the British street artist Banksy once noted, perhaps with a hint of irony, 'Some people become cops because they want to make the world a better place. Some people become vandals because they want to make the world a better *looking* place' (Banksy, 2006: 8, emphasis in original). Urban developers and gentrifiers are attracted to such an 'edgy' aesthetic. In a critique of broken windows, Harcourt (2001: 18) declared that, 'the meaning of order and disorder may not be as stable or as fixed as the order maintenance approach suggests'. For Wilson and Kelling, however, broken windows were entirely negative aesthetic signifiers of disorder, crime and decline.

Conclusion

What this chapter has attempted to demonstrate is that aesthetics have an important role in determining what is acceptable or anti-social and that such assessments have a disproportionate impact on the powerless. In line with Bourdieu (1979/2010), a hierarchy of tastes can be observed with more 'legitimate' tastes being reserved for those with power. The powerful may be shopping-mall owners who exclude hoodie-wearing youths for fear of upsetting the 'consuming majority' (cf. Bannister *et al.*, 2006). They may be gallery owners, collectors, celebrities or media outlets that tell us that certain street artists are worthy of attention, while others are guilty of vandalism. They may be police officers, urban planners or town-centre managers who permit certain types of street drinking, yet are less tolerant of other street drinkers. As Korsmeyer (2005: 275) has noted, 'Those who conceive of themselves as having good taste may condescend to those with "inferior" tastes.' Utilizing anti-social behaviour legislation, those with 'inferior taste' are deemed to be 'broken windows' to be dispersed or 'banished' (cf. Beckett and Herbert, 2010).

According to Scruton (2009: 134), 'Implicit in our sense of beauty is the thought of community – of the agreement in judgements that makes social life possible and worthwhile.' The example given is of planning law, yet would also apply to anti-social behaviour law. It is a majoritarian perspective where the views or tastes of the majority in society take precedence. Thus, having a garden full of mermaids and gnomes is a minority taste – and may be regarded as anti-social. However, I return here to a question I started with: is it right to censure taste, something that is both subjective and emotive? Furthermore, should one person's taste take precedence over another's, even if theirs is a minority perspective? There will always be some whose taste is so harmful or offensive that censure is the right response. For instance, it is sensible to have laws that censure graffiti that is racist/sexist/homophobic or displays other clearly insulting or inflammatory text, what – in the language of anti-social behaviour – would be true 'harassment, alarm or distress'. Or perhaps law that limits who/when certain aesthetic tastes are permitted – such as having age limits on having a tattoo (for example BBC *News*, 2014). However, there is a lot below this level that is open for discussion as being simply 'different'.

Perhaps, instead of seeking agreement in aesthetic taste, we should seek respect for difference. In British policy on anti-social behaviour the word 'respect' comes with the baggage of New Labour's 'Respect Agenda' (Millie, 2009b); yet it is an idea that can still have resonance. Rather than trying to enforce respect (as New Labour did through its anti-social behaviour legislation), the emphasis ought to be on promoting mutual understanding. According to Carla Bagnoli (2007: 117), 'respect requires that we do not impose our views on others, but it also requires that we engage in a frank dialogue with them [...] the conclusion of this dialogue may be informed disagreement'. If decisions concerning what is anti-social – and therefore censured – are informed by aesthetic taste, the idea of always imposing taste on others is not very attractive, especially if those deemed to have inferior tastes are those who already lack power. Instead, promoting the idea of 'informed disagreement' and at least some *tolerance* of difference (Bannister and Kearns, 2009) makes a lot of sense. Of course this does not diminish the serious impact in terms of harm or offence that some people's anti-social behaviour can have on others. However, it does leave hope for the promotion of empathy, or at least recognizing the other's point of view. For Richard Sennett (1970: 108), this is the mature view of city living, to 'grow to need the unknown, to feel incomplete without a certain anarchy in their lives, to learn [...] to love the "otherness" around them'. However, as New Labour has demonstrated – and the Conservative–Liberal Democrat Coalition has reinforced through the Anti-Social Behaviour, Crime and Policing Act 2014 – enforcing standards of behaviour continues to take precedence. However, as this chapter has attempted to demonstrate, it can be a mistake to simply enforce subjective taste and banish the unsightly.

Notes

1. Chav – thought to derive from the Romany for a small child, or from the Kent town of Chatham meaning 'Chatham girl' or 'Chatham average', or even as 'Council House and Violent' (see Hayward and Yar, 2006).
2. Ned – a Scottish term thought to derive from 'non-educated delinquent' (Brown, 2008).
3. Anti-Social Behaviour Act 2003 s.30–6.

Part II

Anti-social Behaviour, the Vulnerable and the Marginalized

10
Addressing Juvenile Anti-social Behaviour in Victorian England: Mary Carpenter and the Reformatory Schools

Aurélie Baudry-Palmer

Although public concern over juvenile anti-social behaviour did not originate in the nineteenth century, it certainly became more apparent during the Victorian period (Gillis, 1975: 96). The 'outburst of concern' over juvenile delinquency was fuelled by the mass publication of pamphlets and enquiries denouncing an alarming rise in juvenile crime (Shore, 2002: 14; PP 1852 (6), vol XLI). As Britain experienced unprecedented social and economic changes, the great reports of the period represented one of the ways in which the nation could make sense of the dramatic transformations that were occurring. Observers who raised concerns about the effects of urbanization, the rise of poverty, the housing conditions of the working classes and the education of the masses, naturally turned their attention to the question of juvenile delinquency.

Commissioned by philanthropic institutions, newspapers and Parliament, a wave of literature commenting on the post-Napoleonic war increase in juvenile anti-social behaviour was thus distributed widely across the country.[1] It diffused the image of a class of urban poor and young criminals whose uncontrollable growth could threaten society's stability: 'juvenile offending became an emblem for social breakdown and domestic instability' (Shore, 2002: 1). The spectre of a class of criminal children exacerbated social anxieties and contributed to shape the Victorians' perceptions of juvenile delinquents. Official surveys such as the 1816 *Report of the Committee for Investigating the Causes of the Alarming Increase of Juvenile Delinquency in the Metropolis*, produced by Whig politician Thomas Fowell Buxton and several Quaker reformers, painted an alarming picture of juvenile anti-social behaviour. Social investigations encouraged the development of the idea of a 'criminal type', which was the product of a race with its own codes and even specific physical features (Davie, 2006: 55–61). In 1838, the character of the Artful Dodger captured imaginations and entertained the image of swarms of young criminals walking about the streets of the Victorian city.

Most pamphlets would attempt to determine the causative factors behind the increase of juvenile crime. They 'contextualized' the problem of juvenile anti-social behaviour; the perceived rise in crime was understood within a broader social and economic context. Urbanization, rapid migration, poverty, factory life, the decline of apprenticeships, demographic changes and the lack of religious education were regularly mentioned.[2] Research in the field of juvenile delinquency has since nuanced the picture of the rise in crime and questioned some of its causative factors. King's analysis, for example, building on the work of Susan Magarey, suggests that the nineteenth-century reform of the administration of criminal justice may have contributed to the increase in young criminals' arrests (King, 1998: 159–60).[3] The 'rise of a more disciplinary agenda' resulted in the adoption of a series of legislative reforms and the criminalization of behaviours previously ignored by courts, which in turn boosted the number of prosecutions (King, 1998: 133–6). Peel's Police Act 1829 represented a revolution in the traditional methods of law enforcement and gave power to police officers to arrest 'all loose, idle and disorderly persons whom he shall find disturbing the public peace, or whom he shall have the just cause to suspect of any evil designs' (Lyman, 1964: 141). Perceived by the liberal Whigs and the Radicals as a threat to civil liberties and an instrument of control in a context of social unrest, the Police was symbolic of the power of the state while the Act constituted an important step in the long-awaited reform of the legal system.

Summary jurisdiction (under the Vagrancy Acts, 1820–22 and the Juvenile Offenders Act 1847) as well as the new powers invested in magistrates contributed to an increase in the number of indictments. Under the new provision, magistrates were empowered to adjudicate over a variety of offences, which until then would have been dealt with at the Quarter Sessions or Assizes. This meant that potential offenders appeared first before a magistrate and, depending on the severity of their crime, might then be committed for trial at a higher court. If summary trials provided magistrates with the right to adjudicate rapidly upon matters and aimed at accelerating procedures, they facilitated the trial-punishment process and may have led to an increase in the number of indictments (Shore, 2002: 5). Similarly, the revision of sentences contributed to a rise in prosecutions. As the sentences incurred became less drastic and the number of offences liable to the death penalty reduced, magistrates tended to prosecute children more readily (King, 1998: 151; Hostettler, 2009: 203).

Nineteenth-century accounts, although often 'impressionistic', contributed to informing the public debate and played a fundamental role in shaping the reform of the penal system (Shore, 2002: 3). Usually based on a series of interviews of young criminals, the reports would describe the children's background, the offence committed, their journey into the justice system and their treatment in jail. In addition to exposing the misery and tragic condition of those children, reformers and observers sought to denounce the inadequacy of the penal system to deal with young criminals. This widespread tendency to lay emphasis on the justice system's downfalls seems to have been a recurring feature of those publications. Investigators denounced soaring rates of recidivism, thereby demonstrating the prison system's failure to act as a deterrent.

The combination of social investigations and their distressing portrayal of the urban poor, together with the series of measures and policies mentioned above certainly had a strong influence on the Victorian psyche. These coincided more generally with the development of campaigns and projects for the moralization of the lower classes through the provision of respectable forms of leisure and better education (Bailey, 1987). Changing attitudes towards childhood and adolescence may also have a played a part in the perception of juvenile delinquency. Besides, the traditional historiography suggests that nineteenth-century debates over social and welfare policies and the 'humanitarian' concern over the condition of the poor brought greater attention to the problem of juvenile anti-social behaviour (King, 1998: 158–9).

Penal arrangements and the punitive system of prison came under severe criticism and the extent to which children prosecuted for anti-social behaviour would benefit more from reformation than punishment became a focus of attention. As philanthropists' views and theories increasingly converged with public policies, reformers got involved in the process of designing a new and separate juvenile justice system. For the first time criminal law would distinguish between young and adult offenders and legislation ruling specifically over the treatment, trial and punishment of juvenile delinquents was adopted (May, 1973: 7). Among such reformers, Mary Carpenter played a decisive role in campaigning against juvenile delinquents' imprisonment and offering alternative penal institutions for young criminals to serve their sentence.

This chapter examines institutional answers to juvenile anti-social behaviour in the 1850s and explores Mary Carpenter's reformatory project. While focusing on the solutions developed by the reformer, I seek to show that Carpenter's discourse reflected a much wider set of ideas about the treatment of juvenile criminals. My second objective consists in studying the workings of Carpenter's first reformatory school (Red Lodge) and in shedding light on a collection of archive records that have received little, if any, attention. The chapter explores the ways in which Mary Carpenter's work contributed to the debate over the treatment of juvenile anti-social behaviour and actively participated in the reform of penal law.

The 'reformation' project

At the beginning of the nineteenth century, criminal law made no distinction between children and adults. In theory, juvenile offenders would be treated in the same way as adults and incurred the same sentences. Children brought before magistrates could, when found guilty of petty theft or vagrancy, be fined, sent to a house of correction, or to jail, whereas those involved in larceny, pickpocketing, or theft from a house could be sentenced to prison, transportation or death.[4] According to the principle of *doli incapax*, only children under the age of seven, who had not reached the age of 'discretion', could not be held responsible for their actions (Kean, 1937: 364).

In the Victorian period, such penal arrangements came under heavy criticism, especially that of children's imprisonment. In failing to segregate children from adults, prisons brought juvenile offenders in contact with hardened criminals. It was feared that such association would result in the 'contamination' or 'corruption' of children. Paradoxically, while custody conditions were deemed inadequate and potentially harmful and that the vast majority incarcerations after arrest resulted in acquittals, children's conviction rate was much higher than that of adults. This indicates that many still believed that such treatment would deter children from committing further offences and that custody would lead to reformation. Advocates of the method would generally argue that a separation from the corruption of the street or from their family environment was most indicated and would prevent further fall into crime.

Faced with a flood of reports commenting on the increase in juvenile crime, surging rates of recidivism, the inadequacy of incarceration arrangements and the general failing of the criminal justice system to deal with juvenile anti-social behaviour, reformers and philanthropists began to argue that one of the ways in which the problem of juvenile delinquency could be more successfully addressed would be by shifting the focus from punishment to reformation. To many the answer to juvenile crime did not lie in punitive or redistributive measures but in reformation. Carpenter's work was instrumental in the creation of penal institutions that would focus on the reformation of young offenders rather than on their punishment.

Carpenter's project is best enunciated in the treatise entitled *Reformatory Schools for the children of the perishing and dangerous classes and for juvenile offenders*. In this work published in 1851, the philanthropist gives a detailed account of the condition of juvenile offenders and points out the flaws of the education system and of the penal system. Both are depicted as unable to address juvenile crime effectively. It is important here to draw attention to Carpenter's distinction between what she calls the children of the perishing classes and those of dangerous classes. Indeed she 'enunciated a two-tiered model of "perishing" and "dangerous" juveniles, [...] echoing the rhetoric of provision for the "deserving" and the "undeserving" poor':

those who have not yet fallen into actual crime, but who are almost certain from their ignorance, destitution and the circumstances in which they are growing up, to do so [...] and those who have already received the prison brand. (Carpenter, 1851: 2)

In the treatise's section concerned with juvenile offenders, Carpenter sought to demonstrate that most young criminals were victims of their circumstances and should therefore, instead of being simply punished, be offered the opportunity to withdraw from their destructive environment. Following the trend set by social investigators and quoting profusely from their reports, Carpenter explored the reasons that turned the many children referred to into criminals (Carpenter, 1851: 63).

The philanthropist was convinced that any young offender could, if placed in a suitable environment, be reformed. So far the treatment inflicted on young offenders through criminal law was inefficient and imprisonment had proved ineffective and had no effect on reformation. The chapters dedicated to prisons and even to Parkhurst are extremely critical of such arrangements. In jail children became 'decidedly more hardened'; several testimonies are transcribed displaying evidence of the corruptive effects of imprisonment on children (Carpenter, 1851: 273–6). Besides, jail was 'injurious to the child physically and mentally'; offenders suffered from 'debility and contraction of the joints; premonitory symptoms of sluggishness and feeblemindedness appeared and there was evident danger to their mind' (Carpenter, 1851: 296).

If prison sentences were inadequate, custody was still perceived as the best vehicle for reformation; offenders needed to be removed from the street and their corrupting environments. The work achieved by the voluntary sector pointed towards a system of reformatory institutions. The Philanthropic Society, for example, was endowed with two establishments; the Reform catered for delinquents, focusing on moral education, whereas orphans or children of offenders would be placed in the Manufactory, where they would learn a trade. A number of charities or voluntary societies had set up similar institutions throughout the country (Shore, 2002: 98). Drawing inspiration from such establishments and especially from successful foreign reformatory institutions, the philanthropist pressed for the necessity to establish schools that would offer a middle ground between educational and penal establishments. The objectives of reformatory schools were thus set forth:

[reformatory schools] will produce the desired effect of checking the progress of crime in those who have not yet subjected themselves to the grasp of law and of reforming those who are already convicted criminals. (Carpenter, 1851: vi)

Penal reformatory schools are to be destined to those children who are absolutely unable, whether from poverty or vice, to receive instruction in the existing schools and who without instruction gratuitously given, must grow utterly destitute of it, and will most probably become a burden to the State, either as paupers, or criminals. (Carpenter, 1851: 67–8)

Reading Carpenter's treatise one cannot help but notice that her vision, and by extension her rhetoric, were very heavily influenced by her religious background. Her political reflections about the justice system interwove with moral and religious considerations. Although several sections of her essay display a more journalistic tone and at times turn into political commentaries, the passages concerned with the ways in which children's reformation could be achieved take on a much more emotional and religious voice.

Carpenter's exposition of the reformatory schools' principles is particularly telling. First and above all, Carpenter argued that it was the belief in men's equality in the eyes of God that must guide the work of people involved in reformatory schools. The 'poor perishing young classes', as worthy of attention and love as any other class of people, therefore needed to receive adequate support. From this original stance derived the idea that 'Love' must be one of the school's ruling principles. Carpenter explained that as man's natural instinct incites him to seek kindness from his fellow men, there is a natural inclination to look for love. At the core of her reflection lay the conviction that when those children, who had long been denied love, were treated with care and attention and realized they were loved for themselves their behaviour was radically transformed (Carpenter, 1851: 73).

For the reformation to be successful, certain principles needed to be observed. For example, force or coercion should not be used to teach children to respect 'the law of man and revere the law of God'. Such methods only bred resistance and resentment. Positive values should be taught to children through setting an example. The behaviour and attitudes of the master should be such that it would enable children to feel the 'brotherhood of man', leading them to emulate their master's behaviour. Children would seek to please their benefactors since 'a desire to please the teacher will inspire a higher moral tone in his presence, and this, enlarged and strengthened by wise instruction, becomes a principle of action' (Carpenter, 1851: 74–5). One of the most fundamental challenges consisted in gaining children's trust; only in relationships based on respect and mutual trust could reformation be achieved (Carpenter, 1851: 74).

Carpenter was deeply attached to the teaching of scriptures and firmly believed in the need to provide children with some intellectual education. Yet, she was also aware that the mere communication of knowledge was, on its own, of little value to the dangerous classes. What was necessary was to provide training to children. This would enable them 'to gain an honest livelihood, and become a benefit to society rather that its bane'. The aim of those schools being to reform and elevate criminal offenders, such ends could only be achieved by removing the children permanently from their perverting environment. Industrial training was the only effective way to reach this objective. Besides, it helped to engage children in an occupation while enabling them to develop certain faculties. Industrial training also had a moral influence; it taught perseverance and bred the love of action. Advocates of the system argued that such training could be extremely rewarding for children who could derive a certain pride from their achievements (Carpenter, 1851: 78–80).

Carpenter was very specific on her ban of corporal punishments. No degrading or revengeful measures should ever be taken against the children for they only served to excite a vindictive spirit and harden children. The use of corporal punishment crushed children's spirit by putting them to shame when the aim of the reformatory school was precisely the opposite, that of elevating and reforming children (Carpenter, 1851: 87).

Changing legislation

Although Carpenter was not alone in campaigning for reform of the penal system, her treatise was the first to have successfully gathered all the evidence proving that penal reformatory institutions would be able to reduce recidivism more successfully than prisons. Her essay on reformatory schools put forward a carefully reasoned and thorough collection of evidence and made suggestions on new lines of action. However, the treatise in itself did not suffice in bringing about change. In the final pages of the essay Carpenter admitted that such schemes could only be carried through effectively if undertaken by the government. In her plea for state intervention, Carpenter explained that her close examination of the work done by the Philanthropic Society and its Philanthropic Farm in Surrey, and by the institution at Stretton on Dunstone, as well as discussions with their managers, had pinpointed the two main handicaps faced by those institutions (Carpenter, 1879: 179). She wrote: 'In both these Reformatory Penal Schools two great difficulties are felt: first that of obtaining funds adequate to the necessities of the establishment, or its powers of usefulness; the other arising from no legal power of detention residing with the master' (Carpenter, 1851: 342). In other words, in the current state of affairs, voluntary subscriptions alone could not suffice to supply a steady permanent income and without legal authority the children could not be kept under the school's influence; they could not be made to stay and serve their time in the school. Indeed, evidence seemed to indicate that many boys, who might have been successfully reformed had they spent a few months at the school, being free to withdraw from the school, had left too early to receive the benefits of the institution. This is particularly explicit in Obsorn's report. To carry out fully their objectives reformatory schools needed:

> clear authority to detain the boys who have voluntarily entered the institution and compel them to submit to reasonable and needful discipline. In consequence of this great defect, very many boys who might have been

reformed by a lengthened stay at the institution have left [and][...], have entirely failed to receive the benefits which our memorialists are anxious to confer upon them. (Carpenter, 1851: 343)

Osborn's report also underlines the inadequacy of voluntary support in meeting the national needs (Carpenter, 1851: 343). The time had come to lobby Parliament and to plead for the adoption of reformatory institutions that would replace prisons and welcome young offenders. The main aspect of the fight consisted in obtaining for such institutions funding by the government and providing legal alternatives to imprisonment.

Carpenter was not alone in this crusade; a number of philanthropists and reformers had being pleading for change. The recorder of Birmingham and liberal politician, Matthew Davenport Hill, was an outstanding figure among the many who wished to set up reformatory schools to deal with delinquents (Saywell, 1964: 5). Davenport Hill met Carpenter in Bristol; his experience as a criminal judge and her knowledge of the criminal classes complemented each other perfectly. In a letter addressed to a relative, Davenport confided that they were 'going to hold a conference at Birmingham to obtain legislative powers of coercion over criminal children and for enforcing criminal responsibility on their parents' (Saywell, 1964: 6). The conference took place in December 1851 and represents a decisive step in the battle for government adoption of the reformatory schools system. Its objective was to gather the reformers in order to agree on a plan of action that could be submitted to Parliament (Carpenter, 1877: 9). It is perhaps no coincidence that the reformers' project gained momentum under Lord John Russell's premiership. The Whig PM had supported the Factory Act 1847, the Public Health Act 1848 and had helped to pass the Prisoners Counsel Act 1836. It was hoped that his government would be more inclined to support the reformers' project.

The 1851 conference gathered the energies of powerful supporters: Rev. T. Carter, Rev. John Clay, Sydney Turner, Sheriff Watson, Mr Wigham and Mr Osborn (Carpenter, J.E., 1879: 155). All shared the same views. First, prison discipline was not adapted to the wants of juvenile criminals. Second, the absence of legal power for retaining the pupil against their will in the present reformatory schools prevented such institutions from achieving their objective. At the end of the conference a scheme was adopted and the establishment of three classes of institutions was recommended: free day schools, industrial feeding schools and correctional and reformatory schools, each category catering for the needs of specific groups of children (Carpenter, 1879: 155).

A deputation was then appointed to bring the project to Parliament and managed, in 1853, to drive the House of Commons to take action. A select committee was appointed to 'inquire into the present treatment of criminal and destitute children and what changes are desirable in their present treatment in order to supply industrial training and to combine reformation with due correction of juvenile crime' (PP 1852–53, vol. XXIII). To carry out its investigation, the committee gathered evidence and examined the participants of the Birmingham conference. Upon examination, Carpenter explained that her observations had led her to conclude that in most instances, children were not deterred by prison but hardened by it. Later, when asked about the most advisable principles upon which to establish reformatory schools, Carpenter insisted on the following points:

– to separate the child from evil associates
– to enable the child to make retribution for the injury he has done to society instead of punishing him
– to enlist the will of the child in work failing which true reformation could not be effected
– to bear in mind that difference between a child and a man and that therefore he must not be treated as such
– to make sure that the children are engaged in a stimulating and relevant occupation, nothing too mundane and repetitive. (PP 1852, vol VII)

In order to counter the objections that could have been raised about the cost of this new measure, Carpenter provided in her essay and during her examination detailed comparisons between the expenses entailed by reformatory schools and those of jails, demonstrating the higher costs of the jail system. Besides, if successful, reformation would prevent re-commitments and therefore rid society of this class of perpetual criminals (Carpenter, 1851: 346–8). This demonstration led the 1853 Select Committee to declare:

> that whatever may be the cost of such schools and establishments they would be productive of great pecuniary saving by [...] diminishing the sources from which our criminal population is now constantly recruited and reducing the great cost of the administration of the criminal law. (PP 1852–53, vol. XXIII)

Following the examination of dozens of experts and participants, the appointed committee resolved that 'penal reformatory establishments ought to be instituted, founded and supported entirely at public cost' and that 'the reformatory schools should be established for the education and correction of children convicted of minor offence'. Consequently, in 1854, Parliament passed the Youthful Offenders Act. The new legislation established that young offenders under the age of 16 would be, upon conviction, sent to reformatory schools to be detained.

Carpenter and her supporters helped turn a new page in the history of juvenile crime law. The expertise she displayed before the parliamentary committee was not simply informed by her research or her treatise, but by experience and experimentation. Indeed, in 1852, prior to the passing of the Youthful Offenders Act 1854, Carpenter had already started her own reformatory school near Bristol. The first school, in Kingswood, was coeducational and its results convinced Carpenter of the necessity to separate boys from girls.

The Red Lodge

Carpenter's next project would therefore be a single-sex reformatory school for girls. As she looked for new premises, an Elizabethan house on Park Row became available. Her friend Lady Byron acquired the premises and, in 1852, Mary Carpenter undertook the sole management of the Red Lodge, the first reformatory school for girls (BRO 40556). The institution was meant to welcome girls under the age of 14 who were described by Carpenter as 'entirely devoid of any good principles of actions; particularly addicted to deceit both in words and actions [...] and of violent passions' (BRO 12693/3). Through the Red Lodge Carpenter was able to put into practice the method and precepts she had enunciated in her essays. The rules of the institutions encapsulated her philosophy:

> The first step towards their reformation will be to awaken a feeling of confidence [...]. Their passions must be as little excited as possible [...] the misdirected energies [...] be called out and wisely guided and the intellectual facilities cultivated in a healthy manner; religious and moral principles must be directly enforced and indirectly, but still more powerfully, taught by the daily life of the teacher and the evident obedience to truth duty. (BRO 12693/3)

Carpenter believed that the girls could be successfully reformed if one could awaken a feeling of confidence in them, by showing genuine concern for their welfare. One of the most essential keys to success would be to gain the girls' trust and respect. In the knowledge that the people surrounding them only had their best interests at heart, children would comply with their rules and seek to work towards the same aim. Besides, Carpenter and her staff would, through their own attitude and behaviour, set an example to the girls and inspire them. In order to fulfil those objectives the girls were submitted to a strict routine (BRO 12693 (3)).

Scriptures would be inculcated through readings and prayer (BRO 40556). The girls would receive regular intellectual training and be involved in some form of industrial occupation, especially those activities that would fit the girls for domestic service. In addition to the daily routine, outings were often organized in order to entertain the girls. Some entries in Carpenter's journal recount the girls' trip to the zoological gardens or a visit to exhibitions at the Bristol Fine Arts Academy. On entering the school, the girls were read a set of rules that aimed at reminding them that they must forget their past life and adopt a proper attitude (BRO 40556).

In exchange for their work, girls would receive a small allowance and would be given five shillings after 12 months service. As exposed earlier, the rescue and redemption of young criminals could only be hoped for if children were provided with the tools that would enable them to be independent after their release. To prevent further anti-social behaviour, children had to be taught a skill or an occupation that would permit them to earn a living and live according to society's rules. Girls were therefore trained in domestic service. To perfect their training and in order to encourage hard work and discipline, Carpenter moved into a building adjacent to the Red Lodge. This enabled her to exercise constant supervision over the girls but also to start up a scheme through which the better-behaved girls would move to the cottage with her and work as domestic servants. The experience would be part of the training of the girls and be perceived as a reward. The girls, still under sentence, would then be allowed as much liberty as the younger servants in an ordinary household. They would be sent on errands and trusted with money to purchase articles and food for the house. This system helped to build the girl's confidence and nurture their sense of responsibility. When suitable, girls could be sent to work as domestic servants in neighbouring houses. The girls were then 'on licence' and would receive the monthly visit of the Red Lodge inspector who was in charge of seeing that the employers kept their part of the compact (BRO 12693/7).

Although Carpenter did not believe in retribution and corporal punishment, misbehaviour at the lodge needed to be addressed. The journal kept by Carpenter indicates that if the girls displayed anti-social behaviour, they would be punished by 'separation' meaning that they would be segregated from the rest of the group for a few days (BRO 12693/1).

Several entries in Carpenter's diary refer to a particular girl, Ackroyd, who was only ever designated in the journal by the letter 'A'. The girl's anti-social behaviour was very problematic. In December 1855 Carpenter wrote: 'A, the last new girl is a terrible thief, stealing from Mrs B's wardrobe just after she came and since stealing the gardener's dinner' (BRO 12693/1). Later Carpenter recounts how having stolen the front door keys and buried them in the garden, 'A' eventually confessed her mischief, but failed to show any shame. In spite of observations and entreaties, 'A' kept stealing. She was segregated from the others, but there was no improvement. The girl was then placed on a special diet of bread and water and kept in her cell, again without success. She continued to pilfer and to behave improperly. The girl's attitude led Carpenter to conclude that 'A' was just devoid of desire to do right and as her anti-social behaviour carried on Carpenter arranged for her to move to Australia (Saywell, 1964: 12). Other episodes of misbehaviour at the Lodge are recounted in the committee's minutes. On 21 September

1852, for example, three girls attempted to set the cottage on fire (BRO 12693/7).

Despite the odd anecdote of misconduct, the Red Lodge achieved extremely positive results. Two years after its creation, the school founded by Carpenter was certified after the visit of one of Her Majesty's Inspectors of Prisons. Through the certificate the school was officially made a reformatory school, the first to cater for girls only (BRO 12693/13). In 1855, a delegation comprising Mr Miles, MP for Bristol, the city's mayor and several ladies and gentlemen, visited the school. Their examination led them to conclude that results of the first year's training were highly satisfactory. Similarly, the 1882 report of the official inspection applauded the work achieved by the institution and its inmates (BRO 40556). Annual reports provide another type of data enabling the school's success to be assessed. Indeed, when looking at the institution's statistics it appears that between 1854 and 1874 the yearly average number of inmates was about 65. Between 1870 and 1874, 87 girls had left the school, either returning to their families or put out to service. Of those 87 girls, ten were living a 'doubtful life', 14 had been lost sight of and 61 were known to be earning a living respectably. For the vast number of inmates, the reformatory school had fulfilled its mission (BRO 12693/7).

Conclusion

It is difficult to appreciate just how much influence Carpenter's campaign for the provision of penal reformatory institutions for juvenile offenders played in the reform of the justice system. However, it is reasonable to say that her experience in education, her investigations and her own experiments in setting up reformatory schools provided her with a knowledge and authority that helped raise awareness. Her expertise helped convince Parliament that juvenile crime could be more successfully addressed through reformation legislation than through punitive or retributive measures. Following the Youthful Offenders Act 1854, the design of penal arrangements for children and their status within the criminal law system changed forever. The variety of acts and changes that ensued has since led academics to label the Victorian era a pivotal period in the creation of the modern justice system. Carpenter's name is intrinsically linked to reformatory schools and to their wider implications for the care of juvenile delinquents. Studying her essays and her correspondence, one cannot fail to acknowledge that her work was entrenched in the trend – encompassing private initiatives and governmental social policies – towards a reassessment of policing strategies and the organization of the justice system. Such a trend has often been hailed as the manifestation of a progressive move towards a more 'humanitarian' penal system as well as of the development of 'child-centred' attitudes in the treatment of juvenile anti-social behaviour. As for Carpenter, having successfully fought for the establishment of a system dedicated to the reformation of criminals, she then embarked on a mission for the prevention of crime. She helped pass the Industrial School Act 1857 and in the 1870s drew legislative support for Day Industrial Schools. In the same way as the fight against juvenile anti-social behaviour and crime had shifted from punishment to reformation, in the second half of the nineteenth century there would be a shift towards initiatives aiming at favouring the prevention of juvenile delinquency; once again Carpenter would lead the way.

Notes

1. Historians Susan Magarey and Leon Radzinowicz have argued that the concept of 'young offender' was a 'Victorian creation' that had been 'elaborated' by the social enquiries of the likes of William Beaver Neale and Henry Mayhew.
2. Drawing directly from the discourse and arguments developed by Victorian investigators and borrowing from their reports, the traditional historiography of juvenile crime has also often adopted the 'causative' analysis model.
3. Another historiographic trend has maintained that the Victorian obsession with young offenders was fuelled by the upper- and middle-classes' fear of social unrest. Historians concerned with theories of social control have argued that juvenile offenders came to be seen as a symbol of the urban poor whose dissolute mores could be perceived as an image of chaos that threatened the stability of the social hierarchy (Gatrell, 1990: 244).
4. It was generally admitted that in the case of children, death sentence would not result in execution but would be translated into transportation. Studies indicate that the image of the child and the gibbet is misleading; few children endured capital punishment (Knell, 1965: 198–207).

11
Truancy and Anti-social Behaviour in England in the late Victorian Era and under New Labour: Plus ça Change

Anne Beauvallet

Introduction

The Elementary Education Act 1870 set a framework for schooling and so it can be considered as the beginning of universal education from five to 13 in England. While the Act did not introduce compulsory education, it did allow school boards to create bye-laws to secure attendance, but they were not obliged to do so. The Elementary Education Act 1876 compelled parents to make sure their children received adequate instruction in reading, writing and arithmetic. It also provided school attendance committees for districts without a school board. In fact, the real turning point was the Elementary Education Act 1880, which required all school boards and school attendance committees to enforce school attendance promptly, or face the intervention of central government. Ratepayers were shocked by 'insistent begging or vandalism' and urged local authorities to deal with truancy and its corollary, anti-social behaviour (Sheldon, 2009).

This chapter compares truancy in the late Victorian era and from 1997 to 2010, by studying both the phenomenon and the government policies designed to address it. First, I define truancy, then I examine the social categories affected by it and the factors behind it. Next, I focus on government policies on truancy and anti-social behaviour, as well as the discourses underlying them in those two periods.

Truancy in the late Victorian era and under New Labour

As Sean Gabb points out, 'none of the various Education Acts defines truancy; nor is this lack supplied in the case law. Nor, indeed, have the various researchers agreed on a definition' (Gabb, 1994). Furthermore, there is the problem of the reliability of school attendance statistics, which are the traditional methods used to measure truancy levels. In a 1974 *Times Educational Supplement* (TES) article, S. Cameron questioned secondary school attendance figures in the Inner London Education Authority because teachers or other individuals might doctor them to further their own interests (Gabb, 1994). Quantifying truancy has also become harder as successive laws raising the school-leaving age have drawn more and more children within the remit of those in charge of school attendance. The official school-leaving age in England and Wales was 11 in 1893, 12 in 1899, 14 in 1921, 15 in 1947, 16 in 1973, 17 in 2013 and 18 as of 2015. Quantifying truancy therefore entails difficulties which educational historian Nicola Sheldon summarizes by arguing that: 'ultimately, the full extent of truancy cannot be measured' (Sheldon, 2009).

This chapter uses the definition of truancy provided by the National Audit Office (NAO) in its 2005 report: 'unauthorized absence' (NAO, 2005: 1). The term is not as neutral as it seems because the distinction between authorized and unauthorized absences relies on what society deems to be justifiable explanations. The ruling classes provide their own definition and impose it on the rest of society. A typical example in the twentieth and twenty-first centuries lies in holidays during term time, which are considered by schools to be acts of truancy. 'The Nottingham education chief who took his children on holiday the week after half-term' (Owen, 2006) probably believed his offspring were not submitted to the very rules formulated by himself and the local authority. Distinguishing between justified and unjustified absences from school is fundamentally a social exercise, which favours the ruling discourse at the expense of other social categories.

There is no academic study on truancy in late nineteenth-century and early twentieth-century England. Therefore, local surveys such as those of Paul Sharp and Peter Gosden on the West Riding, Gordon Vowles on Bedfordshire, John Frederick Parsons and John Anthony Young on Bournemouth, as well as Sarah Wise on the Nichol, a London slum, are crucial research material (Sharp and Gosden, 1978; Parsons and Young, 1992; Vowles, 2003; Wise, 2008). They constitute a series of snapshots from which some common threads emerge regarding the poorest people in late Victorian society in rural and urban areas. Wise studied the evolution of a slum called the Nichol located in the East End (Shoreditch) where 'parental failure to comply with [...] school attendance orders' was widespread (Wise, 2008: 99–100).

Agricultural labourers needed all the help they could get at harvest time and this led to their own children staying away from school. For instance, Parsons and Young quote late Victorian log-books in September with reference to the acorn collection for pig food (1992: 76). Parsons and Young also highlight the fact that children may have lived a long way from school and thus did not attend in order to avoid lengthy walks when the weather was very wet (Parsons and Young, 1992: 76).

There seems to be some continuity when considering the social groups most affected by unauthorized absences under New Labour. This is clear in a report published by the Social Exclusion Unit (SEU) in May 1998, which shows how central truancy and other related issues such as 'anti-social behaviour' (SEU, 1998: par 2.27) were to New Labour. This report states very clearly that truants 'tend to be [...] from poorer backgrounds' (SEU, 1998: par 1.5). Although single-parent family structures seem to constitute 'a risk factor', the SEU notes 'there is no particular sex bias' (SEU, 1998: par 1.5). One particular group is singled out for its high truancy rates: 'traveller children have attendance levels below 50 per cent' (SEU, 1998: par 1.6). According to the *Statistical Bulletin on Pupil Absence and Truancy from Schools in England: 1993/94–1997/98*, 'schools with the highest levels of authorised and unauthorised absence have the largest percentage of pupils known to be eligible for free school meals', that is, of children whose parents receive welfare benefits or are on very low incomes (DfEE, 1998: 4). In particular, schools with 'one in three pupils' entitled to free school meals suffer from high truancy rates (DfEE, 1998: 4).

A report published by the National Audit Office (NAO) in 2005 highlights a major failing in determining the social categories of persistent truants since 'the data is school-level rather than pupil-level' (NAO, 2005: 24). It insists on the limitations regarding the use of the numbers of free school meals to gauge deprivation since this 'does not assess relative economic well-being or capture other social, cultural and environmental factors' (NAO, 2003: 6). In 2003, the NAO recommended other indicators of deprivation should be 'explored' such as 'entitlements to social security benefits or tax credits' (NAO, 2003: 10), but in 2005 such an 'exploration' had not yet made any difference in official statistics (NAO, 2005: 24).

Therefore, some characteristics seem crucial when considering the phenomenon of truancy in both the late Victorian era and under New Labour. First, the poorest and most vulnerable are the most likely to be affected. Second, their material and social living conditions most definitely have an impact on their attitudes to school attendance.

Four interrelated elements underlie the factors behind truancy in the late Victorian era: natural conditions and agriculture, specific events throughout the year, social conditions, and refusal to comply with rules felt as punitive. The first factor affected children in rural areas in particular. For instance, the entry in a Bournemouth school's log-book for a September day sums up the problem: 'Very wet day, numbers in consequence very low' (Parsons and Young, 1992: 76). Harvest times late in the summer or potato picking in the autumn would also be periods of low attendance, as parents needed children to work in the fields (Vowles, 2003: 23). The second factor lies in social events throughout the year which tended to cause a drop in the number of children at school. Here are excerpts from the log-book of an elementary school in Northampton in 1888: 'Northampton races. Very thin school. St George's Fair. Thin attendance' (Speed, 1983: 26).

Some social factors made attendance difficult, if not impossible, at times. These were related to poor health, material deprivation, poor diet, overcrowding and little access to proper medical care. Poor health by itself makes absence from school justifiable and it was the major factor in irregular attendance, as Pamela Horn makes clear in *The Victorian and Edwardian Schoolchild* (Horn, 2010: 26). Poverty was also borne out by children's physical appearance: 'Many of the poorest wore cast-off clothing, which made them a target for ridicule and bullying by more fortunate fellow pupils' (Horn, 2010: 26). Horn refers to an East End school where 'cast-offs were publicly distributed to the worst-dressed scholars by the headmaster, much to their discomfiture' (Horn, 2010: 26). Playing truant meant avoiding social stigmatization from peers and education authorities, which in a perverted way corresponded to the social dimension of truancy.

The fourth and last factor in truancy in the late Victorian era stems precisely from resistance to social codes. As Wise reminds us in her study of the Nichol, a London slum, elementary education was not free at first (Wise, 2008: 161). Although fees were waived for the poorest children, 'this remittance took time and required the parent to give detailed data on earnings and outgoings to a stranger' (Wise, 2008: 161). John Reeves worked as an attendance officer in the Nichol for 16 years. His job first consisted of 'scheduling' 'by which every house in the district with a rental value of £25 or less per annum had to be visited and the presence of school age children established' (Wise, 2008: 161). This was perceived as an intrusion since 'poor families were legally obliged – middle-class families were not – to impart this kind of personal information to the schedulers' (Wise, 2008: 161). Reeves was regularly 'dreadfully abused and harangued' (Reeves, 1915: 35). As Wise underlines, such opposition was 'intimate and fractured' (Wise, 2008: 161). She nevertheless describes two demonstrations organized in October 1889 by Bethnal Green schoolboys against compulsory attendance, corporal punishment and homework (Wise, 2008: 161). Truancy in the late Victorian era can thus be attributed to harsh weather conditions, agriculture, specific events, deprivation and individual resistance to rules considered as punitive.

When Tony Blair became Labour Prime Minister in 1997, many theories were elaborated on truancy and its causes. They fall into three categories pertaining to individual factors, social factors and institutional factors. Individual factors include 'psychological traits such as low level of self-esteem' (Davies and Lee, 2006: 204). Personal interaction may also play a determining role as is illustrated by the survey carried out by sociologists John Dwyfor Davies and John Lee in 2006, although both insist their interviews may not be statistically representative (Davies and Lee, 2006: 205). They found that persistent absentees 'focused on personal relationships with their teachers'

(Davies and Lee, 2006: 207), whereas their parents insisted on the problems of bullying (Davies and Lee, 2006: 206). The latter argument can be directly associated with the considerable role played by 'the influence of friends and peers', as highlighted in the 1998 report of the Social Exclusion Unit (SEU, 1998: par. 1.9). The Unit refers to Home Office figures 'identifying a statistical relationship between truancy and strong attachment to siblings or friends in trouble with the police' (SEU, 1998: par.1.9). The Social Exclusion Unit insists on families' impact on non-attendance, namely 'poor parental supervision and lack of commitment to education' (SEU, 1998: par. 1.8). Education Welfare Services (EWS) staff, who are the very people enforcing compulsory attendance, have tended to share such views, as the first report on *School Attendance and the Prosecution of Parents* clearly shows (Kendall *et al.*, 2003). In the eyes of EWS managers, truancy is caused by 'a combination of pockets of deprivation and a persuasive feeling amongst sections of the population that children's education is not a great priority' (Kendall *et al.*, 2003: 17). Some account for it as the result of the decline in heavy industries and the lack of job vacancies in some areas (Kendall *et al.*, 2003: 17).

Social factors underlying truancy levels also pertain to economic determinants and this is precisely what is highlighted by a London School of Economics (LSE) study: although based on a 1970s American panel dataset (Burgess *et al.*, 2002: iii), it is interesting because it rejects the official description of truancy as 'irrational behaviour by young adults' (Burgess *et al.*, 2002: 1). For Simon Burgess, Karen Gardiner and Carol Propper, the attitudes of young people are 'a rational response to economic forces' (Burgess *et al.*, 2002: 1). They do not deny social factors, but insist on the economic benefits of attendance or non-attendance as expected by youths: 'Those who had higher expected returns from studying were more likely to be in school, whilst those who could command higher returns in the labour market, or who were in areas where the gains from crime were greater, skipped more school' (Burgess *et al.*, 2002: 1–2).

Finally, social factors relate to society as a whole and its responsibility for truancy levels. This is one of the arguments developed by Pat Carlen, Denis Gleeson and Julia Wardhaugh. They insist on 'much pain, hurt and suffering around current educational arrangements' imposed on children from poor backgrounds (Carlen *et al.*, 1992: 159). This is where institutional factors account for truancy levels, but this perspective finds its almost exact opposite in a book by Rhodes Boyson who perceives 'signs of breakdown', among which are rising truancy levels (Boyson, 1975). He is critical of the factors behind this 'breakdown', that is, education policies in the 1960s, particularly comprehensive schools and child-centred teaching methods. For him, the latter diverted schools from their normal functions: 'Schools are for schooling, not for social engineering' (Boyson and Cox, 1975: 1).

The Social Exclusion Unit (SEU) report published in May 1998 summarizes the role of institutional factors: 'The influence of families and peers on truancy is matched by the effects of problems at school' (SEU, 1998: par 1.10–1). The Social Exclusion Unit highlights several areas in need of improvement, such as reading ability, pressure around GCSE coursework deadlines, bullying, lesson quality and the relevance of the National Curriculum (SEU, 1998: par 1.10). In September 2007, the Office for Standards in Education (Ofsted) confirmed the main findings of the SEU report regarding secondary schools: 'Good leadership and management, high quality teaching and a flexible curriculum have a significant impact on attendance' (Ofsted, 2007: 2).

In short, truancy under New Labour was ascribed to individual, social and institutional factors. Individual factors include psychological traits and the role of peers and relatives. Social factors comprise economic elements and society as a whole. Institutional factors relate to academic problems, the curriculum and the organization within schools. Before the policies in the late Victorian era and under New Labour can be analysed, the ideological arguments underpinning them in both periods must be examined.

Policies on truancy and anti-social behaviour and their underlying discourses

Victorians defined truancy by linking it with potentially criminal activities. Through reference to a crime, the example below by Alfred Jones, an elementary school headmaster in 1888, demonstrates the direct consequence of truancy:

> One of our old truants was charged this week with stealing whisky, claret and bottled ale from the racecourse. It is always found that boys who attend badly and during absence receive the education of the streets, have a bad influence on the tone of the school. (Quoted by Speed, 1983: 27)

Augusto De Venanzi analyses the term hooligan first introduced in the late Victorian era and applied by the press to: 'young delinquents, muggers, stabbers, members of youth gangs [...], pranksters and larkers (larking about was a term used to refer to youths engaging into various devious techniques of resistance to authoritarian control)' (De Venanzi, 2008: 204). De Venanzi insists on the fact that there had been 'many forms of nuisance and deviant street activity during the eighteenth century' (De Venanzi, 2008: 210). Yet, in 1901, 'the problem of hooliganism had been taken up by the National Union of Teachers' (De Venanzi, 2008: 208), thus showing worries concerning what could be described in more modern terms as anti-social behaviour.

Late Victorian policies first need to be contextualized, as compulsory attendance did not concern all children below school-leaving age. The half-time system was implemented nationwide with, for instance, the Factory and Workshop Acts 1878 and 1901, which allowed children who found a factory job to work part-time and attend school part-time. Horn shows that attempts to raise the school-leaving age met with popular resistance in Lancashire, for instance, from textile workers (De Venanzi, 2008: 109–10).

Exemption policies were also pursued locally through bye-laws as in the West Riding, Yorkshire. The County Council 'allow[ed] children over 12, whether in employment covered by the Factory Act or not, to take advantage of the half-time system as long as he had reached the Fifth Standard or had made 300 or more attendances in each of five school years' (Sharp and Gosden, 1978: 55). The family had to prove this was 'beneficial employment' in that it needed the child's wages to survive (Sharp and Gosden, 1978: 55). The practice of exemptions gradually disappeared, for example, by 1920 in Bedfordshire (Vowles, 2003: 20) and in the early 1930s in the West Riding (Sharp and Gosden, 1978: 58).

Let us now turn to specific elements of late Victorian policies on truancy, including who was in charge of enforcing compulsory attendance, what measures were carried out and their implementation. Until the Education Act 1902, school boards or local attendance committees were responsible for raising school attendance levels under the Elementary Education Act 1880. School attendance officers such as John Reeves in the Nichol, the London East End slum, were appointed, but the exercise of such functions was patchy as some rural areas were not always covered. The Education Act 1902 ensured greater consistency as enforcement of attendance became one of the legal duties of newly created Local Education Areas (LEAs). This also 'standardised the role of the attendance officer' (Sheldon, 2009). The Act directly linked funding from the central government to attendance levels. As Gordon Vowles shows for Bedfordshire, this had a direct impact on Local Education Authority policies: 'In 1903 it was estimated by the County LEA that a drop of 1 per cent in the annual average attendance would result in the loss of £340 a year in Government grant' (Vowles, 2003: 18). This made school attendance a priority for all, from teachers to LEA authorities (Vowles, 2003: 18).

In her study of the Nichol, Wise details the measures faced by parents of truants. First, 'an A notice was served – warning that if the child's school attendance were not improved, a B notice would follow. The issue of a B notice required the parent to be present at a specially convened meeting of the B Committee, to hear the reasons for the absences' (Wise, 2008: 162). If attendance did not improve, magistrates issued a summons indicating the beginning of legal proceedings against the parents which could lead to fines. The latter, according to Wise, could amount to '2s 6d [...] if the magistrate were in favour of compulsory education' (Wise, 2008: 162). In Bournemouth, in 1892, for instance, ten per cent of absences were found to be unjustified and Parsons and Young thus detail the following measures: '118 parents had been served with official warnings, 66 others had been summoned before the Committee, and 37 brought before the magistrates' (Parsons and Young, 1992: 76). Local studies also highlight the rewarding of good attendance, like in Bournemouth with 'a scheme of rewards and prizes for regular attendance under which certificates and medals – white metal to silver – were awarded' (Parsons and Young, 1992: 21).

Regarding the implementation of such measures, it should first be noted that school attendance officers faced very real risks when carrying out their job. John Reeves, who first worked in the Nichol, encountered 'violent parental hostility' (Horn, 2010: 26). 'Even locating truants could present problems. Reeves would be told that youngsters were ill or dead, only to find later that they were at work' (Horn, 2010: 26–7).

Beyond such practical elements, policies were inherently limited. When prosecution took place, fines were the most common outcome, but their level did not always constitute a powerful deterrent. Peter Speed mentions a boy called William Drage whose parents were fined; however, 'as he earned far more money than they had to pay in fines, they thought it was worth it' (Speed, 1983: 27). Furthermore, prosecution and conviction were used as the last possible resort and not as a routine strategy. Not all magistrates were convinced of the benefits of school attendance, particularly if they knew the survival of the family was at stake. Horn quotes Howard, a member of Her Majesty's Inspectorate, who showed the widespread implications of this reality in 1898:

So long as certain farming operations can be performed by children [...] it appears that employers and parents will continue to break the law, magistrates will be slow to convict, school attendance committees will not press cases against employers and parents, managers will not furnish names of offenders for fear of [...] making the school unpopular, and teachers will not make enemies by furnishing information. (Horn, 2010: 107)

The late Victorian approach to truancy, although framed in highly moralistic tones and based on fears of social unrest, did not lead to repressive policies. Kiron Reid describes this paradox: 'In Victorian times, fear of crime related equally to the perspective that "gangs" of disaffected youths hanging around the streets encouraged crime. Despite calls for action, no special legislation was introduced to deal with the "Victorian menace", however' (Reid, 2003: 90). Prosecution and conviction, in short 'criminalization' of 'the vulnerable child' (Horn, 2010: 91), were not on the agenda. As a result, because fining parents was ineffective and if parents seemed unable to exercise their authority, persistent truants would be sent to industrial training schools (Duckworth, 2002: 221–2). Subsequent developments contributed to a softening of official policies. In 1919, funding and attendance levels were dissociated through block grants to LEAs. School attendance officers became education welfare officers in 1939 and their role, although still featuring the enforcement of compulsory attendance, also centred on the needs of such children and their families.

Sheldon has argued that the focus on truancy reappeared in the 1990s as one of the consequences of the Great Debate initiated by Labour Prime Minister, James Callaghan, in 1976 (Sheldon, 2009). Truancy did not assume great importance in Conservative and Labour policies until the 1997 Labour manifesto. New Labour governments focused on truancy as part of a wider agenda, as the introduction to the 1998 *Statistical Bulletin on Pupil Absence and Truancy from Schools in England* makes clear:

> Promoting regular school attendance is a key component in the Government's strategy to raise educational standards. It is also an important factor in reducing wider problems associated with social exclusion. Pupils who fail to attend regularly experience educational disadvantage at school and impaired prospects later in life. They are also directly at risk of drifting into anti-social and criminal behaviour. (DfEE, 1998: 2)

The same association between truancy and anti-social behaviour features in the introduction to the 1998 Social Exclusion Unit report (SEU, 1998) and in the preface to the 2005 NAO report (NAO, 2005: 1).

Such an approach needs to be further investigated, first by defining anti-social behaviour as New Labour saw it. The Crime and Disorder Act 1998 presents it as acting 'in a manner that caused or was likely to cause harassment, alarm or distress to one or more persons not of the same household as himself' (Crime and Disorder Act 1998: s.1, 1, a). Dan Riley has detailed such activities, although he insists that the list is inherently endless: 'nuisance neighbours, vandalism, graffiti, fly-posting, dealing and buying illegal drugs, begging, anti-social drinking, dumping and abandoning cars, rowdy and nuisance behaviour, yobbish and intimidating behaviour, trespassers and misuse of fireworks' (Riley, 2007: 223). Anti-social behaviour legislation had a serious impact on schools as the 1998 Act enabled them to initiate Anti-Social Behaviour Order (ASBO) proceedings (Riley, 2007: 221), with local authorities also being involved.

New Labour policies on anti-social behaviour raise a number of issues. The statutory language quoted above is part of the problem as defining anti-social behaviour proves 'discretionary' and 'subjective' (Thomas, 2005: 6). The ruling classes and institutions assessed what was 'likely to cause harassment, alarm or distress' (Crime and Disorder Act 1998: s.1, 1, a). It thus saddled schools and local authorities with further social duties. Other issues are both legal and human as the 1998 Act abolished the doctrine of *doli incapax* ('incapable of committing a crime') for children between ten and 14. As a result, it became 'only necessary to distinguish between two groups of children, those under ten and those over ten' (Riley, 2007: 224). Furthermore, although ASBOs 'are not criminal sanctions' (Home Office, 2006: 8) and magistrates act within their civil jurisdictions, breaching the conditions of an ASBO 'is a criminal offence, which is arrestable and recordable' (Home Office, 2006: 48).

The New Labour approach to anti-social behaviour and truancy used apparently benevolent rationales designed to appeal to 'the decent law-abiding majority' as against 'a minority' (Home Office, 2003: 5; 7). The White Paper *Respect and Responsibility* 2003 presents social norms clearly based on Clause 4 of the Labour Party constitution modified in 1995: 'Our aim is a society where we have an understanding that the rights we enjoy are based in turn on the respect and responsibilities we have to other people and to our community' (Home Office, 2003: 6). The approach to truancy may even sound generous because it claims to target youths who will be helped. For instance, in the introduction to a 2002 government video on the 'Truancy and Crime: Tackling it Together' programme, Home Secretary David Blunkett describes 'kids who are not in school, often on the streets and potentially are up to no good' (Home Office, 2002b). He intends to 'give [these] kids a new life' by making sure they get an education (Home Office, 2002b).

The 1997 Labour manifesto (Labour, 1997) promised to 'increase the powers and responsibilities of parents' and as the subsequent analysis of truancy policies will make clear: 'the onus of responsibility for the behaviour of children has moved from state to family' (Riley, 2007: 221) in legal and human terms. Such a perspective also has wider social implications as it focuses primarily on individual duties. In her contribution to a 2010 work on *Blair's Educational Legacy*, Diane Reay summarizes this reality in the following way: 'The dominance of choice discourses and neo-liberal notions of agency seem to have eradicated any understanding of wider structural forces' (Reay, 2010: 9). In her study of *New Labour and Social Exclusion*, Ruth Levitas shows that the ambiguous use of 'social exclusion' by New Labour politicians enabled the party to modify its discourse significantly. She distinguishes three underlying rationales, namely the redistributionist discourse (RED), the social integrationist discourse (SID) and the moral underclass discourse (MUD) (Levitas, 1999: 5). RED, which Levitas calls a 'social-democratic redistributive agenda', focuses on social exclusion as a 'dynamic process' involving 'not only poverty, but the whole gamut of social inequalities' based on ethnicity and gender (Levitas, 1999: 5). SID 'narrows the definition of social exclusion/inclusion to participation in paid work' and 'does not, like RED, imply a reduction of poverty by an increase in benefit levels' (Levitas, 1999: 7). MUD 'presents the underclass or socially excluded as culturally distinct from the "mainstream"' and 'implies that benefits are bad, rather than good, for their recipients, and encourage "dependency"' (Levitas, 1999: 6). In short, 'put (over) simply, in RED, the poor have no money, in SID they have no work, and in MUD they have no morals' (Levitas, 1999: 8). According to Levitas, New Labour bases its arguments on SID and MUD: 'The centrality of truancy and teenage pregnancy to the agenda of the Social Exclusion Unit is bound up with the shift from RED to SID and MUD' (Levitas, 1999: 7). Wider social problems like poverty are therefore conveniently swept under the carpet and some categories of parents are targeted as flouting the social and educational norms.

Specific measures pertaining to New Labour policies on truancy and anti-social behaviour require analysis. Section 444 of the Education Act 1996 stipulates that: 'if a child of compulsory school age who is a registered pupil at a school fails to attend regularly at the school, his parent is guilty of an offence' (Education Act 1996: section 444). This was complemented by section 72 of the Criminal Justice and Court Services Act 2000, which made it possible for parents thus convicted to be sentenced to prison for up to three months and be fined up to £2,500 (Criminal Justice and Court Services Act 2000: section 72). Furthermore, the High Court confirmed in a 2003 ruling that: 'it is a strict liability offence which does not require proof of any knowledge or fault on the part of the parent' (Barnfather v Islington London Borough Council [2003] EWHC 418 (Admin) par 1). In 2003, a fast-track procedure was also phased in to ensure no more than 12 weeks elapse between the first unauthorized absence and court proceedings (Curtis, 2003). Parenting orders were defined in the Crime and Disorder Act 1998 in relation to both anti-social behaviour and truancy (Crime and Disorder Act 1998: section 8). Sections 18 to 24 of the Anti-social Behaviour Act 2003 strengthened the notion of parenting orders and introduced parenting contracts (Anti-social Behaviour Act 2003: sections 18–24). As Riley points out, parenting orders require 'the parents to attend counselling to help them deal with their child [...] and can require the parents to exercise control over their child's behaviour' under the supervision of the local Youth Offending Team (Riley, 2007: 227). Parenting contracts define conditions regarding school attendance and behaviour outside for instance. If parents do not abide by them, the next stages are an assessment by the local Youth Offender Team and parenting orders. Prosecution and criminal proceedings may then appear inevitable, an ASBO being another option available to school and local authorities. Finally, section 23 of the Anti-social Behaviour Act 2003 allowed school heads and local authorities to issue fixed penalty notices to parents of persistent truants (£50 or £100), to which were added on-the-spot fines in 2005 (Anti-social Behaviour Act 2003: section 23).

In 2009, the BBC *News* website estimated that 30,000 truancy-related fixed penalty notices and 19,000 parenting contracts had been issued from 2004 to 2008 (BBC, 2009). In 2003, the first report on *School Attendance and the Prosecution of Parents* gave overall statistics on criminal proceedings (Kendall *et al.*, 2003). The average rate of prosecution was 1.1 per 1,000 pupils and over four-fifths of proceedings resulted in a guilty verdict, fines being the most common disposal given (50 per cent of them were between £50 and £100 (Kendall *et al.*, 2003: v)). The most spectacular outcome has undoubtedly been prison sentences for parents, a Banbury mother being the first in May 2002 (Morris and Smithers, 2002). In February 2009, two BBC journalists, Sean Coughlan and James Westhead, analysed court statistics in England and Wales and found out that on average: 'a parent is jailed for their child's truancy once a fortnight every school term' (Coughlan and Westhead, 2009). Some sociologists have opposed those policies on grounds that they are based on 'punishment not reform' (Davies and Lee, 2006: 209). Through their repeated use of criminal sanctions to address truancy and anti-social behaviour, New Labour governments were indeed more repressive than those in the late Victorian era when conviction was far from systematic.

The question of the effectiveness of New Labour measures must finally be raised. A chart published by the NAO in 2005 showed that from 1994–95 to 2003–4 unauthorized absences 'remained fairly steady' (NAO, 2005: 4). According to government figures released in February 2008, 'truancy rates among pupils in England rose [...] to their highest level since records began in 1997' (Lipsett, 2008). Labour governments' policies do not therefore seem to have made a real dent in truancy levels. In 2004, Ming Zhang, Principal Education Welfare Officer in Kingston upon Thames, published an article in the journal *Pastoral Care in Education*. Although the study focuses only on about a third of local authorities in England and Wales, its results are unambiguous: 'There is absolutely no relationship between the number of prosecutions and the level of school absenteeism' (Zhang, 2004: 30). In 2007, he published another survey and concluded that on-the-spot fines are ineffective (Frankel, 2007). Also in 2007, New Labour stopped laying the emphasis solely on unauthorized absences and adopted a target related to 'overall absence' (Kirkup, 2007).

Conclusion

This study of truancy as a phenomenon and how it was tackled by authorities in the late Victorian era and under New Labour has revealed a number of similarities, particularly in the categories concerned (the poorest being the most persistent absentees), in the factors behind it with deprivation as a key determinant and in the imposition of a norm associating truancy and anti-social behaviour, which were considered in both periods as serious threats to the social order. A difference, however, has emerged in the way those issues were addressed. Late Victorians did not implement repressive measures such as those which were adopted by New Labour governments and did not make a great difference in attendance levels. Although the Conservative–Liberal Democrat Coalition government announced in July 2010 it would phase out Anti-social Behaviour Orders (ASBO) (Travis, 2010), it occasionally puts forward the same argument on truancy, anti-social behaviour and crime as Michael Gove made clear after the summer 2011 riots. In a speech to the Durand Academy in London on 1 September 2011, he asserted: 'There is an ironclad link between illiteracy, disruption, truancy, exclusion and crime which we need to break' (Gove, 2011). Acknowledging the 'controversial connotations' of the phrase, he referred to 'our educational underclass' who 'are the lost souls our school system has failed' (Gove, 2011). Michael Gove thus justified his view regarding the need for greater pressure on 'inadequate parents' (Gove, 2011) and on schools.

12
The Politics of 'Anti-Social' Behaviour within the 'Troubled Families' Programme

Sue Bond-Taylor

Introduction

Family intervention initiatives have appeared within successive governments as a politically popular mechanism for tackling 'anti-social' behaviour, emerging more recently as a central feature within the Conservative–Liberal Democrat Coalition government's strategy for reforming anti-social behaviour policy. Since coming into office in 2010, the Coalition has expressed its commitment to addressing anti-social behaviour, building upon the framework of enforcement tools developed within New Labour's Respect Agenda. Its White Paper, *Putting Victims First. More Effective Responses to Anti-social Behaviour* (Home Office, 2012b) discusses the importance of balancing enforcement action with action *preventing* anti-social behaviour in the first instance:

> Anti-social behaviour (ASB) cannot be addressed long term by dealing reactively with the behaviour of those who already have entrenched and serious behavioural problems. In line with the approach of other initiatives, such as the Government's recently published strategy for Social Justice, we must also prevent anti-social behaviour from happening in the first place, for example by tackling the risk factors that can drive it across society. (Home Office, 2012b: 34)

Along with strategies addressing problem drinking, illicit drug use and mental health problems, the White Paper outlines plans to tackle the problems caused by 'troubled families', referring directly to the role of the Troubled Families Programme in working alongside a new legislative framework in reducing anti-social behaviour in the longer term.

This chapter explores the political agendas underpinning the creation and expansion of the Troubled Families Programme, identifying key themes within government discourse and exploring the ways in which this programme aligns itself particularly closely with wider Conservative Party ideologies. The shifting landscapes of language surrounding such families will be addressed, focusing on the ideological depiction of so-called 'troubled' families as essentially anti-social, marking a shift by the Coalition government away from previous initiatives which have identified families as vulnerable, disadvantaged or having complex needs. The Troubled Families Programme will be contextualized within a wider exploration of New Labour's Family Intervention Projects, and the academic debates which accompanied those projects. These debates sound a note of caution on the Troubled Families agenda, but also serve to highlight the potential for successful outcomes for families and the importance of local policy interpretations in constructing meaningful practice.

'Troubled Families': an emerging discourse

The Conservative Party Manifesto for the 2010 general election set out the Conservatives' commitment to tackling a 'broken society'.[1] This included a commitment to provide 'targeted help to disadvantaged and dysfunctional families' (Conservative Party, 2010), alongside the reinvigoration of Sure Start and a focus upon early intervention strategies.[2] The Liberal Democrats also focused on supporting families within their manifesto, but avoided adopting the imagery of dysfunction, acknowledging that 'families come in all shapes and sizes' (Liberal Democrats, 2010: 49), but also that a child's life chances are still largely determined by the wealth of their parents.

In 2010, the new Coalition government set out their aims to support 'families with complex needs' within their Comprehensive Spending Review by establishing community budget pilots within 16 local authority areas, where departments would pool resources and provide a comprehensive service for such families within a model of decentralized power and local accountability. This emphasis on meeting the needs of the local community through greater local control over spending, service design and multi-agency integration reflects Conservative agendas around increasing localism, the expansion of the third sector, reducing micro-management of public services and the ideological re-shaping of the role of the state 'from big government to Big Society' (Conservative Party, 2010: vii; see Kisby, 2010 for discussion of the 'Big Society').

The language of need and vulnerability was evident throughout this early discussion of community budgets, reflecting the social justice aims of both Coalition parties. A Department for Communities and Local Government (DCLG) press release on 22 October 2010, announcing the arrival of the community budgets, described the aims:

> By having one budget wrapping money and services around the needs of the vulnerable, councils and partners will be able to directly support

those that need help with education, health, anti-social behaviour and housing. (Department for Communities and Local Government, 2010)

By October 2011, however, the language of 'troubled' rather than needy families was creeping into the discourse. The summer of 2011 had seen rioting in towns and cities across England, with Conservative Justice Secretary Ken Clarke blaming the riots on the actions of 'a feral underclass' (Lewis *et al.*, 2011) and 'an appalling social deficit' (*ibid.*), which needed to be tackled head-on. New concerns about criminality and anti-social behaviour were now shaping the emerging policy:

> Support for families with multiple problems has been considered as part of the Prime Minister's review of social policy following the recent disturbances. Building on the current Community Budget approach, new arrangements will be introduced to provide a greater national push to the programme and ensure all local areas can deliver better outcomes for troubled families. (Department for Communities and Local Government, 2011: 7)

This portrayal of families as 'troubled' became more formally entrenched in December 2011, when the government announced the creation of a dedicated Troubled Families Unit headed up by Louise Casey (former head of New Labour's Respect Task Force and so-called Anti-social Behaviour Tzar), making £450 million of cross-government funding available with the aim of turning around the lives of 120,000 of the country's most 'troubled' families before the end of the current Parliament in 2015. Under this scheme, central government funding is available to local authorities on a payment-by-results basis upon evidencing successful outcomes with families. In the Prime Minister's speech at the launch on 15 December 2011, he outlined the problems and proposed solutions within a framework of responsibilization, stating outright, 'my mission in politics – the thing I am really passionate about – is fixing the responsibility deficit' (Cameron, 2011c). On the face of it, his responsiblization strategy is aimed at both the families themselves and at the state, which he acknowledges has let families down in the past, referring to the families as 'victims of state failure'. But it soon becomes clear when he suggests *how* the state has failed them, the extent to which this government is prepared to be held responsible for the underlying structural factors impeding progress in such families. For example:

> Yes, it's the parent's responsibility to look for work... but if the state is paying them more not to work, it becomes a rational choice to sit at home on the sofa. (*Ibid.*)

There is no discussion here of the failure of the state to regenerate local economies where employment opportunities are scarce, to provide training opportunities and adequate transport networks to allow access to them, or to provide support for those with caring responsibilities so that they are both financially and practicably able to work. He goes on:

> Yes, it's the teenager's choice to smash up the bus stop and torment their neighbours [...] but if the criminal justice system doesn't draw a firm enough line between right and wrong, they're more likely to do wrong. (*Ibid.*)

Similarly, there is no discussion of the failure of the state to provide adequate youth services including positive activities and mental health support, or of the impact of recent service budget cuts upon provision for vulnerable young people.

The responsibility of the state is in this way limited to the role of moral educator, providing a range of behavioural incentives and disincentives and promoting the need for a stronger policing role for the state through direct enforcement strategies. Such a depiction of state responsibility misunderstands entirely the experiences of families with complex needs and perpetuates the myth that these families are simply self-interested and unmotivated to change without coercion. Cameron even refers to media depictions of 'families from hell' and the '*Shameless* culture' within his speech (*ibid.*).[3] Drawing upon such imagery reinforces the idea that the Troubled Families Programme is designed to tackle *those sorts* of families, characterized by *anti-social* lifestyles rather than disadvantage and social exclusion. These depictions of an irresponsible 'underclass' (Murray, 1990) are certainly nothing new and resonate clearly with Conservative agendas which emphasize individual responsibility, family values, and traditional moralities. Constructions of the underclass as 'undeserving poor' are also useful in justifying lack of public spending within marginalized communities, and therefore sit comfortably alongside government claims about the extent of the economic deficit and the need for deep cuts across public services.

This is sharply illustrated in recent Conservative Party proposals about the need to regulate the spending of public money by 'irresponsible' families within the Programme, either by receiving their benefits on a smart card which could only be used to make essential purchases, as advocated by Conservative Work and Pensions Secretary Iain Duncan Smith (Ryan, 2012), or by passing control of the benefits received by families within the Programme to their keyworker, a policy apparently blocked by Liberal Democrat ministers within the Coalition (Stratton, 2013). The continued stigmatization and dehumanization of families with complex and multiple needs which this represents does little to address the very real problems which they face on a daily basis.

Identifying 'troubled' families

The financial framework for the Troubled Families Programme (Department for Communities and Local Government, 2012a) sets out clearly the nature of the problems to be addressed by the local authorities, in order to receive their payments-by-results funding with four criteria provided for local authorities to identify their share of the 120,000 families who need to be 'turned around':

(1) Crime and Anti-social Behaviour: An under 18 with a proven offence or any member of the household with an anti-social behaviour related order against them.
(2) Education: A child permanently excluded, or with three or more fixed term exclusions across three terms, in alternative provision or not on a school roll, or with 15 per cent unauthorised absences across three terms.
(3) Work: An adult on Department for Work and Pensions out of work benefits (including Employment and Support Allowance, Incapacity Benefit, Carer's Allowance, Income Support and/or Job Seekers Allowance, Severe Disablement Allowance).
(4) Local Discretion Filter: where families meet two out of the three criteria above, the local authority may use additional local criteria to identify families of concern and in particular who cause high costs to the public purse. Examples of possible local criteria suggested by the Department for Communities and Local Government include a child on a Child Protection Plan, under-18 conceptions, mental health problems, as well as drug and alcohol misuse.

Families meeting the first three criteria should automatically be included in the programme, with the local discretionary filter being applied only where the first three criteria do not identify sufficient families to fill project capacity, thus limiting local discretion to decide which are the most pressing problems for families in that area (in direct contradiction with the aims of the initial community budgets to decentralize decision making and empower local professionals).

Ruth Levitas (2012) has provided the most notable critique of the Troubled Families policy to date. She disputes the 'imputed' existence of 120,000 troubled families as drawn from a 'spurious' reading of survey data which glosses over some of the problems of sampling error and/or bias. Moreover, she reminds us that the criteria for identifying a 'troubled family' within this survey bears little resemblance to the set of criteria outlined within the Troubled Families Programme Financial Framework document. These 120,000 families were in fact drawn from the *Families At Risk* report conducted for the Social Exclusion Task Force (2007) which identified *families with multiple disadvantages* on the basis of having five or more of seven characteristics:

(1) No parent in the family is in work.
(2) Family lives in overcrowded housing.
(3) No parent has any qualifications.
(4) Mother has mental health problems.
(5) At least one parent has a long-standing illness, disability or infirmity.
(6) Family has a low income (below 60 per cent of median income).
(7) Family cannot afford a number of food and clothing items.

These criteria clearly place greater emphasis on the structural and socio-economic contexts of families with multiple disadvantages (which may indeed contribute to or further exacerbate behaviour identified as 'anti-social') than the version of the anti-social troubled family outlined by the Troubled Families Unit. The language of 'risk' or 'disadvantage' has now been abandoned and replaced with the language of 'trouble' (briefly passing 'needs' along the way). Levitas identifies a further discursive move 'from families that have troubles, through families that are "troubled", to families that are or cause trouble' (Levitas, 2012: 7). This new discursive formation appears to dominate government policy in this area, and is used to justify attempts to assert increasing levels of control over, and regulate public expenditure on these families.

This discursive shift is particularly evident within Louise Casey's *Listening to Troubled Families* report (Casey, 2012), which offers in its Foreword an account of families with 'entrenched, long-term cycles of suffering problems and causing problems' (*ibid.*: 1). However, while the report on the surface acknowledges that the families experience problems themselves (in other words, are also 'troubled'), there is an emphasis on those problems being caused by themselves or others within the family, for example, through drug abuse, domestic violence and intergenerational parenting inadequacies. Families are therefore responsibilized for the problems they experience as well as the problems they cause, while the impact of structural and systemic factors is minimized within the report.

Numerous examples within the families' testimonies of their having been failed by the state or other organizations are given little more than a cursory mention. For example, statements include 'nobody was listening', 'they said they couldn't help me', 'they sent me a letter saying there was nothing they could do for me' (cited in Casey, 2012) and yet this failure to respond to earlier cries for help is not identified as a key theme emerging from the interviews with families, a telling omission. The only discussion of such failings is addressed within the section on Anti-social Family and Friends Network and thus buried within a wider theme that returns the problems to the family themselves:

Many of the families complained about professionals of agencies involved with them, and in particular, social services. However, it would not be fair to always lay the blame there when looked at dispassionately. Undoubtedly, some families have reason to feel let down. But there were often unwarranted feelings that their problems were not of their making, and that they had no control over the problem or its solution; that it was they that had highlighted the problems, with services simply failing to intervene and do what they were entitled to expect of them. (Casey, 2012: 51)

The report thus returns responsibility to the family, and suggests that the demands they place upon services are unreasonable (such as requesting a bigger council house, or that their children be put in care). Little stock is given here to Casey's own statement that the families felt that they had no control and how this might reflect their vulnerable and disempowered position within the community and perhaps within their own family.

Similarly, the report identifies 'Abuse' as a key theme emerging from the interviews, but focuses primarily on abuse within the home. Abuse within the context of care by the state is absent from this section, and is discussed within a separate theme of Institutional Care, implying that abuse by the state is a separate and unconnected problem. Even here, only one example from the family testimonies is included (in spite of numerous others appearing throughout the case studies) compared with four examples of family abuse. No commentary is attached to this single story of abuse in care other than to explain that 'some talked of further abuse in foster care' and to contrast this with others' stories of more positive care experiences.

Casey's depiction of 'Troubled Families' therefore paints a very one-sided picture in which the behaviour of the families is open to speculation, while the actions of agencies are not. The report 'does not seek to make wholesale conclusions about services' (Casey, 2012: 5) we are told, although 'some conclusions may be drawn about how services have historically failed to grip the problems of families' (Casey, 2012: 5). The families are in this way depicted as slippery fish who attempt to evade the 'grip' of services, rather than services trying to evade responsibility for supporting families. If families have become difficult to engage, it may be worth locating that within the context of scepticism and mistrust of services which have let them down in the past, and feelings of powerlessness to influence or direct service interventions within the family.

Troubled families and the family interventions model

In December 2012, the Department for Communities and Local Government (DCLG) published *Working with Troubled Families: A Guide to Evidence and Good Practice* (Department for Communities and Local Government, 2012b) which sets out a model for local authorities' work with 'troubled families'. The approach advocated in the report is a family intervention model that builds upon the apparent successes of numerous Family Intervention Projects (FIPs), which have emerged since the 'pioneering' Dundee Families Project began in 1995. This early Intensive Family Support Project was designed to work specifically with families who had been evicted, or were facing eviction from social housing as a result of their housing-related 'anti-social behaviour' (including damage to/neglect of property, conflict with neighbours, verbal abuse, noise nuisance and stealing). Reducing the risk of homelessness was therefore a central focus of the project. It operated within a number of contexts, including an outreach service to existing tenants, more managed outreach support within dispersed tenancies, and most notoriously within a core residential unit, dubbed in the media as a 'sin bin' for 'neighbours from hell' (Dillane *et al.*, 2001). This project was replicated within a number of other areas, largely through the work of National Children's Homes (NCH), and by 2003 an additional six projects were established (Nixon *et al.*, 2006). Evaluations of these seven projects presented evidence of their success in supporting families to avoid eviction and to reduce 'anti-social' behaviour in their properties (Dillane *et al.*, 2001; Nixon *et al.*, 2006). Despite a number of commentators questioning the validity of the conclusions drawn within these reports, the limitations of the data and the small numbers of families involved in the evaluations (see Garrett, 2007a and Gregg, 2010 especially), the Labour government was sufficiently impressed by the projects to roll them out on a national scale.

In January 2006, the then Prime Minister, Tony Blair, launched the Respect Action Plan which introduced, alongside the existing raft of legislative anti-social behaviour tools, a national programme of 53 FIPs, modelled on the Dundee Families Project. Parr and Nixon (2009) describe the significance of this shift in focus:

> Within a remarkably short period of time, however, FIPs had been transformed from a high-risk activity piloted by a handful of local authorities to a national flagship measure heralded as an effective means of 'turning families round'. (2009: 105)

In 2007, the Labour government commissioned the National Centre for Social Research (NatCen) to begin a national evaluation of family intervention services, and a central database for recording family interventions activity became a key tool within this research. Its report in 2012 (Lloyd *et al.*, 2012) captured the activities of services across 159 local authorities based on data from 12,850 referrals to a family intervention service. Of these referrals, 8,841 families received some form of family intervention with 3,675 of these families exiting the service between February 2007 and March 2011. Families are recorded as having left for a successful reason in 70 per cent of cases, compared with four per cent for an unsuccessful reason (with the remaining families leaving for inconclusive or mixed reasons). Over 50 per cent of the families demonstrated successful outcomes in each of the following areas: poor parenting, relationship or family breakdown, domestic violence, involvement in crime and/or anti-social behaviour, lack of exercise or poor diet, drug or substance misuse, alcohol misuse, truancy, exclusion or bad behaviour at school. The Troubled Families Programme therefore employs this as evidence of the capacity of the family interventions model to lead to successful changes for families and communities.

'Anti-social behaviour' and vulnerability – some important critiques

The rhetorical power of the term 'anti-social' as it is applied to vulnerable and disadvantaged families has been a significant criticism of the Troubled Families discourse. More problematic still is the way in which such moralizing discourses, promulgated by policy makers and echoed across the media, then attribute a family's 'anti-social' behaviour and the problems they experience to their own inadequacies, rather than to 'the broader socio-economic antecedents of incivility' (Rodger, 2006: 132). However, this is certainly not unique to the Coalition government and is echoed in the body of work that addresses the wider use of anti-social behaviour legislation to increase social control over vulnerable individuals within contemporary Britain, particularly under successive New Labour administrations (Manders, 2009). Its use against prostitutes (Phoenix, 2008), the homeless (Moore, 2008), juveniles (Squires and Stephen, 2005) and the mentally ill (MacDonald, 2006) are all well documented. There are thus considerable continuities between New Labour approaches to 'anti-social' families and those of the Conservative–Liberal Democrat Coalition.

Parr and Nixon's (2008) account of New Labour's FIPs described how families were constructed as 'other' within government accounts, perceived as a 'hard core' with distinctive characteristics. They identified a tendency to see state failure to support families as a product of families' unwillingness to engage with, and manipulation of, services. The problems they face were therefore seen as the consequences of dysfunctional family structures and lack of self-regulation. Parr and Nixon, however, noted that the political utilization of journalistic 'neighbours from hell' imagery by New Labour in order to communicate their policies to the public impacted upon families' readiness to accept support, given the stigmatizing character of this framing.

Garrett's (2007a) critique of family intervention projects highlights the degree of coercion and control imposed upon families, and the invasion of privacy experienced by these individuals (although it is worth noting that he is concerned mostly with the residential element of the Dundee Families Project and its successors). He expresses concerns about the intrusion into private life, around issues of housework, personal hygiene, use of alcohol and daily routine. A last chance ideology pervades the justification for such residential options, with families at particular risk of eviction, or of losing their children into care. This threat of sanctions is also a key feature of the Troubled Families Programme, with the *Working with Troubled Families* guide stating 'No troubled family should be left 'in trouble' without there being consequences for them if they do not accept an offer from family intervention' (Department for Communities and Local Government, 2012b: 28) and claiming that 'Evidence shows that the threat of sanctions such as loss of tenancy "concentrates the mind" of families and is a key mechanism for bringing about change' (*ibid.*). Therefore, while family interventions ostensibly work on the premise of voluntary engagement, the threat of sanctions suggests that understanding participation as consensual may be misleading.

Family Intervention Projects are one of a range of anti-social behaviour management strategies designed within a 'contractual' framework in which the allegedly anti-social individual becomes an active partner in their own regulation. The family is asked to sign a 'contract' of engagement at the start of the intervention period, which clarifies expectations of the family's engagement and the 'consequences' for failure to engage, as well as the duties of the keyworker in addressing the family's problems (consequences for failure to provide support on the part of the service professionals are not featured in such 'contracts'). This tendency towards 'contractual governance' has been criticized for its lack of authenticity (Crawford, 2003) and deployment as an ideological tool to facilitate 'regulated self-regulation' (*ibid.*: 488). In anti-social behaviour management the balance of power is inequitable between the parties to the 'contract' (for example, tenants and landlord), and most 'contracts' are precursors to enforcement action if the terms of the contract are breached (such as eviction). Indeed, unwillingness to accept a contractual measure may be seen in itself as evidence of intransigence requiring more formal legal sanctions. For example, Parenting Contracts are backed by the threat of the Parenting Order and Acceptable Behaviour Contracts are followed up by Anti-social Behaviour Orders (ASBOs). In the same way, refusal to accept 'support' from a 'troubled families' service may be used against a family as further evidence of their anti-sociality and their irresponsibility during consequent legal proceedings.

Debates in the literature on family intervention services and other anti-social behaviour strategies have therefore questioned whether this combination of welfare and control represents a form of social engineering which effects intrusive and potentially degrading surveillance and coerced behavioural change. Adam Crawford contends that 'the language of effective regulation has come to constitute a benevolent mask for state-sponsored projects of social engineering on an unprecedented scale' (2009: 828). Under the banner of preventing 'anti-social behaviour' and protecting communities from the 'neighbours from hell', we have seen an increasing use of legal sanctions to enforce socially desirable forms of behaviour, or rather those deemed socially desirable by a certain sector of the public. Welfare and support initiatives become backed by legal enforcement strategies for those who do not voluntarily accept the offer of 'help', further individualizing the problem as the product of the incompetent, the lazy or the immoral.

Contemporary depictions of 'troubled families' echo such concerns, with a focus on tackling welfare dependency within interventions. Increasingly, the nation's poorest communities are 'cast in terms of "social pathology", where the poor are blamed for their own predicament, allowing the structural inequalities intrinsic to capitalism to be neatly side stepped' (Law and Mooney, 2005: 6) and social divisions exacerbated further. Welfare in this context may be seen as tending more towards the 'productive' than the 'protective' (Hudson and Kühner, 2009), reflecting the notion of a 'social investment state' which prioritizes investment in human capital in order to promote self-responsiblization and economic productivity (Parr, 2009). Furthermore, Rodger describes the recent 'criminalization of social policy' (Rodger, 2008), characterized by the prioritization of welfare programmes that resonate with public order and community safety strategies, and where the success of social policy initiatives is increasingly measured by their impact upon criminal justice agendas, rather than social justice, empowerment and well-being.

Family interventions and social justice opportunities

Garrett points out that the sorts of outreach provision that family intervention projects provide to families encountering difficulties bear a remarkable resemblance to what 'used to be called "local authority social work" '(Garrett, 2007b) and moreover that this did not come with the stigmatizing label of anti-social behaviour attached. It may be naïve to assume that social work does not also bring with it its own stigma and potentially damaging discourse, particularly where parents are subjected to surveillance for allegedly neglecting or abusing their children.

Furthermore, it is important to account for the differences between family intervention services and contemporary social work. Social workers, operating out of Children's Services departments have as their focus the protection and welfare of the child, and prioritize interventions addressing these issues, working within the contours of the social work discipline and training. By contrast, the development of family interventions operates a more holistic approach, looking at the needs of the 'at risk' child alongside other members of the family. This enables interventions that work with the whole family and understand the obstacles to progress which family members might face, although at times this can be complex and involve challenging some family members in order to make positive changes for others. Morris's (2013) account of vulnerable families' experiences of multiple service use identifies the importance of professionals taking the time to understand and work with family life in order to promote inclusive 'transferable family learning' (*ibid.*: 7). As Parr (2009) identifies, contemporary social work practice has been characterized by processes of bureaucracy, managerialism and proceduralization, along with limited resources, which have limited social workers' opportunities to engage in more intensive or creative work with families. She therefore contends that family intervention projects have the potential to offer some of the best features of social work practice, and cannot be characterized simply as the policing of 'anti-social' or 'troubled' families.

Family-focused strategies therefore offer possibilities that contemporary social work practices may find difficult to achieve. For Mitchell and Campbell (2011), the remit of family interventions extends beyond understanding functioning and building relationships within the family, to a broader understanding of the community context, exploring the ways in which families are connected to or excluded from their community and the processes by which such exclusion is effected. This ecological model therefore attempts to connect individual characteristics, family attributes and systemic and structural dimensions, for example understanding the ways in which attributes such as mental illness, substance abuse or material poverty make it easier for society to exclude a family. The strength of intensive family interventions over contemporary social work practice is therefore in the increased opportunities it supplies for the key worker to obtain a deep understanding of all of the issues affecting the family, including their relationships with the wider community.

Furthermore, Tisdall (2006) describes the tensions between the opposing discourses of local authority Children's Services and anti-social behaviour strategies, and the dichotomous representations of the child in each, as troubled/needy/deserving and troublesome/competent/undeserving respectively. This is echoed in Parr's research, where staff talked about 'walking a tightrope' between the child-focused Every Child Matters strategy and the community-focused Respect Agenda (Parr, 2009: 1265–6). Family interventions therefore provide an opportunity to situate the child within both discourses simultaneously and to respond to the complex and sometimes contradictory realities of young people's experiences of growing up in multiply disadvantaged households. For Parr and Nixon the progressive potential within family interventions is found within the individuals involved in policy implementation on the ground. While there is the danger of Family Intervention Projects slipping into authoritarian and oppressive regimes, buoyed by the populist rhetoric of government and media, there is also they argue, 'the potential to provide opportunities for local agents to be creative, opening up possibilities for genuinely positive interventions built of mutual trust and respect' (Parr and Nixon, 2008: 174). They describe the ways in which local professionals in their research had a much more 'nuanced and sophisticated' (Parr and Nixon, 2009: 104) understanding of the problem than that depicted in national policy discourses, and explore the impact of local political cultures upon the implementation of policy, resulting in the mitigation of the more damaging or demonizing aspects of such policies when applied to vulnerable families.

Issues of social exclusion and vulnerability are explored within Davis's (2011) ethnography of families with complex needs. He describes the perception within such families that 'life is a lottery' (Davis, 2011: 5) in which 'you have to be in it to win it but also you will lose more than you win' (2011: 5). This reflects the perceived inability to shape or affect one's life chances and protect oneself from the arbitrary and unpredictable nature of decisions and actions taken by others. The state is perceived by families as contradictory in what it says and what it does and its language is understood only by the professionals who work within it, further impeding engagement with services. Successful interventions therefore challenge these perceptions by providing reliable, sustained and predictable services, which communicate clearly with families in a way which makes sense to them.

Family interventions delivered through a dedicated keyworker can therefore also support the rebuilding of trust between families and services where family members feel that they have been ignored, let down or demonized by agencies in the past (Bond-Taylor and Somerville, 2013). Central to this is the advocacy role in which family members are supported by their keyworker to challenge service decisions and actions/inaction, and to become more confident citizens, capable of disputing the label of 'trouble', which can in itself impact negatively upon self-esteem and emotional well-being (*ibid.*).

Conclusion

The Coalition government's Troubled Families Programme demonstrates more continuity than divergence from earlier New Labour attempts to prevent anti-social behaviour through family-focused interventions. Family intervention services provide an opportunity to tackle a variety of deep-rooted problems within families, which may sometimes manifest themselves in behaviour labelled as 'anti-social'. Many families are grateful for the support, which they feel has not been available to them in the past, or which has been provided in unhelpful and stigmatizing formats. Nonetheless, service providers must remain alert to the potential for these intensive programmes to generate overly authoritarian, disciplinary regimes.

The dominant discourse emerging out of the Troubled Families Unit caricatures the families within the programme as dysfunctional, inadequate, irresponsible and anti-social, rather than as disadvantaged, excluded and vulnerable. Such inadequacies are attributed to the failings of the families themselves, with broader structural and institutional failings being neatly sidestepped by the Coalition government. However, the significant differences between the responsibilizing discourse of central government and the empathetic ethos and actions of local professionals offers considerable opportunity for successful implementation of the Troubled Families Programme, with more supportive and enlightened work with families taking place at a local level. However, in contrast to the original espoused aims of empowering local professionals (through community budgets) to deliver work with families in the ways that they deem fit, the emerging Troubled Families Programme promotes increasingly restrictive practices.

The current payments-by-results approach to 'troubled families' targets a range of broadly defined 'anti-social' behaviours, including worklessness, school exclusions or truancy, and offending. This focus may deter local authorities from engaging in earlier intervention work with younger children, encourage shorter periods of intervention and promote more narrow practices of intervening with particular family members who meet the criteria (or may be easier to 'turn around'). Research with families identifies the need to provide sustained, creative and flexible interventions to ensure that the keyworker is enabled to build meaningful relationships with the family, to address softer outcomes around feelings of self-esteem and happiness, and to continue to act as an effective buffer between families and enforcement agencies.

Notes

1. The term 'broken society' is originally attributed to Tony Blair (then Leader of the Opposition) in 1995, but has been used more purposefully by David Cameron and other Conservative MPs within the 2005 and 2010 election campaigns and within the work of the Centre for Social Justice (see Thorp and Kennedy, 2010).
2. Sure Start was launched in 1999 as a cross-departmental, early interventions initiative to improve the life chances of children and their families within deprived communities. See Glass (1999) for an outline of its origins and remit.
3. *Shameless*, a British comedy-drama television series which depicts working-class life on a fictional council estate, aired on Channel 4 from 2004 to 2013.

13
Anti-Social Behaviour among Homeless People: Assumptions or Reality?

Jamie Harding and Adele Irving

Introduction

Historically, the visible engagement of homeless people in activities considered to be 'anti-social', such as drunkenness and begging, have made them the target of government action on public disorder, engendering antipathy, as much as sympathy, from policy makers, key regulators and the wider public (Takahashi, 1997, cited in DeVerteuil *et al.*, 2009: 647). Governments have long been keen to blame increases in homelessness on individual failings, resulting from wilful idleness and dangerous criminal/anti-social tendencies (Humphreys, 1999: 167), with policy responses underpinned by the principles of enforcement and exclusion, rather than care and support. During the period 1997 to 2010, the New Labour governments demonstrated a more nuanced understanding of the causes of homelessness, giving increased recognition to the importance of factors beyond the control of the individual. At the heart of government policies towards homelessness was the idea of balancing rights with responsibilities. However, even under this more ostensibly sympathetic approach, concerns to tackle social exclusion among homeless people existed in tension with a perception that their anti-social behaviours needed to be addressed. Following a historical discussion of the key interventions designed to tackle wilful idleness and anti-social behaviour among homeless people, this chapter will focus on policy developments since 1997. It will then draw on recent empirical research in the north east of England, where data collected from homeless people and relevant stakeholders challenged the popular assumptions that have often underpinned policy responses to homelessness. It is argued that such policies have often produced counter-productive effects; reinforcing exclusion and increasing the likelihood that homeless people will be involved in further anti-social acts.

The historical problem of homelessness

Although Lund (1996: 83) argues that the concept of homelessness as we know it today did not exist before the twentieth century, statutes have recognized the status of vagrancy – with the implication of people wandering from place to place – for many centuries. Matthews (1986: 100) suggests that the term 'vagrant' is closely linked with the word 'casual'. The Casual Poor Act 1882 defined a casual pauper as 'any destitute wayfarer or wanderer'. Other names given to this class of pauper included tramp, beggar, loafer and vagabond. Humphreys (1999: 167) notes that throughout history, governments have tended to blame increases in homelessness on the individuals concerned and to ignore 'the factors which at that particular time were causing more of their citizens to wander around poverty-stricken'. The view expressed by Murray (1990: 24), that homeless people are part of an underclass marked by laziness and criminal tendencies (among other factors), reflects a long-standing and influential line of thinking.

Fears about the wilfully idle, and the dangers and costs of providing relief to them, date back to the medieval period. In some cases, these fears specifically related to vagrancy. The first vagrancy statute of 1349 made it a crime to give alms to someone who was unemployed but of sound mind, owing to the risk of incentivizing people to survive by begging rather than employment (Beier, 1985: 4). In 1351, a punishment of 15 days imprisonment was introduced for anyone who left the town where they had worked during the winter if work was available during the summer (Chambliss, 1964: 68). The level of punishment had escalated considerably by 1535, when repeated vagrancy became punishable by the death penalty (Chambliss, 1964: 72–3). According to Chambliss (1964: 74–5), this escalation reflected the loss of goods being transported around the country to vagrants (or 'highwaymen') and completed a shift in perception of homeless people from being merely idle to being criminal. Adler (1989: 209–13), although believing that Chambliss over-emphasizes the criminal element, similarly notes that vagrancy statutes stopped describing vagrants in terms of their lack of employment and instead began to discuss them as 'lusty rogues', beggars and thieves.

Almost five centuries later, the Poor Law report of 1834 continued to reflect concerns about vagrancy being a life-style choice rather than a situation arising from destitution. Whether the result of perceived laziness or anti-social tendencies, the punitive approach taken by the Poor Law to all who sought assistance was escalated for those who were homeless; extremely harsh conditions were maintained throughout the Victorian period. Vagrants were required to live in the casual wards of workhouses and to work breaking stones (Strange, 2011: 245). The two Poor Law reports of 1909 differed little in their treatment of vagrants; the Majority report favoured 'semi-penal institutions', while the Minority report recommended labour colonies where vagrants could be 'kept to work under discipline'

(Matthews, 1986: 110). Matthews (1986: 108) notes two counter-productive impacts of this punitive approach: 'professional' vagrants were encouraged to beg for money in order to stay in common lodging houses rather than workhouses and men who honestly desired work were quickly stripped of self-respect and became habitual vagrants.

Alternative perspectives on homelessness developed in the late Victorian era as it became clear that poverty was much more widespread than had previously been assumed; it began to be questioned whether low moral standards among the most destitute arose from their housing conditions rather than vice versa (Fraser, 1984: 132–7). The housing experiments of Octavia Hill (Thane, 1996: 25–6), charitable provision for homeless people (Strange, 2011: 246) and special measures for areas where there was widespread long-term unemployment (Thane, 1996: 172–3) were all signs of a less harsh response emerging.

However, assumptions that homeless people, particularly single homeless people, were lazy and/or anti-social had by no means disappeared. The most significant pieces of homelessness legislation from the post-Second World War period – the National Assistance Act 1948 and the Housing (Homeless Persons) Act 1977 – concentrated on providing protection to families with dependent children, with single homeless people offered accommodation in 'resettlement units'. While these units emphasized resettlement rather than punishment, section 17 of the National Assistance Act 1948 reflected historic concerns that homeless people may deliberately choose a path of laziness and dependency by insisting that those who persistently used them must undertake work or risk imprisonment (Watson and Austerberry, 1986: 52). Following the units' closure in the 1980s and 1990s, commentators argued that the alternative provision that replaced them reflected continuing negative assumptions about homeless people, by focusing on their assumed housekeeping deficits (Deacon *et al.*, 1995) and their inability to live in a social manner (Garside, 1993: 321).

A similar focus on individual causes of homelessness was evident in the Rough Sleepers Initiative implemented by the Conservative governments of 1979 to 1997, in response to an increasingly visible problem of rough sleeping in central London. The initiative was launched with claims that local housing shortages affected central London only and that the real causes of homelessness were individual, such as 'the breakup of families and other social ties' (quoted in Anderson, 1993: 23). While the initiative originally sought to provide accommodation to single homeless people, Cloke *et al.* (2010: 31–2) highlight a change of approach when anticipated reductions in levels of rough sleeping did not materialize. Ordered to clear a 'hard core' of rough sleepers from the streets of central London, action by the Metropolitan Police increased the number of people arrested under Vagrancy Acts from 192 in 1991 to 1445 in 1992. Later, Conservative Prime Minister John Major criticized 'homeless' beggars and Peter Lilley (Secretary of State for Social

Security) suggested that sellers of the Big Issue magazine should not receive state benefits. The Housing Act 1996 went on to give legal backing to the exclusion of homeless people and others from local authority housing registers for factors such as anti-social behaviour; there was a four-fold increase in such exclusions during the following 12 months, although the large majority were introduced for rent arrears (Butler, 1998).

Homelessness and anti-social behaviour since 1997

In contrast to their predecessors, the Labour governments were largely reluctant to blame social problems solely on individual factors, giving greater acknowledgement to the role of structural disadvantage. As such, there was a concern to balance 'rights' and 'responsibilities'; offering disadvantaged people opportunities to improve their situation, while insisting that it was their responsibility to accept these opportunities (Deacon, 2003: 131–2). However, balancing rights and responsibilities was difficult, as was tackling homelessness and social exclusion while also fulfilling a commitment to act strongly in the area of anti-social behaviour.

The Homelessness Act 2002 restored rights to apply for social housing (housing owned by not-for-profit bodies, such as local authorities and housing associations) by taking away the powers of local authorities to issue 'blanket' exclusion policies against certain classes of applicant – particularly ex-offenders or people with chaotic lifestyles. Instead, a place on the housing register could only be denied to individuals who had neglected their responsibilities through severe cases of anti-social behaviour: cases where a court, if presented with the evidence, would have granted a full Possession Order on the property and where the applicant could not provide evidence of change (Harding and Harding, 2006: 148). In addition, the 2002 Homelessness (Priority Need for Accommodation) (England) Order provided greater legal protection to particularly vulnerable groups of homeless people, including 16–17-year-olds, those leaving prison and those fleeing domestic violence (Crisis, 2013).

The rights and responsibilities theme was clearly evident when the newly formed Rough Sleepers Unit (1999) outlined six key policies to tackle rough sleeping. These included focusing on those in greatest need and not giving up on the most vulnerable. However, there were also direct and indirect indications of the responsibilities of rough sleepers, including an expectation that they would engage with services in support of a change of life-style.

Policies to improve services for homeless people were developed alongside the first specific legislation on anti-social behaviour; the Crime and Disorder Act 1998 created Anti-social Behaviour Orders (ASBOs). Anti-social behaviour was never clearly defined and Parr (2009: 371) notes that many academics 'are highly critical of the dominant discourse of anti-social behaviour, particularly because of the way it demonizes those accused of such conduct'; those accused are often the most vulnerable in society and themselves victims of multiple disadvantage. Brown (2004) suggests that anti-social behaviour policies in this period focused on action; motivation and intention were considered largely irrelevant, as were personal mitigating factors such as mental health problems.

The impacts of New Labour's policies on homeless people were diverse. For example, Harding and Harding (2006: 148) suggest that, despite the intentions of the Homelessness Act 2002, informal blanket bans on the allocation of housing continued to operate, with a particularly severe impact on homeless people who had spent time in prison. However, effective provision was made for the housing of the most serious offenders through Multi-Agency Public Protection Arrangements. Cloke *et al.* (2010: 37–9), in evaluating the impacts of policy towards single homeless people, suggest that, initially at least, there was an emphasis on welfare and care, involvement of the voluntary sector and prevention, which led to a number of successes. Most notably, it was estimated that the numbers sleeping rough fell by two-thirds between 1999 and 2001 (Randall and Brown, 2002). Similarly, Homeless Link (2010; cited in Whiteford, 2013) reported positive changes in the early years, such as policies and practice moving towards disrupting the flow of new rough sleepers on to the streets through the development of more assertive outreach models, alongside more personalized services for homeless people. The government also sought to provide homeless people with opportunities for education, work and training in order to boost self-esteem, build skills and provide connections with mainstream social networks (Whiteford, 2013: 13). It was hoped that, through the combined efforts of the statutory and voluntary sectors, homeless people could be transformed into fully engaged citizens (Jordan, 2001; cited in Whiteford, 2013: 13).

However, there is a consensus that the focus of policy changed during Labour's second term of office (2001–5). The creation of ASBOs had a limited impact until 2003, when the Anti-social Behaviour Act 2003 extended the powers available (Millie, 2008: 379) and the number of ASBOs issued increased sharply, reaching a peak in 2005 (Ministry of Justice, 2011). Furthermore, from 2003, the Home Office's Anti-Social Behaviour Unit was asked to tackle 'problem street culture'. Begging was subsequently made a recordable offence (Cloke *et al.*, 2010: 37) and anti-social behaviour legislation was used disproportionately against homeless people (Whiteford, 2013: 14–15). These changes coincided with the establishment of 'Business Improvement Districts', which created new ways of policing urban spaces. The focus of policy appeared to move away from tackling the social exclusion experienced by homeless people and towards a concern to 'take control of the streets' (Cloke *et al.*, 2010: 37–9) by removing those whose behaviour was considered problematic.

Despite this apparent change of focus, it would be a mistake to suggest that the later stages of the Labour governments simply marked a return to the punitive approaches of previous eras. Money continued to be made available to the voluntary sector to substantially improve the quality of services for homeless people through a range of programmes (Cloke *et al.*, 2010: 242–3). For example, a continuing acknowledgement of multiple causes of homelessness, and a belief in the rights of homeless people to be given opportunities to improve their situation, was reflected in the rhetoric of the Hostels Capital Improvement programme. Launched in 2005, it aimed to make hostels 'places of change' where: 'By encountering good services, they [homeless people] will find routes into education, employment and, ultimately, sustained independent living in their own home' (DCLG, 2006: 5).

In 2010, the Labour government was replaced by a Conservative-led coalition. Whiteford (2013: 26–7) notes that many of the Coalition's policies on homelessness are a continuation of those that began under New Labour. For example, the government's key consultation paper on homelessness, while not using the language of social exclusion, discussed the need to improve access to housing, health care and employment services for homeless people, while also drawing attention to their perceived anti-social tendencies by discussing the 'negative impacts on communities and industries such as tourism from visible rough sleeping and associated activities, such as begging and street drinking' (HM Government, 2011a: 13). Homelessness services have been spared some of the most severe cuts to public spending, although reduced funding for local authorities is, at the time of writing, beginning to have a major impact on these services (Harding *et al.*, 2013).

The above analysis suggests that homelessness policy under New Labour was initially sympathetic, acknowledging complex causes of homelessness and seeking to give homeless people rights to housing and employment opportunities, in order to tackle their experiences of social exclusion. Despite a later shift towards addressing perceived anti-social behaviour such as begging, these elements remained in place throughout the Labour Party's period of office. The twin concerns of providing access to better services while taking action in cases of anti-social behaviour have been maintained under the Coalition. There have been positive evaluations of the development of services for homeless people during the periods of the Labour governments at both national (Fitzpatrick *et al.*, 2011) and local (Harding *et al.*, 2013) levels. However, the focus of the empirical material that follows is to evaluate, specifically, the partial shift away from historical assumptions of laziness and criminal/anti-social tendencies as the reasons for people being homeless, which date back to Victorian times and beyond.

Homelessness and anti-social behaviour in the north east of England

This section draws on a number of studies[1] conducted in the north east of England, which involved interviews with staff of statutory and voluntary organizations dealing with homelessness, and homeless people themselves, in a range of contexts. The studies provided ample evidence of anti-social behaviour on the part of homeless people, with high incidences of drug and alcohol abuse, mental health problems, violent behaviour, familial breakdown, negative social networks, unemployment and dependency on benefits, begging, sex work and crime. The recollections of the homeless people interviewed included: 'I got kicked out [of my last home] for noise', 'If I don't do the sex work, I'll go out and commit crime and shoplift and stuff while, if I go out and make money for like just having sex with someone [...] it's easy money' and 'The assault was because some lad was picking on my pal's girlfriend and he didn't have the bottle to do anything so I done him in.' Staff working in hostels confirmed that there was a group of particularly chaotic homeless people who were involved in (often violent) crime and anti-social behaviour. These individuals were reported to be difficult to manage, particularly when their behaviour was linked to addictions.

In some cases, the anti-social behaviour of the homeless people interviewed was a direct trigger or risk factor for many of the problems they experienced, such as being evicted from the parental home, the marital home, rented accommodation and hostels. Talking about his relationship breakdown, one respondent said: 'What I would do, I would get a half bottle of vodka and drink it neat in like 20 seconds and pass out and then wake up and do the same thing again. See, no wonder, she hoyed us out and divorced us.'

Consistent with historical assumptions, it was clear that some homeless people had deeply ingrained anti-social tendencies and struggled to accept any form of responsibility. Almost half of those interviewed reported that they had rarely attended school and gained few, if any, qualifications. A significant proportion had experimented with drugs and alcohol in their early teens, socialized with negative peer groups and exhibited violent behaviours, saying, for example: 'I got thrown out of school when I was 11 [...] I broke a teacher's nose. I was getting home tutoring for about six month but I hit him with a pool cue so I have basically learnt myself as the years went on.'

Some homeless people also had very limited experience of work. Approximately one-quarter of those interviewed had never worked, with a focus on employment often replaced by prolific offending. Problems of addiction were a frequently cited reason for losing jobs. Furthermore, when asked about their hopes for the future, employment did not always feature in respondents' aspirations.

However, the data also provided much evidence to refute simplistic assumptions that homelessness is a result of individual moral failings. Assumptions about the inherent laziness of homeless people were challenged by a strong ideology of work among the majority interviewed and the lack of indications of a sense of entitlement to welfare or a dependency culture. The motivation of the homeless people to work was evidenced by comments such as, 'I need employment – It's a big problem in my life', 'I've always worked [...] this is the longest that I haven't worked' and 'I really, really want to get my own job, stability, my own wages [...].' A number of respondents were engaged in voluntary work or completing training courses to improve their employability. Securing paid work was linked to a positive sense of identity, the rebuilding of relationships (particularly with children) and continued attachment to mainstream values and cultural norms.

Policy undertones that homeless people are inherently anti-social, as outlined earlier in the chapter, could also be questioned when considering the broader life histories of respondents. Some of the homeless people interviewed had lived 'normal', unproblematic lives, with high levels of educational attainment, positive family relationships, long periods of stable employment and no pattern of substance misuse or criminality. For these people, the pattern of their lives had typically been radically changed by a significant life event – such as bereavement, relationship breakdown or redundancy – which triggered addiction, followed by eviction or the repossession of a home. In one case, a respondent had lived with their partner for six years in rented accommodation; they explained that, following the breakdown of the relationship: 'I just cracked up [...] I basically just left it [...] packed all my stuff, rang the council and says I don't want it and walked away.' Another respondent explained that he had always been in employment and had owned several homes throughout his adult life. However, after the death of his wife, he became depressed and stopped paying household bills, which resulted in his home being repossessed.

The life experiences of respondents also demonstrated that long histories of anti-social behaviour were often linked to traumatic childhood experiences, including parental addiction, bereavement, going into local authority care, neglect and physical and sexual abuse. Descriptions of childhood included: 'I can remember loads, but it is not very good stuff. My dad was a heroin addict. He used to beat [my mam] up and that and then she left him, so we had to leave a go to a refuge', 'I had a pretty crap childhood ... in and out of care ... foster homes ... since about the age of six. Mother, she was an alcoholic' and 'My brother dying, my granddad dying, my Da dying ... unhappy times.' One homeless person reported being set on fire at the age of 12, while another witnessed a murder at a young age. A number of respondents directly attributed their perceived anti-social behaviour to the impact of these events. For example, one said of a life of homelessness, sex work and exclusion: 'If I didn't get abused, I don't think I'd have went on that path.' Another who experienced domestic violence in early childhood said that drugs 'made all my problems go away, especially on the coke'.

A further objection to the idea that homelessness is caused by the anti-social tendencies of the individual concerned was that this pattern of cause and effect was reversed in many cases. A number of respondents reported engaging in begging, sex work and crime as part of survival strategies to secure money and food while living on the streets. Typical comments here were: 'I was going into sandwich shops and being sly and just taking stuff. I wasn't happy about it, but I had to survive somehow' and 'Shoplifting, begging, things like that, you know...just to get by.' In addition, drug and alcohol abuse were commonly reported as coping mechanisms while living on the streets, for example: 'Drink, drugs...when you drink, you don't feel the cold...they don't warm you up, it just numbs the feeling.' In some cases, homeless people reported committing crimes in order to avoid sleeping rough, with prison often seen as a short-term housing solution. One respondent said that, after a conviction, he negotiated through his solicitor for a custodial sentence because he had nowhere to live. Another explained:

> I was dossing on couches like couple of nights here, couple of nights there but people get sick, do you know what I mean, you can't keep putting yourself onto people and, in the end I just thought right, I am just going to go to jail, get myself to court and get myself sent to jail.

Despite the historical reluctance of governments to accept structural explanations for homelessness, it was clear from the interviews with homeless people that structural barriers – in the areas of housing, welfare and employment – often reinforced the cycle of homelessness and anti-social behaviour. A history of rent arrears, offending or violent behaviour (often linked to mental health problems and addictions) prevented many homeless people from accessing housing, despite the measure taken by New Labour to reduce the number of exclusions. Voluntary sector respondents expressed frustration that social housing landlords were often unwilling to consider applications from homeless people. In other cases, the level of evidence of change required before applications would be considered was felt to be unrealistic:

> We have somebody who's been abstinent for a year, he had quite a considerable criminal record, a lot of offences related to alcohol, he had mental health issues as well...he was still barred from housing because of his alcohol related activity...the guy said 'well I want to see two years [of change].' It's absolutely ridiculous.

A number of homeless people held similar views, saying, for example: 'it's a waste of time applying to the council'. The private rented sector was similarly viewed as difficult to access.

It was noted above that some respondents regarded prison as a short-term solution to housing problems. It was clear, however, that such an approach was unlikely to produce benefits in the longer term; one respondent who worked for the local authority noted that being released from prison remained one of the most common causes of rough sleeping. This area has long been acknowledged as a weakness in service provision (Harding and Harding, 2006). Almost half of the homeless people interviewed who had been to prison reported receiving little, if any, support upon release, greatly reducing the likelihood of their finding any form of accommodation.

Indeed, many returned to rough sleeping or could secure accommodation only in a direct access hostel on leaving custody.

The lack of permanent housing available to respondents was resulting in lengthy stays in hostels run by voluntary sector organizations. Although some of this accommodation is of a high standard, having been refurbished as part of the Hostels Capital Improvement Programme, many respondents discussed difficulties associated with addressing problems of addiction while living in this type of environment. Comments included: 'I'm struggling with my drug problem and they've put me in a place where people are going "do you want this?", "do you want that?" and I'm struggling.' Indeed, several reported returning to substance misuse while living in hostels. Nonetheless, some respondents discussed developing positive relationships in this environment, finding benefits from sharing accommodation with those who had had similar experiences and were keen to make positive changes to their lives.

There was also evidence of structural factors creating barriers to employment following homelessness. Where respondents were sleeping rough, lack of sleep and difficulties in accessing hygiene facilities presented obvious difficulties. Other problems included offending histories and a lack of identifying documents, references and/or a bank account. These problems were compounded by the nature of the job market in the north east of England, where high levels of unemployment reduce the likelihood of homeless people securing employment when in competition with those with less problematic lives and fuller employment histories. Criminal records were a particular barrier, as one voluntary sector respondent explained: 'In some cases, you need to do CRB [criminal records bureau] check working on building sites, which is crazy...it stops being about the rehabilitation of the offender and more about risk management from the organization.' Homeless people also reported that the high cost of hostel accommodation often meant that they could not accept work as they would be unable to afford the rent if they lost access to benefits. Their benefits could be cut for being involved in voluntary work, where this was perceived to affect their ability to apply for paid jobs.

Conclusion

The data collected during recent studies in the north east of England highlights a number of reasons for questioning historical assumptions, prevalent since the Victorian period and even earlier, that homeless people have inherent lazy and anti-social tendencies. There was undoubtedly substantial experience of anti-social behaviour on the part of the majority of the homeless people interviewed. However, the data supports the assertion of DeVerteuil *et al.* (2009) that experiences of homelessness are diverse. Some respondents had lived normal, unproblematic lives, reflecting widely upheld social norms, until the occurrence of a disruptive life event.

There was also evidence to support criticisms of New Labour's anti-social behaviour policies (see Parr, 2009 and Brown, 2004), particularly in relation to their impact on vulnerable groups such as homeless people. The anti-social behaviour of respondents was often a coping mechanism for major traumatic events. Despite assumptions that homelessness is caused or prolonged by anti-social tendencies, activities such as crime and substance misuse were frequently responses to, rather than causes of, homelessness.

The data supported the view of Jordan (1996; cited in Scanlon and Adlam, 2008: 534) that, despite fewer personal capacities and societal resources, many homeless people are able to manage their behaviours and participate usefully in a society which offers them effective protection and meaningful opportunities. The policies of the Labour governments in seeking to provide opportunities for homeless people are therefore to be applauded. However, measures that sought to enhance the rights of homeless people often did not produce the benefits envisaged owing to a range of structural barriers. The data confirmed that structural factors play a much bigger role than has historically been acknowledged. The willingness of some respondents to use prison as a short-term housing solution is a particularly striking example of the impact of structural difficulties. It is unfortunate that in Labour's later years in office, the desire to improve services to homeless people existed in tension with more traditional concerns to control their perceived anti-social tendencies, presented as encouragement to accept responsibilities.

While it may seem inappropriate to evaluate policy assumptions dating back to the fourteenth century using evidence collected over the last few years, the data suggests that assumptions that homeless people are inherently anti-social carry similar risks of counter-productive policy responses today to those noted in previous eras by Matthews (1986: 108). Attempts to punish and exclude homeless people tend to create and reinforce the very tendencies that are feared most.

Note

1. The chapter draws on four studies, undertaken between 2011 and 2014. The first study was peer-led research into the pathways to exclusion experienced by a sample of 82 homeless people accessing direct access accommodation and day centres in Newcastle. The second was a cost–benefit analysis of the value of housing-related support for homeless people, using a local homelessness charity as a case study. The project involved interviews with five staff and 14 service users, quantitative analysis of 238 client outcomes records from 2011–12 and a cost–benefit analysis of services. The third study was peer-led research into the experiences and service needs of sex workers in Tyne and Wear; interviews with 36 sex workers and 15 stakeholders were completed. The fourth study was an evaluation of a peer-mentoring scheme, involving 39 interviews with offenders suffering problems of addiction.

14

Is Nomadism the 'Problem'? The Social Construction of Gypsies and Travellers as Perpetrators of 'Anti-social' Behaviour in Britain

Colin Clark and Becky Taylor

Introduction

When it comes to defining and theorizing 'anti-social' behaviour in relation to Gypsies and Travellers in Britain, there is no shortage of historical and contemporary sources.[1] Today, in the Houses of Parliament and on the front pages of tabloid newspapers, in small town council meetings or live talk-show radio programmes, everyone seems to have a view to share on the 'problems' caused by Gypsies and Travellers and their 'anti-social' behaviours. Wherever and whenever a new Gypsy site is in development or a roadside encampment appears on the outskirts of town, a well-worn accusatory list of 'anti-social behaviours' – litter, tax avoidance, noise, crime, welfare fraud, illiteracy and truancy – is circulated and signed (Clark and Cemlyn, 2005; Clark and Greenfields, 2006). It is accurate to state that the vast majority of views are overwhelmingly negative when it comes to public discourses about Gypsies and Travellers (Powell, 2007; Richardson, 2006). Behind statements of their inherent asociality, lies a deep suspicion about their (presumed) mobility, with their marginalization regarded as a 'natural' consequence of their nomadism and perceived lack of 'attachment' to 'fixed' local geographies (Shubin and Swanson, 2010).

Consequently, this chapter examines and challenges perceived notions of anti-social behaviour among Gypsy and Traveller populations within a wider context of urbanization, settlement and social change in Victorian and contemporary Britain. Consistently, government policies have sought to draw links between Gypsies and Travellers and anti-social behaviour, especially those communities with a more nomadic way of life. For example, in 2010 the Department for Communities and Local Government (DCLG) issued guidance that applied pressure on local authorities to deal with issues such as 'fly-tipping, noise, straying livestock and untaxed vehicles' (Irvine, 2010). Despite containing the caveat that 'only a small minority of Gypsies and Travellers behave anti-socially' (DCLG, 2010: 5), the guidance went on to say, in the same sentence, that 'the *mobile nature* of some in this community can present particular challenges in dealing with problems' (authors' emphasis).

In Britain today, Gypsy and Traveller populations are regarded as having no legitimate 'place' in society, with their presence automatically signalling the arrival of anti-social behaviour. So, is the conclusion to be drawn that to be nomadic is to be anti-social? It is this fundamental question we address in the chapter: to trace the development from the nineteenth century of the association of anti-social behaviour with Gypsies and Travellers, and their status as modern-day 'folk devils' (Kabachnik and Ryder, 2013). This allows us to get behind normative assumptions over the innate nature of their presumed asociality, and instead show how such attitudes emerged as a result of the confluence of particular socio-economic trends and cultural understandings from the mid-nineteenth century, which by the end of the twentieth century had become firmly entrenched.

What is 'anti-social' about behaviour?

Anti-social behaviour is both subjective and felt, both public and personal. It is also taken to be both a problem in itself, and dangerous because of the fear that, if allowed to take hold in certain environments, it will lead to more 'serious' criminal behaviour emerging (Kelling and Wilson, 1982; DCLG, 2010). However, what is considered 'anti-social' by one person or group may very well be deemed to be 'sociable' by another individual or group. While typically expressed in normative terms, in fact dominant understandings of 'anti-social behaviour' are profoundly influenced by historical and social context, place and time, community tolerance and quality of life expectations (Nixon *et al.*, 2003).

It is worth briefly reflecting on Stanley Cohen's classic study, *Folks Devils and Moral Panics* (1972). In this seminal text he argued that a 'panic' occurs when there is an identifiable 'threat', whether real or perceived, and whether arising via a group or an episode, to established societal norms, interests and (usually conservative) values. Such 'panics' occur when a localized or national 'concern' emerges that identifies a group as being detrimental to the 'good' of a society. Often this concern is demonstrated and vocalized in overtly hostile and confrontational ways, through illustrating that 'they' are not like 'us' (Thompson, 1998). This is often perpetuated and legitimized at all levels of society: politicians, local councillors, the press and other agencies can all act to reinforce, condone and legitimize the vilification of 'folk devils.' Once a consensus is reached, whereby the majority of the population agree that members of a certain identifiable group are 'folk devils' who pose a

168 Anti-social Behaviour in Britain

'threat' to society then action, in the form of draconian policies, legislation, practices, occurs to dampen the 'threat'. More often than not, the weight and consequences of the action are disproportionate to the perceived 'threat' (Goode and Ben-Yehuda, 1994). In such a context, the aim is not to tackle any underlying material issues that may have caused the initial situation, such as youth unemployment, but rather to radically reinforce established societal norms.

Although Cohen's example was focused around youth culture and the media (the 'Mods and the Rockers' of the 1960s on the south coast of England), his theoretical framework can usefully analyse the position of Gypsies and Travellers in Britain. They habitually face extreme scorn and contempt, while often doing little more than trying to find a place to stay, engage in self-employment practices, such as recycling work, tarmacking or landscape gardening, and raise their children. By turning now to the Victorian period, we can see how Gypsies and Travellers' 'folk devil' status, while always present, started to become increasingly associated with particular 'anti-social activities' relating to public health and particular behaviours.

Gypsies and Travellers in Victorian Britain

From around the sixteenth century, the British state demonstrated its disquiet with both vagrancy and nomadism through enacting legislation against 'sturdy beggars' and 'counterfeit Egyptians' (Beier, 1986). Part of a broader project against the so-called 'idle poor', it was also shot through with a profound mistrust of nomadism *per se*, with nomads being seen as intrinsically untrustworthy and challenging of established hierarchies:

> nomads were seen as offering the worst face of an unacceptable society with their lawlessness, heathenism, promiscuity and barbarism [...] what is more this section of the population presented the amoral face of an uncivilised society, lacking any religion, ignoring acceptable codes of decency and engaging in all forms of promiscuous behaviour. (Mayall, 2004: 60)

Such attitudes may have deep roots, but this does not mean they have been entirely historically static. The Industrial Revolution and the consequent rapid urbanization of Britain in the nineteenth century profoundly altered not only the economy, but also the nation's geography and how it was understood. By 1851, over half of Britons lived in towns and cities, a phenomenon which not only created chaotic and sprawling urban spaces, but also led to the countryside becoming the repository for ideas of a stable and idyllic rural past (Mayall, 2004).

Within this context of urbanization and social change, 'Gypsies' became entangled with both the search for the meaning of landscape in the nation's psyche, and legislative attempts to regulate the physical problems engendered by such rapid urban change (Taylor, 2011; 2014). Motivated as much by preoccupations of the society which was about to be lost, as a desire to understand the lives of Gypsies, a movement of amateur 'gentlemen scholars', self-styled gypsiologists emerged. Artists such as Augustus John, and leading writers like Francis Hindes Groome (1881) developed an interest in recording the origins, language and customs of Britain's Gypsies and Travellers.

Gypsiologists were much less concerned with recording the realities of day-to-day lives of their subjects in late Victorian Britain, than with Gypsies' ancestry and with developing theories which tied 'pure' blood lines to 'uncorrupted' Romani language use and 'proper' nomadic living. They defined Britain's 'true' Gypsy population as fluent Romani speakers living, still (but precariously) untouched on commons or byways in their bow-topped caravan, grazing horses, making and selling traditional crafts. At the same time, gypsiologists lamented the disappearance of the 'real pure-blooded' Gypsies under the pressures of urbanization and modernity: for them the often squalid urban encampments found in towns and cities could not be populated by 'true Gypsies', but rather by various half-bred 'didikais', or mumpers (vagrants perceived as having little or no 'Gypsy blood') whom they viewed with scorn and contempt:

> the Romany notwithstanding his boasted superiority to the peg-peddling 'mumpers' has degenerated, and likes to spend the winter months in the neighbourhood of a town [...]. The real country – the unfrequented by-roads, the fields, the out-of-the-way hamlets – suits him well enough in summer, for then he can occupy himself after his own mysterious fashion. (Brotherton Special Collection, Leeds, DUR Cuttings, Volume 1, 65: 'KM', 'A Romany Chal', 9 August 1907)

Such 'degeneration' was viewed by gypsiologists as the beginning of the end for their desired 'true Romanies'. Given the paucity of engagement with, or solid research into, Gypsy and Traveller communities until the 1960s, the writings of gypsiologists were to have a disproportionate effect on both popular and official understandings of their culture.

There was one other source of writings on Gypsies in Victorian Britain: this period saw a growing band of reformers, educationalists and local authority officials who were offended by Gypsies' continued existence in a modern and civilized nation. Writings of this period cast them as an anachronistic and unwelcome presence in a Britain which increasingly set store by its housing, welfare and sanitary legislation:

> Gipsy idleness, gipsy frauds, gipsy cruelty, gipsy filth, gipsy lies, gipsy thefts, gipsy cheating, gipsy fornication, gipsy adultery, are looked down upon by all enlightened Englishmen and Christians [...]. And he who

encourages they gipsies in this wrong doing is an enemy to the State, an enemy to God, an enemy to Christianity, and an enemy to himself. (Smith, 1882: 209)

Added to this were commonly expressed sentiments that not only were Gypsies and Travellers escaping the controls and taxes which were becoming a fact of modern life, but that they also threatened emerging norms of public respectability and private property – this was another clear strand to Gypsy and Traveller associations with anti-social behaviour. Although such sentiments were initially most pronounced in the Home Counties (Taylor, 2008), they were by no means confined to the more overcrowded parts of England, as revealed by the following incident in the small Scottish settlement of Kincraig, in the Scottish Cairngorms.

In the summer of 1883, a local shopkeeper, Mr Grant, deciding how it was 'very gratifying and profitable that the villas at Kincraig are highly held in the estimation of visitors', bought land and built a villa in order to rent it to summer visitors to supplement his income. Meeting with early success, he rented out two villas in the village for the summer season to a Dr Little from India and Sir Auchland and Lady Dunbar. Knowing that the village was visited every year by Scots Travellers, and anxious that 'the purity of the air by all means ought to be preserved', he fenced off their old camping ground, which could subsequently only be accessed through a locked gate. However, the Travellers, on arrival gained entry to their old grounds, and proceeded to stay there, as usual, for the remainder of the summer. Their presence triggered a bout of correspondence between Grant and the local laird: while he positioned the 'wretched Tinkers' as 'prowling thieves' (without offering any evidence to support this), the main focus of his ire was the 'dirty effluvia of the Tinker Camp and its Surroundings' (National Archives of Scotland, Edinburgh GD176/2629 and /2631, letters from Donald Grant to Alan MacDonald, 20 Jun & 10 Aug 1883). It was their presence, different use of space and how this conflicted with his image of Kincraig as an ideal spot for genteel visitors, which was the main issue at stake. Although a small incident in itself, it can be seen as both emblematic of the growing influence of 'respectable' householders and their concern for property and appearance, as well as a foretaste of the century to come.

Attempts to pass versions of Moveable Dwellings Bills, which sought to regulate the sanitary aspects of living vehicles and tents, as well as requiring Gypsies and Travellers to be registered, were efforts to control or harass nomadic families out of local areas. Likewise, sanitary sections of the Housing of the Working Classes Act 1885 and a host of local bye-laws were used in a similar fashion: as means to control rather than improve the day-to-day lives of Gypsies and Travellers. Indeed, the Chief Constable of Berkshire in his evidence to the 1906 Committee on Vagrancy, made the repressive nature of the legislation explicit when he stated that 'we are running them out very fast by means of the sanitary conditions which are being imposed upon them [...] at Ascot we have nearly run them out altogether' (Report of the Departmental Committee on Vagrancy, 1906: 4818–22).

Here we need to pay attention to the classed nature of reactions to Gypsy and Traveller populations; something present throughout the period under investigation. Although gypsiologists might have depicted Gypsies as separate from the humdrum of modern life; and while reformers, landowners and the aspirant classes focused on their deviancy from the norm, the reality of Gypsy and Traveller lives were that they were intimately bound up with the settled community, and particularly the working classes. Arthur Harding's classic account of the East End of London underworld at the beginning of the twentieth century revealed in passing how Gypsies and Travellers were part of the everyday fabric of poor urban life (Samuel, 1981). Gypsies lived in peri-urban encampments or even cheap lodging in cities over winter alongside working-class populations, making and hawking goods, moving in regular circuits across the countryside in the spring and summer, picking up seasonal work, hawking and attending fairs:

> The annual round of farm work began in late spring with hop training and throughout the summer and autumn Gypsy Travellers moved from farm to farm as each crop needed harvesting. Cherries, strawberries, blackcurrants during high summer as well as peas, beans and other vegetables were needed to be quickly gathered in as they ripened. The hops were ready in September followed by apples and pears in the autumn and potato picking up in early winter [...] Places like Yalding Lees or Hothfield Common near Ashford were traditional stopping places where Gypsy families might stop for a day or two before moving on. During the winter months most local Travellers would find a place to stop on the edge of the larger towns or the urban fringes of south east London where there were large traditional stopping places that had been used by Travellers for generations. (BBC, 2005).

Far from being 'a separate people', their economic survival in fact depended on close interaction with the wider population (Clark, 2002; Okely, 1983). More than this, their lifestyles, if nomadic, were not so far from those of the poorer working classes: both had common experiences of overcrowded, often damp accommodation with no running water and inadequate heating, and were governed by the capriciousness of landlords; levels of literacy were still low and experiences of education by and large alienating; and work was often temporary, seasonal with household livelihoods a precarious 'economy of makeshifts'. Consequently, while the rhetoric of 'Gypsy deviance' (or antisocial behaviour in today's parlance) existed, and was being perpetuated and reinforced by Victorian elites, writers and reformers, it was competing with an everyday lived experience which suggested otherwise.

The build up to 1994

Moving forward a hundred years, to the late twentieth and early twenty-first centuries, it is clear that the trends which emerged in the late Victorian period – the idea of the 'pure-blooded' Gypsy *vs* the deviant 'didikai'; the growing importance of regulation and ideas of social and environmental conformity – have become firmly entrenched in British society. For its Gypsy and Traveller populations, this has been little short of catastrophic. Put briefly, Gypsies and Travellers in the postwar period modernized alongside the rest of society, but crucially the changes in their life-style removed what settled society understood as the markers of 'true' Gypsies (living in bow-topped caravans, speaking 'pure' Romani, etc.). These iconic images increasingly became the rod with which their backs were consistently beaten: failing to conform to romantic expectations, the stereotypes most often deployed within settled society were the negative ones relating to anti-social behaviour and a failure to conform to the standards of 'normal' society (Morris, 1999). In popular understanding 'real' Gypsies lived in bow-topped caravans, travelled the countryside, and were socially acceptable; 'dids', 'pikies', 'travellers' living in modern trailers, who dealt in scrap metal, thievery and are a violent threat to society, are beyond the pale. Such fanciful distinctions, as Thomas Acton (1974) has consistently argued, have been used as much by government as the communities themselves. Officials have consistently argued that services and policy provision must only be made for the 'real' Gypsies, while for Gypsies and Travellers themselves it allows for the creation of internalized hierarchies and creative 'victim-blaming': it is always the 'fake' Travellers on the roadside encampments that are causing the noise, litter and crime, and never the 'genuine' ethnic Romanies on the established private or local authority sites (Clark and Greenfields, 2006).

The inuring of these attitudes has its roots in the material changes of British society after 1945. The new planning system produced local development plans with no space for caravan pitches, while spawning the massive postwar house-building programme, which progressively encroached on many of the long-established peri-urban Gypsy and Traveller camps. This vastly reduced the number of traditional camping grounds, and provoked a crisis of stopping places for mobile Gypsies and Travellers, which was only partly solved by the Caravan Sites Act 1968. This required local authorities to provide sites for the Gypsies and Travellers living in, or habitually using, their districts but did not provide a timescale in which this should happen. While these official sites helped ease matters, they were primarily built in marginal, non-residential areas, such as beside motorways, municipal tips or power stations. Such unattractive locations were both a reflection of, and reinforced, settled society's idea of Gypsies and Travellers as 'outsiders' in urban society (Sibley, 1981).

On top of difficulties with stopping places, patterns of work changed too, and in ways that increased the potential for friction with the settled community. A move towards scrap dealing and trade in higher value items diminished women's economic roles, just at the time when they were expanding in other communities (Okely, 1983). Crucially, it also shifted daily door-to-door and face-to-face interactions to more valuable, but less frequent economic transactions. This simultaneously reduced everyday contact between Gypsies and Travellers and majority society, as well as necessitating the storage of scrap and other materials for trade, which were seen by settled communities as unsightly 'rubbish'. When added to the overall lack of stopping places, this resulted in Gypsies and Travellers spending more time in one place, thus increasingly their visibility and heightening the potential for conflict.

A widening gap between their style of living and mainstream society, a reduction in everyday, economic and unproblematic interactions and their growing physical isolation on ghettoized official sites, all reinforced a sense of alienation. In popular imagination, Travellers became 'delinquent predators' on settled communities, bringing criminality, tax evasion, welfare fraud, rubbish and anti-social behaviour, with their presence to be resisted at any price – within this their nomadism has become a perpetual focus for scorn and blame (McVeigh, 1997). Indeed, although the Caravan Sites Act 1968 was welcomed by Gypsies and Travellers in England and Wales as a means for them to be able to continue a nomadic way of life in increasingly difficult circumstances, in fact the authorities had largely only accepted its measures because it was presented as a means towards Travellers' assimilation into settled society: local authorities who provided sufficient pitches could 'designate' the rest of their area as 'caravan-free', while the existence of official pitches served to further delegitimize those who were forced – through the national and local shortage of pitches – to resort to unofficial stopping places.

1994 and the end of the road?

It is in this context that we can place the passing of the Criminal Justice and Public Order Act 1994 by the then Conservative government led by John Major. Although framed to 'deal with' so-called 'New Age' Travellers and the free festival culture, the Act identified all nomadic populations as 'folk devils' at odds with the Conservative values of the day, as well as transgressing the 'spatial order' of the English 'ruryl idyll' countryside (Clark, 1997; Halfacree, 1996). Clear lines were drawn to enforce 'trespass' in the countryside as a criminal, not civil, offence and crucially that the duty on local authorities to provide Gypsy sites in their areas was removed (James, 2007). In its place was the stated aim of requiring Gypsies and Travellers to take responsibility for buying and developing their own land, with the then Conservative government asserting that the planning system was 'perfectly capable' of facilitating adequate site provision (Home, 2006).

Those opposing the legislation argued that leaving the local planning system to determine individual site applications would make the vicious cycle of unauthorized stopping and increasingly violent evictions worse. Indeed this proved to be the case: local authorities, many of whom had already proved reluctant to build under the Caravan Sites Act 1968, were now expected to decide individual planning applications in the face of intense community hostility. Work by Robert Home (2006) shows that on average, 90 per cent of Gypsy and Traveller applications were rejected at first presentation and a rapidly growing number faced eviction from their own land for breach of planning regulations; so by 2006 there were around 1,200 such sites subject to council enforcement action. In addition, most local authorities stopped building new sites and many allowed existing ones to fall into disrepair, with a net loss of 596 pitches in the seven years after 1995, out of a total of 3,271 (Home, 2006: 87). Such insecurity fed into all areas of Gypsy and Travellers' lives: by the beginning of the new century their life expectancy was on average ten years lower than the majority population, and that the most comprehensive health research carried out with the communities showed that insecure accommodation was consistently and intimately tied up with their poor health status (Cleemput and Parry, 2001; Parry *et al.*, 2004). Indeed, as Ruth Lister (2006) has forcefully argued, Gypsies and Travellers occupy a 'second class citizenship status' in contemporary Britain.

Yet, while *we* would emphasize the importance of understanding the marginalized position of Gypsies and Travellers in contemporary British society within the context of the very real material constraints, the way it was articulated by many politicians and the press was almost exclusively via a discourse of anti-social behaviour. Despite the massive constraints and difficulties the majority face in securing pitches, it is the perennial and contested issues of their mobility and accommodation 'preferences' which remain the focus for blame. Since their inception in the late 1960s, official sites have become loci of hate campaigns, while the arrival of a group of Gypsies and Travellers on an unofficial stopping place is sufficient to generate instant hysteria among the local settled population:

> things are getting worse. Even getting a bit of land is difficult. We go round in a convoy and sometimes we get ten to fifteen of us on the bit of land and the police come and stop the rest of us getting on [...]. Sometimes they dig a trench all round with JCB diggers and say we can't get off unless we take our caravans with us. Well we're trapped then. Can't take out cars to get food even and we can't get out to get to work [...] there was one morning at six o'clock when they had warrants to search for firearms and we were all out of the trailers standing in a row while

they searched [...]. Sometimes people are ill: one time they hitched up a trailer and the midwife looked out and said that a baby was going to be born [...]. The local people we don't see directly but a few have waved sticks at us when we try to get onto a piece of land but [...] [the] worst is what the papers say about us. People panic automatically when we first arrive and too much is written in the papers to frighten people against us. (DOE, 1982: Appendix 3, Gypsy Traveller witness)

Note here the speaker's reference to what is 'written in the papers': since the 1960s, the falling-off in everyday face-to-face encounters between settled society and Gypsies and Travellers meant that the press was increasingly acting as 'key informant' for most of settled society's opinions of Gypsy and Traveller communities and has become paramount. Indeed, a 2004 MORI poll conducted for Stonewall of British attitudes towards Gypsies/Travellers, refugees/asylum seekers, 'ethnic minorities' and gay or lesbian people found that Gypsies and Travellers were the group respondents were most likely to feel 'less positive towards' (35 per cent) (Valentine and McDonald, 2004). Crucially, the 'two groups identified as the most threatening, asylum seekers [34 per cent] and Travellers, were the only two groups with whom most interviewees had had no contact'. The media was for many respondents the source of their knowledge and opinions. Forty-three per cent said television influenced their views of refugees and asylum seekers and 40 per cent cited newspapers (Valentine and McDonald, 2004: 17–18).

Coverage of sites has created, arguably, the worst excesses of racism in Parliament and the British national print and broadcasting press (Turner, 2002; Halfacree, 2006; Holloway, 2005), with *The Sun's* 'Stamp on the Camps' campaign (2005) creating a furore both inside and outside Parliament. The campaign was prompted by a then draft Labour government circular which was depicted as evidence that the government (and John Prescott in particular, as Deputy Prime Minister) was 'going soft' on Gypsies and Travellers and giving them 'special treatment' to create 'eyesores' in the countryside (Barkham, 2005). Seemingly, the automatic equation in the minds of the public of the presence of Gypsies and Travellers with anti-social behaviour was revealed in an ICM poll for the *Sunday Express* ('Cut council tax bill if Gypsies can live near our houses', *Sunday Express*, 23 January 2005: 50). It suggested that almost three-quarters of 'householders' believed they should pay lower council tax if Gypsies 'set up camp' nearby and that they should get a reduction to compensate for any slump in their house prices caused by 'gypsy blight'. More than a third were 'incensed' at current government policy and law enforcement, believing 'gypsies have more rights than others to set up home wherever they choose'; while 63 per cent said 'Labour's stance on gypsies' was 'lacking in common sense' and 'ruled by political correctness and fear of accusations of racism'.

Indeed, the common perception during the 13 years of 'New Labour' rule (1997–2010) was that the government considered the accommodation and welfare needs of Gypsies and Travellers on local authority, private and roadside sites before the needs of 'settled' residents living in houses. This inaccurate perception is one reason for the current Conservative–Liberal Democrat Coalition government's 'tough' stance on Gypsies and Travellers since coming to power in May 2010: a stance that aims to remove perceived 'special favours' in planning regulations from Gypsies and Travellers applying to develop a private site. According to Ryder *et al.* (2012: 1), the Coalition's approach to Gypsies and Travellers is 'hierarchical, does not engage with or adequately promote community groups and opposes forms of positive action; as a consequence of localism it is reluctant to endorse central government interventions' (Ryder *et al.*, 2012: 1). Indeed, although the Anti-Social Behaviour, Crime and Policing Act 2014 does not specifically mention Gypsies and Travellers in its content, the far-reaching definition of what constitutes 'nuisance and annoyance' could clearly be employed with regard to roadside encampments and private site developments. A further clue as to future Coalition plans in this area was signalled in a recent debate at Westminster Hall (4 February 2014), where Conservative Andrew Selous' debate on Gypsy and Traveller planning policy included discussion on changing the current legal definition of those he termed 'travellers'. Selous and other contributors to the debate deployed an argument which would have found favour with Victorian gypsiologists, arguing that only those Gypsies and Travellers who are 'genuinely' nomadic should be classified as Gypsies and Travellers (HC 4 February 2014, Vol 575, Col 1WH).

Alongside debates in Parliament, we have also witnessed the appearance of Gypsies and Travellers into the realm of reality television. This has brought aspects of Gypsy and Traveller life under the spotlight. Recent research has revealed the 'class pantomime' element of programmes such as *'My Big Fat Gypsy Wedding'*, allow the parading for entertainment and media comment the social inadequacies and limited cultural capital of individuals, shorn of the socio-economic context which helps to generate such behaviours (Skeggs and Wood, 2012; Tremlett, 2013). For Gypsy and Traveller communities, this trend was writ large through the aforementioned Channel 4 programme *'My Big Fat Gypsy Wedding'* and its various offshoots (2010–14), which purported to examine the social, economic and political worlds of English Romani Gypsies and Irish Traveller communities in Britain. This invasive programme in actual fact illustrated the dual position that Gypsy and Traveller communities occupy in the British psyche; placed in a kind of social and moral 'other world' that appears to be defined and positioned as inherently anti-social ('anti-British', in fact) in the extreme. From the beginning, the programmes were controversial; especially in terms of the way they portrayed the individuals and families in the programmes. Jake

Bowers, a Romani journalist, suggested that the series 'has as much to do with Gypsy people as Borat had to do with Kazakhstan' (Bowers, 2011). Yet the show had mixed responses; some viewers praised the focus on strict morals within the communities, as well as detailing some of the hardships endured in contemporary Britain. However, other viewers complained to Ofcom and argued that the series exploited individuals and families as well as deliberately misrepresented aspects of Gypsy and Traveller life and culture (McIntyre, 2012).

Indeed, in their submission to the Leveson Inquiry, the Irish Traveller Movement in Britain (ITMB) (April, 2012) argued that in much of the print and broadcast reporting across the different types of media outlets in Britain there is a 'guilt by association' (or ethnicity) factor at play: they note a consistency and a pattern to the way in which there are direct links made between Traveller or Gypsy ethnicity, nomadism, crime and anti-social behaviour. Sometimes, they argue, there is mention of an 'ethnic trait' or 'cultural' reasons as to why the 'community' is tied to anti-social behaviours – the behaviour, such as a violent disposition, is 'ingrained'. Indeed, one of the examples the ITMB highlights is from the Channel 4 TV documentary *Gypsy Blood* (directed by Leo Maguire and first broadcast in 2012) where a journalist, Sam Wollaston (2012), offering a review for *The Guardian* suggests that 'Gypsies and Travellers have settled disagreements with their bare knuckles forever and they continue to do so. And to teach their sons how to [...] I'm not sure they've got much choice really. It's going to be ingrained' (ITMB, 2012: 6–7). As the ITMB stated in their submission to Leveson, this kind of negative and prejudicial reporting of the community can become a self-fulfilling prophecy whereby racialized stereotypes ('the Irish are violent', especially Travellers) are merely confirmed and reaffirmed.

Conclusion

This chapter has been an attempt to locate the (perceived) anti-social behaviour of Gypsies and Travellers within a wider context of mainstream society and social change. It has been argued that reified depictions and social constructions of 'folk devils', such as Gypsies and Travellers, carry strong historical continuities and moments. Emerging concerns in the Victorian period around modernity, the loss of the countryside, ideas of respectability and reform, as well as a need to control the untrammelled expansion of the city led to both charting the culture of 'true' Gypsies before their culture 'disappeared', and regulating the dirty, half-bred 'didikais' of urban encampments. This period also saw the beginning of local government and officials targeting the perceived behaviour of Gypsies and Travellers through sanitary and bye-law measures, which although apparently intended to reform their lives in fact were used to harass them out of a locality.

By the end of the twentieth century, while there was a theoretical acceptance that 'real' Gypsies still existed, in fact policy and public opinion were motivated by the belief that it was only the socially inadequate or 'barbaric' who remained nomadic (McVeigh, 1997). A combination of postwar developments led to the disappearance of stopping places at the same time as Gypsies and Travellers became physically more separate from largely working-class, settled communities. This same period saw a rise in home ownership and consequent preoccupation with notions of house value alongside increasingly precarious employment practices and rapid social change. Taken together, there is little surprise that these coalesced into a particularly toxic formulation of Gypsies and Travellers as modern 'folk devils', often reviled when attempting to find a stopping place and misrepresented in 'reality' television programmes. Contributions from political representatives and local counsellors, as well as the wider media, were often unhelpful. The real sense of continuity and parallels, in terms of the types of legislation enacted in Victorian and more contemporary periods, is both familiar and striking.

Undoubtedly, many more newspaper articles will be published discussing the 'harassment, alarm and distress' allegedly caused by the 'anti-social' settlement of Gypsy and Traveller sites and roadside encampments. Similarly, politicians and local councillors, such as David Blunkett MP, will continue to speak publically of the 'problems' associated with where to locate new Gypsy sites. Indeed, opposing the development of a new site in his own constituency, Blunkett warned that 'a tinderbox of tensions' would be created if the site went ahead (*Sheffield Star*, 2010). Such thinking is planted deep in sedentarist cultures of settlement with legislative frameworks, changing attitudes, as well as laws and policies, sustaining an ongoing tussle. And yet, understanding this dynamic perhaps presents a step towards breaking out of a deadlock created by an obsessive 'anti-social' rhetoric that is both persistent and negative.

Note

1. We appreciate that there are many contested definitions of Gypsy and Traveller populations; definitions employed in the literature, as well as those used within the diverse communities themselves. In this chapter, we mainly discuss Gypsies of English and Welsh descent who have Romani ancestry. We also discuss Irish and Scottish Travellers who are nomadic ethnic groups with their own identity, culture, language and history. What is important here is that all the above groups are recognized in law as being minority ethnic groups, protected by Race Relations and Equalities legislation (Equalities Act 2010). For a much wider discussion of such definitional matters, refer to chapter 1 of the text by Clark and Greenfields, 2006.

15
The Complexities, Contradictions and Consequences of Being 'Anti-social' in Northern Ireland

Sinéad Gormally

Introduction

Anti-social behaviour as a concept has numerous complexities. The definitional slippages and lack of clarity often lead to a range of contextually specific consequences. Although Northern Ireland is in the process of working through and moving away from its violent past, there are times where informal justice responses are still used. The most extreme consequence of being deemed as behaving in an anti-social manner in this context is being physically attacked by a paramilitary grouping.[1] This complex phenomenon will be questioned and analysed within this chapter.

To begin, a brief exploration of the anti-social behaviour policy context in Northern Ireland from 2006 to 2013 will be discussed. The chapter analyses how community activists from Protestant, Unionist, Loyalist (PUL) and Catholic, Nationalist, Republican (CNR) communities view and define anti-social behaviour and asks why, at times, these behaviours are deemed anti-social yet at other times are not. This is followed by an exploration as to the extent of punishment attacks still taking place in Northern Ireland; there is then a discussion around the perceived ineffectiveness of the formal justice system and the impact this has on resorting to informal means of justice to deal with anti-social behaviour. The chapter also investigates the relations between the community and paramilitaries, and analyses why some paramilitary groupings at times justify the use of punishment attacks. It concludes with examples of community restorative justice projects, which not only work with those under threat, but have provided an alternative to violence for both the paramilitaries and the broader community.

Policy and legislation about anti-social behaviour

Anti-social behaviour (ASB) has become a normalized term and a concept that is often used as a catch-all descriptor with few parameters or clear definitional elements. In formal justice systems the practicality of assessing what is deemed anti-social lies with the criminal justice system in arbitrating the implementation of law. The Police Service of Northern Ireland (PSNI) publishes a monthly update on the number of incidences of anti-social behaviour recorded in Northern Ireland. In 2007–8, the year after the category was first introduced, there were 97,548 incidents reported and classed as anti-social. In 2011–12, this dropped to 64,184, raising the question of whether anti-social behaviour policies and policing are 'working', or whether categorization and classification has altered over the years. For example, prior to the 2011–12 data the incident type 'Hoax Calls to Emergency Services' was counted as anti-social behaviour. However, in the new collated data this is not included, thus suggesting a change of categorization rather than a change in the public's behaviours.

Following the Westminster government's introduction of legislation, the Anti-Social Behaviour (Northern Ireland) Order 2004 was created. Anti-social behaviour is now a normalized concept, couched in standardized rhetoric, making it indefinable owing to its diversity of application. Despite this, the legislation derived from the anti-social behaviour agenda can criminalize people for a range of diverse behaviours. The same informal 'criminalization' process can happen within communities in Northern Ireland. The punitive policies demanded by some from the formal justice system are mirrored by the punitive demands made by some community members for informal justice in the Northern Irish context.

Defining anti-social behaviour in the Northern Irish context

Anti-social behaviours are not new in Northern Ireland any more than the rest of the United Kingdom, but the years of the violent conflict resulted in a plethora of informal ways of dealing with these behaviours. Informal interviews have taken place with four community restorative justice focused groups: a community group who work in a traditionally Loyalist community aligned with the Ulster Defence Association (UDA); Community Restorative Justice Ireland (CRJI) which is a Nationalist group traditionally aligned with mainstream Republicanism; Alternatives is a community restorative justice programme that began working with the Loyalist Ulster Volunteer Force (UVF); and the fourth group is a non-mainstream Republican grouping made up of community workers and people with non-mainstream political views. Three of the groups assert the principles of non-violence and condemn any continuing paramilitary attacks, arguing for a restorative justice approach. The non-mainstream Republican grouping also suggest their preference for alternatives to violence, but acknowledge, and at times justify, why informal practices continue to happen against those deemed anti-social. First, it is necessary to articulate the meaning of anti-social behaviour. All interviewees explained that the anti-social behaviour in their communities was varied: one group mentioned activities such as bike stealing or gang culture akin to that found in English cities. The non-mainstream Republicans suggested anti-social behaviour can be nuisance behaviour or can be more serious in nature, such as assaults, fighting, or any behaviour that is perceived as threatening to the broader community. Alternatives also acknowledged that within the community context, the behaviours deemed to be anti-social were wide ranging and often geographically contextual. For instance, behaviours carried out locally may be considered anti-social, while the same behaviours carried out in the centre of town may be seen as criminal. Interestingly, they also questioned whether maintaining the lack of a clear definition of anti-social behaviour was beneficial for policing purposes, to allow them to ascertain the strength of the punishment depending on the person and context.

The issue of drugs was also discussed as a dominant anti-social act. The PUL community group were encountering issues with young people under the influence of illegal drugs. Young people were carrying weapons, bringing about community concerns that addiction issues may lead to criminal activities in order to raise money to fuel their addictions.

The age of those involved in these behaviours was generally seen as between 14 and 19 years old. In contrast, Community Restorative Justice Ireland suggested that anti-social behaviour was not solely limited to young people. From a neighbourhood perspective, they explained, it could be people coming out of bars, vandalism, partying, drug or drink parties or people with barking dogs. In relation to young people what was viewed as anti-social was:

a lot of it is making noise in the wrong place, it's congregating in large numbers and then what goes along with that is they bring ghetto blasters, there is drink, there is some drugs, there is vandalism and some graffiti, there is back chat if some of the neighbours go out to say will they move on and I suppose in many ways that is where it is at. (CRJI)

It was generally recognized that anti-social behaviour was a generic term for a range of behaviours that are often, but not solely, perceived as relating to young people. All those interviewed noted that anti-social behaviour is created by the environment in which the young people find themselves; be that as a consequence of difficulties in family life, feeling disenfranchised, lacking identity or sense of belonging, feeling let down, or marginalized within society. In a more practical sense, it was noted that young people have very little to do and few opportunities available to them. The non-mainstream Republicans argued that the broader political policies of the Conservative–Liberal Democrat Coalition government that came to power in 2010 were anti-social and having negative impacts on youth services that will further cause localized anti-social behaviours.

The interviewee from Community Restorative Justice Ireland (CRJI) effectively summarized the problem with anti-social behaviour: 'There is a continuum in relation to this stuff and I suppose if we see these things through one lens then we have missed the point. It is a multiplicity of lenses.'

While the terminology can be debated, and notwithstanding an acknowledgement of environmental and political factors, the fact that these behaviours can still create community tensions which can have a range of consequences and contradictions must be explored. The most extreme of these is punishment-style attacks.

Paramilitary attacks against anti-social behaviour

The years of open violent conflict (1968–98) resulted in many local communities across Northern Ireland relying on paramilitary punishment-style attacks to deal with unacceptable behaviours. In many CNR communities, this was a result of the conflation of policing with state security forces;[2] the targeting of the police by paramilitary organizations and the rejection of the formal justice systems as illegitimate and reliant on emergency powers. However, the reliance on paramilitary structures to identify and implement informal means of justice and retribution were often highly controversial, with communities varying in their demands and reactions, as well as their relationship to the paramilitaries that carried out punishment attacks. In PUL communities, there was not the same level of alienation from the state, but paramilitaries still commanded a powerful role in the maintenance of control in their communities. Consequently, as a direct result of the conflict, both Republican and Loyalist paramilitaries engaged in localized 'policing' of their communities, often in response to local demand, administering beatings, banishments and shootings (Mika and McEvoy, 2001). The so-called 'informal or alternative criminal justice system', that has evolved since 1969, constituted a range of punitive measures against individuals 'who violate some community norm, as defined by the paramilitary grouping' (Knox, 2002: 172), or indeed that were presented to the paramilitaries by community residents with the invariable demand that action needed to be taken. Since the Good Friday Agreement (1998), there has been an attempt in some communities to move away from the previous physical force approach by using community restorative justice practices, as will be discussed in greater detail below. Nevertheless, there are still some paramilitary groupings who continue to rely on punishment-style attacks to both establish their position in local areas and to respond to expressed community concerns.

Paramilitary violence (Knox, 2002), punishment attacks (Feenan, 2002), punishment beatings (Winston, 1997) or paramilitary vigilantism (Silke and Taylor, 2000) are contested terms used to describe attacks by paramilitary groupings against people seen as engaging in 'anti-social behaviour' and/or criminal behaviour, as well as a means of disciplining those seen as challenging the organization (Jarman, 2004). Andrew Silke and Max Taylor (2000) question the use of the term punishment to describe paramilitary attacks arguing this implies that the behaviour is defensible or appropriate. The 'punishment' for the deemed behaviours can vary from warnings, threats, curfews, beatings, shootings, exiling and execution (Silke, 1998). A variety of weapons have been used within these attacks including baseball bats spiked with nails, power tools (Knox, 2001), hurley sticks, clubs, batons, bars, hammers (Feenan, 2002) or guns: 'The resulting physical damage ranges from bruising to severe laceration and fracturing of bones. Shootings can be through the soft tissue on the legs, but includes bone shattering in the ankles, knees and wrists' (Feenan, 2002: 154).

The true extent of paramilitary attacks is difficult to ascertain as many go unreported (Knox, 2003); but from 2003 to 2013 there were a total of 1,198 casualties as a result of paramilitary-style attacks, both shootings and assaults according to police statistics (PSNI, 2013: 5). The Policing Boards 7th Human Rights Annual Report (2011: 122) notes the number of young people involved in these attacks:

> Between 1 April 2010 and 30 September 2011, there have been 118 casualties reported to the PSNI of paramilitary-style assaults and shootings: this figure accounts for 71 casualties of assault and 47 casualties of shootings. Of those, 52 (44%) were aged between 16 and 24.

Silke and Taylor (2000) found both Republicans and Loyalists were targeting young people under the age of 20 more than previously, with the majority of victims being young men. The PSNI security statistics for 2012–13, state that although, in general, the security situation in Northern Ireland improved significantly over the previous decade from 2003–4, there were still 63 casualties, known of, due to informal means of justice, 27 paramilitary-style shootings and 36 paramilitary-style assaults, 16 in total fewer than 2011–12. These figures were considerably lower than ten years earlier with 149 paramilitary-style shootings and 149 paramilitary-style attacks in 2003–4. Of these attacks, 26 out of 27 paramilitary-style shootings were carried out by Republican groups and of the 36 assaults, 27 were carried out by Loyalist groups and nine by Republicans (PSNI, 2013: 2, 5).

Rachel Monaghan (2002) divides the activities liable to be punished into 'normal' and 'political' crime. Andrew Silke (1999) similarly divides the behaviours into 'civil crime' and 'political crime'. 'Normal' or 'civil' behaviours identified as a target can also be criminal, such as joy-riding (the stealing of cars illegally and racing them), drug dealing, burglary (Silke and Taylor, 2000), vandalism (Jarman, 2004) or muggings (Silke, 1999). They can also be 'anti-social' such as youths engaging in nuisance behaviour or abuse of senior citizens (Monaghan, 2002). Colin Knox (2001) notes that the victims of these attacks are often identified as a type of person who engages in anti-social behaviour and therefore is a 'deserving' victim.

'Political' crime may 'include informing, misuse of the organization's name, collaborating, or fraternizing with the enemy' (Monaghan, 2002: 441). Similarly, actions which are not deemed as criminal but do not conform to the pre-set community norms have also been targeted (Silke and Taylor, 2000). As Anna Eriksson succinctly states:

> Punishment violence exists for a number of interrelated reasons, but the most commonly cited are the absence of legitimate or adequate policing, rising levels of anti-social behaviour, the perceived failure of the criminal justice system to prevent and effectively deal with crime, and a consequent community pressure to 'do something' about crime and anti-social behaviour in both Republican and Loyalist areas. (Eriksson, 2009: 37)

As will be discussed below, this legitimate or adequate policing is a complex matter given that sections of some communities do not see the Police Service of Northern Ireland as a legitimate source of protection, while others feel the move from quick justice cannot be replaced by the lengthy procedures often encountered with the formal justice system.

Leaving aside the organizational or 'political' (Monaghan, 2002) rationale for paramilitary-style attacks, the focus here is on those attacks against, generally but not solely, young people who have been involved in anti-social behaviour activities. In instances where punishment attacks still take place, they generally only occur after a series of warnings or threats have been issued. It is more likely for repeated acts deemed anti-social to be targeted or where restorative practices have been continuously unsuccessful.

Paramilitaries do not however operate independently from their communities (Feenan, 2002). Tom Winston, a former Loyalist prisoner and community worker, clearly explains this in describing the situation in the Loyalist Greater Shankill area of Belfast:

> these individuals do not represent some group of strangers in the community that rule with an iron fist. Rather, these individuals are someone's brother, father, son. They are local people involved in organisations with long histories and family connections. They exist within a long tradition of defence organisation within the Protestant communities in Northern Ireland. (1997: 122–3)

Because of this interconnectedness, young people can be caught in a difficult position, where particular behaviours are at certain times seen as legitimate and defending their community, while at other times can be classed as anti-social and against their community (Jarman, 2004). As one interviewee noted, 'young people are getting caught in the middle of adult game playing'. These conflicting messages can leave young people in a contradictory position resulting in them feeling further marginalized from their communities.

Perceived ineffectiveness of the formal justice system

A further layer of complexity is that communities can at times be unwilling or simply not accustomed to reporting incidents to the police or waiting for the formal justice procedures to run their course. As such, they can tacitly or explicitly support swift community action against people engaging in behaviours deemed anti-social (Knox, 2002).

In Republican communities, the traditional lack of reliance on formalized policing led to a vacuum resulting in local communities putting pressure on paramilitaries to deal with anti-social and criminal activities (McEvoy and Mika, 2002). In Loyalist areas the Police Service of Northern Ireland may not be welcomed due to levels of community-based illegality, including racketeering, drug dealing, etc. (Knox, 2003). Winston (1997) also found that many people saw 'punishment beatings as a more tangible, visible, and immediate form of retribution' (Winston, 1997: 124). This can result in over-reliance on these informal mechanisms to deal with community problems making the 'quick response' popular (Brewer *et al.*, 1998; McEvoy and Mika, 2002; Winston, 1997).

The non-mainstream Republicans acknowledged that violence is not the sole answer, but also held that the state cannot deal effectively with anti-social behaviours. They suggest there is little community trust in the police exacerbated by the fact that they are seen as ineffective in dealing with social problems. Moreover, they felt that people in their community did not want to go to the police for fear of being stigmatized: 'When cops arrive to the door you are seen as a tout [someone who tells tales to the police].'

When asked who would perpetuate this label, they suggested it would be the normalized community response if an incident was reported to the police. Although certain contradictions in relations to the state were apparent in all communities, CRJI suggested:

> see as soon as a rape happens, the police are phoned, see as soon as a murder happens, the police are phoned, see if someone encounters a burglary, the police are phoned, see if there is a body lying in the street, the police are phoned, see if there is a wee child missing, the police are phoned.

This demonstrates the complexities apparent in the perception of the police as a legitimate source of support and justice in the Northern Ireland context.

Community ambivalence towards punishment attacks

Where police interventions are not seen as an option and community-based restorative justice practices have either not worked or not seemed relevant, some community members may still express an understanding for resorting to violence. A mother of a young man in Derry, alleged to be a drug dealer, told BBC Radio 4's *Woman's Hour* that she allowed her son to be shot by a Republican paramilitary group in order to help deal with his problems. She explained that she turned her back while her son was shot twice and then went to his aid:

> In Northern Ireland this is acceptable, it happens and we have to do this. Now he can get the help with his problem. Beforehand he wasn't going to accept there was anything wrong, he didn't feel that he was doing any harm and he has said that he is going to get help now [...]. My son is there, he is alive, he got off lightly, all it was, was just something that had to be done to try to save him. (BBC, 2012)

This suggests that in Northern Ireland certain behaviours are not accepted and are regarded by some within the community as punishable. Colin Knox (2003) notes that this view of understanding is not uncommon with some attacks carried out by mutual appointment, a fact that clearly exemplifies the complexity of these relations and the multi-faceted contradictions and consequences of dealing with anti-social behaviour.

A non-mainstream Republican interviewee stated that there can often be ambivalence towards paramilitary attacks in communities. People who were against the violence with regard to broader political conflict may be more ambivalent in the case of internal community attacks – 'That's awful what happened last night [...] but he didn't get it for saying his prayers.'

Knox (2003) notes this system cannot only become self-perpetuating and reinforcing, satisfying the community demands for justice, but reinforces the power and control that the paramilitaries have in these areas. However, communities are not homogeneous and not all community members call for these actions. It must also be noted that the power and control reinforced by these actions may augment the fear of community members in turning to formal justice structures.

All interviewees acknowledged the historical reliance and normalization of dealing with behaviours through paramilitary action and the community reliance and expectation of quick responses to problems. CRJI effectively summed up these sentiments:

> What I also think happened looking back on it over all the years, definitely in the republican side is they actually spoiled the community;

they disempowered the community in terms of dealing with anti-social behaviour. You went to the local OC [Officer Commanding] and they say 'such and such are messing me about' he would say 'well what are they doing', 'well they are at the corner and they are messing me about' and he would send somebody round to sort it out and it was sorted out in the sense 'move on' or there would be a threat or whatever. Now they come and they say well you need to report that to the cops, then the cops ask them for a statement and they will want them to go to court and they are not used to any sort of [...] they were always used to someone doing it for them.

If, as CRJI promote, paramilitaries refuse to carry out these actions then a 'quick fix' is no longer an option. However, there can be the paramilitary belief that they have a responsibility to the community which further complicates the reciprocal relations: 'Paramilitary groups see themselves as community protectors; their actions are aimed ostensibly at maintaining "law and order" through tackling petty crime such as car theft, joyriding, burglary and drug dealing' (Knox, 2003: 25).

These intersecting dynamics can essentially create a cyclical relationship where there is a community dependency on informal means to deal with anti-social behaviour and/or criminal behaviours, and where it is somewhat normalized, resulting in the danger (Knox, 2001) that these people, often young people, are seen as legitimate targets.

In the Northern Ireland context, there are extensive layers of complexity concerning anti-social behaviour. There are policy demands to deal with these behaviours, popular demands and support for punitive policies (Pearson, 1983; Cohen, 1972) elaborated by governments, and then in Northern Ireland, there is the added complexity whereby communities and paramilitary groupings make a decision on what is deemed anti-social and independent action can follow. Permission for certain behaviours can shift, with them being regarded as acceptable at certain times and in certain circumstances, whereas at others individuals engaged in such behaviours are chastised, threatened and/or subjected to punishment attacks. Further, there is the added issue that the role and authority of the police service is undermined resulting in a lack of trust, engagement or belief in them as a means of procedural justice. This has resulted in the creation of community-based restorative justice practices in an attempt to engage with these complexities and find solutions that are acceptable to the multi-faceted communities in which they are based.

Community-based restorative justice initiatives

The change in the political landscape, married with internal discussions within the Republican movement, resulted in an exploration of alternatives to these paramilitary punishment practices. Community-based restorative justice practices began to emerge as a means to facilitate paramilitaries to move away from the punishment attacks (McEvoy and Mika, 2002).[3] Despite critics (McGrattan, 2010) of community-based restorative justice, paramilitary attacks were, and are, occurring at a community level and it is at a community level that solutions are utilized (Mika and McEvoy, 2001; Eriksson, 2009). As such, ex-prisoners and those who were involved in the conflict have played a significant role in restorative justice practices within Northern Ireland in an attempt to move away from punishment attacks and more broadly to maintain the peace process.

Two of the most established community restorative justice initiatives are Community Restorative Justice Ireland (CRJI) from the Republican community and Alternatives from the Loyalist community; others are in the early stages of developing these practices. These initiatives are working to prevent paramilitary-style attacks and to find community-based alternatives to violence. They not only work with those under threat, but can negotiate with paramilitaries and provide support for the broader family circle, both during the situation and after it has been resolved.

Alternatives began in 1996 and started by working with people who were referred to the initiative, highlighting the importance of the need for the broader community 'buy-in' to community restorative justice practices. 'Those referred would be individuals who had come to the attention of the community and paramilitary organisations as a result of their involvement in anti-social behaviour' (Winston, 1997: 125). A process of negotiation and mediation would occur and support work would ensue. The central focus of Alternatives is to work with young people who are involved in persistent or serious cases of anti-social behaviour (Eriksson, 2009). They work on community-based disputes and have also set up a proactive engagement with young people in the form of youth work. This is in an attempt to prevent behaviours getting to a stage that they are seen as damaging either by community residents or by the paramilitaries.

In contrast, CRJI had the ability to adopt a wider remit owing to the support from the Republican movement (Mika and McEvoy, 2001). There is a broader 'buy-in' from the community and thus they can deal with a greater range of community issues. This support was not instantaneous and nor was it an easy process. It took the paramilitaries to agree not to engage in the punishment-style attacks as much as the workers to engage with a range of key people and to build up a positive representation through working with individuals. Eriksson explains the importance of the paramilitary support for non-violence:

> Occasionally, people would go to the IRA instead after realising that they would not receive the desired results. However, the IRA generally referred people back to CRJI, saying that they were no longer offering to shoot

or beat people as a result of their involvement in anti-social behaviour. (Eriksson, 2009: 72–3)

This approach not only provided an alternative for community members, but also for the paramilitaries engaged in these activities. CRJI explained that during the transitional period from violence to restorative practices, they had to deal with the changing role of particular members:

> there were people who would have been dealing with those issues within a neighbourhood whose power was removed, whose rationale for being had changed, whose role within life, or role within a struggle or role within a political space had changed.

Both these established initiatives have been involved in the restorative process for many years. For others the process is newer and they are still trying to get people on board with the ideas. As Neil Jarman (2004) warns:

> the political and social leaders of Loyalism and Republicanism have to be patient in convincing their supporters that political and community activity is more effective than violence and may risk being outflanked by more radical groups who may be seen to be more effective in responding to a threat either from within their own community or from the other side. (Jarman, 2004: 433)

Today paramilitary attacks are still occurring, albeit at a lesser rate, and can be seen as effective answering to a community call to engage in swift, violent action against people engaging in anti-social-style behaviours. Of course it must also be questioned whether the continuation of these attacks is being carried out for political or social benefits by those who are not in political dominance.

Community-based restorative justice practices are not going to create a solution overnight, but while there are still paramilitary groupings that are willing to administer paramilitary attacks for anti-social behaviours, then there may be some community members who ask for these practices. Violence against any acts deemed anti-social or not, is not conducive to a more peaceful Northern Ireland and importantly these types of attacks rarely have lasting positive impacts:

> From the physical punishment point of view we are on the wing that says – it doesn't work. Let's understand it didn't work when the Republicans were doing it, what it did do was it gave a sense that something was happening, or someone was doing something or someone was making an effort. (CRJI)

In contrast, community-based restorative justice can take time, takes dedicated workers and takes community 'buy-in' but being grassroots will surely ensure longer-term solutions. These projects are now being inspected and certified by the criminal justice authorities and can deal with cases referred by the police and public prosecution service, meaning they are legitimized and promoted by the formal justice system as well as the community structures. However, as Alternatives explains it can be a difficult process that involves commitment from all involved.

> [I]t works because it is relational; it is about building a holistic, long term, sustained relationship with the young person and their family, it is not an in/out intervention, it is not a one off and that's really important. [...] it is underpinned by cognitive approaches. [...] One young person said to me 'I wish I had just taken the beating' and I said 'why son?', 'because it is so, so much easier than being asked these difficult questions, so much easier than having to reflect on who I am and the choices and the decisions I am making' and that is the reality, this goes beneath the surface.

This demonstrates the need for a relational and sustainable process of engagement both for the victims and those committing punishment-style attacks, in an attempt to move away from the severe and negative consequences for some people engaging in what are deemed as anti-social behaviours.

Conclusion

The chapter has explored the complexities, contradictions and consequences of being anti-social in Northern Ireland. Applying a vague and elastic concept of anti-social behaviour has resulted in punitive policies and punitive responses that criminalize people for, at times, relatively minor incidents in the formal justice system. Similarly, in the informal justice system, in Northern Ireland, the same process of applying an unclear descriptor has resulted in community criminalization and violent punitive responses. Despite the potential usefulness for the formal justice system to criminalize and prosecute, it can also cause contradictions in terms of community-based reactions as to what is deemed anti-social. Young people in particular may be engaging in these behaviours due to difficulties in family life, feeling disenfranchised, lacking identity or sense of belonging, feeling let down or marginalized within society. This is only furthered by the lack of clarity and consequently the level of punishments delivered depending on the wider political or social context at the time. The disengagement from the formal justice system and the perceived ineffectiveness of them to deal with anti-social behaviour, as well as the historical reliance on paramilitary groupings to resort to informal means of justice, only serves to muddy the waters further.

Nevertheless, the continued support for community restorative justice projects that work with those under threat and have provided an alternative to violence for both the paramilitaries and the broader community should be promoted. Although behaviours which are deemed anti-social may still lack clarity and yet continue to be the target of punitive policies, the use of violence to control these various behaviours must be marginalized in order to maintain Northern Ireland's transition to a peaceful society. Furthermore, the highlighted complexities, contradictions and consequences should be drawn upon to question whether the concept of anti-social behaviour should continue to be used in any guise, without clear definitional clarity and without a well-defined statement of purpose.

Notes

1. There are five main paramilitary organizations in Northern Ireland that are currently on ceasefire. These include three Republican groups – The Official IRA, The Provisional IRA and the Irish National Liberation Army. Within Loyalism there are the Ulster Freedom Fighters/Ulster Defence Association, the Ulster Volunteer Force, and Red Hand Commandos. In addition to these there are a number of 'dissident' Republican groups that are not on ceasefire which include the Real IRA, Óglaigh na hÉireann and a range of other groupings, as well as some splinter Loyalist groups.
2. The Police Service of Northern Ireland (PSNI) and the British Army.
3. For a detailed explanation of the history of community based restorative justice in Northern Ireland see Eriksson, 2009 and McEvoy and Mika, 2002.

16
Policing the Margins: Anti-Social Behaviour and the 'Underclass Discourse'

Didier Lassalle

Introduction

The concept of 'underclass' can be traced back to the 'problem family' debates of the 1950s through two related notions: the 'cycle of deprivation', fashionable in the 1960s, and the 'culture of poverty' that attracted much attention in the 1970s (Macnicol, 1999). The aim of this chapter is to clarify the relationship between anti-social behaviour (ASB) and the 'underclass' discourse that developed in Britain in the 1980s, and which has continued to inform political thought and social policies since 1997. First, I outline the rise of anti-social behaviour as a policy concept based on Charles Murray's work and its subsequent use by both the Labour and the Conservative parties in their quest for power. Then, I turn my attention to the main socio-demographic characteristics of the people targeted by this policy. Finally, I examine the scope of the changes introduced by the Conservative–Liberal Democrat Coalition government that came to power in 2010.

Controlling the 'dangerous classes'

The rise of anti-social behaviour as a policy concept dates back to 1992 when the social problem posed by persistent young offenders was first brought to the forefront of British politics. In a bid to turn the tables on the Conservatives, Tony Blair, then Shadow Home Secretary, launched his well-publicized pledge 'tough on crime, tough on the underlying causes of crime' (Blair, 1993: 27–8). He was countered by Conservative John Major's support for new powers to deal with repeating young offenders (Kirbee, 1993). This political one-upmanship took a more dramatic turn after the murder in Liverpool of two-year-old Jamie Bulger by two minors in 1993, following which Major declared that 'society needs to condemn a little more and understand a little less' (Major, 1993). Although Blair had first suggested that the killing had deeper causes in the breakdown of communities (Callinicos, 1996: 16), retribution became the dominant philosophy of both the Conservative Party and the Labour Party, a trend that was considerably strengthened by their fierce political competition on the theme of law and order. The Criminal Justice Act 1993 introduced by the Conservative government reinstated the right of the youth courts to take account of offenders' previous criminal records; then the Criminal Justice and Public Order Act 1994 lowered to ten years the age at which custodial sentences could be passed in cases involving serious crimes.

The regulation of anti-social behaviour was first implemented on council estates where unruly tenants were advised that local authorities had been granted the power to take action against them, which could lead to their eviction in the most serious cases. Probationary tenancies and other assorted measures were also introduced under the Housing Act 1996, which made it explicit that maintaining a tenancy was to become conditional on behaviour (Department of the Environment, 1995: 3). Finally, Major endeavoured to focus attention on certain groups of people, beggars in particular, whose behaviour was deemed unsettling for members of the public and whose mere presence was an 'eyesore' in many cities (Garrett, 2009: 89).

Meanwhile, a more general preoccupation with the advent of an 'underclass' that needed to be kept in check was clearly emerging in some politicians' proposals. In 1993, a few Conservative ministers such as Tom Sackville (Health) and Alistair Burt (Social Security) had launched a campaign against single mothers and the social security system, which they claimed encouraged lone parenthood. Their idea that social housing should be geared primarily towards parents who had tried to create stable relationships before having children was supported by David Blunkett, then Shadow Health Secretary, which suggested that some in the Labour Party had already started to follow the same line (Wynn Davies, 1993). The backlash against single parents (mostly single mothers) had been triggered by Charles Murray's work, in particular, his articles *The Emerging British Underclass* and *Underclass: The Crisis Deepens* commissioned and published by *The Sunday Times*, in 1989 and 1993 respectively. The American political scientist claimed that the rise in illegitimacy encouraged by 'well meaning' (*sic*) government intervention heralded the emergence of a crime-ridden urban underclass in the United Kingdom similar to the one in the United States. Murray's controversial arguments were taken up at face value by right-wing Conservatives (John Redwood, Peter Lilley and David Green) who used them to denounce the culture of dependency generated by the welfare state (the 'nanny state') that led to the creation of a self-excluded 'underclass' unwilling and/or unable to function in the workaday world (Braid, 1993). Moreover, Murray's definition of the 'underclass' gave some credit to the questionable view that poor people who did not conform to prevailing social values should be controlled and disciplined:

> By underclass, I do not mean people who are merely poor, but people at the margins of society, unsocialised and often violent. The chronic criminal is part of the underclass, especially the violent chronic criminal. But so are parents who mean well but who cannot provide for themselves, who give nothing back to the neighbourhood, and whose children are the despair of the teachers who have to deal with them. (Murray, 2001: 2)

Murray's arguments were also taken up, although in a slightly watered-down version, by Labour politicians such as Frank Field (Field, 1989) who specifically targeted very young single mothers and young males. For him, countering the growth in the underclass among single-parent families and the unemployed implied that young lower-class girls should be made to understand within school that having a baby at an early age meant a one-way ticket to the nearest sink council estate. Similarly, young would-be fathers should be made to understand that the state would force them to provide for their offspring. However, Field insisted that there was no 'racial basis' to Britain's underclass that was made up of people who occupied the most vulnerable positions in British society (Field, 1996: 58–61). His views on the underclass and on the best ways to deal with it soon became mainstream New Labour thinking, and tackling these issues was now a top priority for the party.

Jack Straw, then Shadow Home Secretary, set up an agenda for reclaiming the country's streets which, according to him, had been given over to 'squeegee merchants', graffiti artists, beggars, drunks and addicts (Mills, 1995). He also promoted the party's *A Quiet Life* document which detailed proposals to tackle the root of the problem of anti-social criminal activity in neighbourhoods (Straw, 1995a, 1995b). One of Labour's pledges in its 1997 general election manifesto was the introduction of the Community Safety Order (CSO) to fight chronic anti-social behaviour. However, in New Labour discourse it was not poverty *per se* that led to crime, but rather marginalized and dysfunctional families were seen as its main cause. Therefore, 'social exclusion', now deemed to be solely responsible for the emergence of an underclass in the country, was to be carefully monitored and brought under control. Behind the political rhetoric, the party now acknowledged the need for individuals to accept their responsibilities and was clearly treading the same path as its Conservative rival in its response to youth crime and its causes.

Drawing on a communitarian discourse, which emphasized the use of the law to rebuild social cohesion and stability (Etzioni, 1993), Blair introduced his vision of the 'modern civic society' based on 'an ethic of mutual responsibility or duty' in his famous speech at the Aylesbury Estate, on 2 June

1997. He added: 'It is something for something. A society where we play by the rules. You only take out if you put in. That's the bargain' (Blair, 1997). Therefore, the two main features of his new policy designed to bring the 'underclass' back into mainstream society were the fight against all forms of social exclusion and the enforcement of a new code of laws to crack down on crime and other anti-social behaviour. On the one hand, the Social Exclusion Unit (SEU) was set up in 1997 to help the excluded groups identified by the New Labour government: the five million families where no one of working age was employed, the three million people living on the 1,300 worst housing estates in Britain, the unemployed 18- to 24-year-olds, low achievers leaving school without qualifications and the young homeless (Macintyre, 1997). This policy had also the advantage of bringing together those in the Labour Party who favoured a class-based analysis and those who preferred a cultural interpretation of the cause of poverty and deprivation. In the process, the word 'underclass', with its connotations of fecklessness and criminality, vanished from the New Labour government's lexicon. On the other hand, the Crime and Disorder Act 1998 introduced the Anti-Social Behaviour Order (ASBO) whose scope was first expanded by the Police Reform Act 2002 and then by the Anti-social Behaviour Act 2003. The official line on ASBOs was that they were civil orders aimed at stopping problem behaviour in order to protect communities from intimidating activity, not at punishing individuals. Moreover, the Home Office was keen to stress that they were by no means a last-resort measure, but rather just one of a range of tools available (Community Care, 2006).

Anti-social behaviour was a particularly well-suited target for New Labour governments which were anxious to deliver on their law and order election pledges. They felt it endangered their pet policy of 'social inclusion' by corroding community cohesion and undermining their efforts towards social and economic regeneration (Squires, 2008a). From the start, their mainstream anti-social behaviour rhetoric focused on children and teenagers because anti-social behaviour was construed as a dispiriting metaphor for the condition of contemporary Britain, particularly of its underprivileged youth said to have developed an 'underclass culture' (Rodger, 2008: 48–71). Commenting on the rapid rise in the number of ASBOs issued in England and Wales between April 1999 and September 2005, Hazel Blears, Minister of State at the Home Office with responsibilities for policing and crime reduction, declared that she was 'extremely encouraged' by their 'enthusiastic take-up' because it showed that local authorities, the police and the courts did not hesitate to use this tool to 'clamp down on the problem'. However, children's charities, as well as numerous youth workers were much less fervent about the orders, calling them a 'blunt tool' and deploring, as did Martin Narey, formerly of Barnardo's, that the use of ASBOs on children was becoming 'entirely routine' (BBC *News*, 2006). During this period, large amounts of public funds were invested into schemes in the most deprived neighbourhoods. However, endless struggles over budgets and the distrust of the very people it was supposed to help limited the scope of this very ambitious project.

Subsequently the emphasis on trying to control behaviour slowly receded into the background, while the focus was set on the new leading catchword of 'Respect'. The Anti-Social Behaviour Unit (headed by Louise Casey) was renamed the Respect Task Force and the newly appointed Minister for Respect, Hazel Blears launched New Labour's Respect Action Plan in 2006. Although the link between bad behaviour and area deprivation was recognized and promises to tackle causes were made, the main thrust of the policy paper was a concern for the values of the majority and the need to enforce standards of behaviour. Poor parenting was held responsible for children's involvement in anti-social behaviour and the idea put forward was to compel 'problem families' to accept support to change their ways. State-funded parenting classes and Family Intervention Projects (FIPs) for 'challenging and anti-social families' were set up to address this objective (Burney, 2009: 44–9). Presenting his Real Respect Agenda, the new Conservative Party leader, David Cameron, put forward his own plans for social enterprise zones and a national school-leaver programme presented as 'long-term solutions to the causes of social breakdown, not just short-term sanctions and punishment' (Travis, 2006). However, the Conservatives shared New Labour's view that a culture of respect was needed and that coercive methods could be used to implement it.

As soon as Gordon Brown replaced Blair as Labour Prime Minister in 2007, the emphasis was placed on positive outcomes for young people. The Respect Taskforce was closed down, and Casey was moved to a job inside the Cabinet Office looking at community policing, partly because her approach was too evocative of Cameron's 'Broken Britain' rhetoric.[1] A Youth Taskforce was set up instead inside the Department for Children, Schools and Families (DCSF), headed by a civil servant specializing in youth issues, Anne Weinstock (Wintour, 2007). The departmental head, Ed Balls, was clearly in favour of a more balanced approach to youth crime 'emphasizing the causes of crime as well as being tough on crime itself'. He even went as far as to declare that, although ASBOs were sometimes necessary, he would be glad to do without them (Branigan, 2007).

The change of tone had probably something to do with the slew of criticism levelled at the overuse of ASBOs in relation to young people, particularly young lower working-class males living in ghettoized neighbourhoods with high crime rates (White and Cunneen, 2006). This most disadvantaged and structurally vulnerable segment of the British population was also continually reviled in the press and presented as 'yobs', 'chavs', 'no-hopers', and 'hoodies', that needed to be controlled and chastised. According to many researchers, this ideological representation of the young poor and deprived as an irresponsible, 'feral underclass'[2] threatening social order was built, from the beginning, into the very policies designed to fight anti-social behaviour that stressed individual or familial responsibility rather than failing social and economic conditions (Millie, 2009a; Waiton, 2009). David Blunkett's pamphlet published in 2008 showed clearly that the concept of 'underclass' was also taken for granted in New Labour's higher circles when he called for measures to prevent the formation of an 'entrenched underclass' and rebuild social mobility. Finally, the focus on anti-social behaviour linked with the 'tacit acceptance of the development of an underclass' (Blunkett, 2008: 14) was seen as contributing to the maintenance of an 'exclusive society' that the New Labour government had pledged to reform in the wake of Cameron's political attack on Britain's 'broken society' (Cameron, 2007).

Targeting the usual suspects?

In total, 21,749 ASBOs were issued during the period from 1 April 1999 to 31 December 2011. The highest annual number of ASBOs issued was 4,122 in 2005. The steep rise in ASBOs in 2004 and 2005 resulted mainly from the introduction of the criminal ASBO (CRASBO) in the Police Reform Act 2002. Between 2004 and 2011, more ASBOs were issued following convictions for a criminal offence, rather than following an application made by the police or local government authority. In total, 60 per cent of all ASBOs were in fact CRASBOs over the period considered (Ministry of Justice, 2012).

Although ASBOs were never originally intended for children, the Ministry of Justice statistics show that the government had clearly decided otherwise at least until 2005, when they reached their highest number of 1,551. Afterwards, the number of ASBOs issued to young people fell steadily year-on-year down to 375 in 2011. However, between 1 April 1999 and 31 December 2011, the 10–17 age group accounted for between three-fifths and one-third of the total number of ASBOs issued by all courts in England and Wales, with an average of 37.7 per cent, over the period considered. From June 2000 to December 2011, 8,160 ASBOs were issued to young people of this age group, of which 762 (9.3 per cent) were issued to females and 7,398 (90.7 per cent) to males (MJ, 2012). In 2008, when the downward trend had become clear, Home Secretary, Jacqui Smith insisted that it reflected an increased readiness by local authorities, police and magistrates to use Acceptable Behaviour Contracts, Parenting Orders and Individual Support Orders to encourage improved behaviour. By contrast, the Shadow Home Secretary, David Davis claimed that the real reason for the fall in the number of ASBOs was that they were being breached in increasing numbers, which questioned their usefulness in controlling young people's behaviour (Darwar and Wintour, 2008). Furthermore, between 2005 and 2009 the total number of Penalty Notices for Disorder (PNDs), more commonly known as 'on-the-spot fines', given to young people aged 16–17 for being drunk and disorderly, or for causing harassment, alarm or distress was 41,992, an average of 8,398 a year (Ministry of Justice, 2010: Table 2.1). The figure was down to just 2,403 in 2011–12 (YJB, 2013: 19–20). This sharp drop in the number of PNDs issued does not necessarily reflect a change in youth criminal behaviour, but rather the way in which the police run through the use of managerial targets and incentives. For instance, the Offences Brought to Justice Target (OBJT) was replaced in April 2008 and dropped entirely in December 2010 to allow police to use their discretion more. Moreover, Youth Offending Teams and other partners are using alternatives, such as restorative justice disposals and Triage schemes that also have contributed to this fall (YJB, 2013: 18).

Another area of concern has been the number of Individual Support Orders (ISOs) issued in addition to an ASBO. Indeed, from 2004 to 2011, only 11.4 per cent of all ASBOs issued on application (367 out of 3,216) included an Individual Support Order meant to address the underlying causes of the behaviour that brought the juvenile to justice (Ministry of Justice, 2012: Table 5). This has been heavily criticized by children's charities with the argument that imposing a punitive framework on young people without trying to make them understand why their behaviour is inappropriate or helping them to change it is a complete waste of time. Moreover, these charities have also pointed out that ISOs ensured that young people would be less likely to breach their order and end up in prison and that it also allowed changes in individuals' behaviour to be taken into account (Community Care, 2006). Indeed, by the end of 2011, juveniles accounted for 44.9 per cent of all ASBOs breached while they only represented 37.7 per cent of those issued. Furthermore, just over two-thirds of juveniles (68.3 per cent) had breached their ASBOs at least once, compared with only 51.5 per cent of adults. This had significant consequences for some youngsters, since 226 children aged 12–14 received a custodial sentence (6.1 months on average) for breaching their ASBO. Over the same period, 1,207 young people aged 15–17 received a custodial sentence (6.3 months on average) for the same reason. Altogether, 17.9 per cent of all the young offenders from the 12–17 age group were given a custodial sentence for breaching their order, compared with 38.5 per cent of adults (MJ, 2012).

Centrally collected data on the social circumstances of individuals being served with ASBOs are not available. In the same way, centralized statistics on ethnicity are difficult to obtain although, in its guidance on ASBOs, the Home Office clearly states that agencies should monitor the ethnicity of both victims and perpetrators. However, specific research has been published on these issues. For instance, the Youth Justice Board for England and Wales published a report on ASBOs in 2006, which shed some light on the perpetrators. The young people in the study sample were mainly White males, although 22 per cent were from Black and Minority Ethnic (BME) groups. They mostly belonged to a highly disadvantaged group characterized by: family breakdown and inconsistent supervision from parents or carers; educational difficulty and under-achievement; previous abuse, bereavement and loss; residence in high-crime neighbourhoods, with relatively few age-appropriate facilities. Many of these features were shared by other young people involved in the youth justice system. Finally, the majority (77 per cent) of the sample had at least one previous criminal conviction, half of the sample had two previous convictions, and one in five had none (YJB, 2006).

Research concerning BME perpetrators is scarce and often relies on other variables to assess the impact of ASBOs on this specific population. For instance, the over-representation of BME groups in served ASBOs should be expected since they are more likely to live in social housing, and therefore more likely to be subjected to the discretionary powers conferred on Housing Action Trusts or Registered Social Landlords to serve them (Isal, 2006: 7–8). Also, an Edinburgh-based study has suggested that young working-class males, especially from ethnic minorities, who lead an active 'street life' are disproportionately targeted by the police and tend, once the process of being identified as trouble-makers has been set in motion, to be sucked into a spiral of amplified contact with the police, even if they have stopped behaving badly (Newburn, 2011; McAra and McVie, 2010). A more recent study on interventions to address anti-social behaviour, has shown that in all the cases where ethnicity is known, 88.5 per cent of the perpetrators are White, 7.5 per cent are Black, 1.7 per cent are Asian, and 2.2 per cent are Mixed (Clarke *et al.*, 2011: 36). Even though these figures should be considered with caution since ethnicity is often missing (here for two-thirds of the sample considered), they are roughly in line with ethnic representation within the English Youth Justice System (YJS).

In 2010–11, young people from a White ethnic background accounted for 82 per cent of the total Youth Offending Team caseload, eight per cent were from a Black ethnic background, four per cent from an Asian background, and six per cent from a Mixed one (YJB, 2006: 77). More worryingly, according to the report of the Independent Commission on Youth Crime and Anti-Social Behaviour, there is some evidence that the YJS discriminates against particular ethnic groups: 'young people from mixed race backgrounds are more likely to be prosecuted than white defendants and less likely to be reprimanded or given a final warning. Black and mixed heritage defendants are more likely to be remanded in custody' (IC, 2010: 14). This is borne out by statistics published by the Youth Justice Board. In 2010–11, 64 per cent of the young people held in custody belonged to the White group, whereas 17 per cent were from a Black ethnic background: their corresponding representation being respectively 86 per cent and three per cent in the general population aged 10–17. In the same way, 22 per cent of young people from the White group in custody were held on remand, compared to 34 per cent of young people from a Black ethnic background (YJB, 2012: 30–1).

Changing the piper not the tune?

The report of the Independent Commission on Youth Crime and Anti-social Behaviour (2010) also emphasized responsibility and responsiblization, the need for early intervention and prevention and the principle of restorative justice. The Commission deplored the use of custody for children and young people (except in the most extreme cases), but saw no need to raise the age of criminal responsibility (one of the lowest in the European Union). They also accused politicians of taking part in a punitive 'arms race' over sanctions despite the general fall in youth crime. Finally, the report stressed the distinction to be made between children and young people who commit criminal offences for a relatively short period during adolescence and a 'much smaller group whose behaviour is often seriously anti-social from an early age and who are much more likely to develop into prolific, serious and violent offenders' (IC, 2010: 40), thus giving renewed credit to the existence of a residual underclass. The report was endorsed by both Labour and Conservatives.

A study published by the Audit Commission, in 2010, also took for granted the existence of the underclass although it carefully avoided using the word. It found that 9.2 per cent of the 16–18 age group (183,200 people nationally) were NEETs (Not in Education, Employment or Training), and were at risk of falling into long-term joblessness, ill-health and criminality because of the current recession. This was often linked with other social issues such as being in care, teenage parenthood or homelessness, and mapping the NEETs' location mirrored the country's most deprived areas. The study also painted a portrait of young people who were often the sons or daughters of parents who had dropped out of school early themselves, and who had become trapped in a cycle of unemployment, living in households where no one had a job. The general idea being that without better targeted help these young people were likely to swell the ranks of the 'residual underclass' of unemployed career offenders, and thus add to the already heavy financial burden that society had to bear (Audit Commission, 2010).

When the Conservatives entered government in May 2010 in a Coalition with the Liberal Democrats, increasing criminalization of anti-social behaviour was high on their law and order agenda. In a bid to distance herself from her New Labour predecessors and to be seen to be giving more severe punishments, Conservative Home Secretary Theresa May declared that the term 'anti-social behaviour' should be rebranded 'crime and disorder' to make sure that the victims were taken seriously by the police. She also announced a plan to 'give victims and communities the right to force the authorities to take action where they fail to do so' (Slack and Chapman, 2010).

During the August 2011 riots, the terms 'underclass', 'feral' and 'feckless' resurfaced and were widely used in the British press, as well as by many

Conservative politicians to qualify the undeserving and dangerous poor who were burning and robbing their own communities in their 'mindless thuggery' (Wilson, 2011). The Conservative Work and Pensions Secretary, Iain Duncan Smith, put the blame on family breakdown and a 'benefit system that had helped generate a growing underclass of people living unproductive lives' (Mulholland, 2011). However, the seriousness of these riots that took place against the backdrop of the worst global economic crisis since 1929 forced the Conservatives to soften their harsh, punitive rhetoric.

In 2011, David Cameron introduced a £448 million plan, involving local councils, to help 'problem families'. His proposals are largely derived from ideas and policies developed by Louise Casey and ministers when Labour was in power. The scheme is voluntary, but councils have the powers to evict troublesome tenants, take children into care or issue ASBOs should a family refuse to co-operate (Wintour, 2011a). Another consequence has been the reprieve from abolition of the Youth Justice Board of England and Wales (YJB) by the Secretary of State for Justice, then Ken Clarke, on the grounds that the body had proved its worth during the riots (Travis, 2011). The YJB was set up in 1998 by Jack Straw when he was Home Secretary to provide custodial places for juvenile offenders and to oversee the network of youth offending teams across England and Wales. Even more striking has been the appointment of Blair's former 'respect tsar', Louise Casey, to head a Troubled Families Unit in the Department for Communities and Local Government whose task will be to find workable and lasting solutions for Britain's 120,000 problem families by the end of the Parliament in 2015 (Wintour, 2011b). Ironically, it was also Casey who developed the much criticized concept of ASBO when she was working in the Home Office, a tool that has often been derided by Conservative politicians, including David Cameron himself, as too cumbersome and inefficient.

The Conservative government's White Paper, *Putting Victims First – More Effective Responses to Anti-Social Behaviour* published in March 2012 proposed replacing ASBOs and some other court orders by two new tools which, unlike ASBOs, could have positive requirements, as well as prohibitions attached to them: the Criminal Behaviour Order (CBO) and the Crime Prevention Injunction (CPI). Other, less marginal, reforms have been introduced. First, professionals will be given more discretion in responding to anti-social behaviour. Second, a potentially hazardous Community Trigger system will be set up to give victims and communities the right to require agencies to deal with persistent anti-social behaviour that has previously been ignored. Third, the Community Remedy will give victims of low-level crime and anti-social behaviour a say in the punishment of offenders out of court. Although the main element of the strategy put forward is prevention, tackling the risk factors is also very high in the government's priorities. The clear aim is to impose acceptable standards of behaviour on irresponsible and uncontrollable individuals through the courts if necessary, but also by devolving more policing powers on communities and victims. Moreover, the underclass discourse is being recycled under the new approach of 'tackling the drivers of anti-social behaviour' (Home Office, 2012b: 34). Indeed, even though the word 'underclass' is never mentioned in the White Paper, the designated targets of these new measures leave no doubt as to their social extraction: problem drinkers, illicit drug users, troubled families, mental health cases and owners of dangerous dogs (Home Office, 2012b: 34–9; Strickland, 2012). All of these proposals were included in the Anti-Social Behaviour, Crime and Policing Bill 2013–2014.

Conclusion: smoke and mirrors

Since 1993, the Conservative Party and the Labour Party have mostly followed the same ideological path in terms of the fight against anti-social behaviour, periodically reviving or conjuring away the concept of 'underclass' to justify their policies. The latter's resilience and flexibility stem from the fact that it is impossible to decide which of the behavioural or structural factors play the most important role in the causation of poverty and deprivation. Therefore this concept constitutes the perfect political tool since it can be easily adapted to suit any government's needs. In times of political tensions, economic uncertainty or both, it also presents a convenient scapegoat on which to project undefined fears and anxieties. Thrust upon deprived White and BME lower working-class people, the young in particular, it has been highly successful at masking the 'de-civilizing process' (Rodger, 2088: 30–7) generated by economic restructuring and welfare state retrenchment in the United Kingdom and at exonerating it from all responsibility in the matter by putting the onus on the shortcomings of the individual. Finally, it has allowed the two main parties of government to hide their powerlessness at relieving the plight of this much reviled segment of the British population.

Notes

1. The term started to be used in *The Sun* newspaper in 2007 and was subsequently taken up by David Cameron and the Conservatives as a useful catchphrase in their bid for power (Easton, 2008).
2. This expression was used by columnist Simon Heffer in the *Daily Mail* on 6 January 2007. He had also used a similar expression ('[...] feral children from the underclass') in a previous column in the same newspaper on 31 July 2004.

17
Anti-social Behaviour and the Vulnerable Public

Stuart Waiton

Introduction

Sociological discussions about 'late-modern' society are often confusing with regard to the nature of what is repeatedly described as our 'neo-liberal' times (Hay, 2007). Not only is it difficult to find any group of individuals who would describe themselves as neo-liberal, but in policy, in law and in the nature of policing today, there is little trace of a 'liberal' sentiment (Ramsay, 2012). We may live in a market society, but we also live in a therapeutic culture (Furedi, 2004; Nolan, 1998). At the level of culture and politics, this is not a society that treats its citizens as liberal subjects, but as diminished vulnerable individuals. This is in stark contrast to the Victorians, who were passionate about the need for personal responsibility and autonomy (Himmelfarb, 1989). The rhetoric of freedom and responsibility may continue today, but they often mean something very different from anything the classical liberal John Stuart Mill (1999) proposed in the nineteenth century. Freedom, for example, since the mid-1990s, has been discussed with reference to the 'freedom from fear', while responsibility is more often than not an instruction to people to 'behave', rather than something adopted by the self-willing action of independent minded individuals (Mill, 1999). Central to this change has been the transformation of the ontological understanding of the individual. The Victorian ideal of the robust, free individual has been replaced by the 'ideal' of the vulnerable public – made up of dependent potential victims who need to be protected, not only from crime (or harm) but from an increasing array of behaviours.

The ideal of moral independence faced constant difficulties in the Victorian period regarding the poor, with the conflicting need to support those in desperate need while at the same time ensuring personal responsibility was not undermined (Payne, 2005: 35). There was an elitist suspicion, by some at least, that certain sections of society lacked the capacity to develop their moral independence. However, this remained a contested area, one often reflecting the elites' own belief or disbelief, in the liberal project of the time. Charitable support was discouraged from being given to the 'undeserving', especially when the Charity Organisation Society (COS) was set up in 1869, unless there was evidence of potential moral improvement and self-reliance within the individuals and families in question. Through the process of encouraging the development of character, it was believed that 'demoralization' would be prevented (Jordon, 1974: 26). Despite radical criticism of 'Liberal Britain' at the time, and a fervent critique of the economic and political barriers to human emancipation, for Marxists, like Frederick Engels, the belief in the human subject was not questioned (Engels, 2009). Indeed, for Engels, as for Karl Marx, there was an absolute belief in the capacity of the public to act, organize and fight for a better world.

At this time, the question of crime was often discussed with reference to both a 'scientific' and/or a moral approach towards the individual. The 'residuum' was seen as being naturally inferior or morally degenerate. However, in general it was assumed that this group of 'degenerates' was relatively small compared with the majority of the population who it was assumed should and could aspire to be upstanding, sturdy and vigorous individuals (Cullen, 1996). The idea that the public in general could be classified as 'vulnerable' would make no sense to the Victorian elites. Indeed, at a wider cultural and political level the liberal ideal of autonomous robust individualism and a belief in the importance of cultivating strength of character were widespread throughout British society regardless of political beliefs (Himmelfarb, 1991).

Today, social policies and laws are not developed with this robust liberal individual in mind: we do not have a liberal or a neo-liberal culture. In many respects, the opposite is the case. Rather than new initiatives to regulate behaviour reflecting a belief in the capacity of the individual, they reflect an ontological approach that epitomizes a sentiment of diminished subjectivity (Heartfield, 2002). Consequently, new laws are developed, not with the free, autonomous individual in mind, but with a new normative framework that is predicated upon the idea of our essential vulnerability, or what Peter Ramsay has described as our 'vulnerable autonomy' (Ramsay, 2012). In this chapter, I situate the growing concern about anti-social behaviour within the emerging anxious elite who have helped to construct an image of the 'vulnerable public' out of the disaggregated post-Cold War citizenry. This process was assisted by the loss of belief of both the moral right and the radical left, who became claims-makers for the 'victim of crime' and the newly caricatured 'vulnerable groups'.

Vulnerable autonomy

In his legal analysis of society's preoccupation with safety, a preoccupation that emerged in the 1990s, Ramsay attempts to explain how and why new laws that protect our feeling of security have emerged in the last two decades. For Ramsay these new laws have been able to develop and proliferate, despite our apparently liberal form of justice, because of the transformation in the normative sense of the human subject. Anti-social Behaviour Orders (ASBOs), he argues are novel, not because they attempt to protect our *feeling* of safety (something other laws have done), but because ASBOs are specifically and directly concerned with our subjective feeling of security. Unlike previous laws, ASBOs, Ramsay notes, are solely concerned with our feelings, specifically with our feeling of fear. Unlike the Public Order Act 1986, ASBOs are not about acts we have committed, but acts we may do in the future that may create fear; with the authorities determining on our behalf what type of behaviour may cause such fear.

Under section 1(1)(a) of the Crime and Disorder Act 1998, anti-social behaviour is described as 'conduct that would, more probably than not, cause the *most sensitive person* actually present in the particular context to fear for their safety' (Ramsay, 2012: 23, my emphasis). Consequently, the ASBO can be seen as an administrative form of risk management, a risk management that aims to prevent anti-social behaviour. The ASBO, Ramsay concludes, is essentially about reassuring the public, a public that has been defined through the feelings of an imagined or constructed 'most sensitive person'. Explaining why hearsay evidence should be used when dealing with anti-social behaviour Lord Hutton argued that this created a fairer balance between individual rights and the demands of the community. Once again however, this is a particular type of 'idealized' community; as Lord Hutton specifies, 'the community in this case is represented by weak and vulnerable people' (Ramsay, 2012: 60). The principles of law, of evidence gathering and forms of proof can be undermined because the law, as was, is no longer sufficient; no longer sufficient Ramsay suggests, because the nature of the legal subject in question has been transformed and reclassified in our more therapeutic culture, as sensitive, weak and vulnerable.

The assumption being made is that there is a reassurance gap in society that must be filled through the use of orders that regulate further the behaviour of citizens. Here we see the new framing of rights and responsibilities, where citizens are no longer simply free, but are free based on prior positive obligations centred on the necessary recognition that people and communities are fundamentally vulnerable and must be protected from fear. Once conceptualized in this way, previously defined 'nuisance' behaviour that was seen as relatively trivial and not serious enough to be dealt with by the law, or conduct that it is believed can create any level of insecurity, is transformed into a profoundly significant thing, something that undermines both individuals and communities.

Citizens need reassurance. But, asks Ramsay, what sort of citizen/subject is it that needs this level of reassurance? The answer is that it is the *vulnerable* person who no longer receives sufficient protection from existing laws who now needs this *right* to be reassured.

Universalizing victimhood

Discussing the rise of the New Labour Party in the 1990s, a party that was to be in government for 13 years, and which promoted the idea of Third Way politics, James Heartfield notes:

> The Third Way connected with the electorate, not on the basis of their collective purpose, but instead playing upon their individuation and the anxieties that arose from it. The voters were no longer represented in the polity as the collective subject of the democratic process. Instead they were recognised by the state as the isolated and persecuted victims of events beyond their control. (Heartfield, 2002: 199)

Central to Heartfield's discussion of diminished subjectivity is the understanding of a transformation in politics. A transformation that saw the diminution of what C. Wright Mills (1968) described as an active *public*, and as significantly, a transformation that saw the emergence of an increasingly disconnected or liquid elite (Bauman, 2000). As politicians searched for a 'Big Idea', Zaki Laïdi argued that in the post-Cold War era we had entered a *World Without Meaning* (Laïdi, 1998): a world that lacked political imagination (Furedi, 2005) or moral purpose (Lasch, 1977: 187) and which resulted in the formation of a culture of fear (Furedi, 1997) or what David Garland (2002) described as a culture of control.

Safety increasingly became a framework for developing policies and engaging with the public. In the 1990s, everyday activities were rebranded, and safety became a framework around which institutions organized. Consequently, terms like safe-play, safe-sex and community safety emerged as part of what Furedi described as a new culture of limits (Furedi, 1997). Within this context, concerns about crime were extended to incorporate wider anxieties about safety and, importantly, increasingly began to engage not only with crime, but the (perceived) fear of it. The role of local authorities, politicians and the police incorporated a need to reduce public insecurities and so, it was believed, help to strengthen, perhaps even rebuild, communities. As Garland argues, fear 'once regarded as a localized, situational anxiety, afflicting the worst-off individuals and neighbourhoods, has come to be regarded as a major social problem and a characteristic of contemporary culture' (Garland, 2002: 10).

Illustrating the way in which the public was being conceptualized and engaged with by politicians at this time, in 1997 the Labour Home Secretary Jack Straw described the fear of crime as something that essentially imprisons entire sections of society. The extent of the problem of the fear of crime, Straw believed, meant that:

Two thirds of women pensioners are scared to leave their house at night. Our pensioners are prisoners in their own homes who only want to live in peace. Surely the prisoners should be those who commit the crimes, not those who are the victims of crime. It cannot go on. (*The Guardian*, 26 April 1997)

With this permanent and fundamental sense of fear, which was understood to be hovering above communities, the basis for police intervention was transformed into a more subjectively constituted defence of the public's emotional well-being. In a sense, the community being engaged with was a community of vulnerable individuals, a community victimized by fear. This perceived sense of victimhood was understood to be the potential common bond between individuals – and the basis of state engagement and legitimation. As Garland explains:

The symbolic figure of the victim has taken on a life of its own [and has become] [...] a new social fact. The victim is no longer an unfortunate citizen who has been on the receiving end of a criminal harm, and whose concerns are subsumed within the 'public interest' [...] The victim is now, in a certain sense, a much more representative character, whose experience is taken to be common and collective, rather than individual and atypical. (Garland, 2002: 11)

Diminishing subjects

The universalizing dynamic of 'the victim' relates not simply to objective changes in society but arguably more significantly to the interpretation of the social, political and cultural changes that occurred from the 1970s. For conservatives like James Q. Wilson (the inventor of the 'broken windows' theory of crime), the new focus upon the victim of crime in the United States reflected his understanding that morality was no longer a credible force for good in society. Christian ethics and morality, he believed, had held people together but in the twentieth century (of the self) even the middle classes had abandoned this outlook and as morality declined little was left to control people's impulses (Wilson, 1985). Most significantly, for Wilson there was no going back to a moral world. Pragmatism or 'realism' was needed in politics and in addressing crime in society. Consequently, Wilson argued that we needed to take a 'more sober view of man', foolish aspirations needed to be abandoned and 'utopian things forgotten' (Wilson, 1985: 250).

Wilson was one of the most significant conservative thinkers who first proposed the need to elevate the importance of the victim of crime. As Best notes, this had become a trend among right-wing politicians in the United States at the end of the 1960s (Best, 1999: 98). But this elevation of the victim must be situated within the wider pessimism of Wilson's sense of loss. It was not simply the problem of crime that led to his focus on 'the victim', but more importantly his diminished sense of the moral capacity of 'man' and society.

Similarly, in the United Kingdom in the 1980s, it was the loss of belief of some of those on the left that led to the emergence of left realism and to a similar elevation of the victim and indeed the construction of entire groups of people as 'vulnerable'.

In the United Kingdom, the prioritization and representation of the victim emerged most fervently within the feminist writing of the 1970s and 1980s with the 'discovery' of violence and abuse against women and children (Jenkins, 1992: 231). Despite often contradictory evidence of the significance and even the extent of the victimization under study, this approach had an underlying and in-built acceptance of the vulnerability of those people being studied. For example, Hartless notes with 'surprise' that, of the young women who said they had experienced sexual harassment of some kind, 'only 8% [...] said they had been "very scared"' (Hartless *et al.*, 1995: 119). Surprise at any level of robustness and at the ability of 'vulnerable' individuals to cope with unpleasant experiences was coupled with a trend to interpret any evidence of fear as a product of harassment. Rachel Pain, in her analysis of fear among elderly women, raises the question of why older men fear crime more than young men. Despite the myriad possible reasons including physical frailty, social isolation or a sense of powerlessness and estrangement from society which could be the cause, Pain speculates that perhaps it is due to their *vulnerability to harassment*, 'especially in very old age, to abuse from carers inside or outside the immediate family' (Pain, 1995: 595).

Whereas previously radicals had attempted to challenge the official statistics on crime and deny the 'social problem' of crime, increasingly this feminist criminology reversed this approach and attempted to prove that crime, harassment, and what would later by called 'anti-social behaviour' was even more of a problem than was officially accepted. Being a 'victim' of crime and anti-social behaviour was no longer simply a passing event, but became something that defined the lives and identity of 'vulnerable groups'.

In the 1980s, feminist and left realist concerns about the impact of crime on individuals and society drew closer to the official criminological approach at the time – especially with the common use of victim statistics. 'Establishment' criminology had however undergone its own transformation during this period moving from a positivist belief in society's capacity to overcome the problem of crime to an 'administrative criminology' (Young, 1988: 174). This administrative criminology, associated with Wilson's (1985) approach to crime, was a more pragmatic method of dealing with the effects of it. Despite the political nature of much of the feminist and particularly the left realists approach to crime, the common bond that had brought them and the official criminologist closer to one another was a diminished belief in moral or political and social possibilities to resolve the problem of crime. With a greater pessimism about society and a greater sense of distance from social change and outcomes, radical and conservative thinkers became more preoccupied with the plight of the victim. The public, or at least substantial sections of it, were now increasingly conceptualized as being what Betsy Stanko described as, 'universally vulnerable' (Pain, 1995: 596).

The significance of crime and behaviour for New Labour in the 1990s was assisted by the work of feminist and new realist thinkers of the left in the 1980s, who helped to formulate an understanding of the public as vulnerable. In Philip Jenkins' analysis of *Moral Panics in Contemporary Great Britain*, in which he analyses the emergence of panics around child abuse in the United Kingdom, he notes the significance of feminist as claims-makers:

> From the mid-1970s on, there evolved in Britain a strong feminist movement, which had had an enormous impact on many aspects of society and politics [...] [f]eminist ideas soon prevailed in radical and left-wing journals [...] and were commonly expressed in liberal newspapers like the *Guardian* [...] [and] by the mid-1980s, fifty local authorities had women's committees. (Jenkins, 1992: 35-6)

This form of feminism, as Jenkins notes, had a substantial impact upon politics in the United Kingdom – as did the left realists, led by Jock Young, who, like these feminists, had become disillusioned with the idealist beliefs of the radical left. Crime for these left realists needed to be taken seriously and victims needed to be placed at the centre of concern for criminologists and the state. As Matthews and Young argued – expressing sentiments that were later to be echoed by the likes of New Labour's David Blunkett:

> Crime is of importance because unchecked it divides the working class community and is materially and morally the basis of disorganisation: the loss of political control. It is also a potential unifier – a realistic issue, amongst others, for recreating community. (Matthews and Young, 1986: 29)

Developing out of the radical framework of the early 1970s, a number of feminist and realist criminologists became disillusioned with the fight for political and social change and, rather than challenging the issue of crime as an elite concern or method of social control, increasingly identified crime as a major issue, particularly for the poor, women and blacks who were now understood as being 'victims of crime' (Jones *et al.*, 1986). Discussing the shift in Labour councils from radicalism to realism Young noted that:

> The recent history of radical criminology in Britain has involved a rising influence of feminist and anti-racist ideas and an encasement of left wing Labour administrations in the majority of the inner city Town Halls. An initial ultra-leftism has been tempered and often transformed by a prevalent realism in the wake of the third consecutive defeat of the Labour Party on the national level and severe defeats with regards to 'rate capping' in terms of local politics. The need to encompass issues, which had a widespread support amongst the electorate, rather than indulge in marginal or 'gesture' politics included the attempt to recapture the issue of law and order from the right. (Young, 1988: 172)

It was sections of the left who, with the support of their victim surveys, both discovered and advocated on behalf of women, blacks and the poor as *victims* of crime, the problem of fragmented communities being located within the prism of crime, anti-social behaviour and the fear of crime. From this perspective, the tendency was for Young and his co-authors both to exaggerate the significance of crime and to generalize an understanding of the public as fundamentally vulnerable – within the narrow parameters of crime and anti-social behaviour. In particular, previously radical political issues were transformed into victim claims for newly conceptualized 'vulnerable groups', incorporating black people, women and homosexuals into this new and diminished caricature. In the demoralized and poverty stricken inner-city areas of London, like Islington, where crime rates were five times the national average, the equally demoralized realists concluded that it was the problem of crime that 'shaped their lives' (Jones *et al.*, 1986: 201). While correctly noting that crime was not a fantasy for the people of Islington, these realists noted that a third of the women of the area avoided going out after dark, concluding that this represented a 'virtual curfew of the female population' (1986: 201). This misrepresentation of one-third of women being transformed into the entire female population reflected not simply an exaggeration, but a newly developing conceptualization of the public more generally as vulnerable – something which was to become more central to the Labour Party's understanding of social problems in the 1990s and would help to transform the relationship between citizen and state.

The rise of anti-social behaviour

By the turn of the millennium, the Labour Party in Britain had made antisocial behaviour into a major political issue. Labour MP Frank Field went so far as to describe the problem of anti-social behaviour as the 'newest horseman of the apocalypse' (Field, 2003: 64). In 2002, Prime Minister Tony Blair used the Queen's Speech (where the priorities for the government are set out) to explain that anti-social behaviour – and specifically vandalism, graffiti and fly-tipping – was 'probably the biggest immediate issue for people in the country' (*The Guardian*, 1 November 2002).

Looking at past newspaper articles discussing the problem of 'anti-social behaviour', it is noticeable that, for example in *The Guardian*, there were only one or two stories a year in the 1980s that mentioned anti-social behaviour. This contrasts with 2006, when then there were over 600 articles in *The Guardian* alone discussing anti-social behaviour: there were over 17,000 such articles in all United Kingdom newspapers in 2013.

The term anti-social behaviour has existed for a long time, but in the 1990s it became a specifically political terms connecting the everyday nuisance behaviour of people with a wider sense of disorder and social breakdown. The term itself grouped together a number of relatively minor forms of bad behaviour, collectivizing them in a 'broken windows' type representation of the collapse of community. Interestingly, when looking at the newspaper articles about anti-social behaviour, it is noticeable that in the mid-1990s it was promoted as a significant problem with reference to crime, thus the often quoted problem of 'crime and anti-social behaviour' was how the issue was elevated as a problem. By the end of the decade however, the problem of anti-social behaviour was the problem in and of itself, no longer needing the crutch of crime to give it significance. And as we have seen, for Labour politicians and the Prime Minister it became an apocalyptic problem – the biggest immediate issue facing the people of Britain.

For Labour Party promoters of ASBOs, their focus on anti-social behaviour was portrayed as a new way to rebuild communities. In 2004, the then Home Secretary David Blunkett explained the government's approach to civic republicanism, arguing that, 'People say that actually feeling safe to walk down the street, is the first and primary goal that they want us to achieve. That way, they'll come out to public meetings, they'll go down to their local school, they'll join in in being part of the solution' (Cummings, 2005: 6).

For Blunkett, fear, often generated by anti-social behaviour, was undermining communities and overcoming fear would recreate an active political public. However, fear in communities, to the extent that it can be taken at face value, is often generated by far more than misbehaving youngsters and 'neighbours from hell'. As Elizabeth Burney (2005: 9) notes, 'poor people do suffer more from crime and disorder but they also have more things to worry about and are more likely to feel things are out of control.' Fear of anti-social behaviour, Burney believes, can be seen as simply part of a wider culture of fear, or of risk consciousness:

> Risk consciousness besets modern society and anti-social behaviour is only one among many of the issues which seize public attention. Pollution, paedophiles, food scares, medical errors and many more threaten our peace of mind as ever-present dangers which from time to time throw

up peaks of alarm triggered by fresh events or 'expert' reports. (Burney, 2005: 11)

At the risk of being one sided, the suggestion being made here is that *it is not anti-social behaviour that creates fear – but rather, fear became expressed through the issue of anti-social behaviour.*

The criminalization of behaviour that was previously not seen as worthy of legal sanction has developed alongside the growing importance of the 'victim' within the criminal justice system. With the growth in legislation and initiatives to deal with anti-social behaviour an ever wider net has been cast that has helped to redefine more things as being 'anti-social' and equally to see more people as victims of this behaviour. What is seen as being harmful to people has expanded – as has the government's attempt to prevent harm happening.

For some the growing concern with harmful behaviour is justified and relates to the changing form of behaviour itself. Stuart Jeffries for example argues, 'That growing vulgarisation points up a problem for Mill's principle – what one person believes causes harm or thinks intolerable will be very different from another. But surely vulgarity and rudeness harm others and steadily make our culture uncivilised? Mill's principle needs to be recast for a new age' (*The Guardian*, 19 September 2005). Why Mill's principles need to be recast is unclear. Mill and those of his generation did not accept vulgarity and rudeness – but they did expect individuals to be able to deal with these issues without the use of the state and the law. What Jeffries' approach represents is perhaps less the growing problem of behaviour than of a growing fragility within society and an increasing reliance on the state to resolve problems that individuals were previously expected to be able to deal with.

Indeed, since the emergence of ASBOs and legislation to deal with anti-social behaviour was first introduced, society has moved 'forward', and today with legislation dealing with hate crime, singing at football matches and increasingly with the regulation of what is 'said' on the Internet, on Facebook and Twitter in particular, we have moved, as philosopher Joel Feinberg has argued, 'from the harm principle to the offence principle' (Cohen, 2012).

The reason for this shift and for the emergence of anti-social behaviour as a major political issue is in large part due to the dialectical relationship between the diminishing sense of moral and political purpose in Western society, and the construction of the vulnerable victim – the powerless 'subject'. With a diminished sense of political possibilities, politics has increasingly become about the micro-management of society and the increasing use of law and regulations to enforce correct forms of behaviour, with safety being elevated as a framework for policy developments and fear being the key emotion that is recognized and engaged with. Simultaneously the individual has diminished in the mind's-eye of the elite, and new initiatives and forms of policing have developed with the thin-skinned, chronically offended person as the representative character of (post) modern Britain. The community in this case, as Lord Hutton outlined above, consequently 'is represented by weak and vulnerable people' (Ramsay, 2012: 60). Entire populations of people are imagined to be 'vulnerable groups' and the 'most sensitive person' becomes emblematic, a newly framed diminished individual around which experts and politicians orient themselves. Essentially what we are witnessing is the replacement of J.S. Mill's liberal individual with the newly construction vulnerable person and group.

In *Violence* Slavoj Žižek discusses a new norm developing in Western society, to 'fear thy neighbour as thyself'. Discussing the transformation of the meaning of tolerance, from a Millsian idea of free speech and the importance of tolerating different ideas, to one where tolerance means respect, not being offensive and indeed the criminalization of words and behaviour. He argues:

> My duty to be tolerant towards the Other effectively means that I should not get too close to him, intrude on his space. In other words, I should respect his *intolerance* of my over-proximity. What increasingly emerges as the central human right in late-capitalist society is *the right not to be harassed*, which is a right to be kept at a safe distance from others. (Žižek, 2009).

Tragically, despite its pretentions to the contrary, anti-social behaviour legislation is helping to enforce Žižek's asocial society, where connections between people are undermined by ever increasing initiatives to protect our 'right' to be protected from everyone around us.

18
Anti-Social Behaviour: Marginality, Intolerance and the 'Usual Suspects'

Peter Squires

Introduction

In most contemporary accounts, and especially in anti-social behaviour (ASB) performance management publications, anti-social behaviour is often regarded as if it were a discrete and recognizable class of behaviours occurring in society. It is frequently seen as a particular attribute of the poorest and youngest: the self-evidently 'undisciplined' or 'anti-social'. In this chapter, however, an alternative perspective will be developed. This view sees the emergence of anti-social behaviour as part of a wider project of 'cultural governance' where support for the dissemination of broadly framed anti-social behaviour management powers, prompting and recycling a growing intolerance of the discomforting consequences of rising inequality, marginality, poverty and dependency is indicative of a significant shift in the purposes of social policy. Rather than engage in the consciously political and resource-intensive process of addressing the causes of this debilitating inequality and marginality, anti-social behaviour encourages the view that this low, stigmatized or symbolically troubling behaviour is, by itself, the primary cause of the problems experienced by those associated with perpetrating the behaviour. Thus far, and expressed this way, however, there might seem to be little more to this observation than the familiar response of a critical criminologist to the criminalization of working-class street activities.

It is certain we have been here before: Horn (1980), for example, described the local regulatory onslaught against the sins and indiscretions of rural life during the eighteenth century and the final collapse of the traditional agricultural economy; Linebaugh (1991) outlined the punitive turn against the customary pilfering by tradesmen as a new era of capitalist commercialism was installed; and Chambliss's (1964) famous analysis of the introduction of laws against vagrancy emphasized the combination of social order and 'free' (although fixed) labour so crucial to industrialization. Stepping a little closer to our times and our core subjects, since the 1950s a great volume of commentary, up to and including the present British government's 'gang violence' prevention strategy (HM Government, 2011b) has sought to unravel the 'deprived/depraved' relation presumed responsible for the supposedly 'feral' or perhaps merely 'anti-social' behaviour of contemporary working-class youth – this group being consistently the most strongly identified with the troubling behaviours in question (Squires and Stephen, 2005; Bottoms, 2006). Such 'enforcement waves' have frequently singled out the visible and disorderly challenges that such behaviour has appeared to pose to vested interests and moral authority at key points in our recent history. Today, however, the wide range of behaviours encapsulated by the, typically highly subjective, conception of anti-social behaviour which has become the target of (often pre-emptive or 'precautionary') enforcement proceedings (Squires and Stephen, 2010) points instead to broader and deeper social divisions formed around contemporary inequalities, ethnicities and identities.

New powers in the land

Concern about what we *currently* call anti-social behaviour arises especially at times of fractured and changing expectations of governance and sociability such that, today, even as recorded crime is falling – and likewise falling across most of Western Europe (Van Dijk *et al.*, 2012) – the fabricated perception of anti-social behaviour distils a diverse range of social anxieties, preoccupying and displacing political energies into the realm of the criminalized and manageable, just as other social and political problems appear either more intractable or otherwise off limits (such as creating jobs, tackling poverty and homelessness, managing immigration). This may not quite amount to 'governing through crime' in Jonathan Simon's terms (Simon, 2007), but clearly represents a growing popular intolerance of poverty and marginality (also represented in the demonization of supposedly 'feral' working-class youth; in demeaning humour directed at the poorest (Jones, 2011); in the genre of 'poverty porn' television programming (Hancock and Mooney, 2012); and the populist contempt displayed towards teenage 'welfare mothers' and benefit claimants (Duncan, 2007) – itself a resurrection of much older notions of the 'dependency culture'.

Picking up on these attitudes, journalist John Carvel, writing in *The Guardian* newspaper, reporting on an Office of National Statistics (ONS) *Social Trends* analysis, remarked that, according to the evidence, twenty-first century Britain had become 'a more anti-social and less tolerant society' (Carvel, 2007). In reality, anti-social behaviour and intolerance were just two sides of the same coin. Following its politicians, England's mainstream and respectable middle classes came to label as 'anti-social' anything which they found contemptible, immoral or which they were reluctant to tolerate. And as Michael Tonry (2004: 57) noted, this provided neither explanation nor remedy; deploying the labels of anti-social behaviour simply made a small problem worse, raising unrealistic expectations that people could be forced to behave (Burney, 2005) or 'made good' by law, a policy once rejected as foolhardy and self-defeating by an earlier generation of liberals. It follows that we have to explain, not just the onslaught of new behaviour management, but also the material intolerances sustaining it, with each as a prism for viewing the other. David Downes' insightful analysis *Contrasts in Tolerance* (Downes, 1993) can help us here, locating the explanation in structural, cultural and historical characteristics of the society in question rather than the merely symptomatic intolerances of some regarding the behaviour of their perceived subordinates.

Nevertheless, the two-dimensional character of anti-social behaviour helps explain, in part, both the imprecise – often contradictory – definitions provided for it as well as its wide resonance as an idea. Who, after all, has never passed covert judgement on other people: 'L'enfer, c'est les autres' (Sartre, 1947) or, especially, as contemporaries like to add, their kids? On that very point, 'mission drift' has been an aspect of anti-social behaviour from the very outset (Squires, 2008b); when the Anti-social Behaviour Order (ASBO) was first conceived, it was never intended to be applied to juveniles, yet, very soon, youthful misbehaviour had become the quintessential definition of the 'anti-social' (Campbell, 2002; Bottoms, 2006). These ambiguities also suggest why, in simple terms, there has always been such a strong element of performance about anti-social behaviour politics and, not least, such a precisely orchestrated 'othering' (naming and shaming) of the allegedly anti-social. It also reveals the important role that *perceptions* play in the definition of anti-social behaviour for, central to the definition of anti-social behaviour, is an idea of the 'harassment, alarm and distress' instilled in third parties which is necessary to the definition of anti-social behaviour (Crime and Disorder Act 1998: Section 1). However, even this notoriously elastic definition of what constitutes anti-social behaviour represents far too empirical a foundation for, in practice, the determination actually rests with an assessment arrived at by a police officer, neighbourhood warden or other enforcement functionary, that the behaviour in question is *likely to cause* 'harassment, alarm and distress' to third parties. In fact, it hardly mattered whether any private citizens became alarmed or distressed by the behaviour in question, for guidance to prosecutors later confirmed that distress caused to enforcement officials *alone* would be sufficient to constitute anti-social behaviour. Courts could even grant 'interim' orders, 'on application', even though the persons whose behaviour was under consideration might be unaware of the court proceedings and therefore unable to represent themselves and answer any allegations made.

In effect, anti-social behaviour became a flexible and convenient catch-all enforcement tool and an exemplary instance of 'net-widening' (Austin and Krisberg, 1981) or the 'dispersal of discipline' (Cohen, 1985; see also Squires and Stephen, 2005: 84–123). Not only was the threshold of unacceptable behaviour selectively lowered, but the enforcement process was streamlined and evidential requirements lightened. These features of anti-social behaviour enforcement were retained in the Conservative–Liberal Democrat Coalition government's anti-social behaviour reforms after it came to power in 2010. Given the 'precautionary' framing of anti-social behaviour, the age at which anti-social behaviour interventions into families were permitted extended below the statutory age of criminal responsibility (at ten, already significantly lower than the Western European average), implying that children as young as eight could be subjected to 'Acceptable Behaviour Contracts' and the whole family liable to be evicted from social housing if such 'contracts' were breached (no similar sanctions overhung the misbehaviour of the children of home owners).

Aside from these relativist redefinitions of the field of delinquency, in due course it became abundantly clear that another vital aspect of the new regime of anti-social behaviour management lay in the flexible enforcement opportunities it presented. Although many early claims about anti-social behaviour seemed to rest upon the discovery of a new form of deviance that was offensive, anti-social and disrespectful (pre-delinquency or 'pre-crime' even) it soon transpired that a significant majority of 'Anti-social Behaviour Orders' (or ASBOs) were being issued for behaviour that was *already* criminally prohibited. The utility of the order, in other words, rested entirely upon its enforcement potential: the additional five-year prison sentence that could follow breach of an ASBO. In respect of younger delinquents, broad-ranging anti-social behaviour powers were said to be useful for challenging the sense of 'impunity' which, it was often claimed, surrounded young people in trouble and who, according to a Home Office evaluation, could persist in their delinquent activities 'in the full knowledge that there were few criminal sanctions that could touch them' (Campbell, 2002: 2). Aside from the bizarre idea that 'impunity' might be treated as if it were a characteristic of a type of offender as opposed to a failure of law, policy or practice, the putative solution, Individual Support Orders (ISOs) to help young people comply with the requirements of their anti-social behaviour supervision, were only given to a quarter of the young people appearing before the courts (Ministry of Justice, 2011). ISOs were introduced, in part, as a supposed solution for the high proportion of younger offenders who breached their ASBOs. Young people came to breach ASBOs at a rate of around 70 per cent (Jamieson, 2012), and the relatively limited numbers of ISOs handed out failed to make much of an impact upon these breach rates.

More officials became involved in the 'policing' of anti-social behaviour; for instance, many people are aware that these include housing, education and welfare personnel as well as police auxiliaries, but it is less well known that (under section 40 of the Police Reform Act 2002) community safety 'accreditation' and selected police (ASB management) powers (drawn from an overall list of 32 distinct powers) were also made available to a wide range of public or private sector security personnel. Finally, in a thoroughly Foucauldian embrace of self-surveillance designed to engage and promote public support for the new measures (the 'localization' agenda), members of the public came to be able to nominate their neighbours or fellow community members for anti-social behaviour intervention, an idea which became the basis for the 'community trigger' proposed by the Coalition government in 2012 (Home Office, 2012b: 18–19). The broader justification for these measures involved former Prime Minister Tony Blair's contention that contemporary criminal justice was unfit for purpose and needed 're-balancing' in favour of the so-called 'law-abiding majority' (Tonry, 2010) and against the 'selfish minority' he defined as criminals, louts, drug pushers, abusers or 'neighbours from hell' (Blair, 2004a; 2004b).

Many of these elements of anti-social behaviour management – the enforcement led approach, the wider nets, the dispersal of discipline, the up-tariffing effect (prison sentences) when orders were breached, the cultivated intolerances, the early intervention and pre-criming and the specific demonization of youth – when allied with Blairite re-balancing, can certainly be seen as part of the 'punitive turn' identified by a number of prominent commentators on Anglo-American criminal justice (Pratt *et al.*, 2005; Wacquant, 2009). For Prime Minister Blair, however, they marked a still more dramatic turning point: 'the end of the 1960s liberal, social consensus on law and order' (Blair, 2004b).

The neo-liberal, 'anti-social' consensus?

The Thatcher government, first elected in 1979, is often credited with having broken with the 'postwar consensus' said to have characterized British politics until 1979 (Kavanagh, 1989). However, as Farrall and Hay (2010) have argued, although Thatcherism promoted a very strong and pro-police 'law and order' ideology, criminal justice policy-making itself was actually much less to the fore. Things certainly began to change especially following the mid-1990s with the Blairite capture of the 'law and order' agenda. Yet it was only after 1998 that a newly institutionalized and expansionist conception of anti-social behaviour, the especial domain of the youthful and marginal, became established. A series of preoccupations with contemporary manifestations of 'anti-sociability', aspects of a wider neo-liberal backlash against the alleged 'permissiveness' of post-1968 youth cultures and social welfarism (see Squires, 2006), now implied that social discipline had been undermined, the sense of personal responsibility and self-respect upon which the stability of families and communities rested had been eroded, and the work ethic dissipated. The dominant justification for social policy also shifted from 'welfare', tackling poverty and inequality, to one of facilitating social inclusion in the market place, specifically the labour market (Levitas, 1996). Individuals had to learn to 'market' themselves to potential employers; communities came to be judged in terms of the 'social capital' they might represent to potential investors. Failure to do so was not simply irresponsible and anti-social, it could also be criminalized (Rodger, 2008). Although welfare policy had always entailed subtle distinctions and discriminations (between, for instance the 'deserving' and 'undeserving' poor) (Squires, 1990), it now began to acquire more punitive and conditional characteristics. At the same time, honouring social and behavioural responsibilities became a central requirement for citizens of the neo-liberal social consensus.

One specific indication of how dramatic this shift, from social democracy to neo-liberalism, has been is evident if we look back to Hermann Mannheim's conception of 'anti-social behaviour' contrary to the 'spirit of postwar reconstruction' in the immediate postwar era. In 1946, Mannheim singled out the 'anti-social behaviour' of the propertied and powerful for attention; he specifically referred to 'profiteering' and the non-payment of taxes (Mannheim, 1946), something we might do well to reflect upon again today as European economies still struggle to extricate themselves from a self-imposed politics of austerity occasioned by the often less than ethical, and profoundly anti-social, practices of large financial institutions and banks. By contrast, as we have seen, in the curiously myopic neo-liberalism of British crime and disorder governance, anti-social behaviour has been conceived almost entirely as a characteristic of individuals, their choices and behaviour (Jamieson, 2012: 453).

We can observe this individualized attribution of responsibility in the continuing evolution of anti-social behaviour management strategy in Britain. The flagship Blairite White Paper *Respect and Responsibility* (Home Office, 2003) construed the task of assuming responsibility and conferring respect as a wholly personal performance. Accompanying the legislation which followed (the Anti-social Behaviour Act 2003) was a small *Action Plan* booklet containing uplifting and supposedly motivational slogans designed to inspire individuals towards social purpose and self-respect. Yet the assumption implicit in many of these homilies to self-improvement was that the barriers to achieving respect and responsibility were entirely to do with issues of choice and personal motivation. Irrespective of structural questions concerning needs, support and opportunities, addressing anti-social behaviour came to be redefined as a kind of '12-step programme' which the virtuous or resilient might choose to ascend – at times prompted by the threat of sanctions. That said, there is a great deal of truth in Richard Sennett's (2003) insightful remark that policy makers have often been 'poor psychologists'. The comment has a substantial bearing on anti-social behaviour policy implementation. After all, how is respect promoted for those whose legal rights are restricted, whose simple presence is deemed troublesome, whose motivations are questioned, whose integrity is cast under doubt, whose behaviour is condemned and whose scowling mugshots are reproduced on 'name and shame' leaflets distributed throughout their communities. When such routine humiliations are added to the frequent scapegoating by tabloid media and politicians alike, it becomes difficult to reconcile real 'respect and responsibility' with anti-social behaviour management and the 'Respect Agenda' (Scraton, 2007: 126–47). Despite the discourses of support and empowerment often reflected in this version of anti-social behaviour management strategy, actual practice rather more closely resembled enforcement activity backed up with sanctions for whenever individuals and families failed to live up to the values and standards articulated by right-wing media sources, voiced by politicians and, reinforced at the community level, by a new cadre of anti-social behaviour management officials. In effect, *conformity* to the rigours of neo-liberal family life, education and job-seeking, has been promoted and supported rather more than access to welfare, opportunities or resources (Gillies, 2005).

While the austerity politics and social security benefit cuts of the Coalition government after 2010 rolled back the welfare arm of state social policy still further, in one sense the strategic transition was seamless. First, in its long-awaited alterations to anti-social behaviour management interventions (Home Office, 2012b), in its strategy to tackle gangs and violence (HM Government, 2011b) and, finally in its Troubled Families Programme (DCLG, 2012d), the new government closely followed the lead of its predecessor. Consistent with Blairite ambitions, *Putting Victims First* was the focus of the Coalition government's White Paper on anti-social behaviour reform (Home Office, 2012b). The Anti-social Behaviour, Crime and Policing Bill 2013–2014 promises simplified and streamlined, faster and more effective orders and injunctions, new police powers to deal with the 'anti-social', enhanced operational discretion for anti-social behaviour management professionals, speedier evictions as well as longer-term enforcement solutions for some of the underlying problems.

Some indication of these longer-term measures became apparent in the Coalition government's gang strategy, brought forth, in part, as a response to the summer 2011 riots. In common with Iain Duncan Smith's Centre for Social Justice (CSJ) report, on gangs and gang cultures, which preceded it (CSJ, 2009), the government's *Gang Strategy* (HM Government, 2011b) articulated a wholly inverted interpretation of the evidence base upon which it rested. Thus crime, disorder and anti-social behaviour, seen as personal and behavioural choices, were construed as causes of marginality, social exclusion and poverty. This same central paradox was echoed in the government gang strategy document. For although the document presented clear and unambiguous evidence – drawing upon research by Bellis *et al.*, (2011) – of the extent to which area deprivation levels influenced assaultive violent injury rates, it still went on to describe an intervention strategy almost entirely focused around individual choices, decision making and what it called the 'life stories that lead to murder' (2011, 11–12). Tackling deprivation was off limits, the best that could be achieved would be to help young men negotiate their way through the dangerous risk-scape that working-class urban masculinity had apparently become.

Accordingly, strategic efforts to address poverty and social exclusion were overlooked; instead, individuals had to be led towards better choices and dysfunctional families had to be 'turned around'. As has been argued, this 'politics of behaviour' has been established to conceal the social and structural problems which often underlie much anti-social behaviour (not to mention a great deal of criminal behaviour too), by promoting the view that anti-social behaviour primarily resulted from the 'poor choices made by uninformed, unmotivated, incompetent or irresponsible individuals' (Crawford, 2009a: 814).

The Troubled Families Programme (TFP) became the vehicle through which such crimogenic circumstances were to be accessed and dysfunctional families 'turned around'. 'Troubled families' were defined by reference to four criteria: households where no adults are in work; where children were not in school; where profoundly dysfunctional internal family dynamics existed and where family members were frequently involved in crime and anti-social behaviour. While the last two or three decades have seen much debate about the existence, or not, of a new 'underclass' in contemporary Britain (Morris, 1994; MacDonald, 1997), few public policies have done quite so much to bring it into being as a discrete object of social policy intervention as the TFP. Where, once, the anti-social behaviour management strategy had become the *sine qua non* of the new youth justice, turning public policy into pest control, under the TFP, anti-social behaviour management has become the driving and defining focus of neo-liberal social welfare strategy: perhaps *regulating the poor*, revisited (Piven and Cloward, 1972).

Essentially, the programme provides all local authorities with targets based upon the estimated number of designated 'troubled families' – the worst of the worst – in their areas, proceeding next to guide the authorities towards producing a definitive list of those families that required 'turning'. It is recognized that such families will often have been well known, deprivation recycling across several generations, to local service delivery agencies. The language is also significant, this 'turning around' suggests an apparently wilful and anti-social family, intent on pursuing a course that is both self-destructive, a nightmare for their neighbours, and a blight on their communities. And yet, true to the delegated form of neo-liberal governance, the TFP is designed not to develop policies to meet the needs of these multiply-disadvantaged families, rather it is intended to *incentivize* local authorities (and their partners) to get a grip upon these problematic households through a three-year tapered regime of payment by results. The document spends time carefully spelling out the new financial arrangements. For each 'troubled family' identified and *successfully* engaged with, the Department for Communities and Local Government (DCLG) will make available a fee of

£4,000. Part of this will be paid up front with the rest to follow subject to successful family outcomes, such as: reduced rates of offending, a 60 per cent drop in reported anti-social behaviour, a reduced frequency of school exclusions, members of the household gaining employment or 'satisfactory progress' towards work, or, finally, 'at least one adult in the family moving off out-of-work benefits into continuous employment in the last 6 months' (DCLG, 2012d: 9). The DCLG document notes that 'based on the average length of a successful intervention with a family and the time frame for showing results, you should be able to claim your results-based payments around 12 months after the intervention has started' (DCLG, 2012d: 8). The document falls short of referring to these 'results-based payments' as 'winnings', but one is left with a distinct impression, for which there are clear historical precedents, that the government has placed a bounty on poverty and problem families and, not unlike the results-based regime for financing offender management services more generally, will be rewarding those authorities demonstrating the greatest diligence and success in regulating the marginal and anti-social.

Already encouraged to act earlier and more swiftly, to respond to public complaints more certainly and deploy a range of flexible powers more promptly, local authorities are now financially incentivized to deal with problem families more quickly and cheaply. Two historical and political observations resonate, although not entirely consistently, with this new infrastructure of marginalization. On the one hand, the new regime of behaviour management recalls the, perhaps apocryphal, story of the efficient 'overseer of the poor' or 'relieving officer' under the Victorian Poor Laws. The really efficient relieving officer, it was said, was the one with the fewest paupers to manage, the majority being deterred by the austere promise of 'less eligibility' within the forbidding walls of the workhouse (Squires, 1990). On the other hand, as revisionist histories of Victorian government growth have shown (Williams, 1981; Rose, 1985; Garland, 1985; Weiner, 1990) successful governance did not rest merely upon simple repression and effective control of the poorest but, rather, as Michel Foucault (1977) has argued, upon the successful recycling of 'useful delinquency'.

Foucault's argument, perhaps expressed most completely in *Discipline and Punish* demonstrated how the refinements in nineteenth-century prison discipline helped perfect the para-sciences of social administration which came, in time, to have a fully societal application. They were, furthermore, creative and constructive interventions, both reforming the criminal while also using him to relay a message about the work ethic and personal responsibility to the law-abiding. By extension, the chief contribution of contemporary neoliberal governance has been not, in the words of the global campaigners, to 'make poverty history' but rather to make it *useful* – and even economic – and a site for the closest attention to the behavioural dysfunctions of the poorest. Currently, the value of the poorest and the anti-social is as a lesson in political economy and personal responsibility. It follows that the importance of recruiting members of the public into reporting their supposedly 'irresponsible' or 'anti-social neighbours', via the anti-social behaviour or 'Benefit Fraud' hotlines (a similar mechanism deployed in each case) lies in constantly re-establishing the distinction between 'us' (the socially responsible) and them (the anti-social). The, apparently, self-evidently anti-social 'usual suspects', have been extracted from their marginalized and deprived environments, reified and illustrated, and portrayed as if they were the primary source of our current social problems. Their needs, except their declared need for self-control, are no longer of concern to government, their behaviour is everything. Phoenix (2009) has described these new arrangements as marking the return of a 'repressive welfarism', but perhaps an older expression of disciplinary powers, once articulated by Jacques Donzelot, *The Policing of Families* (1979), is also suggested.

This time around, however, these 'policing' activities are not primarily inclusive, educative or rehabilitative; the broader political economy of positive social mobility no longer operates. Instead, the new interventions, carrying many of the hallmarks of the original anti-social behaviour programme, condemn, contain and exclude. They are stigmatizing, low-intensity/high utility, swift, local, visible, cheap, responsibility-oriented and 'entry-level'. Such interventions, whether 'diversions from' or 'alternatives to' criminal justice, facilitating control and containment without involving the consequences of costly criminalization or substantial new resource implications (little in the way of new resources accompanied the TFP), while the 'results-based payment' system established a regime of perverse and anti-social incentives by which local authorities might select those to 'support' or those to neglect. Taken together they represent a neo-liberal form of limited (superficial and short-term) 'crime and disorder management' activism making poverty pay while side-stepping the heavy symbolism of crime or the expensive requirements of justice – let alone social justice.

Conclusion

The poorest and most marginal families of what the Coalition government and its supporters have lately referred to as 'broken Britain' (CSJ, 2006; Hayton, 2012) have come to bear the brunt of the new 'cultural governance'. Neo-liberal politics has fostered a renewed acceptance of inequality and, in its competitive wake, has cultivated a diminishing tolerance and a growing enmity towards the poorest and excluded whose predicament serves as a useful 'natural' reminder to the rest of us of the need for economy and compliance. Neo-liberalism has evidently effected a fundamental shift in the popular conceptions of citizenship and responsibility since Mannheim's day, market competence and commodification have acquired the trappings of sociability, while acting in one's self-interest has now acquired the veneer of pro-social behaviour, and it has become 'anti-social' to fail and to be poor, or to need or require public support. Neo-liberal anti-social behaviour management has crossed the first threshold of the failing state – it is already failing the poorest.

19
The Anti-sociality of Anti-social Behaviour Policy

Emma Bell

For Theresa May, Home Secretary, introducing the Conservative–Liberal Democrat Coalition government's White Paper on anti-social behaviour, *Putting Victims Fist: More Effective Responses to Anti-Social Behaviour*, it is quite obvious what such behaviour entails: it may include anything from vandalism to disorderly behaviour and even harassment:

> No one should have to accept graffiti on their walls, public drunkenness on their streets or harassment and intimidation on their own doorstep. But for too many communities in this country such crime and anti-social behaviour remains a fact of everyday life. (May in Home Office, 2012b: 3)

It may be criminal or simply anti-social – the two terms are conflated as if they were indistinguishable. In terms of the official response, both forms of behaviour may attract criminal sanctions, notably a prison sentence. Yet, behaviour which is considered as anti-social rather than criminal is targeted by civil measures and is to be subject to the lower civil standard of proof under the Anti-Social Behaviour, Crime and Policing Act which received Royal Assent on 14 March 2014. When determining whether anti-social behaviour did or did not take place, a court need no longer be satisfied 'beyond reasonable doubt', as was the case under the previous anti-social behaviour (ASB) legislation, but instead may take its decision based on a simple balance of probabilities.

This represents a considerable extension of the criminal law to encompass behaviour which would normally fall outside its remit, not being defined as a criminal offence. While the House of Lords rejected plans to widen the definition of anti-social behaviour to include 'conduct capable of causing nuisance or annoyance to any person', the new Act does go further than the original legal definition provided by the Crime and Disorder Act 1998. Anti-social behaviour is defined not just as (a) 'conduct that has caused, or is likely to cause, harassment, alarm or distress to any person'[1] but also as (b) 'conduct capable of causing nuisance or annoyance to a person in relation to that person's occupation of residential premises, or (c) conduct capable of causing housing-related nuisance or annoyance to any person' (Anti-social Behaviour, Crime and Policing Act 2014, Part I, section 2 (1)). Anti-social Behaviour Orders (ASBOs) were to have been abolished but remain and it seems that they will continue to target not just at any kind of behaviour capable of causing 'harassment, alarm or distress' but specifically the forms of behaviour most likely to be engaged in by narrowly-defined sub-groups of the population, namely the poorest and most vulnerable groups in society: beggars, prostitutes, children and young people. The new power to exclude adults responsible for anti-social behaviour from their homes is likely to exacerbate this trend.

While there has been much official concern about the vulnerable victims of anti-social behaviour, there has been little official or media concern expressed about the vulnerability of those who perpetrate anti-social behaviour or about the socially exclusive consequences of anti-social behaviour legislation on their lives. Similarly, there has been little official or media concern expressed about the vulnerable victims of forms of anti-social behaviour committed by the most privileged members of society. The very notion of *anti-social* behaviour has served to place it outside its social context, rendering the measures destined to tackle it futile in terms of preventing either its causes or its consequences. Poor communities have remained blighted by anti-social behaviour, but not just that perpetrated by the members of those same communities. Arguably, a much greater source of harm has been that caused by the anti-social activities of the powerful, whether by the state or private companies. Yet, the ideological construction of anti-social behaviour has meant that these significant harms have been ignored. Despite rhetoric to the contrary, there is every indication that the anti-social behaviour of the powerless will continue to be the focus of repressive legislative interventions in the United Kingdom for the foreseeable future. It is in this sense that anti-social behaviour policy may be considered as anti-social in itself.

This chapter begins by looking at anti-social behaviour policy in practice, outlining the way in which anti-social behaviour policy works to exacerbate existing social divisions, before moving on to examine the multiple kinds of anti-social behaviour which are left unchecked by such policy.

Criminalizing the vulnerable

There are no official statistics available on the actual offences subject to anti-social behaviour legislation. Nonetheless, official discussion of the causes of anti-social behaviour reflects who is likely to be targeted by the legislation. For May, the 'issues that drive much anti-social behaviour' are, for example, 'binge drinking, drug use, mental health issues, troubled family backgrounds and irresponsible dog ownership' (Home Office, 2012b). 'Troubled families' have been identified as a key source of anti-social behaviour – they are those families which suffer from unemployment, drug addiction, alcohol abuse, low income and poverty, in other words, poor and vulnerable households. Crime and anti-social behaviour are thus linked to an underclass made up of those people who form the ranks of the 'broken society'. This would appear to be borne out by the large number of people served ASBOs for prostitution (Phoenix, 2008) and begging (Statewatch, 2012a).

From the official statistics on the use of anti-social behaviour legislation that are available, it is clear that young people aged between 10 and 17 have been disproportionately targeted by ASBOs. Out of a total of 21,749 ASBOs issued in courts in England and Wales from April 1999 to December 2011, 8,160 were issued to young people aged between 10 and 17, representing 37.5% of all cases (Ministry of Justice, 2013). The new law also allows anti-social behaviour injunctions to be implemented against children as young as ten, while children aged 14 or above may face a prison sentence for breach. As with adults subject to ASBOs, these children tend to suffer from a whole host of social problems, representing some of the most vulnerable people in society. A Youth Justice Board Study into the early use of ASBOs found that children and young people subject to them tended to suffer from family breakdown, educational failure, emotional difficulties, bereavement and abuse (YJB, 2006). In addition, many of them have been found to suffer from mental health problems (BIBIC, 2005).

Youth are also disproportionately targeted by other forms of anti-social behaviour legislation, notably dispersal powers. Introduced by the Anti-social Behaviour Act 2003, these give senior police officers the power to disperse groups of two people or more from a public place when they have reasonable grounds for believing that *their presence or* behaviour has resulted in, *or is likely to result in,* one or more people being intimidated, harassed, alarmed or distressed. The powers tend to target groups of youths, responding to public fears concerning young people 'hanging around on the streets'.[2] They have been rebranded as police 'direction' powers under the new law but they will continue to allow police to direct any individual who they have 'reasonable grounds to suspect' that their behaviour 'has contributed *or is likely to contribute to* harassment, alarm or distress' or the 'occurrence in the locality of crime or disorder' (Anti-social Behaviour, Crime and Policing Act 2014, Part III, section 35 (2), my italics). Barnardo's, a major children's charity in the United Kingdom, has criticized these powers, claiming that children sent back to 'abusive or unsafe households' or moved on without any attempt to address the reasons underlying their anti-social behaviour could be placed in even greater danger (Barnardo's, 2011).

In addition, these powers to exclude certain individuals from public spaces have been extended by the new Public Spaces Protection Orders introduced by the 2014 law. These orders may be made by local authorities when it considers that '(a) activities carried on in a public place within the authority's area have had a detrimental effect on the quality of life of those in the locality, or (b) it is likely that activities will be carried on in a public place within that area and that they will have such an effect' (Anti-social Behaviour, Crime and Policing Act 2014, Part IV, section 59 (2)). Yet again, anti-social behaviour is extraordinarily widely defined and there is no need to prove that the offending behaviour has actually occurred – only that it may occur. There are concerns that such powers may be used to further limit the right to protest or to penalize the simply 'annoying' behaviour of children and young people.

The parents of children may also be targeted by the Conservative–Liberal Democrat Coalition government's 'Troubled Families Project', the successor of New Labour's Family Intervention Project, which targets 120,000 'problem' families across England and Wales,[3] using a combination of support and coercion. Families are offered practical help, such as parenting advice and assistance with drug and alcohol abuse. Yet, if they refuse the support offered to them, they may be subject to a range of sanctions, including injunctions to prevent anti-social behaviour and demotion orders whereby tenants in social housing may be stripped of their secure tenancy and threatened with eviction. For those families who are evicted from their homes, local authorities may provide short-term family intervention tenancies which are made conditional on good behaviour and cooperation with family intervention social workers.

The culture of anti-social behaviour

The use of coercion to tackle the multiple causes of anti-social behaviour as it is currently defined by the government highlights the fact that anti-social behaviour is seen to result from individual behavioural problems rather than from structural factors. Indeed, the very notion of 'troubled families' just mentioned immediately focuses attention on the families themselves, rather than on their problems. A discursive slip is regularly made in government discourse between families that have troubles to families that cause troubles (Levitas, 2012). Anti-social behaviour is essentially regarded as a cultural problem which is passed down from one generation to the next. For David Cameron, it springs from 'a culture of disruption and irresponsibility that cascades through generations' (Cameron, 2011c). Even poverty, with which anti-social behaviour is inextricably linked in the eyes of the government, is regarded as a cultural problem. For Frank Field, the Coalition's poverty tsar:

> a modern definition of poverty must take into account those children whose parents remain disengaged from their responsibilities. I no longer believe that the poverty endured by all too many children can simply be

measured by their parents' lack of income. Something more fundamental than the scarcity of money is adversely dominating the lives of these children. Since 1969 I have witnessed a growing indifference from some parents to meeting the most basic needs of children, and particularly younger children, those who are least able to fend for themselves. I have also observed how the home life of a minority but, worryingly, a growing minority of children, fails to express an unconditional commitment to the successful nurturing of children. (Field, 2010: 16)

The Conservative–Liberal Democrat Coalition government's approach to the issue of anti-social behaviour and its social causes thus represents a classic case of victim-blaming. This means that its strategy is unlikely to be successful, neglecting the wider structural causes of anti-social behaviour, such as poverty and unemployment. Furthermore, the use of sanctions such as eviction and imprisonment are likely to exacerbate the problem of social exclusion ensuring that the perpetrators of anti-social behaviour are permanently cast out from mainstream society (the lasting effects of a criminal record are well known). Yet, as Cameron himself has claimed, 'When one group in society seems to lead a life apart from the rest, that can have a corrosive effect on others' (Cameron, 2011c). The strategy of tackling anti-social behaviour which condemns those responsible for it to 'live apart from the rest' may therefore be regarded as *anti*-social in itself.

In addition, instead of calming public fears about anti-social behaviour, the government is participating in the stirring up of a genuine *moral* panic about anti-social behaviour whereby it is not so much behaviour in itself which is regarded as problematic, but rather the fact that this is seen as symbolic of the wider moral disintegration of society (Cohen, 2005). Stuart Waiton argues that the current panic about anti-social behaviour is amoral rather than moral, claiming that it focuses on the amoral notion of safety and expects little in the way of moral transformation on the part of those deemed responsible for it (Waiton, 2008). For him, almost any behaviour is deemed acceptable, provided that it is 'safe and does not disturb the safety of others' (*ibid.*: 134). Yet, it would seem that the intensive and intrusive intervention projects targeted at the poor and vulnerable are indeed a serious, if largely ineffective, attempt to transform their values. Furthermore, the moral dimension of the problem is repeatedly highlighted over the safety aspect of anti-social behaviour. For Cameron it is all 'about blame, about good behaviour and bad behaviour, about morals' (Cameron, 2011c). What constitutes good behaviour is not radically different from the behaviour expected of individuals during the moral panics of the 1970s (contrary to what Waiton suggests). It is about assuming responsibility for oneself and one's family, preferably within the confines of the traditional two-parent family (*cf.* the Conservative Party's declared support for marriage and the introduction of married couples' tax breaks in 2013).

In a climate of moral panic about anti-social behaviour, it is particularly difficult to have a rational debate and to consider policies which may be truly *social*, aimed at reintegrating those who are seen to be cut off from mainstream society. Instead, the perpetrators of anti-social behaviour are demonized, regarded as morally and culturally different from the rest. Repairing the so-called 'broken society' becomes chimeric as social fissures widen into chasms.

In addition, communities are encouraged to become involved in the exclusion of those who do not share dominant norms and values. Already, communities have been encouraged to report anti-social behaviour to the authorities and to 'name and shame' those responsible for anti-social behaviour. The naming and shaming of children attracted the criticism of the European Commissioner of Human Rights for violation of article 8 of the European Convention on Human Rights which protects one's right to a private life (Gil-Robles, 2005). Furthermore, under the new Anti-social Behaviour, Crime and Policing Act 2014, children as young as ten responsible for anti-social behaviour will continue to be named and a new 'community trigger' has been introduced which means that local authorities and police will be obliged by the local community to take action regarding a persistent problem. While such a measure may help to ensure that serious anti-social behaviour is not ignored, there is a danger that involving communities in this way will pit individual citizens against each other, again accentuating rather than healing community divisions. The community itself may thus become rather anti-social, characterized by a 'defensive exclusivity' (Crawford, 1998: 245). So, it is not just anti-social behaviour itself which may harm communities but also the measures taken to address anti-social behaviour.

The ineffectiveness of anti-social behaviour measures

It may be argued that the potential anti-social effects of anti-social behaviour legislation outlined above are a risk worth taking if this means protecting the public from the undeniably harmful effects of some forms of anti-social behaviour. Yet, this legislation is arguably rather ineffective in terms of public protection. It is also likely to remain so despite the Coalition's promises to develop what it terms as 'more effective responses to anti-social behaviour' (Home Office, 2012b). The legislation is to remain fundamentally the same as at present as ASBOs are simply replaced by various forms of injunctions and Criminal Behaviour Orders (CBOs)[4] and dispersal powers as police direction powers. The system is to be somewhat streamlined and simplified with injunctions for low-level behaviour now being easier to obtain, subject only to the civil standard of proof.

It is hard to see how the new system will address the problem of breach, despite claims to the contrary (see, for example, Home Office, 2012b). It is estimated that out of a total of 21,645 ASBOs issued between 1 June 2000 and 31 December 2011, 57.3 per cent were breached at least once (Ministry of Justice, 2013). The proposed new legislation claims to address the problem by, for example, adding 'positive requirements' to the new ASBOs obtained on conviction – the Criminal Behaviour Orders (CBOs) – which it is hoped will enable offenders to address the underlying causes of their behaviour. Yet, if breach of these positive requirements is to be sanctioned, breach rates of the new orders could be even higher. Furthermore, given that prison is still to be used as a penalty for breach of CBOs and, as a last resort, for breach of other injunctions made against adults, the potential 'anti-social' impact of these disposals, in terms of their failure to reintegrate the perpetrators of such behaviour into society, remains unaddressed.

In addition, the disposals claim to empower victims of anti-social behaviour while in reality they tend to distract their attention from many more serious forms of anti-social behaviour perpetrated by those living *outside* their own communities. Indeed, while the Conservative-Liberal Democrat Coalition government can be criticized for its overly broad definition of anti-social behaviour which can lead to the criminalization of many forms of mere nuisance behaviour not usually defined as criminal, it can also be criticized for defining anti-social behaviour too narrowly, associating it only with the underclass that belongs to 'broken Britain'. There are in reality various forms of behaviour which may be regarded as thoroughly anti-social, given their capacity to cause 'harassment, alarm and distress' and to create considerable social harm, but which are not targeted by either criminal legislation or anti-social behaviour legislation.

The anti-social behaviour of the powerful

David Cameron has recognized the need to tackle 'problems at the top of our society', recognizing that 'some at the top [...] have behaved appallingly' (Cameron, 2011c). He claims to be tackling these problems by rendering MPs' expenses more transparent, by examining media corruption via the Leveson Inquiry, by placing new taxes on banks and closing some tax loopholes. Yet, he does not envisage using anti-social behaviour measures to tackle this form of anti-social behaviour, despite the fact that these would get around the notorious difficulty of proving *mens rea* with regard to white collar crime (Whyte, 2004). Perhaps a new focus on the anti-social behaviour of the powerful would also help to draw public attention to *their* 'responsibility deficit'[5] rather than to that of 'troubled families'. For Hazel Croall, anti-social behaviour measures could be a very effective way of targeting 'economic crime' perpetrated in the course of business since its wide definition would allow it to encompass many forms of harm which may cause real distress, such as harassment in the home by doorstep and telesales people (Croall, 2009). Indeed, the anti-social behaviour of business is particularly concerning, yet the notion of 'anti-social business' has not yet entered either the popular or government lexicon. An Internet search for the term 'anti-social business' throws up results from companies such as IBM focusing on the failure of business to use new social media tools in the most effective way possible.[6]

One particularly harmful form of anti-social behaviour committed by big business in the United Kingdom and throughout the world is environmental harm. This may cause extreme damage, not just to the natural world, but also to human beings, resulting in anything from simple nuisance to injury and even death. Here again, the official definition of environmental anti-social behaviour is extremely limited, concerned only with acts such as criminal damage, vandalism, graffiti and fly-posting, littering, nuisance vehicles, disposing of used needles in the street and the misuse of fireworks. It does not refer to, for example, the environmental nuisance caused by the erection of mobile phone masts which are not just unsightly but often cause a considerable amount of worry and stress among local populations concerning the real or perceived health risks that they may have. Nor does it refer to the smoke, fumes and gases emitted by industry. These kinds of nuisance are regulated by existing statutory nuisance legislation such as the Environmental Pollution Act 1990. Yet, the sanctions are hardly dissuasive, usually consisting in a caution or a fine, the amount of which is often wholly insignificant when compared to the multimillion pound annual turnovers of the industries which are fined (Walters, 2009). A number of environmental nuisances identified as 'significant' air pollution by the Environment Agency, the regulatory body charged with enforcing such legislation, are often treated with a simple caution. For example, one case involving the deliberate release of kerosene and aviation fuel into a waterway resulted in a mere caution (*ibid.*: 8). Most of the matters taken to court were breaches of licences or cases involving the illegal burning or disposal of waste. Arguably, the threat of imprisonment underpinning much anti-social behaviour legislation would be a more effective deterrent, helping to ensure that big business refrains from causing environmental nuisance which can cause not just 'alarm or distress' but even death. Indeed, it is estimated that 24,000 British residents die prematurely every year because of air pollution (cited by Walters: 1).

The social harm caused by the failure of employers to respect rules and regulations regarding health and safety in the workplace may also be regarded as serious forms of anti-social behaviour. It has been argued that instances of such anti-social behaviour are likely to swell as a result of the planned cuts to the tune of 35% to the budget of the Health and Safety Executive, leading to an estimated 11,000 fewer inspections a year.[7] As things stand, a British company can expect a visit from the Executive only once every 20 years (Whyte, 2007: 32). The failure of employers to respect their duty of care towards employees is of course punishable by the criminal law[8] but the lack of state regulation means that these crimes are very rarely ever prosecuted.

These breaches of health and safety legislation are in reality serious crimes, even if they are rarely treated as such.

Businesses are also responsible for a range of anti-social behaviour with regard to their employees, frequently causing 'harassment, alarm and distress' when they restructure, relocate (Ramsay, 2004) or simply fail to respect the basic integrity of their workers, demeaning or denigrating them. Employees can complain to an employment tribunal when they feel they have been subject to some form of discrimination covered by the law, such as sexual or racial discrimination. However, there is nothing they can do about other harmful behaviour which remains entirely unregulated.

Recently, public attention has been drawn to the extremely anti-social practice of tax avoidance by huge multi-national companies such as Amazon, Starbucks and Google. Current anti-social behaviour measures would obviously constitute a wholly inadequate response to such behaviour but it would at least be useful to highlight the anti-social nature of these practices. There is a strong case for formulating new legislation in order to tackle the real social harm caused by such behaviour, in terms of it hindering the funding of social services and the redistribution of wealth. Yet, the Coalition government has only proposed introducing a limited anti-abuse rule which will affect just a tiny minority of cases as opposed to a more general anti-avoidance rule which would prevent large-scale tax avoidance (HM Revenue and Customs, 2012; War on Want, 2012).

Another way in which businesses have behaved anti-socially is via the 'regeneration' of urban centres which has caused serious damage to the fabric of community life, often being just as, if not more, destructive than behaviour that is more traditionally regarded as anti-social. Within the context of urban 'regeneration', there has been considerable focus on the need to tackle anti-social behaviour. Yet, the kind of behaviour targeted is not that which tends to affect the lives of deprived communities but rather that which threatens to deter potential consumers from new commercial centres. Partnerships have even been developed between businesses and the police in an effort to tackle crime and anti-social behaviour against business. These partnerships have thus developed strategies to prevent criminal acts, such as shoplifting, but also merely troublesome behaviour which is seen to deter potential customers from newly regenerated urban areas such as the playing of outdoor games and sports and begging (Coleman *et al.*, 2005; Minton, 2006: 14). The exclusionary effects of such measures may be described as being extraordinarily anti-social. In addition, local people may find their lives severely disrupted by regeneration programmes, often forced to move away from their area as housing costs escalate. Local businesses may also be forced to close, unable to afford the new rents (Monbiot, 2000). As large areas of Britain's cities fall into private hands, public space has become increasingly regulated, killing off many remaining forms of local diversity.

Far from being perceived as anti-social, business is usually presented as being a victim of anti-social behaviour. Yet, it could just as easily be argued that business benefits considerably from anti-social behaviour measures. It benefits from exclusionary measures such as dispersal powers and new Public Spaces Protection Orders which can exclude people who may be considered a threaten to commercial interests. In addition, businesses have used ASBOs to protect their interests from protesters (Statewatch, 2012b). Under the Conservative–Liberal Democrat Coalition government, businesses are actually profiting in a pecuniary form from schemes aimed at tackling the perceived social causes of anti-social behaviour. The private welfare-to-work company, A4e (Action for Employment) is involved in Family Intervention Projects via the 'Working Families Everywhere' campaign which aims to get families back into work. Furthermore, private companies can benefit more indirectly from anti-social behaviour measures when those who breach them find themselves placed in prison. It is estimated that 13.1 per cent of the prison population of England and Wales is held in privately-run penal establishments (Prison Reform Trust, 2011: 71).

The state may also be seen to benefit from current anti-social behaviour measures. Despite the ineffectiveness of such measures, they do at least allow government to appear to be doing something about crime and the problem behaviour which blights not just the lives of the middle classes but particularly those of the very poorest members of society. For the current Conservative-led coalition, such measures allow it to convey a more caring image, concerned with the problems of those who suffer from anti-social behaviour and with the social causes of anti-social behaviour itself. Anti-social behaviour measures are presented as a key element in the project to repair Britain's supposedly 'broken' society.

A focus on the anti-social behaviour of the powerless also enables the state, intentionally or not, to deflect attention from its own anti-social behaviour. Indeed, the anti-social behaviour of the state itself should not be overlooked. Agents of the state may engage in anti-social behaviour, either actively or passively. Police officers, for example, may passively fail to regulate the crimes and anti-social behaviour of the powerful while focusing their attentions on the powerless. Actively, the police have been engaged in anti-social policing methods, undermining the right to protest by harassing demonstrators. A recent report has expressed concern over the use of pre-emptive arrest, the control of movement using kettling techniques (officially known as 'containment') and the gathering of personal data on protesters by Forward Intelligence Teams[9] (Netpol, 2012). Such policing methods do not just threaten to infringe civil liberties, but also risk causing considerable 'harassment, alarm and distress' to the individuals subjected to them, particularly during kettling, whereby protesters are confined for long periods of time without access to basic hygiene facilities or to food or water.

Conclusion: the future of ASB legislation

Over half-way into the Conservative–Liberal Democrat mandate, it would seem that little is likely to change. Despite claims to be creating 'more effective responses to anti-social behaviour' (Home Office, 2010b), measures to tackle anti-social behaviour are to continue to be ineffective in terms of tackling the anti-social behaviour of the poorest and most vulnerable members of society. Rebranded as anti-social behaviour injunctions and police direction powers, these measures will remain anti-social in themselves, failing to reintegrate the perpetrators of such behaviour into society. Furthermore, a significant amount of anti-social behaviour perpetrated by the powerful will remain unaddressed, leaving members of the public exposed to serious harm and nuisance. As the government itself has noted, 'Anti-social behaviour still ruins too many lives and still damages too many communities' (Home Office, 2012b), yet the damaging effects of anti-social behaviour perpetrated by the powerful and of anti-social behaviour legislation itself must also be recognized if the lives of people in these communities are to be improved.

Nonetheless, the current political climate is far from favourable for a change of direction. Indeed, it is unlikely that the current government, with its strong links to the world of business, will risk offending its core supporters by targeting their anti-social behaviour. In addition, in the context of the current recession, it is probable that the government will continue to attempt to offset its failure to provide social and economic security with an attempt to provide security from crime and anti-social behaviour to the public at large. Furthermore, the strategy of involving communities themselves in the fight against anti-social behaviour (via the 'community trigger' for example) fits very well into the government's wider aim of building a 'Big Society' of volunteers, ready to supplant the state in the search for solutions to social problems. Moving away from state solutions to such problems is also facilitated by the increasing role played by the private and third sectors in tackling the perceived causes of anti-social behaviour, notably the problems of unemployment, poor parenting and drug abuse associated with 'troubled families'. For the foreseeable future then, official responses to anti-social behaviour are to continue to be anti-social in themselves.

Notes

1. Behaviour is no longer limited to that which causes 'harassment, alarm or distress to one or more persons not of the same household as [the perpetrator]', as per the 1998 Act.
2. According to the British Crime Survey, this was, until recently, considered to be the most serious worrying form of ASB for the general public (Home Office, 2010a).
3. This figure of 120,000 problem families is spurious, based as it is on an outdated estimate from a survey originally carried out by the New Labour government's

social exclusion task force which attempted to count the number of families which had at least five characteristics identified with social exclusion (Levitas, 2012).

4. The CBO replaces the CRASBO, an ASBO specifically designed for those already convicted of a criminal offence.

5. The expression is borrowed from David Cameron (2011).

6. One exception was an article by Aditya Chakrabortty from *The Guardian* suggesting that tax-evading business leaders ought to be given 'Anti-Social Business Orders'.

7. Numerous 'safety crimes', such as those perpetrated in the workplace, are not regarded as health and safety offences (Hillyard and Tombs, 2008: 9). Consequently, it is suggested that a 'social harm' approach should be taken to the problem of criminality, whereby attention is focused not just on crime as it is formally defined but also on physical, financial, emotional, psychological and sexual harm (*ibid.*: 14–16).

8. The Corporate Manslaughter and Corporate Homicide Act 2007 intended to facilitate the prosecution of companies who breach their duty of care in this way, specifically ensured that company directors would not be made personally liable.

9. These teams of police officers photograph and/or take video footage of individuals involved in political protest. They may also note down other personal information regardless of whether or not the individuals concerned have a criminal record.

Part III

Anti-social Behaviour, Recreation and Leisure

20

'Roughs on the Turf' and 'Suburban Saturnalia': Anti-social Behaviour on Victorian Racecourses

Emmanuel Roudaut

Introduction

Horseracing has a paradoxical status and is 'possibly the best example of a sport that remained very exclusive in social terms but also had a huge popular following' (Holt, 1992: 181). Well into the twentieth century, social exclusivity was unchallenged in the membership of the Jockey Club, the ruling body of the sport, or in the attendance at Newmarket meetings, while Ascot and a number of fixtures were key moments of the London season. Even in preindustrial England, the presence of plebeian spectators in less exalted venues, occasionally resulting in disturbances, was 'disapprovingly acknowledged' (Malcolmson, 1973: 51). The association of 'the sport of kings' with popular entertainment was seen more favourably when horseraces were included in the traditional holiday calendar, during Wakes Week for instance, thus contributing to the paternalistic, cross-class nature of rural recreations. This paradoxical status did not disappear with the Industrial Revolution. On the contrary, it may have been reinforced by various innovations in the late eighteenth century and the development of the railways a few decades later. These arguably turned horseracing into the first mass spectator sport, with attendant concerns of crowd control and unseemly behaviour. This chapter will first outline perceptions of and attitudes to what would now be called 'anti-social' behaviour on the racecourse. It will then assess the effectiveness of attempts to deal with it, from the Victorian period to the interwar years.

Racing in the age of urbanization

Traditional horseraces were long-drawn-out affairs, which consisted of a series of heats culminating in a final 'match' between two horses. It was a test of stamina for five- and six-year-olds over four miles. An innovation known as the sweepstake became popular in the second half of the eighteenth century. Larger fields were encouraged, so as to increase prize money. More importantly, sweepstakes turned races into captivating tests of speed, as they were run over a shorter distance by younger horses (three- or two-year-olds). Some of these experiments were so successful that they came to be known as 'classic races', especially the St Leger, first run in 1776 at Doncaster, and the Derby, first run in 1780 at Epsom. Thanks to Epsom's accessibility from nearby London, the popularity of Derby Day grew rapidly, attracting five to ten thousand spectators in the first years. By the mid-1830s, many London employers had declared it a holiday, albeit unofficial, and the return journey had become 'a drunken traffic-jam unequalled anytime, anywhere in the kingdom' (Wynn-Jones, 1979: 73). Likewise, most major urban centres had a racecourse in their vicinity and race week became a key part of the working-class leisure agenda. Even at the start of the century, major races attracted crowds estimated at over 100,000 (Huggins, 2000: 92–4, 119). People travelled to races on foot, on horseback or by carriage, until the railway revolution drew more spectators from further afield. The start of organized steeplechasing in the 1830s supplemented an already growing number of flat-racing fixtures, and the Grand Liverpool Steeplechase, better known as the Grand National, became a truly national event, the equivalent of the Derby in steeplechasing. All these changes were instrumental in the survival of a rural pastime in the age of industrialization and urbanization. What remained was the cross-class nature of traditional recreations. If social classes did not mingle, at least they came in contact with each other.

Victorian crowds, however, could turn into mobs, and occasionally race-goers became riotous. In 1838, when the first Derby Special failed to provide enough seats, some five thousand frustrated passengers stormed the railway station and created havoc until mounted policemen were called in. However, it is generally assumed that racing could 'offset the potential for class conflict and division' (Huggins, 2000: 88). This seems to be confirmed by the absence of sedition when crowds gathered to attend races on the Manchester moor a few months after the Peterloo massacre in 1819, although urban expansion and Irish migration led to serious ethnic violence at some races in large industrial towns during the 1850s and the 1860s. Racecourses were also affected by agitation linked to women's suffrage, culminating with the death of Emily Davison at the Derby in 1913 (Huggins, 2000: 134–6). Nevertheless, moral reasons, rather than politics or issues of law and order, were put forward when horseracing, which had been banned under Oliver Cromwell, came under renewed attack in the first decades of the nineteenth century.

A moral crusade

Despite sporadic condemnation of betting, horse races had benefited from royal patronage since the Restoration in 1660. Cross-class participation, with the exception of Newmarket, was generally encouraged by paternalistic attitudes to popular recreations. The development of sustained attacks on horseracing in late Hanoverian England can be correlated with the growth of Nonconformity and the rise of the evangelical movement in the Anglican Church. Preachers would castigate not only the gaming and betting, but also the 'loose behaviour' which accompanied these festivities, in particular drunkenness, brawls and prostitution. A noted example was the campaign launched in 1827 against the Cheltenham races by the local vicar, Francis Close, who in a widely circulated sermon clamoured against the Christian race grounds 'exceeding the Heathen festivals of Venus and Bacchus' (Close, 1827: 8).

Similar evangelical pressure was exerted throughout the country, sometimes with the support of the local press. Petitions were signed, and occasionally reformists would attend the meetings and confront race-goers. Even observers hardly likely to be hostile to the turf acknowledged that people went to the races more for the 'raciness' than for the races. According to the Earl of Suffolk, thousands flocked to the Epsom Downs 'in the hope or on the pretence of seeing a race which not one man in fifty ever really sees, nor one in twenty cares about seeing' (Vamplew, 1976: 135), while a famous trainer objected to 'drinking [being] carried to excess followed by dancing in semi-darkness' (Day, 1880: 285). Questioned by a parliamentary select committee in 1844, several leading racecourse executives also expressed the view, backed by informed argument, that most of the public did not attend the fixtures for the racing *per se*. People came for the gambling opportunities, and also for the funfair attractions (House of Commons, questions 1270, 1360, 1361, 1381).

Both fairs and horseraces came under regular attack from moral reformers owing to the disreputable characters they were liable to attract. Magistrates and the police were also worried about the drunkenness and rowdy, possibly violent, behaviour they were likely to provoke. In his classic study of the turf, Wray Vamplew devotes a whole chapter to the unruly crowd behaviour which characterized racing events. The most emblematic event was the Epsom Derby, described by a contemporary observer as 'a national carnival-cum-public-saturnalia, [...] a licence for behaviour that would not be tolerated elsewhere' (Vamplew, 1976: 135). A graphic description of the 1851 Derby can be found in *Household Words*, where Charles Dickens depicts 'all the variety of human riddles who propound themselves on race-courses'. Alongside jugglers, acrobats, fortune-telling gypsies, black-faced singers, ventriloquists and confidence tricksters features the enigmatic mention of a transvestite, possibly suggesting that this was not an unusual sight *on* the course: 'Now a coarse vagabond, or idiot, or compound of the two *never beheld by mortal off the course*, hurries about, with ample skirts and a tattered parasol, counterfeiting a woman' (Dickens, 2009: 195–6, my italics). There is no significant difference between these scenes and descriptions of the Derby published later in the century, as in the first chapters of *The Christian*, a best-selling novel of 1897. In 1878, a parliamentarian declared that 'every vice that could be imagined had full scope at the Derby' (Vamplew, 1976: 137). Similar accounts concerning other meetings abound, as in the memoirs of a late nineteenth-century police inspector who

> cursed these race meetings [at Musselburgh near Edinburgh]. They were nothing else than carnivals of drunkenness, crime and misery. They collect from all the lowest and most degraded centres of population the worst of their elements. Debauchery and criminal pollution always follow horseracing. (Vamplew, 1976: 142)

In 1856, the Liverpool journalist Hugh Shimmin noted the conspicuous presence of prostitutes at the Aintree racecourse, where organizers seemed to turn a blind eye to illegal dog-fights and prize-fighting (Walton and Wilcox, 1991: 75–6, 84–5).

Other reports, spanning the eighteenth and nineteenth centuries, detail the activities of confidence tricksters and various categories of crooks and thieves operating at race meetings, sometimes using young women as baits to lure their victims. A study of prosecutions in York during races has highlighted the convergence of prostitutes from Leeds, Bradford, Hull and Nottingham for the occasion, confirming similar anecdotal evidence for other cities. The pattern of regional circuits of prostitution could take on a national dimension, with reports of London prostitutes visiting Doncaster for the St Leger (Vamplew, 1976: 137; Finnegan, 1979: 25). Travelling gangs of pickpockets would also operate on regional race circuits. Their range of action extended with the railways, as evidenced by prosecutions of London pickpockets on northern courses during the 1860s, and it was not unusual for them to operate on the train. In the Midlands, the so-called 'Birmingham Boys' were notorious for their brutality, and as gangs made incursions into other regions, territorial disputes were not uncommon (Huggins, 2000: 127). Rowdy behaviour was not confined to gangs or the poorest sections of society, as evidenced by a drunken assault on police constables by the scions of prominent Liverpool families returning from the Grand National in 1879. Considerable pressure was exerted on the victims, the magistrates and the local press to avoid undue publicity. It is therefore likely that similar incidents went largely unreported (Pinfold, 2004: 64–5).

Some of these testimonies seem to suggest that, 30 or 40 years on, little had changed since the attempt to drive the races out of Cheltenham in 1827. In fact, Francis Close was only able to secure the temporary relocation of races to nearby Tewkesbury, and little more was achieved than the temporary abandonment of racing by some town councils in the 1830s. Most campaigns failed altogether (Huggins, 2000: 206–7). It is interesting to compare this lack of success with the fate of similar movements. The first decades of the century saw a resurgence of religious and humanitarian attempts to improve moral standards. A Society for the Suppression of Vice, founded in 1802 and popularly known as the Vice Society, sought to emulate the efforts of previous Societies for the Reformation of Manners and launched prosecutions on a wide range of issues. The Society for the Prevention of Cruelty to Animals, founded in 1824 (later the RSPCA), set itself a wide remit, as indicated by its name, but focused on the eradication of animal fights. The Lord's Day Observance Society (LDOS), founded in 1831, campaigned for more rigorous restrictions on non-religious activities on Sundays. The 1830s also witnessed the development of an organized temperance movement. It was at the racecourse that the immoral practices combated by these crusades could be found all in one place, making it an obvious target for reformist zeal. On the surface, the most successful organization had been the RSPCA, which had secured the passing of the Cruelty to Animals Act in 1835, although the upper-class pursuits of hunting and coursing were not included in the clause banning animal fights such as bull-baiting and dog-fights. However, Shimmin's observation of animal fights and pugilism at Aintree was not unusual, and the ban proved difficult to enforce, as evidenced by numerous cases of prosecution in the late nineteenth century (Holt, 1992: 57–8) and the need for further legislative moves. The LDOS suffered similar setbacks (Harrison, 1965) in its attempts to strengthen restrictions on Sunday trading and pub-opening hours. The so-called Victorian Sunday was a gradual and patchy achievement. As for the most formidable of these pressure groups, the Temperance movement, it had to contend with powerful commercial interests supported by the Conservative Party. Its major legislative victory, the Licensing Act 1872, although falling far short of its initial aims, led to rioting and was rapidly amended when the Conservatives returned to office in 1874. It took the exceptional circumstances of the First World War to secure drastic restrictions on opening hours in drinking places. These various attempts to curb the pursuit of sensual pleasures had been hampered either by fear of arousing public unrest, or the opposition of the governing class, when it did not come from business interests. This was also the case when it came to reform horseracing.

Reasons for failure

As with fairs, interference with race meetings, by the police or moral reformers, could meet with violent resistance. A witness declared to the Select Committee on Gaming set up in 1844 that he had been 'pelted on [his] way home' after his attempt to create an Anti-Gambling Association to suppress gambling in Doncaster during race week and that 'the consequence of this *émeute* was that the association fell to pieces' (HC, 1844: Q. 1019). The same witness recounts a pitched battle in 1829 between the police and 'thimblemen' or 'thimble-riggers', a category of confidence tricksters present in large numbers on most racecourses throughout the nineteenth and twentieth centuries. Armed with sticks, the thimblemen had confronted the police instructed to expel them from the Doncaster racecourse (HC, 1844: Q. 1020). Similar incidents involving organized groups were reported, especially between 1820 and 1840: dragoons had to be called in on at least one occasion. If such levels of disruption were unusual, anti-racing preachers who ventured on to the racecourse could be threatened or even molested throughout the period (Huggins, 2000: 135, 216).

Upper-class support of racing was indisputable, and its apologists often quoted King William IV's description of 'the manly and noble sport of a free people'. Any attempt to eradicate a disreputable activity associated with the turf could be presented as a covert attack on the sport itself, and consequently an attack on manliness, British heritage and liberty (Huggins, 2000: 230). The lingering suspicion that turf reformers were keen on banning racing itself, and not simply its most disreputable aspects, was not always unfounded. It appears to be the case of an anti-gambling witness who declared to the panel of the 1844 Select Committee on Gaming that 'as long as the racing system is what it is, no gentleman can go without sanctioning the vices as well as the amusement' (HC, 1844: Q. 1062) and persisted in saying that it was impossible to suppress betting 'without abolishing horse-racing' (HC, 1844, Q. 1082).

The full statement of the witness, who later bemoans 'the great percentage who come to the races for the other sensual gratifications provided for them', such as eating and drinking and 'much worse' (HC, 1844: Q. 1127–8), reads like a perfect illustration of the gap between a leisured upper-class panel and a dour, possibly Nonconformist, middle-class reformer whose inflexibility was more likely to antagonize his audience than promote effective change. In fact, middle-class attitudes to leisure, including racing, were extremely varied, and he probably represented a small, if vocal, minority (Bailey, 1986: 84–5; Thompson, 1988: 260). Mike Huggins (2000: 68–85) has also found that, contrary to previous assumptions, there was a significant middle-class involvement with racing throughout the period and that some 'respectable' families did attend meetings.

Attempts to rid the turf of its rowdier aspects were also hindered by economic interests. The presence of refreshment-booths and gambling-booths alongside various sideshows of dubious legality increased the incidence of drunkenness and brawls. However, organizers were reluctant to dispense with facilities which represented a major source of income. This becomes apparent in the declarations of race managers to the 1844 Select Committee. Without the letting of these booths, it was claimed, they would not have been able to finance the stakes and pay the lord of the manor. The most profitable source of income was the gambling-booths, which were allocated by auction. They were outnumbered by refreshment-booths, which could be rented at much lower rates. The manager of the Goodwood racecourse, for instance, declared that each of the two gaming-booths was let for £125. With the rent for a refreshment-booth of the same size at around ten or 15 shillings, and total receipts of £50, the number of drinking places can therefore be estimated at nearly 100, excluding catering premises within the grandstand. Huggins cites comparable figures for northern tracks. The Epsom manager mentioned 12 or 14 gaming-booths, and it can be safely assumed that the number of drinking places in this leading racecourse amounted to several hundred. Unsurprisingly on the defensive, witnesses insisted on the precarious state of their finances. Indeed the manager of Goodwood told the panel that all receipts from the letting of amenities went to the racing fund, which was heavily in debt (HC, 1844: Q. 1185). Commercial agreements could include more controversial activities. Whereas at Goodwood thimble-riggers had their tables broken by the authorities, at Epsom they were tolerated for a fee, prompting an apologetic response from the witness: 'Yes; when you rent a race-course you must make the most you can of it' (HC, 1844: Q. 1387–92). Likewise, the management at Aintree could not be unaware that a tent was devoted to dog-fights in the 1850s, even though they preferred to turn a blind eye against the payment of rent. It appears that at least until the 1870s some racecourses would raise revenue by charging for activities which were either illegal or on the fringe of legality (Huggins, 2000: 132).

According to Huggins (2000: 127–8, 136), this relative tolerance of illegal or disreputable activities was also due to the fact that they were often regarded as part of the attraction. The most famous representation of Derby Day, a painting by William Powell Frith first exhibited in 1858, could almost suggest that they were the *main* attraction. While the race and its spectators are relegated to the background, the attention of the viewer is drawn to scenes of seduction, conspicuous consumption and deception. The central scene shows acrobats and gypsies in tatters next to a family of wealthy racegoers. A thimble-rigger and a pickpocket are seen plying their trade on the left. Various scenes of courtship and at least two prostitutes can also be identified. It could be argued that this emblematic picture conformed to, and perhaps reinforced, the expectations of a show in which anti-social activities and the misfortunes of gullible victims, quite conspicuous here, were an essential ingredient. In a rougher vein, some northern songs described the scuffles, 'black eyes an' broken shins' resulting from drink and excitement as part of the 'mirth and fun' of going to the races (Gregson, 1983: 13).

Ambivalent attitudes to violent behaviour or petty crime could be found higher up the social ladder. The memoirs of several upper-class race-goers reveal that they were on relatively good terms with the 'swell mob', that is, the gangs of pickpockets who also toured the racing circuit, with a mutual understanding that regular race-goers would be spared at the expense of credulous newcomers. For Huggins, 'the relatively few convictions associated with individual meetings [...] show a clear tolerance of behaviour'.

Although their presence did deter some criminals, 'there was little evidence that the local police was effective with more organized and expert criminals, *especially where there was public opposition to their actions'* (Huggins, 2000: 137–8, my italics).

Violence on the turf

Victims who protested about losing their money through cheating or stealing could be dealt with violently by the gangs. Other preys included the bookmakers, who were submitted to various forms of extortion, ranging from plain protection money to menial tasks being performed by a self-proclaimed 'assistant' for exorbitant wages. Such practices, documented throughout the second half of the nineteenth century, were still widespread in the 1920s (Chinn, 1991: 200). A more dangerous method was to call the uncooperative bookmaker a 'welsher', in other words to accuse him of being dishonest and refusing to pay a winning bet. Such an accusation would invariably start a flare-up and the thrashing of the suspect by the crowd, which could degenerate into a lynching. Some victims were *bona fide* bookmakers wrongly accused, whereas others were real welshers, as in a brutal episode, resulting in the death of the victim, vividly related in 1869 by James Greenwood in *The Seven Curses of London* (399–401). A fierce critic of bookmakers, Greenwood could hardly be suspected of trying to arouse undue sympathy for their plight, and incidents of this kind were frequently reported in the second half of the nineteenth century. Frustrated crowds would also vent their anger on trainers and jockeys in cases of suspected race rigging. However, the most violent episodes concerned bookmakers accused of welshing (Huggins, 2000: 133–7).

To protect themselves against racketeering, many bookmakers resorted to the services of bodyguards, or 'minders', usually recruited among professional pugilists (Chinn, 1991: 199–201). These moves were often interpreted negatively, and the deterring, sometimes sinister-looking, presence of these escorts was regarded as further proof of the dishonest nature of the bookmakers' activities. Such views were relayed by reformist groups, especially when a moral panic, largely prompted by the perception that the increase of betting among the lower classes constituted a threat to society (Clapson, 1992), began to develop in the 1890s. A telling example can be found in an article in the *Birmingham Mail*, reproduced in the *Bulletin of the National Anti-Gambling League* (NAGL) of May 1905:

> If it be true that a man's character shall be known by the company he keeps, then the bookmaker stands condemned at once, for it must be admitted that a more villainous looking horde than the 'bookie's' retinue would be difficult to find. [...] Also, when favourites are running up a

series of wins, ['Jack Thick Ear'] the retired pugilist is a force to be reckoned with if it be necessary to 'pacify' an obstreperous client.

These accusations were not always unfounded, and some organized groups did try to pass themselves off as bookmakers, finding strength in numbers to get away with sharp practices if discovered. This was particularly true of smaller racecourses which had sprung up on the outskirts of London in the 1860s. Usually set up by publicans and unscrupulous bookmakers, these metropolitan meetings were regularly marred by rigged races and general affray. As an example, Vamplew (1976: 36), who describes them as 'suburban saturnalia', relates a pitched battle opposing groups of welshers and their customers at Bromley. Concern about crowd disorder led to the passing of the Racecourses Licensing Act in 1879, which eliminated the rowdier metropolitan fixtures by introducing drastic licensing conditions for horseraces held within a radius of ten miles from Charing Cross. Parliamentary interference, however, was extremely rare, if only because of the opposition of the Jockey Club, which preferred to remain the sole regulator of racing. The only reason why the 1879 bill was allowed to pass was that a recent tightening of Jockey Club rules had no impact on the targeted venues. Indeed the promoters and jockeys of these sham metropolitan races were undeterred by an exclusion from the *Racing Calendar,* as they had no intention of taking part in recognized fixtures (Vamplew, 1976: 95, 98–9).

The impact of commercialization

More than a piece of legislation which only applied to the London area, it is a commercial development pioneered at Sandown Park in 1875 that is usually credited with ensuring a sharp fall in crowd disorder at the end of the century. New venues, most of them limited companies, were fully enclosed, which enabled them to charge a general entrance fee. As dividends were capped, gate money was mainly invested in improved facilities and higher prize money, in order to attract better horses and enhance the quality of the racing. The success of the new meetings compelled established fixtures to follow suit. Within 30 years, most racecourses in Britain had created enclosures and charged for public admission. The new source of revenue also made it easier to discontinue the renting of booths used for illegal practices. Traditionally, paying access had been limited to some select areas of the course, especially the grandstand, already ensuring a segregation which kept the 'riff-raff' out. Now an alleged additional benefit of the turnstiles was to secure 'the absolute exclusion of troublesome spectators' from the whole course (Vamplew, 1988: 57, 275), while heavy investments provided extra incentive for racing companies to minimize the risks of disruption. In their attempt to present an upgraded image, Sandown led the way in encouraging the attendance of respectable female spectators. Improvements in the organization were also instrumental in the reduction of frustration disorder. The enclosed courses ran to a much stricter timetable and there were fewer false starts, thanks to the use of the starting-gate from the 1890s onwards.

Huggins (2000: 138) notes, with caution, 'some hints of a reduction in physical violence from the 1890s'. According to Vamplew (1988: 271), 'there is some evidence to suggest that crowd behaviour improved at the more commercialised race meetings and soccer matches'. This was certainly the opinion of many commentators, one of whom claimed that 'ruffianism [and] racing hooliganism [were almost] a thing of the past [since the advent of] the park meetings with their well-policed enclosures' (Mortimer, 1958: 116–17). Such views, often expressed in mainstream as well as sporting publications, may have been complacent, possibly self-serving, at a time when anti-gambling campaigners were targeting racecourses and upper-class institutions like the Jockey Club (Dixon, 1991: 82–108). In November 1898, the *Bulletin of the National Anti-Gambling League* reproduced a series of articles, originally published in the *Daily Telegraph* under the generic headline 'Roughs on the turf', which denounced the continuing violence at some racing venues. In its number of August 1913, the press was still accused of minimizing the seamy side of racing:

> It must not be supposed that the roughs have discontinued their practices, but it is only at times when they burst all bounds that a portion of the Press can be got to report their saturnalia *in extenso*. As a general rule anything which will disgust the public, and perhaps increase the danger to Turf monied interests, is rigidly boycotted.

Abundant proof that disruptive and delinquent behaviour had not deserted racing fixtures was provided by the upsurge in violence during the 'racecourse wars' of the 1920s, arguably sensationalized by the press, unlike the alleged self-censorship of the late Victorian and Edwardian press (Chinn, 1991: 200–5; Shore, 2011). Press coverage focused on the territorial wars between London gangs dominated by the Sabini brothers and the 'Brummagem Boys', a coalition of Birmingham gangs. As already noted, racketeering and enforced 'protection' of bookmakers continued Victorian practices. Razor fights were a regular occurrence, and newsworthiness was enhanced by the occasional use of firearms and the origins of the protagonists, as some were of Italian or Jewish descent. Oral evidence collected by Carl Chinn (1991: 198) also confirms that organized confidence tricksters were still active throughout the 1930s on the racing circuit.

The moral panic of the 1920s led to a stepping up of repressive measures, supplementing the organizational changes of the late nineteenth century. In 1924, a body of inspectors, whose duties included keeping out undesirables, was set up by the Jockey Club. The following year, after the outcry provoked by some murders, the Home Office instructed the recently created Special Duties Squad, better known as the 'Flying Squad' and renowned for its muscular methods, to tackle racecourse crime (Bean, 1981: 109). These moves followed the formation in 1921 of the Bookmakers and Backers Racecourse Protection Association, designed to provide real protection and act as a representative body. Initially, they remained dependent on the services of minders, with ambivalent relationships with gang leaders. A crucial step was their recognition as an institutional pressure group, which gave them the official right to allocate pitches in partnership with the Jockey Club in 1929, a right that ensured their protection by the authorities. If low-level delinquency continued, racecourse gangsterism subsided significantly afterwards, although it remained a serious problem until the war in some unenclosed courses, notably Epsom and Brighton.

Conclusion

Vamplew points out that 'almost any event in Victorian England which brought together a large gathering of people could result in crowd disorder' (1988: 266). Race meetings were no exception. Vociferous crowds were a regular occurrence, and more than elsewhere the festive atmosphere of the course guaranteed a measure of tolerance for rowdy or unseemly behaviour. Stringent measures were only taken in cases of large-scale disorder. The standard response was a policy of containment, which included an ostensible police presence. County police and specials were often hired to supplement the local forces, perhaps chiefly with a view to mollifying the reforming groups, as suggested by the low rate of prosecutions and convictions until the First World War (Huggins, 2000: 138).

Another enduring strategy was spatial segregation through differential pricing and strict social vetting for access to some areas. The decisive, but exceptional, action taken in 1879 can largely be explained by sociological factors, as the targeted meetings were exclusively attended by lower-class elements, unlike the traditionally mixed attendance at races. There may also have been a lowering of the threshold of tolerance in the second half of the nineteenth century; however, commercial considerations appear to have played a more significant role in curbing anti-social behaviour. Racing was first and foremost a business venture for the companies that emerged in the last quarter of the century, and it was essential for them to screen out undesirable elements to secure their profitability. Similar trends could be observed in other developing leisure industries, as with the drive towards respectability of the Moss music hall empire. This sanitizing process was dismissed as cosmetic by an increasingly vocal anti-betting movement in the 1890s. In fact, it may have been confined to the newly created 'park meetings', whereas older meetings retained many characteristics of a traditional fair, including the rowdiness. The 1920s saw stricter policing and the recognition by the Jockey Club of the bookmakers as joint partners in the regulation of betting. Nevertheless, these changes were mainly concerned with gang violence and criminal activities. It seems that, at least until the Edwardian era, there was a remarkable degree of continuity in racecourse life. Huggins (2000, 138–9) argues that it 'may be seen as a liminal area where petty crime was tolerated by both the racing and the urban authorities, where a range of popular cultural forms [and a climate of anti-bourgeois behaviour] were able to shelter and survive'. Racing, he concludes, provides an example where reformist attempts to impose respectable mores were 'both spasmodic and relatively ineffective'. Racecourse life has also been analysed through its carnival dimension, as it was a strikingly cross-class experience, with residual aspects of preindustrial England, unlike football crowds for instance. The argument is partly undermined by the strong amount of decorum and clear zoning policies that preserved an unambiguous display of social status. Nevertheless, a day at the races remained a festive outlet in which a degree of transgression and disruption was not only tolerated, but perhaps also regarded as part and parcel of the show.

21
Victorian Respectability, 'Anti-social Behaviour' and the Music Hall, 1880–1900

John Mullen

'Anti-social behaviour' is often a label used for social regulation (Brown, 2004). Among other things, it participates in the construction of a 'denigrated Other', whom we can reject, but its specific content is determined by the society and the political forces which invented the term. There is no shortage of concepts which have been used to define who is valuable and who is less valuable in human society: chivalry, decorum, godliness, good taste and anti-social behaviour have all played this role in different periods and different social milieux. In nineteenth-century Britain, respectability was no doubt the most powerful of these ideas. But what did it mean for the Victorians?

First, respectability was a very flexible and complex concept. Indeed its vagueness constituted part of its function. A working-class person had never definitively gained the label of 'respectable': it could always be lost again by reprehensible behaviour of some kind. In this it can be compared to other labels of social and moral regulation such as 'godliness' in some Christian contexts or the 'integration' demanded of Third World migrants to Western industrialized countries today.

Secondly, its presence was felt everywhere in Victorian Britain: it seems that 'respectability talk' was a constant pastime for many sections of the population. Robert Roberts, writing about life in a poor part of Manchester at the turn of the twentieth century, portrays the incessant commentary and analysis concerning the level of respectability of different neighbours (Roberts, 1990: 32–7). In the newspapers which discussed the entertainment industry (*The Era*, or *The Encore*, for example), the subject was an inexhaustible source of analysis and redefinition.

Peter Bailey, the leading historian of the music hall, summarizes respectability as:

> a highly specific value system of considerable normative power, whose most important consequence was to incorporate a minor but significant

sector of the working class into the social consensus that assured mid-Victorian society in particular its overall cohesion and stability. (Bailey, 1998: 30)

Historian Elizabeth Roberts, author of an oral history of working-class life, underlines the tremendous influence of the idea:

> Social historians studying the working class in the recent past, are almost overwhelmed at times by the total devotion and dedication shown towards the concept of respectability. (Roberts, 1984: 14)

This chapter will deal with the role of 'respectability' in Victorian society, and particularly in late Victorian music hall, and will seek to compare the concept with that of 'anti-social behaviour' today.

The power of an idea

It seems that the 'minor but significant sector' of the working class which Bailey says was wedded to this ideology became far larger as the decades of the nineteenth century went by. The rise of new white-collar shop and office workers gave this ideology more purchase among the lower classes, while successful trade union struggles and increasing democratic rights obliged elite thinkers to hesitate before dismissing the idea that lower-class people could be worthy of respect. Historian Geoffrey Best says that respectability exerted 'a socially soothing tendency, by assimilating the most widely separated groups (separated socially or geographically) to a common cult' (quoted in Bailey, 1998: 31).

It was extremely rare for late Victorian commentators to openly oppose respectability ideology; only the most radical might do this. Friedrich Engels, for example, complained about British trade union leaders:

> The most repulsive thing here [in England] is the bourgeois 'respectability', which has grown deep into the bones of the workers [...]. Even Tom Mann,[1] whom I regard as the best of the lot, is fond of mentioning that he will be lunching with the Lord Mayor. (Engels, 1889: 1)

Another radical, Bertrand Russell, brought up in an elite family in Victorian England deplored that, for the sake of respectability:

> men and women make great moral efforts, [...] but all their efforts and all their self-control, being not used for any creative end, serve merely to dry up the well-spring of life within them, to make them feeble, listless, and trivial. (Russell, 1916: 122)

These were rare voices indeed, and both recognize the massive influence of the concept of respectability.

The view of this ideology as necessarily an effective force for social stability has been queried by some writers, who have emphasized that the acceptance of 'respectability' did not stop working people from having radical ideas. They would often, on the contrary, *redefine* respectability to move it closer to their own interests. For example, when music-hall artistes went on a long strike and organized picketing in 1907, their newspaper presented this as a move towards being respectable workers who would fight injustice, and a move away from being 'common' casualized workers (*The Performer*, 31 January 1907).

Peter Bailey suggests, further, that 'respectability' could be a matter of playing a role, rather than a set of ideas with deep psychological roots. He says we must remember that working-class institutions such as friendly societies or working-men's clubs were obliged to parrot the ideology of respectability in order to get middle-class support or to be safe from bourgeois attacks. 'Mouthing a few passwords about respectability', he suggests, 'might secure immunity from the badgering of middle-class charity workers or district visitors' (Bailey, 1998: 38). In general, he underlines what he sees as 'the tenuous hold of the normative sanctions of respectability' (Bailey, 1998: 41).

Despite these various caveats, respectability ideology certainly was successful as a scapegoat identification mechanism. To believe in respectability was to believe in the dangers, at all levels of society, of its necessary opposite: the 'indecent', the 'vulgar', the 'common'.

Respectability in different social classes

Respectability looked somewhat different, however, in diverse social milieux. In the elite groups, its commandments could merge into questions of etiquette. As social mobility became a little easier, established groups developed ever more complicated rules to ensure the maintenance of class image barriers. Books gave detailed advice about behaviour at dinner:

> Never allow a servant to fill your glass with wine that you do not wish to drink. You can check him by touching the rim of your glass. Bread is broken at dinner. Never use a napkin in place of a handkerchief for wiping the forehead, face or nose [...]. (Young, 1881: 26)

New rituals, such as the calling card, became ever more complex (Bailey, 1998: 17). One was expected, in bourgeois circles, to know that a calling card with the left-hand lower corner turned down signified a condolence visit, whereas if it was the upper right-hand corner, this meant the lady or gentleman had called personally rather than sending a servant. These rituals served to reassure the elite about the relative impermeability of social barriers.

In lower classes, respectability looked quite different. Avoiding the appearance of destitution was an important part of it. Robert Roberts writes about how using newspaper, instead of lace curtains, to cover windows was considered, in the slum he lived in, a sign of having abandoned hopes of respectability. The concept was a contradictory one for working class people. It included elements of respecting oneself: no excessive indulgence in alcohol, no excessive violence within the family and a certain level of cleanliness. It would include limiting swearing, not fighting in the streets, paying rent on time and not talking of sexuality to your children, or allowing them to see naked bodies. Being seen as respectable counted as social capital, even amid poverty. As Elizabeth Roberts explains: 'To be respectable was to be respected, and in closely knit communities it was very difficult to live comfortably without the respect of one's family and neighbours' (Roberts, 1984: 14).

Yet it also included strong elements of respecting existing social hierarchies, and accepting one's own 'inferiority' to elite groups. In the world of entertainment, there was the not untypical case of the orchestra in Cheltenham in the 1910s. The musicians earned only one pound five shillings a week – less than a skilled manual worker, and only just enough for a family to eat. However, to ensure respectability, they were banned by their employers from wearing caps on the way to and from work (Ehrlich, 1985: 188), since caps would mean that they belonged to the working class and were therefore assumed to be suspect in their respectability. Similarly, working-class corps de ballet dancers at the central London music halls were under pressure to wear very 'respectable' clothes when leaving the theatre (Carter, 2005: 115).

An earlier commentator clearly suggested that if the music-hall entertainers were recruited among higher social classes, they would tend to favour more respectable material:

> the high salaries which good singers who can act are able to earn just now on the stage has had the effect of materially increasing the supply. Some well-educated girls train for the stage as a matter of course. [...] It is from this quarter we must look for an improvement of the music hall stage. [...] If they are educated, trained and refined they will give no support to the vulgar and the suggestive. (*Western Times*, 5 July 1900)

Being respectable, finally, included having (or faking) a taste for 'improving activities' – high culture and reading – elements which could be profitable to ordinary people, but were wedded to the idea that only leisure which corresponds to elite tastes is of any value. Indeed, there was a powerful campaign during the whole of the late Victorian period to ensure that the newly found leisure time of the industrial workers be used in an 'improving' manner. This is the period of the rise of local museums, parks and libraries, brass bands and bandstands, choral societies, penny classical concerts, and so on. These elements constituted both an improvement in working-class lives, instituted partly as a result of the fear of class revolt after the Chartist movement,[2] and also an attempt by the elites to make sure that the newly found leisure was used in ways which could not become threatening.

The campaign for respectability in the music hall

We shall now see specifically how the idea of respectability was imposed and negotiated around the mass entertainment industry of the music hall. At the end of the nineteenth century, music hall was the most popular cheap entertainment form, with millions of tickets sold every week. At its origins in the 1850s and 1860s, the genre had been far from respectable. In the following decades, the gradual acceptance that working-class people needed or deserved or had to be given leisure time was accompanied by no shortage of advice from different sections of the elite as to how this leisure time should be spent. This Victorian campaign for 'rational leisure' aimed at opposing 'frivolity or unmeaning mirth' (Waters, 1990: 22).

As the decades went by, the 'rational leisure' idea was obliged to become a little more flexible, and the wholesale condemnation of music hall became much rarer. At the same time, the genre was being transformed. The concentration of capital led to bigger theatres and increasing domination of the industry by theatre chains such as Moss Empires. Music-hall entrepreneurs and managers now wanted to join local elites, whereas previously the non-respectable image of their business would have prevented this. In the audience too, new white-collar groups wanted music hall to fit with their modest but real social pretentions, whereas the threat of magistrates refusing licences to non-respectable music halls ensured that pressure was maintained.

For all these reasons, from the 1880s on, music-hall proprietors threw themselves heart and soul into the 'cleaning up' of the genre. Maloney comments:

> It seems likely that [managers were attempting] to install middle-class values or notions of respectability [...] in the music hall, so that upwardly mobile sections of the lower classes would feel they could attend music hall without compromising their social aspirations. (Maloney, 2003: 86)

What methods did music hall owners use to ensure and police respectability? First, there were changes in the architecture of the new variety theatres being built after 1880. The circle and the stalls had separate entrances and separate corridors, and one could not pass from one part of the theatre to another. Everything was done to ensure that the more privileged classes did not meet the working classes in the theatre itself. In particular, there was a fear that middle-class women would meet working-class men, with supposedly unfortunate consequences. The number of private boxes in the theatres also increased. Chasing after respectability meant accepting the social hierarchies which were in place.

Secondly, where possible, premises were moved to more respectable parts of town. Thirdly, the promenades of some of the music halls (lounge areas for walking, sitting and relaxing), were often closed down, as they were suspected of being places where prostitutes solicited clients. Fourthly, the drinking of alcohol was very much curbed. It was no longer permitted in the auditorium; and in a large number of halls there was no drinking at all. Fifthly, the new music halls tried to trumpet their respectability by including in their night's entertainment ever more elements of high culture. Extracts from Shakespeare, or short ballets, or extracts from Wagner's or Verdi's operas were introduced.

Sixthly, there were increasing efforts to attract married women and their families to the variety theatres; their presence would be brandished as proof of respectability. Finally, there was a consistent attempt to control strictly what comics and singers said during their act. It became standard to ban all ad-libbing. The Britannia music-hall programmes of the 1890s included a request to inform the manager of 'any suggestive or offensive word or action upon the stage that may have escaped his notice'. This was not unusual (Maloney, 2003: 62). The standard contract in use by 1907 included a clause specifying that 'Any artiste giving any expression to any vulgarity, or words having a double meaning [...] will be instantly dismissed' (*The Performer*, 31 January 1907). The emphasis on respectability was underlined in advertising: a typical Manchester advert for a pantomime promised 'No dull moments, no vulgarity, honest healthy fun throughout' (*Manchester Courier*, 4 January 1900).

Government and moral authorities

How were the government and other institutions involved in the campaign for respectability? Unlike the case of the twenty-first century campaigns against anti-social behaviour, politicians were not at the origin of the campaign for respectability. Moralist organizations were the most active. There is the well-known case of Mrs Ormiston Chant, who ran a crusade against vulgarity and immorality at the music halls in the 1890s. A complex figure, involved in the campaign for women's suffrage and in voluntary work aiming at getting women out of prostitution, as well as in the campaign for cleaning up the music halls, she was criticized both by those who found her attitude prudish, and by those who considered that as a woman she did not have the right to speak out on such questions (Faulk, 2004: 78).

In 1894, she alleged, concerning the Empire theatre, that 'the place at night is the habitual resort of prostitutes in pursuit of their traffic', and that 'portions of the entertainment are most objectionable' (Faulk, 2004: 79). She attacked the richer class of men, who, she said, went to the Empire to pick up working-class prostitutes. Chant also criticized the short ballets which were produced in the halls: 'Ballet dancers cannot see that the absence of clothing is an offense against their own self-respect. They do not realize that they are exhibited well-nigh undressed for the men in the lounge [...]' (Faulk, 2004: 84). Chant's campaign dominated the letters page of papers such as the *Daily Telegraph* for a whole month. As a result, the promenade at the Empire was closed for some time.

Although the moralist crusaders were a small minority, and were frequently mocked even in respectable newspapers,[3] they had real power. When the licence of a music hall came up for renewal they could and frequently did lobby magistrates to have licences refused because of the low moral tone of an establishment. A hearing to decide whether to grant a licence for the opening of a large music hall in Manchester was opposed by a large number of clergymen and charity workers in 1904, who firmly believed that it would 'lead young people astray' and make work harder for churches and educational institutions (*The Guardian*, 10 June 1904).

If elected authorities did not launch the campaign for respectability, they did sometimes intervene strongly in its favour, and members of moralist organizations included many local politicians who sat on the committees dealing with entertainment licensing. So, from 1890, the London County Council decided to employ inspectors to go to music-hall shows in order to report back on problems of public morality. At the beginning of its new responsibilities, the London County Council proposed a radical system of individual licensing for music-hall and other artistes. Singers would be compulsorily certified once a year, and fined or suspended if they sang 'indecent songs' (*Sheffield Evening Telegraph*, 25 February 1890). The music-hall milieu responded vigorously. A mass meeting was held in March 1890, denouncing the project as 'vexatious and unnecessary'. Protest was powerful enough to force the London County Council to backtrack: the licensing of artistes was abandoned, although fines for indecent singing were increased (*The Era*, 8 March 1890).

The artistes

We shall now see how music hall-singers dealt with the question. All of them claimed to be respectable – it seems it was socially and professionally impossible to do otherwise – but the public obsession with the issue encouraged a significant number of artistes to explore the subject in song, and several specialized in moderate transgression of the boundaries of respectability.

The songs are particularly useful as sources because of the nature of music-hall performance. The singer normally had to succeed in getting the entire audience to sing the chorus. Sentiments which half the audience did not wish to sing would constitute a real professional danger to most artistes who worked in a precarious profession where reputation was everything. For this reason, there was strong pressure in favour of consensual songs (Mullen, 2012: 188).

Music-hall audiences were far more masculine before 1870 than afterwards (King 1993: 24) and we have some evidence that the content could be very much more vulgar in the early period. George Speaight has collected, from the very early music hall, booklets of very explicit songs which can in no way be described as suggestive (Speaight, 1975). It is very difficult to know how common this bawdy content was, but certainly by the end of the Victorian period, the moralists were campaigning against suggestive material in general, and not against bawdy material as such.

We find out details about artistes' attitudes when cases came before magistrates. This was not a frequent occurrence: normally informal pressures were sufficient to keep artistes in line. Nevertheless, every year there were two or three court cases. In 1890, a licensee, conductor and manager were charged with 'conspiring together to procure the singing of an alleged indecent song'. The summonses in the case were taken out by the Society for the Prevention of the Degradation of Women and Children (*Manchester Evening News*, 7 February 1890). The fact that the case was reported in a series of local newspapers across the country shows both that it was not a common occurrence and that the question deeply interested contemporaries.

Singing star G.H. McDermott had his contract cancelled in 1892 for singing an indecent song (*Manchester Evening News*, 2 June 1892), whereas in 1897 (*Manchester Evening News*, 6 February 1897) another singer was sacked because of a song entitled 'Oh, Sir, you'll have to marry me now!' The theatre director claimed the song was vulgar, but the singer successfully claimed unfair dismissal since, she maintained, the manager had heard the song in rehearsal and not objected. The singer's words show how much of a battle over interpretation was going on 'It might perhaps have a double meaning', she said, 'but there was nothing offensive or suggestive about it unless it were taken "the other way"'. We feel here the tensions and confusions involved in public debates about respectable intentions, debates which could have real material consequences for artistes. Another music-hall artiste was sacked without pay in 1900 because of a 'vulgar' sketch; the magistrates found the sacking justified (*Nottingham Evening Post*, 22 November 1900).

Most singers proclaimed loudly their opposition to 'vulgar' or even 'suggestive' songs. Miss Harriet Verbon, a singer interviewed by *The Era* made a typical declaration, saying 'I never sing a song that the most prudish dame could take exception to. Managers should exercise a censorship over improper songs. The British public do not want tainted songs' (*The Era*, 25 August 1900). Nevertheless, several top stars in the period from 1880 on specialized in the suggestive. The most famous among them are Marie Lloyd (whose songs included 'I asked Johnny Jones so Now I Know'), Whit Cunliffe ('Tight Skirts have Got to Go!') and Harry Champion ('The End of my Old Cigar'). Their suggestiveness did not stop them being among the best-paid artistes at the turn of the century.

Lloyd portrayed on stage a working-class woman who knew about life, love and men, and knew how to have a good time: not a paragon of respectability. In 1897, complaints were made about a song she sang which suggested that the father of the narrator frequented prostitutes (Baker, 1990: 98). Another of her songs 'Wink the Other Eye' encouraged her reputation as daring, though the daringness only seems to go as far as to suggest that a woman might kiss a cabbie instead of paying the fare. After the relief of Mafeking (a British victory in the Boer war in 1900), Llyod performed a new song, 'The Girls in the Khaki Dress', suggesting that British soldiers were having illegitimate children (Baker, 1990: 117). For many years, Moss Empires, the most powerful of the variety theatre chains, refused to hire Lloyd despite her stature as an international star.

Lloyd retaliated by singing a song directed against the puritans, inviting her working-class audience to join her in indignant protest. Entitled 'They can't stop a girl from thinking', it included the following lines:

> I mustn't tell you what I mean
> Mustn't tell you what I've seen
> Everything that's risqué must be dropped!
> While I've been stopped from winking
> Mustn't tell you what I've heard
> Mustn't say a naughty word
> So help my Bob, it's a jolly good job
> They can't stop a girl from thinking!

From the safety of her star status, Lloyd was one of the rare public personalities to defend suggestiveness:

> They don't pay their sixpences and shillings at a music hall to hear the Salvation Army. If I was to try to sing highly moral songs, they would fire ginger beer bottles and beer mugs at me. I can't help it if people want to turn and twist my meanings. (Farson, 1972: 57)

We can see here she is treading a difficult path – on the one hand rejecting a perceived 'high morality' of bourgeois society, on the other maintaining that the vulgar meanings are produced not by her, but by those who wish to distort her meanings. This contradictory discourse shows the tension between accepting social norms and celebrating dissenting voices.

Who could be blamed for vulgarity?

There was always, indeed, a tension in the campaigns against vulgarity and in favour of respectable entertainment. Sometimes working-class audiences were presented as innocent victims of vulgar entertainment they did not want, whereas at other times it was claimed that the vulgarity was what the degenerate public demanded. So a 1900 news article emphasized that the vulgarity on stage 'was hissed and booed' by the audience (*Nottingham Evening Post*, 22 November 1900), whereas a commentator in *The Era* the same year insisted 'you have to satisfy, to play to your audience. A manager must not stage what he likes, but what his audience likes' (*The Era*, 15 December 1900).

Similarly, there was, towards the end of the period, no general agreement as to whether the stage content of music hall had effectively become more respectable as the years went by. An interview with a comic singer, J.H. Milburn in 1891 claimed it had:

Many things have changed over twenty years I've been working [...] Why, now, the more refined a thing is the better the audience like it. Take my word for it, it's only with a very small few that double entendres go down now. [...] I wouldn't sing a vulgar song anywhere for anything or anybody. (*The Era*, 18 July 1891)

The *Western Mail* claimed the introduction of elements of high culture as proof of the vanquishing of vulgarity:

the metamorphosis of the English music hall from mere places of vulgarity to palaces of artistic creation has been of striking growth during the Victorian era. Many excellent ballad and operatic vocalists have long presented genuine music to enthusiastic music hall audiences. (24 October 1900)

Here, normal music-hall singing is presented as 'not genuine music', and the introduction of elite tastes is presented as allowing the betterment of the audiences. One Member of Parliament claimed that the main improvement had come at the very end of the century owing to new forms of regulation: 'since the London music halls were placed under the county council they have wonderfully improved' he insisted (*Pall Mall Gazette*, 16 May 1900).

In other quarters, however, there was no shortage of commentators to claim nothing had changed. In 1896 an invited speaker at the quarterly meeting of the mid-Essex teachers' association 'denied that these halls had produced anything either in novelty of form or merit of substance [...]. All had been vulgarising and lowering' (*Chelmsford Chronicle*, 1 May 1896). In 1900, many still thought vulgarity very frequent. A critic wrote in the

Edinburgh News 'I have listened to scores of songs sung, some of them, by men earning huge salaries [...] which as regards their character could not be sung before any respectable and decent household' (*Edinburgh Evening News*, 3 July 1900), whereas the *Pall Mall Gazette* complained 'vulgarity, at least, is as rampant as ever' (16 May 1900).

We can see, then, that contemporary debate about the nature and presence of vulgarity seems to produce more heat than light, in the absence of an objective definition of what vulgarity actually is. One might see parallels in debates today about anti-social behaviour and its prevalence in Britain.

Conclusion: Respectability and anti-social behaviour

Having explored, then, the question of respectability in Victorian England and the campaign within music hall, how can we compare its content and power to that of the campaign against anti-social behaviour in Britain in recent years?

There are some similarities. They are both ways used by elites to try to control the behaviour of individuals belonging to subordinate classes. Both concentrate on individual behaviour rather than on social justice. Both try very hard to recruit the dominated classes into the same world view, by setting up a denigrated Other, a type of person to be rejected: the hoodie, perhaps, or the vulgar performer. They both involve a central concept which is open to some negotiation and redefinition. Both are highly selective as constructions of objects of moral reprobation: respectability did not involve being opposed to racism, for example (Blackface minstrelsy was considered more respectable than music hall, for example), while 'anti-social behaviour' is not defined to include exploitation or workplace injustices in general.

But there are very important differences. First, anti-social behaviour as an ideology is very recent. The Labour Party manifestos of 1997 and 2001 are the only ones, since the birth of the Labour Party, to mention the term. The Conservatives mention it in the same years. 'Respectability' ideology, on the other hand, dominated an entire historical period. The agents, too, are different: the campaign against anti-social behaviour originated from a political elite, whereas the campaign for respectability came more from a social elite. Only one of the two was a popular obsession. In addition, today's adjective 'anti-social' is explicitly attached to 'behaviour', and not to the essence of groups of people as such, whereas in Victorian times, one would often hear of 'respectable classes' or 'respectable parts of town': people rather than simply behaviour were praised or reviled.

'Respectability' grew up and was imposed at a time when democratic ideas were very slowly affirming themselves in Britain, but where egalitarian ideas remained weak, especially among the elites. Its meritocratic and moralistic aspects made it an appropriate ideology for this period. The ideology of 'anti-social behaviour' on the other hand comes in a period where democracy is taken for granted, as is the idea that all social classes deserve to be respected and integrated into society. The denigrated Other is no longer, in this ideology, the majority of the 'lower' classes, but smaller groups from among them who are presented as threatening the serenity of 'normal' social existence.

Notes

1. Tom Mann was a left-wing trade unionist and leading figure in the 1889 dockers' strike.
2. From 1838 to 1848, Chartism constituted a mass working-class movement. It had many currents within it, but, particularly in the context of the European revolutions of 1848, seemed to the elite to threaten their very existence.
3. *The Era*, 1 December 1900 mocked the moralists as a 'tribe of culchawed persons' who would never have any significant effect on the music hall.

22
Drunkenness, Anti-social Behaviour, Class, Gender and Alcohol in the Making of the Habitual Drunkards Act, 1870–79

An Vleugels

Introduction

Being drunk can be understood as both social and anti-social behaviour. If – as Mary Douglas has stated – drink constructs the world, then the defining of boundaries between acceptable and unacceptable drunkenness is central to the making of culture (Douglas, 1987: 8). In Britain, by the end of the nineteenth century, an Inebriates Act granted the state powers to provide asylums in which habitual drunkards could be forcibly detained. In the discussions surrounding this legalization during the later decades of the century, ideas of biology and heredity were central to the understanding of the problem and the threat drunkards posed to the health of the 'race' was much discussed. Studies show that 80 per cent of the population of these institutions were women, a finding that has posed 'a particular puzzle for historians' (Hunt *et al.* 1989: 244 and Zedner, 1992: 6). By tracing the origins of the inebriate asylum movement in Victorian Britain and the ideas on drink, class and gender that surrounded it, this chapter aims to contribute towards solving that puzzle.

Historians have located a broad shift at the end of the nineteenth century from an interpretation of alcoholism as a vice, a moral analysis of the problem, towards an interpretation whereby alcoholism was perceived as related to biological disorder: a pathological condition (Greenaway, 2003: 36). These new narratives of drunkenness as a disease were mostly forged by medical men who thus broadened up their field of expertise and consolidated their professional reputations (Sournia, 1990: 14). They did not use a shared language when exploring the problem of excessive drinking: they talked about drunkenness, intemperance and dipsomania and rarely used those terms consistently. Languages of biology, medicine and morality were always intertwined in this multifaceted and culturally complex shift. The ways in which the distinctions between the different types of drunkenness were established remained ambiguous and are still very unclear today (Nicholls, 2009: 162). Drinking and drunkenness were constructed differently, according to who drank. This makes the subject historically specific and it can thus contribute to our understanding of the ways society was organized in the past (Cohen, 1993: 53). Exploring the different cultural meanings of drunkenness in the public debate in the 1870s will help us understand the different ways in which excessive drinking became constructed as anti-social behaviour.

Lower classes, drinking as a vice: 'their normal and natural state'

Excessive drinking and public drunkenness had been always prevalent in British society, and since the eighteenth century had provoked debate among lawmakers (Warner, 2003: 207–8). When the Industrial Revolution and growing cities propelled modernity, public drunkenness became a threat to the efficiency of the running of mills and mines. By the mid-nineteenth century, a radicalized temperance movement had become a mass movement, whose members took the pledge not to drink or provide alcohol. Temperance societies promoted self-control and abstinence to curb working-class drinking habits (Shiman, 1988: 1). In so far as there were doctors involved in the temperance movement, they spoke the language of sanitary reform (Harrison, 1994: 31). In much the same way as they would consider the cleaning out of sewers and the whitewashing of slums or the crusade against contagious disease, medical men called the campaign against drunkenness 'a great sanitary object' (*The Lancet*, 15 March 1873: 387). When the celebrated alienist Dr Forbes Winslow explained in 1872 that drunkenness could sometimes also be considered a disease, it was mentioned to him that surely this was not applicable to the 'enormous mass of drunkenness in the lower classes' (Select Committee on Habitual Drunkards, 1872: 77, 1345). He readily agreed, declaring: 'I think there are habitual drunkards as well as there are habitual prostitutes and persons who habitually indulge in any other form of vice. It is their normal and natural state' (*ibid.*).

In the narratives of anti-social drunkenness that the temperance movement divulged, the work-shy drunkard was male and with his drinking he ruined the lives of his wife and children, who were represented as innocent victims (Harrison, 1994: 311). The drinker in this scenario was responsible for his own actions and needed to be educated in order to change his behaviour. From the 1870s onwards, however, the optimism of this temperance rhetoric of self-betterment and self-help started to weaken. The revolutionary street violence of the Paris Commune at the beginning of the decade had been received in Britain with concerns about working-class uproar at home (Beaumont, 2006: 467). A perceived rise in criminality and unruliness and its supposed link with anti-social drinking started to preoccupy reformers ever more (Stedman-Jones, 1971: 15).

In 1872, a far-reaching Licensing Act was passed in the British parliament that allowed people to be arrested for being drunk in public. It also greatly increased fines for those who were found to be 'guilty while drunk of riotous or disorderly behaviour' (Licensing Act 1872 35 & 36 Vict. c. 94 s. 12). On the streets, arrests for drunkenness rose significantly and newspapers were packed with miserable stories of criminal drunkards and of people who died from delirium tremens or who were left 'dead drunk' in prison (MacLeod, 1967: 218–19). The Licensing Act 1872 also drastically reduced the opening hours of public houses, which immediately provoked popular protests. Workers who claimed the right to drink when and where as their own, came on the streets of Britain's towns singing 'Rule Britannia' (Harrison, 1994: 255), in much the same way, it seemed to many, that the Communards had sung the 'Marseillaise' on the streets of Paris a year earlier, in the Spring of 1871.

Uncontrolled drunkenness and revolutionary fervour were so easily interchanged that they could be embodied within the same figure. Illustrator George Cruickshank for example, had called the Communards in 1871 'ignorant drunken brutes' on a remarkable poster, which depicted a screaming wide-eyed figure with arms and legs stretched out engulfed in flames, called 'Liberty, the leader of the Parisian Red Blood Republic' or a 'Fiery Devil'. Two years later, Cruickshank replicated that exact same figure of the 'Fiery Devil' to illustrate a passage in a temperance tract aimed at the masses, only this time the same frantic figure was to represent a drunkard 'haunted by drink', surrounded by ghosts of his self-induced madness. Drunkenness had always been linked to madness and revolution, in manifold ways, but now in the 1870s, this relationship was most eagerly explored in the public domain.

A very worrying aspect of the violence on the streets in France for Europe's ruling middle classes, had been the participation of women: profoundly irrational, anti-social behaviour that resonated powerfully within the British imagination. Drunken women in public appeared the ultimate representation of chaos and the tyranny of the rabble (Gullickson, 1996: 104). As a result, an additional dramatic female role in the shared narratives of drunkenness had now become available aside from the part of suffering wife. After 1871, we read ever more about the sexually predatory, drunken woman. This portrayal fits in with wider contemporary concerns about prostitution, in a discussion whereby the topics alcohol and sex were always closely intertwined (Lee, 2013: 53–5). A Select Committee of the House of Lords, appointed in 1878, 'for the purpose of enquiring into the prevalence of habits of intemperance and into the manner in which these habits had been affected by recent legislation and other issues', expressed special concern about what they observed was the increase in female drinking. Mr William Smith, prison governor of Ripon, North Yorkshire, for example, explained that the greatest number of committals for drunkenness was of women and that the prison authorities would have more trouble dealing with their behaviour than with that of the men they apprehended (*Report*, 1878–9: 36).

Drunkenness as a disease: 'wholly free from the taint of vice'

In the same year the Licensing Act 1872 was passed, a Select Committee of the House of Commons had started its hearings to legislate for another type of drunkenness (MacLeod, 1967: 220). It was chaired by Dr Donald Dalrymple MP, a retired physician and lunatic asylum proprietor, and was to enquire into a bill he had proposed for the 'Cure and Treatment of Habitual Drunkards' that advocated the provision of state-controlled homes where men and women suffering from the disease of drunkenness could be detained and cured. Dalrymple proposed two types of institutions. First, he recommended the creation of so-called 'industrial hospitals' for criminal lower-class drunkards who repeatedly appeared before police courts and whose deviant behaviour impeded on society and was a burden on the tax payer. Second, he advocated a state-regulated system that would allow privately owned homes for drunkards to legally confine their patients.

Among the expert witnesses who were invited to give evidence before the Committee were many physicians who wanted to convince the House that they were indeed dealing here with drinkers whose problem was different from the vice of drinking that affected society's lower classes so much. The interest of physicians for the establishment of lower-class inebriate asylums was limited (McLaughlin, 1991: 306) and when the Bill was enacted in 1879 the section of the proposition pertaining to 'industrial hospitals' was completely abandoned. It would, however, be taken up again in a different context at the end of the century as the Inebriates Act, and women would bear the brunt of its implementation.

In 1872, the members of the Committee were much more interested in remedying a different type of drunkenness than what the temperance societies were battling. Wealthy drinkers, who had crossed the boundaries of what was socially acceptable, would generally not be arrested. Instead, doctors could diagnose them with the disease of dipsomania: an uncontrollable craving for alcoholic substances, 'wholly free from the taint of vice' (*The Lancet*, 6 April 1873: 512). While for 'ordinary drunkards', the indulgence was voluntary, for the dipsomaniac it was not; instead it was 'attributable to an impulse which the patient could not control' (*Report*, 1872: 34, 642). The *Gentleman's Magazine* advised its readers that when dealing with female dipsomaniacs: 'the overstimulator [...] must be treated as if insane and her mental infirmity recognized as a disease, requiring treatment and control' (Daly, 1879: 120).

Most of the specialists on the Commission agreed that the illness of habitual drunkenness was a mental disease, an overpowering urge to drink alcohol: a mania such as, for example, kleptomania. Although physicians had always perceived a close relationship between excessive drinking and madness, they did not clearly explain how the two functioned together. Especially hard to account for was the origin of the urge for drink; the irresistible craving for alcohol which made the drunkenness 'habitual'. As this urge was considered uncontrollable, it was not only the faculty of reason, but also that of will and moral power that was affected in patients (Johnstone, 1996: 47; Valverde, 1997: 255). Therefore, although habitual drunkenness was here understood as a disease, the language used to talk about it always continued to carry moral meanings about what was socially acceptable behaviour.

The eminent asylum doctor Dr Charles Bucknill was one of very few physicians who campaigned against licensing special treatment homes for inebriates and he called the proposed law 'distinctively a class measure'. He denounced the double standard of an Act for which middle-class drunkenness was 'the uncontrollable result of disease, while upon the poor and ignorant wretch, I must still impose the penalty of vicious excess' (Bucknill, 1878: 12).

Middle and upper classes: 'the wear and the tear of modern life'

The Licensing Acts that were in place to control anti-social drinking generally did not affect well-to-do people who drank at home, in hotels or in clubs, but even when drunk in public well-off heavy drinkers would be treated differently (Hoppen, 1998: 354). The head constable of Liverpool told the Committee how every person arrested for drunkenness should appear in front of magistrates the next day, but 'if a man is known to be a respectable person, or if his friends follow him up and say "we will take care of him and he does not live far off, he is not locked up" ' (Report, 1872: 120, 2075).

Although heavy drinking was mostly constructed as a working-class vice, there had always been a considerable amount of middle- and upper-class drinking in Britain that was not necessarily considered anti-social. Men sat for hours following dinner, drinking wine, boasting of their capacity for 'tucking' so many bottles of claret or tumblers of punch 'under their belt' (Hansard, 1871: 1516). Gradually, with the rise of a new industrious middle class and its emphasis on frugality, propriety and sobriety, there was no longer time and space for such indulgences (Barr, 1998: 68; Harrison, 1994: 301). The decadent gentleman's drinking habits in Anne Brontë's *The Tenant of Wildfell Hall* of 1848 for example, were both recognizable and objectionable and their candid and condemning portrayal shocked contemporary readers (Hyman, 2008: 451). By 1870, 'as drunk as a lord' had changed into 'as drunk as a beggar' (Anon, 1875: 402) and private excessive drinking had also become anti-social behaviour. Conspicuous sobriety by members of upper and respectable middle classes revealed the influence of the temperance movement.

In the 1870s, the members of the Select Committee on Habitual Drunkards had noticed a worrying new increase in middle- and upper-class habitual drunkenness that seemed to be related to the appearance of what were called, 'new values' in society. Especially the 'new rich', those who had made their fortune in industry and commerce, were thought to be susceptible (Report, 1872: 728, 543). Their habit, though, was not the traditional upper-class 'convivial and jovial sort of drunkenness', but rather a 'secret and a sottish' one (Report, 1872: 21, 441).

It is important to remember that in the mid-nineteenth century alcohol was considered nutritious and was used as a stimulant (Warner, 1980: 235). This idea was much discussed among physicians in the 1870s and it helped to explain this particularly contemporary preoccupation with a rise in drunkenness among the business and professional classes. As their new-fangled, very active lifestyle and stressful work exhausted their powers, they were driven to make more use of stimulants and to take up a habit of 'nippin':

> a new danger that has sprung up among the more favoured classes [...] The wear and the tear of modern life, the heavy draughts upon the reserve-fund of the nervous system, the necessity of keeping oneself 'up to the mark' are asserting themselves with imperious force and are driving many of our most active and intelligent leaders in society, female as well as male, into surreptitious stimulation or open addiction to alcohol. (*The Lancet*, 11 July 1874: 52)

The introduction of the new medical term 'addiction', juxtaposed with the financial terminology used to refer to the 'economy' of the body, indicates clearly how different and indeed modern this type of drunkenness was. Specialist 'inebriate asylums', as were proposed in the Habitual Drunkards Act 1872 and discussed by the committee, were already well established in the United States, and it was indeed there that Donald Dalrymple had found inspiration for his Bill (Crowley and White, 2004: 10). For as much as working-class drunkards on the streets could be confused with revolutionary Frenchmen, the taking of drink as a 'pick me up' would turn wholesome Britons into effeminate Americans.

Notwithstanding, the advertising columns of *The Times* and *The Lancet* in the 1870s suggest a considerable supply of private care for wealthy inebriates and especially for women in Britain. Private lunatic asylums were populated to a very large extent by alcohol and other addicts (Scott, 1879: 212). Like lunacy, 'habitual drunkenness' was a problematic diagnosis, a judgement for which people had to rely on the knowledge of specialists. Where eccentricity could be confused with lunacy, there was the fear that convivial drinking could be taken for habitual drunkenness. At what point did drunkenness become habitual and anti-social? After the introduction of the idea of forceful confinement in the first Bill an angry editorial in *The Times* appeared: 'Beware al ye frequenters of races, cricket matches, agricultural shows, regattas or rifle meetings during this thirsty season [...] imprisonment may come from a picnic and hard labour from a conservative festival' (Anon. 1872, *The Times*, 11).

The problem of personal liberty was the main motive put forward by MPs to reject the Bill when it was first introduced. Liberal Home Secretary Henry Bruce responded to the proposal that although 'it might be convenient to shut up many an erring wife and many a young man ruining the fortunes of himself and his family, it was not within parliament's remit to provide this possibility' (Hansard, 1870: 1247). It was feared that profit-seeking asylum owners would wrongfully convict healthy people at a request of someone wanting to get rid of a troublesome relative (Brown, 1985: 54). Suspicion was raised by real life events whereby deceitful family members had locked up innocent people in lunatic asylums. Such incidents played heavily on the public imagination and inspired popular fiction. A stage version of Wilkie Collins' sensational novel from 1859, *The Woman in White*, for example, which told the story of a cruel husband's conspiracy to commit his wife to a lunatic asylum to obtain her money, had opened in London at the end of 1871 and it was still running when the Committee started its hearings (Lycett, 2013: 315). When Dalrymple's proposal finally became law in 1879, it was in a much watered-down version and only for a limited period of ten years. It now essentially offered legal recognition to private asylums for habitual drunkards through a licensing system and the idea of compulsory confinement had been completely abandoned.

The bill had been unacceptable in its original form as it did not only concern *public* drunkenness, as other alcohol-related legislation had done before, but *all* drinking that could be considered habitual and therefore anti-social. It potentially also included the drinking of the middle-class lawmakers themselves, which explains its fierce opposition. The anxieties about wrongful confinement that were expressed and the worries about against state intervention in private affairs that were voiced, laid bare how the boundaries of what was considered habitual anti-social drinking were dictated by established cultural categories of class and gender.

Working-class people had always been locked up with little argument for being 'drunk and disorderly' no matter whether just drunk on occasion or in fact habitual drunkards. Likewise, in the mid-1860s when the Contagious Diseases Acts had been passed which permitted forced medical vaginal inspection of women whom the police labelled common prostitutes, no reservations had been expressed in Parliament about loss of personal liberty or possible wrongful confinement (Walkowitz, 1980: 73–9). Precisely because the principle of coercion had been used in the fight against sexually transmitted diseases, some supporters of the Habitual Drunkards Bill had reasoned that there 'ought to be no hesitation in extending it in the case of this disease' (Hansard, 1878: 710). This argument proved thoroughly unconvincing: there could not possibly be an analogy between both laws. Those who had been the target of the Contagious Diseases Acts were prostitutes, lower-class women, while those who would be affected by a Habitual Drunkards Act were not only women but also men, and of the middle and upper classes.

Drinking ladies: 'the most repulsive object on the face of the earth'

A significant part of the public debate surrounding drunkenness in the 1870s focused on the 'increasing evil' of female middle- and upper-class drunkenness, which was considered especially anti-social (Anon, 1871 *Saturday Review*: 75). Dr Forbes Winslow told the members of the Select Committee he knew numbers of 'ladies moving in very good society who are never sober, and are often brought home by the police drunk. They are wives of men in a very high social position' (Report, 1872: 75, 1332). Dramatic reports appeared in the press about young girls of the upper classes succumbing to drink. Their intemperance would spring from 'excessive night fatigue, undergone by delicate and nervous persons' (*The Lancet*, 25 February 1871: 277). This could lead to potentially very dangerous situations, as it was also believed that 'liquor impairs chastity in women more than in men'. When out and about during the London season, a young girl 'naturally looks for some artificial support, for a whip to keep her from flagging [...]' (Anon., 1871, *The Spectator*: 11). The young women here under scrutiny, being compared to racehorses on the track, played an unusual publicly active role when thrown into the marriage market, contradictory to what was believed to be their natural female passive dispositions.

As they were believed to be weaker, women were also thought to have generally more need for artificial stimulants and they could become casualties of their doctors' generous alcoholic prescriptions. Justified by female 'natural weakness', drinking alcohol could then become a legitimate, social act for ladies, but only when used as medicine with a cultural meaning completely detached from what was happening at the same time in their husbands' clubs or in the public house. A letter to the editor of *The Times* – criticizing the rise of intemperance among ladies – ironically sketched a contemporary situation:

> How common is it for a lady to call upon another when the hot spirit and water is on the table, and the hostess will say 'you see my dear, I am

very vulgar, I am taking at this time of the morning some gin and water, but it is by the 'doctor's orders', for I do suffer so much with the spasms (gin spasms), dear, do me get you just a little, pray do. (Cartwright-Reed, 1872: 5)

One of the specialist witnesses on the Select Committee of 1872 was Dr Alexander Peddie from Edinburgh who was an expert not only on drunkenness, but also on female maladies. In 1858, he had already started a campaign for specialist asylum provision. In an essay titled: 'Legalised Arrangements for the Treatment of Dipsomania' he had laid out a definition of the dipsomaniac as opposed to the habitual drunkard and he had explained that drunkenness as a disease could be recognized by a tendency towards solitary, rather than social drinking. Since social norms for middle- and upper-class women did not allow them to be unaffected social drinkers, their drunkenness therefore necessarily had to be dipsomania and was necessarily always unacceptable and anti-social; drinking ladies were seen as 'the most repulsive object on the face of the earth' (Daly, 1879: 119).

Dr Andrew Wynter, who wrote on female drunkenness as one of the diseases inhabiting what he called the 'borderlands of insanity', was one of the few voices in the debate to acknowledge a link between female drinking and middle-class women's social conditions: women would drink because they were bored and frustrated with their allocated roles:

Were it not that women are beginning to rebel against the barriers that are placed against their taking their proper place in society as the helpmate and in certain sense the equal of man, we should indeed fear that the habit of intemperance, once fashionable among men, would root itself among what some are pleased to term the softer sex. (Winter, 1877: 4)

This unease about the drunken woman breaking out of the mould of respectability did indeed correspond to a spread of new feminist ideas. John Stuart Mill had only just published *The Subjection of Women* in 1869 and a year later, at the same time Dalrymple presented the Habitual Drunkards Act proposing mandatory custody for dipsomaniacs, the Married Women's Property Act 1870 had given women greater power over their own possessions, opening the long way to legislative reform towards women's liberation. In the coming decades, middle-class women would start to challenge the traditional sexual divisions in society and would leave the drawing room to enter the public sphere (Rappaport, 2001: 86). On the streets of city centres where it became ever more difficult to distinguish who were 'real' ladies (Nead, 2005: 63), public drunkenness always continued to be a very important marker of respectability. The physical effects of alcohol would alter women's natural state of virtuousness and obedience, which resulted in 'unnatural', promiscuity and therefore profoundly anti-social behaviour, as one writer for the *Saturday Review* remarked:

> We are sensible of a distinct moral relaxation among women, and of a new sort of unwomanly recklessness in the presence of men [...] it would seem that alcohol has something to do with this disorder, for the physical effects of it on women are proved by medical investigation to be precisely that what would denaturalise them [...]'. (Anon, *Saturday Review*, 1871: 76)

The efforts to transform drinking ladies into diseased patients in the last quarter of the nineteenth century were informed by ideas of appropriate female behaviour. When it became clear that the keepers of moral values, middle- and upper-class women, were also affected by intemperance, drinking as a 'vice' had to be fundamentally reviewed. During the 1870s, the topic of female middle-class drunkenness was at the forefront of the public and political debate on drunkenness. In these narratives, it was configured as a separate condition, as a disease caused by biological weakness rather than moral failing.

Conclusion

While, in fact, the problem of habitual drunkenness was to be found in all classes of society, and while men as well as women drank, it was necessarily represented in a distinct way according to different cultural categories, establishing essential differences between gender and class. The 1870s saw an increased preoccupation with drunkenness as anti-social behaviour and a desire to regulate it. When legislating for drunkenness – setting down behavioural codes that were to be adhered by all – it was clear to those studying drunkenness how ambivalent the topic was and how its meanings needed to be negotiated very carefully. The extensive debates between 1870 and 1879 surrounding the Habitual Drunkards Act 1879, demanding asylum care for habitual drunkards, illustrate this very well. All engaged in the public and political debate in the period agreed that anti-social drunkenness had to be curbed, but they also insisted that both the type of drunkenness and the way to remedy it could take many forms. Anti-social drunkenness could be a private and a public matter, the drinker could be held accountable for his or her behaviour or responsibility could be relinquished depending on the scenario in which it was set. Drunkenness in the 1870s was discussed by a group of new specialists on mental disease, who did so on their own terms, as middle-class professional men, which resulted in distinctive legislation. The public debate surrounding the regulation of drunkenness and the making of anti-social drinking in the decade of the 1870s, provide an exciting insight into the way society worked. The construction of the meaning of excessive drinking affected and was at the same time influenced by a fast changing society in which moral and medical ideas were contested, where the free market promoted the rise of professionals and businessmen, while workers and women started to demand equal rights. Narratives of vice and that of disease, of responsibility and biology in Victorian Britain always intersected and they revealed a constant overlapping of old and new discourses, intertwined with changes in ideas and shifts in attitudes towards categories of gender and class.

23

Symbolism and the 'Free Market': The Regulation of Alcohol and Anti-social Behaviour Past and Present

Deborah Talbot

Introduction

The concept of anti-social behaviour (ASB) was a product of New Labour's 'third way' thinking, yet concepts of disorder and incivility, which have a strong interrelationship with the idea of anti-social behaviour, have a long tradition in English sensibilities and civil law. This is nowhere more obvious than in the regulation of alcohol and entertainment.

The earliest law concerning alcohol was passed in 1381, but it was aimed merely at the regulation of price to prevent inflation and the cheapening of the coinage (Dorn, 1983). Statutes dating from the fifteenth century established a connection between the consumption of alcohol and labour discipline. As Nicolas Dorn (1983) and Brian Harrison (1994) argued, alcohol consumption was identified from this point onwards with lax attendance and productivity, political agitation among the working class, riots, disorder and revolution. Drinking and entertainment were seen as a barrier to a longer more regular working week and the intensification of work required by industrialization. Legislation throughout the early to mid-seventeenth century dictated where and when drinking could take place, ranging from restricting drinking in inns to residents, banning entertainment on religious days and making drunkenness an offence (Dorn, 1983).

Drink and entertainment, therefore, has, in English history, held a symbolic meaning, speaking to a discussion about the nature of a newly emerging industrialized society, class formation, and political agitation. This chapter will explore this symbolism, first of all focusing on the emergence and formation of licensing law in history, secondly of New Labour and Conservative–Liberal Democrat Coalition policy in relation to alcohol consumption.

George Orwell (1940: 41) pointed to the hypocrisy embedded in English licensing laws that were 'designed to interfere with everybody but in practice allowed everything to happen'. I will argue that beyond the rhetoric, Orwell's description is indeed correct; elites in England and Wales were not so concerned about alcohol and entertainment to prohibit both, although they may be forced to respond to particular health campaigns, or for other self-serving reasons. However, licensing law has served governance well in certain instances of threat and needful social engineering where it *has* been enforced. This chapter will explore the contradictions of licensing law in its historical emergence and post-1997, and how and when it is enforced. To this end we might reframe Orwell's quote that licensing law is 'designed to interfere with some but in practice allowed most things to happen, under a *symbolic* criminalisation of all'.

These two themes – symbolism and contradictory motivation and enforcement – run throughout this chapter. It begins by exploring the rationale of licensing law as it emerged in conjunction with the slow developing industrialization of England and Wales. This section provides case studies of selective enforcement. The chapter then moves on to consider the reframing of alcohol regulation and its symbolism in the New Labour government and beyond. The argument of this chapter is that legislation enacted around concepts of disorder and anti-social behaviour not only serve to regulate individual and group conduct, but also relationships between capital and state.

Symbolism and licensing practice in the regulation of alcohol and entertainment in the eighteenth and nineteenth centuries

This chapter has already outlined some of the early symbolism of alcohol consumption and its relationship to concepts of anti-social behaviour and disorder. Licensing regimes and the official attitude to alcohol have been shaped by economic, as well as political and moral, considerations. Attempts to restrict the consumption of alcohol from the sixteenth century, for example, were closely connected with the new vagrancy laws aimed at controlling labour and ensuring discipline, alongside concerns about the close connection of alehouses with working-class radicalism (Dorn, 1983). Furthermore, theorists have understood fears around nightlife and popular culture to be intimately connected to fears about the 'dangerous classes' in the rapidly growing cities from the eighteenth century (Schlör, 1998). The social reaction to this culture was organized by largely middle-class movements ranging from the Reformation of Manners Movement (Hunt, 1999) to the Temperance movement in Victorian England, aimed at introducing a (presumed absence) of manners and civility[1] into the poor by reforming their conduct (Dingle, 1980).

The symbolic nature of licensing law can perhaps be seen most clearly in the introduction of the Disorderly Houses Act 1752, which formed the model for even contemporary forms of entertainment licensing. It became part of statute as a result of a petition by writer and magistrate Henry Fielding to the Lord High Chancellor, which drew attention to the growth in 'criminal' activities in the lower classes and speculated as to their cause. In Fielding's reasoning, the decoupling of the lower orders from feudal bondage had steadily inculcated new customs into this section of society, chief among them a demand for 'luxury'. While vice and ruination associated with the pursuit of luxury was unproblematic in the upper classes, among the lower classes, who were the source of labour and wealth, Fielding considered it destructive to society. Moreover, he feared the spectacle of riot and sedition. He therefore argued that the entertainment and consumption habits of the people should be restrained. The problem was how, when, according to Fielding, people took no notice of oppressive law and would reject any measure that constrained their individual liberty. Further, a system of control had to take account of what Temperance campaigners Sidney and Beatrice Webb (1903: 2) later noted as 'the absence of police'. The answer was found in liquor licensing law, and the Disorderly Houses Act was modelled on its structure. Fielding's pamphlet is a fascinating document both because it expresses the symbolism of the regulation of alcohol, but also how it carefully balances the preoccupations of control and liberty.

The Webbs (1903) observed that state involvement in the sale and consumption of alcohol was motivated by two conflicting interests. First, the revenue derived from taxes on liquor on the one hand, combined with the growing power of the 'free-trade' breweries, facilitated the growth of consumption. Lobbying by the breweries resulted in the passing, for example, of the Beerhouse Act 1830, which removed the right of magistrates to license public houses for the sale of beer and allowed any householder to sell beer for a small fee. Secondly, the Webbs argued, was the 'social disease' – the combination of economic deprivation, moral dissolution and indiscipline that appeared to originate from alcohol. Licensing law could not stop powerful interests, but it could regulate the conditions of alcohol use within what were perceived as acceptable outlets for supply (Dorn, 1983). The way that licensing law reflected such practices of inclusion and exclusion in the ability to control outlets for alcohol consumption and entertainment often coincided with the interests of the breweries and ensured cooperation and 'self-regulation'.

Any entertainment that fell outside of the bourgeois economy ('fairs and festivals') were treated as potential sites for incivility and disorder and targeted for surveillance by the emerging police forces (Storch, 1976). The aim of the first entertainment licensing law, the Disorderly Houses Act 1752, was to permit and restrict, so long as the authorities retained control over the premises. What is central here is that licensing law, whether aimed at deregulation or re-regulation depending on the historical period, had the impact of consolidating the *permitted* capitalist industry. Free or unregulated activities outside of that industry were successively restricted. The differentiations made were cultural ones. For example, the apparent difficulty of distinguishing between places frequented by the upper classes as opposed to the lower classes was exemplified in the Disorderly Houses Act 1752 through a clause which stated that a premises did not need a licence if it were an important theatre (with specific places listed in the text), or were already licensed by the crown or Lord Chamberlain. More recently, the fate of the 'beat clubs' in London's West End and Manchester in the 1960s, closed because of the so-called 'moral dangers' to young people (Public Records, 1964 HO300/24; Lee, 1995), and the domestication of the rave scene in the 1990s are also indicative of these dual standards.

The industry was often compliant with respect to regulatory controls for entirely strategic reasons, which belied the prevailing ideology of the laissez-faire market. For example, between 1890 and 1900 the industry saw a drop in revenue due to falling sales and prices. As a consequence, a struggle to control retail outlets ensued. An industry in fierce competition then favoured the closure of a number of outlets, which accorded with the growing Temperance mood of regulators (Dorn, 1983). Further, licensing law has flowed from the nature of economic policy. During the twentieth century, the trade was defined by the eroding boundaries of capital and state. Andy Lovatt (1996) referred to a 'Fordist' mode of regulation where the state regulated supply, by restricting the number of public houses and hours of opening. This form of regulation persisted until the 1980s with the growth of laissez-faire economics (Baggott, 1990) and renewed support for the liberalization of the trade. Yet, whatever constellation of licensing law was proposed, the result was a differentiation made between permitted and non-permitted industry.

The ability to mediate this differentiation derived from the structure of licensing law and its institutional implementation. As Webb and Webb (1903: 4) noted, licensing law regulated supply in four key ways: first, through the payment of taxes and fees for sale and manufacture; secondly, through the registering of individual licensees so they were 'brought to public notice'; thirdly, through the limitations placed on the number of alehouses in localities and on the qualifications needed to be a keeper; lastly, through the imposition of special rules or conditions of sale. The local operation of the law involved three forms of control exercised by magistrates: the 'power of selection', the 'power of withdrawal' and the 'power of imposing conditions'. The first power came with a 1552 statute (5&6 Edward VI.c.25) in which a licence became a privilege, not a right, and magistrates had the power to select through the exercise of discretion who should be given that privilege. The second power came earlier, with the 1495 (11 Henry VII.c.2) and 1504 (19 Henry VII.c.12) Acts, by which two justices could suspend what were seen as superfluous alehouses (Webb and Webb, 1903: 6). The third power came from a combination of the first two, and before the Beer Act 1830 magistrates had total autonomy to impose conditions, such as closing times, the number of licensed venues in areas, where public houses could be situated in the locality and so on (Webb and Webb, 1903: 9).

These three basic powers have been negotiated and altered in different historical periods depending on prevailing opinion. As already mentioned, in a unique drawing back of statute law, the Beer Act 1830 restricted judicial discretion, specifying that it was limited to making sure the applicant was of good character. The power of withdrawal was placed within the jury system, and Parliament argued significantly that the publican should be free to do whatever Parliament had not expressly forbidden (Webb and Webb, 1903: 98). The consequences of this liberalization was that the number of retailers of liquor grew, and as fears spiralled with regard to the growing level of drunkenness and incivility, magistrates and bishops agitated for a repeal of the Act. In the winter of 1830, a Parliamentary Committee was formed led by James Silk; the Committee was Temperance in character, and the following Beerhouse Acts of 1834 and 1840 enhanced the powers of the justices with regard to the owners' 'qualities'. Despite these shifts and reversals, the basic structure of licensing law and the powers granted to the state to control places of drinking remain similar to the structure of law today; further, that these specificities of quasi-legal practice embedded in licensing law conferred the ability of magistrates and other empowered authorities to control and differentiate between cultural and social spaces.

It is obviously the case that both liquor and entertainment licensing law have mutated beyond their original form. It is also the case that the development of police forces in the nineteenth century significantly enhanced the power of the state to enforce law and moreover develop alternative routes to controlling popular entertainment and incivility, such as direct repression and surveillance (Storch, 1976). Much of the language has changed while the symbolism has become more muted. Regardless, the licensing of alcohol and entertainment follows basically the same principles outlined by the Webbs, that is, a system of control aimed at controlling or containing the conditions of supply and of selecting who is a 'fit and proper' person to be licensed.

The state itself has historically been, and continues to be, in the contradictory position of modulating different interests while displacing blame. As illustrated by Dorn (1983), the production and consumption of alcohol has been subject to the twin political forces of free-marketers and Victorian Temperance (and its predecessors). The working class itself acts as a mass market for the consumption of alcohol (Gofton, 1990), particularly given, as Harrison points out, the psychological strains of industrialization combined with an erosion of 'traditional sanctions on conduct' (1994: 41) predispose people to over-consumption. What can never be admitted by governance is an economic and cultural causation; thus individuals – drinkers and licensees – are blamed for its socially deleterious effects, an early example of a responsiblization (Rose, 1999) agenda. Licensing law – with its supervisory and differentiating possibilities – has been innovated to contain these contradictions.

New Labour and beyond: consumption, anti-social behaviour and disorder

New Labour thinking on alcohol and licensing emerged in policy form with a report from the Better Regulation Task Force 1998, which advocated the rationalization of existing licensing law. The result of this report and subsequent consultations was the Licensing Act 2003. The Act proposed to 'liberalize' hours of opening by allowing licensees to apply for differentiated hours within a structure of considerations about the effect on crime and disorder, nuisances and anti-social behaviour, public safety and the protection of children. It aimed to release the burdens on 'responsible' businesses, while retaining a range of sanctions against 'irresponsible' ones; thus the legislation was firmly couched in New Labour's 'third way' politics, balancing rights and responsibilities (Talbot, 2006). It was also explicitly aimed at engineering particular forms of cultures over others; the purpose of this supposed liberalization was to create a 'cafe society' (DCMS, 2002). At the time it was felt that restrictive licensing laws encouraged a culture of excessive drinking (the enticement of deviance); conversely, increased availability would normalize consumption and encourage responsible drinking. Such thinking had particularly emerged out of the work of the Institute of Popular Culture in Manchester Metropolitan University (MMU) and the Manchester City Council and the experiment in cultural regeneration conducted in Manchester.

The Act produced a widespread reaction, reigniting a decade-long debate on the impact of later licensing and the 'growth' of bars and clubs on the supply of alcohol and consequentially drunkenness. The argument, put forward by a loose alliance of London councils, some key residents associations, voluntary organizations such as Alcohol Concern, academics (Hobbs *et al.*, 2003), policy-makers and the Home Office, was that the growth of the 'night-time economy' prompted 'binge drinking' and consequently a growth of 'alcohol-related' (Alcohol Concern, 2004), or 'alcohol-fuelled' (DMCS, 2005: 3) disorder. The implementation of the Licensing Act 2003 in particular provoked the potential spectacle of 24-hour opening and of city centres therefore descending into an annoying or fear-provoking chaos of drunken 'yobs' (of both genders) creating violence, noise and anti-social behaviour. Intersecting with such activity was the public health lobby, where the British Medical Journal (BMJ) and hospitals pointed to the increased pressure arising from alcohol-fuelled violence on hospitals and emergent health problems arising from excessive drinking. I will return to this when considering Conservative–Liberal Democrat Coalition policy.

A consultation document produced by the Department of Culture, Media and Sport (DMCS), the Office of the Deputy Prime Minister (ODPM) and the

Home Office in January 2005 as part of a National Alcohol Strategy argued that while 'most people drink responsibly', there was 'general agreement that the scale of alcohol-fuelled disorder is much too high' (DMCS, 2005: 3). The document discussed making binge and under-age drinking 'socially unacceptable' (DMCS, 2005: 3), and highlighted the problems of street massing (when large numbers of young people are on the street at the same time after standard closing times), street drinking and large numbers of people in particular areas 'intimidating, harassing, alarming or distressing the public' (DMCS, 2005: 6). So extensive was the social reaction to the Licensing Act 2003 that in the course of its long passage through Parliament, the Criminal Justice and Police Act was passed in 2001, which included a bewildering array of measures from 'on the spot fines' to Closure Orders. Since then, other Acts have been passed that constrain the workings of the Licensing Act 2003 (July), including the Anti-social Behaviour Act 2003 (November) and the Violent Crime Reduction Act 2006, which introduced Alcohol Disorder Zones (ADZ).[2]

Of course disorder, like anti-social behaviour,[3] is a concept that can 'mean anything, while also being a strongly symbolic and evocative term' (Brown, 2004: 204), and generally studies cited in order to prove a correlation between alcohol and disorder actually have a more narrow focus on violence or aggression (see Alcohol Concern, 2004; Finney, 2004). The diffuse nature of the social reaction permitted by this terminology recalled some elements of a moral panic (Borsay, 2007) and historically common fears concerning the entertainment habits of the lower orders, women, and minority ethnic groups (Erenburg, 1981; Kohn, 1992).

Efforts to direct attention towards the (mostly northern) disorderly binge drinker being produced by the excesses of the Licensing Act 2003 ignored some salient facts about government economic and social policy. One is that the deregulation of licensing hours that began with the end of the afternoon break (where pubs closed after lunch until early evening) in the mid-1980s (Baggott, 1990) was part of a broader ideological commitment to laissez-faire economics and deindustrialization initiated much earlier than the New Labour government. The second is consequential from the first, that the night-time economy was an idea born out of the need to regenerate decaying inner-city areas (Department of the Environment, 1993). Nightlife would be an economic driver as part of a service-driven sector of symbolic goods that would dominate our postmodern and post-Fordist landscape. A third aspect is also key, and that is to remind ourselves that the night-time economy was a policy of social control aimed at driving rave culture into private and licensed space, thus rendering them visible and ordered (Garratt, 1998; Collin, 1997). One consequence of this was that at least officially the intoxicant of choice had to be legal, that is, alcoholic, despite the continued prevalence of illegal drugs. Moreover, breweries were happy to innovate to suit new tastes and chemically 'facilitate' use. Summaries of research by Alcohol Concern (2001) illustrate that the content of alcopops (alcohol and other ingredients including sugar and a variety of stimulants) conceal the taste and strength of alcoholic drinks and thus are more likely to appeal to the young. Finally, in many ways, focusing on bars and clubs as a source of disorder ignored the rise of drinking outside those spaces. Statistics on licensing over a century show that the most dramatic increase in the number of licensed outlets has been in off-licensed premises, from around 25,000 in 1905 to 46,582 in 2004; while restaurants and public-house licences have shown an increase of nearly 15,000 from 1980 from a historic low point in the postwar period (DMCS, 2004): the era of privatized family-based 'leisure' (Mass Observation, 1943) and the public marginalization of women. In fact, the number of clubs licensed remains small (Home Office, 2002a; DCMS, 2004). Latest figures show a continuance of such trends, with an increase in off-licensed sales and an increase in the loss of licences in the club sector (Home Office, 2013). Figures from 2010–12 showed an 18 per cent increase in the number of licences awarded to supermarkets and general stores (Home Office, 2012a). Finally, in 2012, pubs, bars and clubs accounted for only 11 per cent of 24-hour licences, compared with 24 per cent for supermarkets and stores, and 54 per cent for hotel bars (Home Office, 2012a). In terms of availability for drinking, therefore, pubs, bars and clubs are not the most significant sector, and yet have attracted the most negative attention.

These four points illustrate, as in prior history, that licensing law and the regulation of spaces of drinking and entertainment is enmeshed in contradictions. Economically it was viewed as a critical driver, hence regulators moved towards the laissez-faire position of 24-hour opening. Support for the *business* of drinking is critical to government policy. Yet someone must be blamed when things go wrong; to centre stage moved the violent 'binge drinker' and to a lesser degree the 'irresponsible licensee'. Meanwhile, off-licences and supermarkets have escaped notice. The 'free market' and alcohol-fuelled disorder or anti-social behaviour exist in an important symbiosis, which recalls the relationship between free-marketer breweries and the disorderly working-class of Victorian Temperance thinking.

In addition, the supposedly new regime of licensing regulation did nothing to stop the continuing dualism historically evident in licensing of inclusion and exclusion regarding particular cultural spaces and peoples. As research by Paul Chatterton and Robert Hollands (2002, 2003), Deborah Talbot (2004) and Martina Böse (2005) showed in different contexts, licensing and regulation continues to operate with clear notions of unacceptable and acceptable cultures and peoples; however, in contemporary subjectivities, they are entwined with beliefs correlating commercial viability with orderly spaces. Talbot's (2007) research – conducted in an anonymous locality in London – demonstrated the racialized nature of regulatory subjectivities; black licensees were simply not viewed as trust-worthy or commercially competent by the police or even local authori-ties (who might be expected to take a more enlightened view, but who were reliant on police warnings and objections). The regulation of licens-ing therefore coalesces with cultural regeneration strategies to ultimately favour big business over independent or alternative spaces, or white con-trolled spaces over those owned by black licensees, and so on in a com-plex process that intertwines moral norms and cultural habits with com-mercial development. These observations reconfirm geographical research on culturally differentiating processes occurring within cities in the con-text of 'gentrification' (Zukin 1989, 1991, 1995; Smith, 1996; Ferrell, 2001).

If New Labour policy represented the ambiguity of the 'third way' approach in that it tried to balance the 'free market' and 'consumerism' against social engineering, the Conservative–Liberal Democrat Coalition government which came to power in 2010 represented a hardening of a more free-market-, 'choice'-led ideology, although it took some time to emerge. In the immediate sense, the rhetoric of condemning binge drinkers and disorder, with 'tough action' against irresponsible licensees continued. The Coalition's alcohol strategy, produced by the Home Office,[4] promised to 'tackle the scourge of violence caused by binge drinking' (Home Office, 2012c: 2). The measures proposed included: minimum pricing for alcohol, enhancing powers of local authorities to control density of premises, Early Morning Restriction Orders which allow local authorities to restrict the sale of alcohol by area between 12–6am,[5] a late night levy on businesses to force them to contribute to the cost of policing, a Responsibility Deal to encourage businesses to act responsibly and health advice. Significantly, proposals to introduce minimum pricing – the only policy to practically influence super-markets – was shelved in 2013 in favour of a ban on selling alcohol lower than the price of duty and VAT (*Independent*, 17 July 2013), while in Scotland blanket minimum pricing was removed from the Alcohol etc. (Scotland) Act 2010 over fears that it contravened European Union (EU) price competition rules (Nicholls, 2011). In addition, it has been noted that the government has fostered close links to the drinks industry in line with its libertarian, laissez-faire leanings (Sheron *et al.*, 2011). Research commissioned by the BMJ (Gornall, 2014) has found that the government was intensively lob-bied by supermarkets, breweries and right-wing research institutes, such as the Institute of Economic Affairs, while public-health experts were excluded, even as minimum pricing was being consolidated into policy. Enacted under the ideology of the free market and choice, the outcome illustrates that – with the close cooperation of the state and business – the 'free market' is anything but free. Nevertheless, powers still prevail to target individually 'unacceptable' premises, while providing an environment of tolerance for the activities of big business.

Conclusion

This chapter has put forward the argument that the regulation of alcohol and entertainment mediated through licensing law and other indirect legislation has a strong symbolic quality of criminalization, while in practice creating the means to discriminate between acceptable and unacceptable cultural forms and behaviour. This tells us much about the nature of the 'free-market' both at particular historical junctures such as the Victorian period and today. A historical and current consideration of legislation concerned with the regulation of anti-social behaviour and disorder shows that it aims both to regulate conduct and provide a means to discriminate between 'acceptable' and 'unacceptable' business, a process of regulation that big business is involved in and benefits from. What does this mean for the nature of drinking alcohol and what we might broadly think of as subcultural (meaning those that may be designated unacceptable) spaces?

Orwell noted in his sentimental account of English culture that the working classes were 'inveterate gamblers, drink as much beer as their wages will permit, are devoted to bawdy jokes, and use probably the foulest language in the world' (1940: 16). There is something to be said for understanding drinking cultures in this context; yes, excessive drinking is driven by the nature of capitalist economies, whether this is about expanding markets or alienation. However, there is also something in Fielding's lament that the English are too attached to liberty. Nightlife historically is both an expression of the separation of work and pleasure characteristic of market and industrialized societies *and*, because of the dominance of class segregation and the official response to popular culture, a form of rebellion, conceived in its broadest (apolitical) sense. There are doubts about the efficacy of control. Peter Ackroyd (2000), in his 'biography' of London, describes the unruly and disorderly nature of everyday life in a capital city; its very size eludes attempts at control and sanitization (Raban, 1974). Free-market ideology has its reflection in contemporary popular culture.

While in this conclusion I have noted both the perverse effects of free-market thinking and the limits of intervention, it seems useful to consider how nightlife can be a source of creativity, and how urban policy and licensing law might facilitate diversity in urban landscapes irrespective of the multiplicity of concerns about health and disorder. This in particular means a better understanding about the relationship between regulation and more subcultural forms of expression, which have often been at the forefront of reshaping economic, cultural and political agendas, aptly seen in places as geographically diverse as Manchester and Brixton (London). In Brixton (Talbot, 2004), Manchester (Böse, 2005), or through mass events like raves where alternative culture was able to express itself in a spatial form, the possibilities of encountering the 'Other' – whether this be an expression of class, ethnic, gender or other forms of difference – were high (Sennett, 1970;

Raban, 1974). The impact of such encounters was both a challenge to conventional identities and the assertion of mainstream values such as work or family (Pryce, 1976; Willis, 1978). Transgressive spaces and behaviour were at the same time destructive and creative, allowing for personal dissipation, internalized and externalized violence and vandalism, but also opening a space for cultural and political expression (Lessing, 1969). The importance of understanding the dynamic of subculture, emergent in disciplines such as cultural criminology, appears key.

While what we have today seems far removed from those possibilities, it seems important not to close them down for the future. Current debates and policies around alcohol-related disorder and anti-social behaviour, as simplistic policy discourses, have served to expand the scope of regulatory control and police powers; while we imagine they are aimed at unwanted behaviours, they also have negative consequences for alternative spaces and subcultural expression. In making nightlife a 'law and order' issue, the prospect of night spaces being inhabited by subcultural entrepreneurs becomes narrower. The colonization and control of nightlife, alongside the moral disapproval about its behaviours, will not aid the potential for the recreation of a more interesting and creative nightlife and politics.

Notes

1. This section will refer to 'anti-social behaviour' as incivility, the term more commonly used pre-1997.
2. It was reported that as of 2009 no Alcohol Disorder Zones (ADZs) had been implemented (http://www.alcoholpolicy.net/2009/07/no-alcohol-disorder-zones-set-up-.html) and in 2011 they were repealed under the Police Reform and Social Responsibility Act 2011.
3. The difference between the terms seems to lie in the collective versus the individual in contemporary discourse, although anti-social behaviour (ASB) can refer to behaviour by groups.
4. Significantly, the main responsibility for licensing moved back to the Home Office from the Department of Culture, Media and Sport (DCMS) in 2010 after the Conservative–Liberal Democrat Coalition came to power.
5. This was an uncommenced power from the Licensing Act 2003 and extended in the Police Reform and Social Responsibility Act 2011.

24
Psychotic (e)states: Where Anti-social Behaviour is Merged with Recreational Drug Use to Signify the Social Problem Group

Shane Blackman and Andrew Wilson

Introduction

In 2012, grime artist Plan B's album title track 'Ill Manors' used a critical tone to convey the reality of young people's experience of poverty and inequality under the Conservative–Liberal Democrat Coalition government. These 'gritty' representations of psychotic (e)states affirm young people's culture and define their urban locality. In the video of the song, the popular images are reflected back to 'fuel the fear' with an ironic sneer at misrepresentations in the media, an irony that is lost on governments which have used images of anti-social behaviour, drugs, and young people on stigmatized social housing 'estates' within their programme to regulate the conduct of a social problem group. Young people's actions are allowed no margin for error as youthful exuberance is seen as having 'intent' and interpreted as a sign of future criminality. Activities that previous generations engaged in as a rite of passage are now regarded as not just anti-social but as risk factors to predict potential misdemeanours. Drawing on Ian Hacking's (1986) notions of 'making up people', that is, classifying people through 'looping effects' (Hacking, 1996), we examine the way that the recreational drug use of youth in poorer neighbourhoods has been merged with an anti-social behaviour agenda and problematic drug users to create a 'criminogenic group' who are deemed likely to cause criminal behaviour.

The approach used in this chapter is to critically address policy documents, media representations and popular culture, focusing on young people and anti-social behaviour as a field of knowledge and a social arena where institutions such as the tabloid press and government seek to secure regulation and control (Bourdieu, 1996). Government policies and media perceptions have aimed to elicit moral repugnance in their presentation of different forms of deviance impacting on people's everyday life. We suggest that the construction of moral disapproval has been achieved through merging two types of drug use, recreational and problematic (DeScioli *et al.*, 2012). Set within the context of disadvantaged neighbourhoods both types of drug use have been merged into one category, that of the social problem group who are then defined as criminal through their engagement in anti-social behaviour. Here we investigate the contradictions and misrepresentations associated with anti-social behaviour and drugs, where negative images shape a perception of everyday actions and fuel hostility towards the normal actions of youth.

The twin social evils: anti-social behaviour and drugs

The nineteenth century saw the emergence of the concept of juvenile delinquency as part of penal policy (Shore, 1999: 17). Armed with this new concept, John Gillis (1975: 98–9) argues that the state saw crime increasing at a fast rate, as 'types of juvenile behaviour previously dealt within informal ways became the subject of prosecution'. Broadly speaking, disorderly misdemeanours which were part of what E.P. Thompson (1991: 9) called 'plebeian customary practice' were tolerated. According to Natalie Zemon Davis (1971), writing about sixteenth-century France, these formed part of young people's traditions of the 'reasons of misrule', where challenges to social order were dealt with informally within the local community. During this period, the role of the state increased and Ian Hacking (2007: 161) points out that counting different forms of deviance 'generated its own subdivisions and rearrangements', both created a 'problem' and affected the response to it. For Jock Young (1971: 140), 'there was an increasing proportion of young people at the margin of society who were perceived as outcast, neglected, idle and – most important – uncontrollable'. In essence, as Gillis suggests, the rise in juvenile crime is a result of a new willingness to prosecute behaviour on the basis of new offences. Elizabeth Burney (2009: 50) identifies the historical and contemporary broadening of the definition of what constitutes anti-social behaviour along with the creation of drug-related anti-social behaviour, as possessing a long lineage from the 1890s onwards, which thrives on institutionally driven anxiety with the resolve to produce a popular preventive to control youth.

During the early 1900s in America, a pioneering investigation into juvenile delinquency by William Healy (1915) brought a new focus on the individual 'deviant'. He considered that statistics and pathology were not enough to understand deviance, which was also shaped by culture, and environment. In contrast, during the 1920s in the United Kingdom, the concept of subculture was applied to young deviants who were defined in biological terms as being socially evil, according to a range of social issues impacting on young people, including intoxication, criminality and unemployment

(Wood Report, 1929; Lewis, 1933). In the United Kingdom, the social problem group was defined and identified as being subnormal and unproductive. We argue that the contemporary construction of problem drug users into a social problem group drawn from the poorest tenth of the social scale has a legacy in the nineteenth century (Blackman, 2014: 499) and has implications for the way recreational drug use by young people in poorer areas is perceived.

We suggest that the emergence of juvenile delinquency in the Victorian period and the consequent increase in young people being prosecuted, has contemporary resonance with increased attention to anti-social behaviour (Crawford, 2009a: 821). Since 1998, in government white papers, legislation, and media reports there has been a tendency to present anti-social behaviour through opposites. The contrast is usually made stark between 'hard-working citizens' and 'yobbish' youth who engage in low-level criminality. Within the anti-social behaviour debate, we are encouraged to see anti-social behaviour as not just bad, but also a sign of future criminality, signalling the decline of the family, community and individual. All signs of anti-social behaviour are deemed unacceptable, and as needing correction or punishment to prevent a real or an imagined decline (Ruggiero, 1999: 123). Linking recreational drug users with problem users within the anti-social behaviour agenda has helped to distort perceptions of drug use through the policy focus on 'problematic youth'. The most appealing social constructs have an empirical basis that serves to add enough substance to give shape to their over-inflated explanatory power. There is little doubt that social context plays an important part in drug use trajectories (Zinberg, 1984), but that does not make any of the negative factors inevitable or even likely for recreational drug users in poorer neighbourhoods. In fact, there is good evidence to show that the presence of heroin or crack users can inoculate future generations against the use of addictive substances (Parker et al., 2001). These distinctions are known but ignored within the framing of a social problem group.

The construction of what constitutes 'anti-social' is a good example of the kind of 'looping effects' that Hacking (2007) identifies as fulfilling a crucial role in the dynamic process of 'making people up'. Once created, the anti-social category brings with it an expectation that others will take sides and support sanctions against what is upheld as deplorable, dangerous and threatening behaviour. The legislative details in the Crime and Disorder Act 1998, the Anti-social Behaviour Act 2003 and the new Anti-social Behaviour, Crime and Policing Act 2014 were based on survey findings that interpret opinions as of fact and uses them to inform policy. In contrast to this 'abstracted empiricism' (Mills, 1959: 64), Hayden and Martin (2011) recognize that anti-social behaviour is rooted in subjective experience, feelings and standards. Here we want to separate some of the strands that have woven three constructs, young people, anti-social behaviour and drugs, into an emotive category which, when set in poorer neighbourhoods, draws on community stigma to attribute negative intent to normal actions.

Although empirically unproven, the gateway drug thesis has common currency in anti-social behaviour settings (Blackman, 2004: 153). Matthew Bacon's (2013) research with the South Yorkshire police gives a good example of the way police officers view the move to stronger substances as inevitable. Both the subjective nature of the term anti-social behaviour and its elevation in the political discourse have been intensified by media images and tabloid descriptions of anti-social behaviour that draw on terms like 'the yob', 'reign of terror', 'hate', 'thugs', 'tearaway teenage' and 'chaos'. The invective shapes a 'pervasive image of a generation of thoughtless, uncouth, obnoxious teens' (Hughes, 2010: 9). In terms of how public perceptions are influenced, it would seem that the British media when reporting on drugs and anti-social behaviour could be accused of a 'lack of balance in what is covered and how' (UKDPC, 2010: 59) For Doolin *et al.* (2011: 16) 'drug related crime and youth centred anti-social behaviour continue to dominate newspaper headlines', which they see as shaping the public perception of crime, resulting in punitive legislation.

The growth of the new right from the 1980s onwards with its accusatory agenda of blame defined a neo-classical shift to individual responsibility, promoting an image of anti-social youth as a social pariah, an object of fear and described as receiving their 'just deserts' (Kubiak and Hester, 2009). The latter has appeared in contemporary British television through the representation of anti-social behaviour by comedians such as Matt Lucas and Catherine Tate who portray fictional anti-social behaviour characters such as the chav Vicky Pollard (Lucas) in *Little Britain* and the stroppy schoolgirl Lauren (Tate) and her catch phrase adapted by the Labour Prime Minister Tony Blair in the House of Commons: 'am I bovvered?'. Characters that teenagers may see as funny or cool may be differently understood by figures of authority. Alternative comedians present accessible but complex representations of young people's anti-social behaviour but, at the same time, these representations have been simplified and used against young people by the tabloid press. Furthermore, the right-wing tabloid press has used absurd examples of anti-social behaviour to mock Labour government policy, see for example the *Daily Mail* and *Daily Express* coverage of anti-social behaviour including: 'Buddy the ASBO parrot' (9 November 2012), 'Oscar the "ASBO cat"' (23 August 2013) and 'Giggling toddler warned of ASBO for laughing too loudly at "Thomas the Tank Engine" on television' (*Daily Express*, 14 May 2013). At some distance from real people's lives, the Home Affairs Select Committee Report on Anti-Social Behaviour (House of Commons (2005: para.19) has argued: 'we do not believe that the problem of anti-social behaviour has been exaggerated by Government or played up by the media'. The end result of a popular discourse that has made the notion of ASBOs a laughing stock is, first, the removal of the term ASBO and, secondly, the creation a new term 'nuisance'. This had been predicted by Peter Squires (2008) in his study on the criminalization of nuisance. The contradiction apparent in the tabloid coverage of anti-social behaviour from serious moral stand to crass jokes has kept anti-social behaviour on the agenda as an object for reform described by Adam Crawford (2009a: 810) as producing 'bouts of hyper-active state interventionism'.

In opposition to government claims and media assertions, recent evidence suggests that, rather than increasing, both anti-social behaviour and drug use have been declining. The British Crime Survey (2013) has suggested that there has been a fall in the level of crime, although this has not significantly affected the public perception of disorder. Also, the United Nations Drug Report (2009) and the recent UK Drug Policy Commission (2012) have commented on the decline of drug use and drugs as a problem in society. The public perception of the extent of anti-social behaviour according to Furlong (2013: 193) is 'not supported by crime statistics'. Even at the height of the anti-social behaviour frenzy, Girling *et al.* (2000) found that anxieties about young people had become out of proportion with the risk they pose. The UN Committee on the Rights of the Child (2008) observed that young people have been marginalized and adults have been guilty of systematically portraying young people in a negative light and confronting them with, at best low expectations and at worst a hostility that invites a negative response. The Committee concluded that intolerance and inappropriate characterization runs through the heart of the British government and informs its policy response to the anxiety spiral that the authorities have helped create. Thus anti-social behaviour and drugs form part of the looping process with empirical examples, replayed through the media, feeding the perceptions of the public and the responses of the authorities (Lee, 2007).

Merging problem drug use and anti-social behaviour to inform policy

We argue that anti-social behaviour has developed into a form of governance to promote a popular preventive to regulate deviant life-styles (Paterson and MacVean, 2006). This policy discourse has its own energy. The 'loop effect' promotes public fear and anxiety about crime, drugs and youth with apparent public consent. For Alan France (2009: 430), young people are being projected as a 'symbol of decline' for a society in crisis. In this debate, there is little opportunity to challenge this circular process because it is self-reinforcing, and is driven by an apparent logic and rationality that feeds into political and electoral rhetoric (Hughes, 2011). Toby Seddon's (2011) piecing together the move from addiction as a category to 'problem drug users' provides useful insight into the way that drug use has become intertwined with the response to crime through a series of looping effects. Since the term was first used by the Advisory Council on the Misuse of Drugs in

1982 to describe a particular type of user, whether a heroin user or first time teenage glue sniffer, it has come to describe a particular category of user who is primarily defined by use of problematic drugs and their involvement in crime and anti-social behaviour (Mackenzie *et al.*, 2010).

After the election of the Labour government in 1997, drugs and anti-social behaviour became intimately connected as strategy through the Crime and Disorder Act 1998 linked with drugs policy set out in 'Tackling Drugs to Build a Better Britain' (Home Office, 1998). It would be wrong to reduce the drugs strategy to its focus on crime and disorder, but its emphasis was on a specific notion of drug use, stating 'drugs and crime are of concern to all communities' with 'acquisitive crime committed by drug misusing offenders to feed their habits, and the anti-social behaviour and feeling of menace that the drug culture generates within neighbourhoods'. There was substance to these claims as the research into social exclusion by the Centre for Analysis of Social Exclusion (CASE) found in a longitudinal study of families and neighbourhood regeneration. Interviews with families in Leeds, Sheffield and East London in 1999 and 2000 recorded concerns about drug use in stairwells, discarded needles in play areas, and the wider negative effect of the drug market (Bowman, 2001; Mumford 2001). John Graham (2000), then Deputy Director of Strategic Policy at the Home Office seconded to the London School of Economics (LSE), visited two of those areas plus one in the north east as a 'kind of pilot study' into the neighbourhood effects of the different drug markets. Research with a direct focus on the negative impact of the drug market revealed a more problematic picture than the CASE research suggested, in turn justifying further research.

The follow up study commissioned by the UK Anti-Drugs Co-ordination Unit (UKADCU) took a closer look at the impact of the drug market on attempts to regenerate poorer neighbourhoods and found that the anti-social behaviour associated with drugs had reduced significantly by the time of the research. Discarded needles were less of a problem as mobile phones had made fixed-site drug dealing a thing of the past. The key remaining negative image was the apparent affluence of the drug dealers as a role model (Coomber, 2006). Lupton *et al.* (2002) detailed the shortage of treatment options for dependent users, but their main emphasis was on management of the drug market. These reports emphasized the distinction between the established cannabis – recreational drug use and the drug market for heroin and crack that was associated with neighbourhood problems. There was common agreement within the areas that cannabis use was routine practice, in contrast with 'a negative stereotypical image of heroin and crack users' (Wilson *et al.*, 2002: 68). The police agreed that the 'amphetamine market, along with other recreational drugs such as ecstasy and cannabis, was confined to users who fund their drug use through legitimate means' (75). In relation to 'sensible drug use', Parker *et al.* (2002: 960) state that users can be seen as 'primarily educated, employed young citizens with otherwise conforming profiles'. The Commons' Home Affairs Select Committee's (2007: 7) report 'The Government's Drugs Policy: Is it working?' arrived at a similar conclusion arguing that there should be a 'clear distinction between the use of Class A drugs' and less harmful drugs like cannabis. Subsequently emphasis turned to problematic drug activity that was causing problems for the police and neighbourhoods, with heroin and crack, diverting attention from less problematic recreational drugs.

Council Estate of Mind[1]: the criminalization of hanging around

The description British Prime Minister David Cameron set out in his December 2011 speech launching the post-London riots programme to tackle 'troubled families' left little to the imagination:

> Officialdom might call them 'families with multiple disadvantages'. Some in the press might call them 'neighbours from hell'. Whatever you call them, we've known for years that a relatively small number of families are the source of a large proportion of the problems in society. Drug addiction. Alcohol abuse. Crime. A culture of disruption and irresponsibility that cascades through generations.

During the mid-2000s, as part of the National Reassurance Policing Programme, Martin Innes and colleagues (2004) developed the notion of 'signal crimes' (Innes and Fielding, 2002) to help explain the disjuncture between experience and perceptions of crime and to explain why people are fearful of minor incivilities. Innes describes the importance of unwanted risk. The way this connects with the effects of a signal crime or signal disorder are made explicit in the following extract, taken from a man talking about people in his neighbourhood who were dealing drugs. As he described:

> It just gives an air of... almost an air of fear because it is not just the two of them – if it was just the two of them you could handle it and do something about it, but it is the fact that now they have got all their cronies.... (S9)

For Innes young people featured as a touchstone for social anxiety, where any fear was channelled through the notion of 'youth'. In these studies on drugs markets, more than one police officer commented on the fact that residents calling the police about youths 'hanging around' often added that the youths were 'using drugs' as a way of adding to the seriousness of the nuisance behaviour. Lupton *et al.*'s (2002) survey of residents in one neighbourhood in the drugs market study provides a good example of the way headline figures can give grounds for misinterpretation. Its finding that '85% of residents were worried about drug use' was put in perspective by the neighbourhood manager who 'believed that drug use was widely tolerated on the estate'.

> Most residents accept it, there's wide use of cannabis, and wide knowledge of heroin and crack. There is dealing from houses; five properties are labelled as crack houses by residents. Most people don't care about the use of drugs, they are more concerned about crime in the area, or their child being harmed. (Wilson *et al.*, 2002: 24)

The suggestion that crack houses were tolerated may have been an exaggeration given the high level of fear after a spate of shootings that were associated with the heroin and crack market, but it illustrated the problem of generalizing drugs across the user spectrum. For example, use of drugs can be used to escalate a perceived concern, making the subjective criteria of anti-social behaviour appear to be objective. As a result, identifying young people as using recreational drugs or drinking alcohol becomes a way of justifying a phone call to the police or of adding a 'seriousness' to the otherwise normal activity of 'hanging around'. This punitive process started with the criminalization of dance music within rave culture. Young people's involvement in recreational subcultural activities from raves and gigs to hanging around on street corner or at parks, became key points of intervention whereby youth become the object of control. For Donna Brown (2013: 540–1) this amounts to criminalizing 'hanging around'. Her concern is that we seem to be moving backwards to 'pathologising young people'. Hanging around is normal for young people: it is part of their everyday activities (Banks, 2013).

The government and media intensification of promoting intolerance towards youth is linked, according to Donna Brown (2013: 538), to young people 'being excluded from public space'. Cara Robinson's (2010: 53) ethnography on young people and public space, found that one of her subcultural groups that occupied public space encountered police and public disapproval for their recreational drug use and graffiti, but for the young people themselves these spaces were home, and held memory and belonging for them. For her, anti-social behaviour policy in practice through the creation of specified 'youth shelters' in isolated, unlit spaces in parks 'is at a cost to the safety and welfare of the young people'. This is closely related to the perceptions of young people's presence in public space, which is then seen as an instance of anti-social behaviour in itself. This type of argument demands young people's removal from public space confirming the notion that young people have both lost their position in the community and cannot participate in the normal daily activities because they are defined as untrustworthy and a danger. Increased regulation and closer inspection of youth presence within the community through the negative lens of macro media and young people's self-driven use of social media have affirmed the view that young people do not deserve sympathy (Helm, 2013). The use of legislation that demands the removal of young people from public space confirms the idea that young people's public presence is not required and their exclusion is justified by the notion of the problem drug user as the cause of community hostility towards youth (Crawford, 2009b).

The merger of recreational drugs and problematic drug use has not only been part of government policy, but it has also occurred at local government level. For example, the most significant divide forms between councils which see drugs as a police matter, such as High Peaks Borough Council (Derbyshire) which sees drug use as a criminal offence that the police should deal with, and the councils who make no distinction between criminal and anti-social conduct. North Wandsworth Borough Council (London) warned that drug use and drug dealing is a breach of tenancy agreement so may result in eviction. The common theme to emerge is that anti-social behaviour and drugs are strongly related to visibility, specifically related to dealing. In some cases, this is expressed under the generic term 'misuse of public space'. The Cheshire Constabulary website suggests the space may be misused by drug dealers and users and provides an example of the way perceptions are blended to blur the lines between crime, anti-social behaviour and everyday action:

> People loitering on the street waiting for drug dealers can also be perceived as anti-social behaviour. Drug dealing is a crime – but sometimes it's first reported as anti-social behaviour. Such threatening behaviour causes alarm and distress for the people it affects, and that is why it is vitally important that it is dealt with. (Cheshire Police, 2014)

Nicholas Hall (2013: 4) outlining the Strategic Assessment for Community Safety Partnerships, for Richmond upon Thames, states 'Drugs-drives acquisitive crime. Recreational drug use linked to anti-social behaviour'. Throughout this local policy document there is no differentiation between drugs, and importantly recreational drugs are being brought into the policy regulation framework in relation to anti-social behaviour. The failure to adequately distinguish between the different effects of drug use and the asserted link between recreational drug use and anti-social behaviour has allowed for the creation of legislation to regulate and criminalize young people's leisure. These examples drawn from local government policy are likely to be those constructed from the national profile of the problem group (Girling *et al.*, 2000). Essentially this is likely to appeal to a common sense perception of users of Class A drugs, specifically heroin and crack, because since the introduction of mobile phones dealers of these substances tend to prefer to retain a distance between their home, the product and the customer. Recreational drug users tend to be supplied through social networks and so buy in more private settings or commercial settings associated with the night-time economy (Chatterton and Hollands, 2003). Consequently, they do not occupy the same space physically, nor do they occupy the attentions of the authorities as a specific anti-social behaviour problem. The policy emphasis on 'problem' drug use with its extension to anti-social behaviour draws heavily on the stereotypical images of the drug user, not just the association with acquisitive crime, but also the associated behaviours of drug-market violence and loitering. The key misrepresentation according to Bottoms (2009) is based on the different ways in which teenagers are perceived to be a problem and specifically 'hanging around' together gets transferred to the perception of drug dealing or using as a problem irrespective of actual drug consumption or dealing.

Confusion between recreational and problem drugs is apparent at the United Nations. Yury Fedotov, executive director of the United Nations Office on Drugs and Crime (UNODC) has defended the current system of drug control. Speaking to BBC Radio 4, *Today Programme* (13 March 2014) he stated:

> I would not say the international drug control system is falling apart. The most serious thing about cannabis is that it is a gateway drug [...]. Polls show users start to move towards more dangerous substances.

In their comprehensive review of the gateway thesis, Hall and Lynskey (2005: 46): maintain that:

> The role of cannabis in the 'gateway pattern' of drug use remains controversial because of the difficulty of excluding the hypothesis that the gateway pattern can be explained by the common characteristics of those who use cannabis and other drugs.

The British government reclassification of cannabis in 2001 took place on the basis of a clear distinction between drug markets that could be identified and separated into the recreational and the problem markets. This led the then Home Secretary David Blunkett to downgrade cannabis to Category C and to support measures to sift out problem drug users, primarily through drug testing offenders on arrest and coercing them into treatment. This begs the question that if crime shaped the emphasis on problematic drug use, how and why has recreational drug use been drawn into the anti-social policy framework? We suggest that young people's recreational drug use is based on collective social behaviour that encourages group cohesion in the pursuit of excitement as a normal expression (Parker *et al.*, 2002; Wilson 2007). However, this thrill-based cultural practice is an unstable discourse, which becomes subject to the construction and promotion of public intolerance of young people's behaviour. We assert that recreational drug consumption while being illegal and criminal is not a primary cause of anti-social or criminal behaviour, but it is used as justification for the regulation of both.

Conclusion

This chapter has argued that the expansion of anti-social behaviour combining recreational and problem drugs use under the present Conservative–Liberal Democrat Coalition government will promote further intolerance towards young people where their behaviour is deemed as 'unruly activity' or capable of causing nuisance. This will potentially elevate more young people into the crime and disorder framework through focusing on the apparent incivility (hanging around) of young people. This makes a link back to the nineteenth-century problem of an increase in juvenile delinquency resulting from a new willingness to prosecute behaviour previously regarded as not deviant. We identify the anti-social behaviour as a governing discourse for the taming of youth that promotes public intolerance of young people's behaviour. Using the ideas of 'looping effects' and 'signal crimes' as a way of linking media coverage of drug problems and anti-social behaviour, we have tried to highlight how recreational drug use particularly in low-income settings is framed by the presence of problem drug use and its links to anti-social behaviour and crime. We tried to highlight how recreational drug use particularly in low-income settings is framed by the presence of problem drug use and its links to anti-social behaviour and crime. As a result, recreational drug use has become over-identified with crime and disorder. Without evidence, the anti-social behaviour agenda has contributed to the promotion of non-deviant recreational drug use as a serious indicator of risk and potential crime. We conclude that anti-social behaviour has brought misinterpretation to understanding recreational drug use by young people. Under this merger recreational drug use and anti-social behaviour become identified as wasteful and deviant behaviour, which destroys communities defined as belonging to a criminogenic group, who are theorized as possessing no capacity for self-control and therefore are an easy moral target for the media to promote a blame culture and for government to increase punitive policies.

Note

1. Skinnyman (2004). *Council Estate of Mind.* London: Low Life Records.

25

Regulating Anti-Social Behaviour and Disorder among Football Spectators

Mark James and Geoff Pearson

Incidents of anti-social behaviour and public disorder at and around British football matches have been well documented in the media since the late Victorian period (Dunning *et al.*, 1988) and more recently have been the focus of a plethora of academic studies across a range of disciplines including in particular Sociology, Law, Psychology and Criminology (Frosdick and Marsh, 2005; James and Pearson, 2006; Stott and Pearson, 2007: 37–58; Hopkins, 2013). Since 1924, nine official enquiries have been commissioned by various government departments to examine the regulation and management of sports stadiums, crowds and crowd disorder, each repeating and endorsing the recommendations of its predecessors (see in particular Popplewell, 1986; Taylor, 1990). Despite growing political concern about the impact that football-related disorder was having on society as a whole (Pearson, 1998), it was not until the 1980s that specific legislation was introduced with the aim of reducing instances of football-related anti-social behaviour and violence. A combination of direct governmental action through legislative interventions coupled with the police's interpretation of how both general and football-specific measures should be interpreted have framed the state's response to football-related disorder.

These legislative strategies were, however, often based on the indiscriminate application of wide-ranging laws, both generally applicable and football-specific, and the use of police powers that failed to distinguish between a person's potential to engage in anti-social behaviour or public disorder and contextually acceptable fan culture. Restrictions on access to, and the consumption of, alcohol at and while travelling to football matches were introduced by the Conservatives through the Sporting Events (Control of Alcohol) Act 1985 (Pearson and Sale, 2011). This was followed closely by the creation of Exclusion Orders, the forerunner of both Football Banning Orders and Anti-Social Behaviour Orders (ASBOs) by section 30 of the

Public Order Act 1986, which enabled courts to ban anyone convicted of a 'football-related' offence from attending football matches for a period of three months.

At the same time, the policing of football spectators became more strategic following the creation in 1988 of the Football Intelligence Unit (now renamed the UK Football Policing Unit) within the National Criminal Intelligence Service. In particular, the creation of Football Intelligence Officers with specific responsibility for individual teams and the use of 'spotters' whose job it is to observe fans suspected of being 'risk supporters' has improved significantly the police's ability to identify, locate and place under surveillance those most likely to engage in football-related disorder. Further, improvements in evidence-gathering technologies have enabled the police to prosecute fans for football-specific offences, such as throwing missiles inside a stadium, racial chanting, pitch invasions and ticket touting (sections 2–4 of the Football (Offences) Act 1991 and section 166 of the Criminal Justice and Public Order Act 1994 respectively) and to build dossiers of information about suspected 'risk supporters' that can be used when making applications for Football Banning Orders against them (James, 2013: 207–30).

Indiscriminate policing strategies based on invasive surveillance techniques and containment strategies that severely restrict free movement continue to be used against some football crowds, particularly where travelling supporters are considered by local police to pose a risk of public disorder while attending away matches. Furthermore, statutory responses remain entrenched in the idea that order can best be maintained by curtailing the behaviour of everyone who attends live matches.

The year 1997 saw the election of an avowedly pro-football New Labour government that sought to engage with the sport proactively. This approach was epitomized by its commission of a review of the evidence relating to the Hillsborough disaster (Stuart-Smith, 1998). However, its law and order agenda was epitomized by the introduction of quasi-criminal civil prevention orders, typified by ASBOs and the Crime and Disorder Act 1998. As part of this framework, and in response to the disorder involving England fans at the 1998 World Cup in France and the 2000 European Nations Championships in Belgium and the Netherlands, the banning order regime that applied to football was overhauled, most notably by enabling the police to apply for a Football Banning Order against a fan who had not been convicted of a football-related offence, but in anticipation that they might engage in disorderly conduct in the future (section 14B of the Football Spectators Act 1989). This chapter will begin by examining how and why football supporters behave, or are perceived to behave, in an anti-social or disorderly manner before analysing whether such regulation as supported by governments of all political persuasions since 1997 has been effective from both a legal and a practical perspective.

Anti-social behaviour or non-normative behaviour? The concept of the 'risk' supporter

Anti-social behaviour at and around football matches has been given many and varied definitions. In an analysis of cases carried out in the early 1980s, the courts had labelled as 'football hooliganism' the following activities:

Looking aggressive, jeering, shouting, jumping up and down, waving fists...running in groups, issuing bloodcurdling and obscene threats... invading the pitch; wrecking motorway service stations...fighting with fists; kicking rival fans who are on the ground...stampeding round railway stations...vandalising and overturning local people's cars after a match...assaulting local residents...shouting...racist abuse...and... throwing missiles at each other, local people, oncoming cars and the police. (Salter, 1985: 352)

This all-encompassing explanation of what is colloquially referred to as 'football hooliganism' is mirrored by the UK Football Policing Unit's similarly wide definition of a risk supporter as: 'A person, known or not, who can be regarded as posing a possible risk to public order or anti-social behaviour, whether planned or spontaneous, at or in connection with a football event' (National Policing Improvement Agency, 2010: 10). This is a definition that replicates the standardized version provided by the Council of the European Union in its recommendations for police cooperation where football matches have an international dimension (2010: 1–21).

Neither of these definitions has legislative force, nor is there any definition in law of football-related disorder or football hooliganism. The closest analogy that can be drawn is with the conditions that must be fulfilled in order to impose a Football Banning Order on a person under either section 14A or 14B of the Football Spectators Act 1989. Where a person has been convicted of a football-related offence, the court must impose a Football Banning Order if it is satisfied that there are reasonable grounds for believing that doing so would help to prevent violence or disorder at or in connection with any regulated football matches (section 14A). Where the respondent is suspected of being involved with football-related disorder but has not been convicted of a football-related offence, the court must again impose a Football Banning Order if two conditions are met. First, that there are reasonable grounds for believing that doing so would help to prevent violence or disorder at or in connection with regulated football matches and secondly, that the respondent has at any time caused or contributed to any violence or disorder in the United Kingdom or elsewhere (section 14B). In both cases, the scope of the term 'regulated football matches' includes all professional football matches and international representative games that take place in the United Kingdom and any international club or representative matches or tournaments outside the United Kingdom that are organized by UEFA and FIFA, respectively the European and World governing bodies of football (Football Spectators (Prescription) Order 2004/2409).

Thus, there is a disconnection between what is required at law and what is being used by the police as a means of identifying anti-social or disorderly football supporters. A supporter can be categorized as a 'risk' simply by engaging in, or 'posing a possible risk' of engaging in, anti-social behaviour, whereas the Football Spectators Act 1989 requires a higher degree of misbehaviour before legislative intervention can take place. However, in collecting the evidence required for a successful application for a Football Banning Order under section 14B, the police regularly adduce evidence of multiple counts of 'risk' behaviour to prove that the respondent will be involved in future acts of violence or disorder, despite the lack of evidence that the supporter's behaviour will actually escalate in this manner (James and Pearson, 2006). This position is compounded by a failure on the part of the police to distinguish between behaviour that is normal at a football match, but would be anti-social in many other contexts, and behaviour that is anti-social or disorderly in any context, including among football supporters.

English football fandom has grown out of a highly complex fan culture consisting of a range of often overlapping sub-cultures (Pearson, 2012). Within these many sub-cultures, two are of particular importance here; 'hooligans' and 'carnival fans' (Pearson, 2012: 1–13). The hooligan group can be defined as attending matches with the primary intention of engaging in violence and disorder with like-minded members of other team's supporters. Although trends change over time, and there are significant geographical differences, 'hooligans' rarely wear their team's colours and, where possible, keep themselves apart from the main body of supporters. 'Hooligan' groups are generally small in numbers, but have a disproportionately high impact on responses to the policing of all football supporters because of the media, police and parliamentary interest in their activities (Pearson, 2012).

In contrast, the primary intention of the carnival fans is to create an atmosphere of transgression from the norm (the non-football world) where collective gathering, chanting and social drinking are central to their enjoyment of supporting their team. This much larger group regularly attracts the interest of the police because of an apparent assumption that this kind of behaviour will, almost as a matter of course, degenerate into violence and disorder. As the carnival fans also often eschew wearing team colours, it can be difficult to distinguish between these two groups of football supporters, particularly when for practical reasons they may end up travelling to and from matches on the same modes of transport or drinking in the same public houses.

Further confusion can arise as many of football's other supporter sub-cultures also have as part of their defining behaviour the consumption of alcohol and singing of songs that may be seen as indecent, intimidatory or aggressive when taken out of the context of a football match. For example, in the case of *R v Thomas* (2006), the defendant, a professional footballer, was acquitted of a charge under section 5 of the Public Order Act 1986 on the basis that there was insufficient evidence to prove that any of the fans watching the game were harassed, alarmed or distressed by his gesturing at them with his middle finger. Thus, conduct that would be unacceptable in many other contexts is acceptable, or at least tolerated, when it occurs in connection with a football match. The malleable boundaries between these different groups can make it particularly difficult for the police to determine whether or not individual fans, or groups of fans, are risk supporters likely to engage in disorder or boisterous fans simply engaging in behaviour that is normal for its setting: watching live football matches. Public order responses to the risk of 'hooliganism' that treat football supporters as an homogeneous group has led, to a greater or lesser extent, to all football fans being treated as potential hooligans.

Football Banning Orders

This inability to distinguish between contextually normalized behaviours has resulted in conduct that is acceptable by the norms of football crowds and football supporters being categorized as anti-social by the police to the point of demonization and moral panic (Cohen, 1972 and 2002). This moral panic has resulted in 'panic law' and in some cases panic legal interpretations, ensuring that existing laws are used to regulate situations for which they were not designed and new laws are promulgated to close off actual or perceived legislative loopholes.

The origin of all modern behaviour-regulating civil orders can be traced back to the Conservative government's creation of Exclusion Orders in sections 30–37 of the Public Order Act 1986. The aim of the Exclusion Order was to prevent the respondent's engagement with football-related disorder by preventing the banned person from mixing with others likely to be engaged in such disorder and stopping them from attending football matches for a period of three months. This regime was extended by the creation of Restriction Orders in section 14 of the Football Spectators Act 1989, which could be imposed to prevent fans from travelling abroad to watch international football matches involving the England national team.

Further name changes, amendments and extensions were made to this regime by the Football (Offences and Disorder) Act 1999 and Football (Disorder) Act 2000 following further incidents of disorder at international tournaments in 1998 and 2000 (Stott and Pearson, 2007: 83–167). These developments followed quickly after the New Labour government had introduced ASBOs in the Crime and Disorder Act 1998 and epitomize its blurring of the distinction between civil and criminal interventions.

These various legislative developments culminated in the creation of a single Football Banning Order, replacing the separate Domestic and International Orders that had previously been in place. These new Orders can be applied for on two distinct grounds. First, under section 14A of the Football Spectators Act 1989, the prosecution can apply to the sentencing court for a Football Banning Order to be imposed on a person who has been convicted of a football-related offence. Secondly, and in a significant departure from what had happened previously, under section 14B of the amended Football Spectators Act 1989, the police can apply for a Football Banning Order to be imposed on anyone who has been involved with any violent conduct in the past, not necessarily football-related or prosecuted to conviction, and who is believed to be likely to engage in football-related disorder in the future. Thus, the police can now apply for a Football Banning Order as a pre-emptive measure against supporters suspected of being involved in football-related disorder based on evidence collected on them over a period of up to ten years through surveillance of football crowds undertaken by police spotters, police using hand-held and body cameras and analysis of CCTV footage. Although developed by the New Labour government, the Football Banning Order framework that is now in place was again a panicked response to external incidents, the riots at the 1998 World Cup and 2000 European Nations Championships, as much as it was the embodiment of a political philosophy. The lack of any serious parliamentary debate on these provisions, on the basis of the pressing need to be seen to be acting before the start of the next football season, highlights the lack of engagement with the human rights issues that are engaged by bans of this nature.

The Football Banning Order has become a cornerstone of police attempts to regulate the behaviour of football supporters and has resulted in extensive campaigns of overt surveillance against all fans, conduct that is often justified by police as being to deter 'risk supporters' from engaging in violence or disorder. When targeted at those who have been proven to be engaged in football-related disorder, as was its original purpose, it is claimed that the imposition of a Football Banning Order can be a powerful deterrent, although there is also some evidence that they may be seen by some as a 'badge of honour'.

The standard conditions imposed by Football Banning Orders include: a ban from attending all professional football matches in England, Scotland and Wales, all international football matches involving England, Scotland or Wales dependent on the respondent's nationality, and all international football tournaments organized by UEFA and FIFA; an exclusion zone around the home stadium at which the banned person's team plays for 24 hours before kick-off and lasting until 24 hours after the end of the game; an exclusion zone around any stadium at which the banned person's team is playing; bans from using specific public houses and/or transport interchanges and in some cases the inclusion of a secondary city centre exclusion zone to incorporate potential disorder hotspots; and surrender of the banned person's passport five days before their team or the relevant national team plays a match abroad and ten days before an international football tournament takes place and for the duration of the tournament (see for example, Football Spectators (2012 European Championship Control Period) Order 2012/340). This final condition ensures that a banned person can be prevented from travelling abroad for up to 100 days in any calendar year. What is less widely known is that these conditions apply to all Football Banning Orders, whether imposed on conviction for a football-related offence under section 14A or following an application by the police on the grounds that the respondent has the potential to be involved in football-related disorder under section 14B.

Since the introduction of the section 14B procedure by New Labour in 2000, the purpose of the now ubiquitous surveillance of football supporters has extended beyond the evidence-gathering necessary for pursuing to conviction those who have been involved in football-related anti-social behaviour and disorder to building behaviour profiles of those spectators who are suspected of being, or who might have the potential to be, involved in anti-social behaviour. Once constructed, these profiles then form the basis of police applications for Football Banning Orders under section 14B of the Football Spectators Act 1989.

As the securing of Football Banning Orders against potentially disorderly supporters has become an increasingly important part of police operations, the focus of Football Intelligence Officers has shifted subtly. These specialist officers now spend significant amounts of their time gathering evidence of supporters engaging in anti-social behaviour or posing a risk to public order (National Policing Improvement Agency, 2010: 10), instead of engaging in operations to identify and apprehend those who are actually involved in the orchestration of serious disorder and violent conduct. This in turn has led to an increase in the surveillance of football supporters, particularly filming them at and on their way to matches, in order to discourage disorderly or anti-social behaviour or, where it is occurring, to assist in compiling a case for an application for a Football Banning Order under section 14B. As a result, these applications are often based on evidence that supporters have engaged in anti-social behaviour, rather than committing criminal acts or public disorder (*Chief Constable of Avon and Somerset v Bargh* (2011)), or have simply been nearby when an outbreak of disorder occurred (*Chief Constable of Greater Manchester v Sutton* (2006)), or failed to dissociate themselves from a group that had been attacked by opposing fans (*Chief Constable of Greater Manchester v Messer* (2012)), rather than proving that they are actively engaged in football-related violence and disorder. Thus, the current legislative framework in place in the United Kingdom for regulating football supporters enables the police to conduct almost unprecedented levels of surveillance, in particular through the use of police spotters and both overt and covert filming, on citizens who have done little more than attend a football match.

The evolution of police tactics to control anti-social behaviour and football-related disorder

Alongside these legislative developments have been changes in the ways that football supporters and football crowds are policed. Although developed for the folk devils of the last Conservative government (striking miners, travellers and ravers) and in response to Labour concerns about binge drinking respectively, the power to stop and search people under section 60 of the Criminal Justice and Public Order Act 1994 and the use of alcohol-related dispersal orders under section 27 of the Violent Crime Reduction Act 2006 have been used extensively as a means of regulating carnivalesque behaviour associated with football matches. When using these powers to stop and search or requiring a person to leave an area, the opportunity to gather additional intelligence, such as videoing a person while they provide the police with personal information, has become the norm. This information can, and often is, then used in applications under section 14B to demonstrate a tendency to be in locations where stop and search or dispersal powers had to be used, leading to a conclusion that the respondent has been, or is about to be, engaged in football-related disorder. The lack of either an evidential or logical link between location, association with others and alcohol consumption to engagement in football-related disorder is assumed instead of proved.

Further, the long-standing use of proactive policing strategies against football supporters, such as the kettling of crowds and the corralling of spectators from one venue to another (or 'bubbling'), have only attracted mainstream comment following their use in other more media-friendly contexts, such as political protests (*R (Laporte) v Chief Constable of Gloucestershire Constabulary* (2007)). Regular match-going football supporters accept as normal that they will be kettled or marched from the local train station or the public house where they have been told by the police to congregate in a bubble (Pearson, 2012: ch. 6). However, two recent cases have provided much clearer explanations of the parameters within which containment strategies can be used. First, containment of groups of people by the police in a kettle or bubble must be only a temporary restriction on liberty in order to prevent an imminent breach of the peace or outbreak of public disorder (*Austin v Commissioner of Police of the Metropolis* (2009)). Thus, the routine containment of football supporters without intelligence that disorder is imminent is of questionable legality. Secondly, the police cannot require as a condition of release from containment in a kettle or bubble that those who have been contained provide personal information or submit to being filmed, nor is it lawful to collect such information under a section 60 stop and search (*Mengesha v*

Commissioner of Police for the Metropolis (2013)). Thus, once again, the routine collection of personal information and filming of football supporters when they are not engaged in disorderly conduct is unlawful.

The court observations underpinning this analysis suggest that almost none of the evidence being relied on for the imposition of Football Banning Orders applied for under section 14B shows actual engagement in disorder or violence, but was instead evidence of belonging to a certain sub-culture of football supporter or of expressing certain (non-criminal) modes of behaviour. In particular, many of the profiles provided to the courts contained evidence that the respondent was associating with others identified by the police as 'risk supporters', usually fans whose Orders had expired or who were also having profiles built against them. Where Football Banning Orders were secured on the basis of guilt by association, the process became self-sustaining as the now banned fan could be used as the basis for implicating others with associating with a 'risk supporter'. The most extreme occurrence of this was in two cases heard in the same week when the imposition of a section 14B Order on one supporter on the Monday was used as evidence at an application on the Wednesday to prove that the second respondent associated with someone who was banned from attending football matches; obviously, at the time they were associating with each other, neither was the subject of a Football Banning Order (*Chief Constable of Greater Manchester v Clarke* (2006) and *Chief Constable of Greater Manchester v Reilly* (2006)).

Conclusion

The regulation of football supporters has been driven by a wide variety of factors, with no single one providing the definitive explanation of why this particular group has been the focus of such extreme state intervention. From the Conservatives' desire to protect the image of the country abroad to New Labour's post-1997 law and order agenda, and an obsession among all political parties with the organized violence engaged in by a small number of hooligan gangs, each viewpoint has informed state interventions in this area. Further, despite annual decreases in the number of football-related arrests and the imposition of fewer Football Banning Orders, the official narrative remains that violence and disorder are problems at football matches and that excessive consumption of alcohol remains a key cause of this behaviour.

Following the Court of Appeal decision in *Leeds United Football Club Ltd v Chief Constable of West Yorkshire* (2013), this approach could be confused further if policing tactics become informed by financial considerations as there is now much less scope for the police to charge for 'special police services' than was previously the case. Whereas the police had been able to charge host clubs for all additional policing related to a football match, the

Leeds United case determines that charges can only be made for additional policing inside and in the immediate environs of a football stadium. The cuts imposed on the police by the Coalition government and the apparent linking of funding for Football Intelligence Units to successful Football Banning Order applications under section 14B (Hopkins, 2013) could see police tactics driven by fiscal pragmatism rather than intelligence. Compiling evidence against those suspected of involvement in violence or disorder is resource-intensive, particularly in times of austerity and government cut-backs of public services; however, additional funding is available for successful police operations that result in the imposition of section 14B Football Banning Orders. If police forces are pursuing what are effectively financial targets in their decisions on whether to pursue applications under section 14B instead of prosecuting to conviction, then doubt is cast on whether the most effective public order strategies are being pursued and whether the justifications for imposing section 14B Orders set out by the Court of Appeal in *Gough and Smith v Chief Constable of Derbyshire* (2002) are still valid.

In contrast, some police forces are taking a different approach to policing football matches; treating them as sporting events first and foremost and as potential locations for public disorder as an important, though secondary, consideration that requires a proportionate response based on a genuine intelligence-based risk assessment. These forces recognize the value of communication with supporters in advance of events, increasingly through social media, as a means of supporting the intentions of fans to enjoy their experience, even where that involves heavy alcohol consumption, in a way that can be managed safely. One case study of interest comes from the policies and practices adopted by South Wales Police to manage the travelling support of Cardiff City, dominated by the 'Soul Crew' hooligan firm and the 'Valley Boys'. Following regular disorder, police strategies to manage the complex crowd dynamics focused not on imposing increasing restrictions, but on facilitating legitimate expectations of the fans and in doing so isolating the small minority intending on using matches as a vehicle to engage in disorder (Stott *et al.*, 2012).

These approaches provide examples of diametrically opposed paradigms for policing football matches. One views the game through a 'hooligan lens' where there is an assumption that disorder will occur and that everyone present has the potential to be a risk supporter. This 'riot control' philosophy can lead to excessive restrictions being imposed on supporters and ultimately to the use of indiscriminate force, where everyone present is treated as an actual or potential hooligan. The other polices the event on the basis that the vast majority of football supporters wish to avoid disorder and violence and that they will respond to police direction if it is communicated clearly, has a valid objective and is not perceived to restrict unjustifiably their lawful objectives. This 'public order management approach' is intelligence-led, resulting in targeted interventions that differentiate between fans on the basis of their actual behaviour, not predetermined assumptions about what they might do (Stott and Pearson, 2007: 250).

As each police service defines its own football policy and assesses the accompanying risks differently, there is little in the way of a standardized approach to policing football matches, leaving supporters unsure how they might be treated at each game. Whichever approach is eventually seen as being the more effective, and following the Court of Appeal's decision in *Leeds United Football Club Ltd v Chief Constable of West Yorkshire* that might include being the more cost-effective approach, will inform future policing policy.

The success of the current regulatory framework, however that is measured, is not attributable to the creation of football specific offences, the imposition of section 14B Football Banning Orders on suspected risk supporters or either indiscriminate overt surveillance of fans or 'show of force' policing tactics. It is impossible to say that this regulatory framework has enabled the police to identify in advance when disorder will occur, who will be involved in the outbreaks and who will be attacked (Stott and Pearson, 2007: 245). Instead, more progressive policing strategies such as those identified above have been a key factor in the observed reduction in violence and disorder inside and immediately around football stadiums. Changes in stadium design, the demographics of football supporters and societal tolerance of anti-social behaviour have also played their part in reducing disorder at and around football matches (King, 2001). Further, there is anecdotal evidence that Football Banning Orders imposed following conviction for violent football-related offences under section 14A Football Spectators Act 1989 may be helping to reduce risk in the immediate vicinity of stadiums.

Despite the apparent improvements in public order at and around British stadiums, there remains a failure on the part of many police forces to understand the motives of football's many sub-cultures. This in turn makes it more likely that football supporters will be treated as an homogeneous group who, at away matches in particular, are a risk to public order by their very presence en masse. This viewpoint has been facilitated by the current regulatory framework that encourages applications for Football Banning Orders against those acting in an anti-social manner, or who are on the periphery of disorderly groups, at the expense of pursuing to conviction those who are actually guilty of engaging in football-related violence and disorder. The introduction of football-specific public order offences by the Conservative government in the Football Offences Act 1991 and changes to the Football Banning Order framework by New Labour post-1997 have had significant impact on the strategies associated with policing large and potentially disorderly crowds; it has also ensured that football spectators are among the most extensively surveilled and strictly policed groups in the United Kingdom.

Pre-1997, the Conservative government adopted the approach of criminalizing aspects of fan culture that they thought would lead to outbreaks of disorder. Post-1997, New Labour enabled increasingly draconian Football Banning Orders to be imposed on fans who had the potential to be disorderly. The Coalition government has not directly amended the Football Banning Order framework; however, the cuts imposed on the police through the Spending Review have resulted in the creative use of police powers transplanted from other contexts. Despite all three main parties being keen to demonstrate pro-football sympathies, it is likely that the 'ideology of vulnerable autonomy' (Ramsay, 2012: 84–113) will continue to drive the panicked responses of government to high-profile incidents of football disorder.

Conclusions

Sarah Pickard

The purpose of bringing together diverse and comprehensive analyses of anti-social behaviour in Victorian and contemporary Britain in this book was to attempt to reveal any analogies regarding anti-social behaviour and governmental approaches to it. Through the 25 cross-disciplinary chapters, clear continuities stand out between the two periods examined.

The opening part of the book discusses 'Anti-social Behaviour, the Urban Environment and Public Spaces', which is where 'unacceptable' conduct first drew attention in Victorian Britain and continues to be the focus of interest today. Large numbers of people living in proximity inevitably leads to scrutiny of the behaviour of groups or individuals being under scrutiny along with attempts to manage it. The contributors show how the moral imperatives of a 'respectable' Victorian elite led to heightened surveillance and policing of public spaces in towns and those frequenting them. The mid-nineteenth century witnessed increasing intolerance and tighter regulation of public and street activities. In particular, visible incivilities, such as 'rowdyism', 'ruffianism' and blasphemy among the 'degenerate' working class were the target of ever stricter legislation and social control (the social processes by which the behaviour of individuals or groups is regulated). This was undertaken mainly in order to please the 'respectable' and 'endangered' middle and upper classes, who became increasingly intolerant of 'deviant' and 'dangerous' behaviour among the lower orders. This was all the more true as a result of distinct changes to the social, political and environment within a context of growing industrialization, immigration and political unrest. Nevertheless, in Victorian Britain, there was a tendency to turn a blind eye to certain incivilities of the working class as long as they remained in their own neighbourhood and they did not interfere or affect the more gentile inhabitants of a town. Contemporary political concern for anti-social behaviour stemmed primarily from behaviour in public spaces especially social housing. At the end of the twentieth century, the New Labour government became interested in controlling anti-social behaviour through an aspiration to curtail unruly behaviour in social housing and to improve community cohesion and reduce social exclusion. Subsequently, public spaces and town centres have been increasingly surveilled and controlled in an attempt to reduce public disorder and anti-social behaviour. Similarly, over the past two decades, a host of activities has become criminalized in a political attempt to mend the neo-liberal and individualist 'broken society'. Thus, both periods have witnessed a growth of intolerance and control of anti-social behaviour in public spaces and the urban environment, leading to large amounts of legislation to regulate, manage and curb what is deemed to be anti-social behaviour.

In the second part, 'Anti-social Behaviour, the Vulnerable and the Marginalized', contributors reveal how the social control of anti-social behaviour has tended to focus on particular kinds of at risk or marginalized individuals and groups. In this way, an 'insecure elite' blames the 'vulnerable individual' for crime and anti-social behaviour. In the Victorian era and today, this has meant the targeting of the lower classes, but also others who tend to live on the margins of society, especially the poor who constitute an underclass. In Victorian and contemporary Britain, children and young people are very often the focus of criticism and legislation too, for example, regarding truancy from school where policy has become increasingly punitive. There are clear parallels in the rate and type of legislation pertaining to youth justice. Indeed, youth justice underwent significant changes at the end of the nineteenth century and at the start of the twentieth century, as well as at the end of the twentieth century and the start of the twenty-first century. In the Victorian era, despite Mary Carpenter's efforts to rehabilitate wayward juveniles in her reformatory schools, many punitive attempts were introduced by Parliament through the workhouse, new legislation and the creation of the national prison system. Under New Labour, controversial Anti-Social Behaviour Orders (ASBO) were introduced to control 'neighbours from hell', but they became a means to curb the behaviour of 'a feral youth' criticized for being unruly. The Conservative–Liberal Democrat Coalition government has taken further steps to criminalize non-normative actions, especially in relation to anti-social behaviour and young people. Targeting or persecuting vulnerable persons is evident in the politics of 'anti-social' behaviour within the Troubled Families Programme launched by the Conservative–Liberal Democrat Coalition government. Specific communities or groups of people have also been targeted in both the nineteenth century and the twenty-first century. Gypsies and Travellers have been the subjects of social constructions and are widely portrayed during both periods as perpetrators of 'anti-social' behaviour. It would seem that underlying the management of anti-social behaviour among the most vulnerable and marginalized in society is a wider project of neo-liberal 'cultural governance', by dismantling 'welfare' and discrediting those most reliant upon it. Furthermore, many aspects of anti-social behaviour policy is itself anti-social. In this way, the relationship between anti-social behaviour and 'underclass' discourse in Victorian Britain is similar to that of contemporary Britain, but it is now even more punitive and widespread regarding the vulnerable and at risk.

The contributors to the last part of the book, 'Anti-social Behaviour, Recreation and Leisure', show how Victorian governments tried to reduce the errant and 'immoral' pleasures of the working class in various settings. Recent governments have attempted to control and legislate against diverse activities associated with the lower classes too. Disreputable, vulgar and common behaviour on the Victorian racecourse or in the music hall led to anxieties among the elite who wanted to impose the upper class social norms of respectability and morality. In contemporary Britain, recreational drug users have been defined by some as a social problem group, while football spectators have been increasingly regulated. During both periods, the consumption of alcohol by the working class is construed as a vice and 'alcohol-related disorder' has been increasingly controlled and criminalized. New Labour introduced a whole raft of management measures: ASBOs, Parenting Orders, Dispersal Notices, Closure Notices, child curfews to name but a few. Thus, the pleasures and pastimes of the working class in both periods have been more and more regulated and controlled by the ruling classes.

The powerful and the powerless

The powers that be generally consist of an elite powerful minority who decides what represents suitable, moral and acceptable or unsuitable, immoral and unacceptable behaviour; these social norms are then imposed on the majority of the population. In addition, the ruling classes also decide how to sanction undesirable and 'inferior' behaviour. More often than not, it is the behaviour of the working class, the 'criminal class', the 'undeserving poor', 'the dangerous class' and more recently, the 'underclass' who is subject to censorship and control, be it the workhouse in Victorian Britain or a dispersal order today. However, our understanding of what constitutes anti-social behaviour needs to be more nuanced than simply opposing the elite and the lower orders in Victorian Britain because the middle classes suffered from zealous restrictions too. Nevertheless, lawmakers' attempts at social control mainly aim at 'civilizing' the Other in their own image – the powerless should behave more like the powerful. Moreover, despite the commonly portrayed image in the media that it is the lower classes who tend to behave anti-socially, today the powerful impose their own corporate anti-social behaviour and anti-social laws on the powerless.

Overwhelmingly the target for social control is 'the Other' in relation to those making the laws. The labelling of the Other as anti-social is present in both periods under study. This 'othering' takes many forms, but it is consistent, for example, the vagrant in Victorian times or the homeless in contemporary times. This very visible 'Other' is the embodiment of someone who will not or cannot abide by social norms and whose very existence and way of life are considered by the elite to be anti-social and in need of social control. In a similar vein, the life-style of Gypsies and Travellers disturbs and is the focus of social control in both the nineteenth and twenty-first centuries. In this way, the poor, the young, the vulgar and the troubled are troubling and represent the greatest threat. Under the Conservative–Liberal Democrat Coalition government, we are witnessing a push towards personal responsibility, which is creating a climate where the individual, the family or the community are held to blame for what is considered by others to be anti-social behaviour, reinforcing the 'them and us' sentiment. In this way, the latter are personally responsible for their own problems, rather than the state which increasingly sanctions anti-social behaviour, deviancy and public disorder. Thus, poverty is the fault of the poor and not the fault of structural problems, meaning that society and the government are not held responsible.

Anti-social behaviour is in the eye of the beholder

Another theme that features throughout this book is the subjectivity of anti-social behaviour and responses to it. What one individual or community find harassing, alarming, or distressing, in other words, anti-social behaviour, another will find acceptable, even agreeable or possibly necessary depending on their circumstances. Social norms – tastes, tolerance and threats – regarding behaviour differ considerably; what is 'normal' varies not only from one person or community to another, but also from one point in time to another and one geographical area to another. But there existed and there still exists a hierarchy of tastes among decision makers where some tastes are deemed more desirable or legitimate and reserved for those with power. This variance is pointed out in a recent Home Office document: 'Just as individuals will have differing expectations and levels of tolerance so will communities have different ideas about what goes beyond tolerable or acceptable behaviour' (Home Office, 2011a: 14). Anti-social behaviour is thus open to perception and interpretation, and this ambiguity is augmented by the fact that the term covers a vast array of different conducts, as did incivility and 'immoral' behaviour in the Victorian era.

Both periods under study are characterized by a form of moral panic emanating from the behaviour of certain elements of its population. Geoffrey Pearson writes that in the Victorian era 'respectable England felt itself to have been suddenly engulfed in a new rush of crime' (Pearson, 1983: 76), while sentiments of 'Broken Britain' have been rife in the twenty-first century. The media in its Victorian and contemporary forms have both exacerbated this moral panic through the deviancy amplification spiral (Cohen, 1972), which boosts the image of social breakdown of social values and creates ever greater social anxieties and measures by legislators to control anti-social behaviour and further social cohesion by the labelling of the deviant as the 'Other'. Lawmakers of all political orientations have contributed to these moral panics through their discourses on anti-social behaviour (see Pickard, 2014d).

From respectability to respect

Anti-social behaviour is by no means new phenomenon. Incivility existed during the Victorian era, as it does today. Both are periods of rapid social and economic change associated with a moral panic regarding anti-social behaviour. Similarly, political responses to anti-social behaviour are fundamentally similar during the two periods. Anti-social behaviour was spotlighted by governments in Victorian Britain and became a focus of government policy in post-1997 neo-liberal Britain. During both these times, governments have tended to condemn and control anti-social behaviour from vulnerable and marginalized groups in public areas via surveillance, policing and justice policies. Both periods are marked by a willingness to prosecute behaviour that had previously not been regarded as deviant and in need of social control and increasingly punitive measures. This has led to the introduction of new legislation that has criminalized hitherto non-criminal behaviour that had up until then been ignored or tolerated. The scope for regulatory control and police powers have been significantly expanded – be it the right to consume alcohol or the right to protest in public spaces. Moreover, there is a parallel differentiation of control according to social class with the targeting of lower-class elements – be it horse-racing or absenteeism from school. This cultural governance had led to the criminalization of non-normative anti-social behaviour in both periods. The policies of the Labour Party (1997–2007) were particularly forceful in the criminalization of anti-social behaviour, which came to dominate criminal justice policy under Tony Blair and this marked a clear return to Victorian values. This continues under the Conservative–Liberal Democrat Coalition government. Therefore there is a clear parallel between Victorian Britain and twenty-first century Britain, as illustrated by the Anti-social Behaviour, Crime and Policing Act 2014.

Lastly, in Victorian and contemporary Britain, immoral and anti-social behaviour is frequently portrayed by the elite as evidence of personal weaknesses or personal choices because perpetrators 'don't know better' or don't want to change. They are thus represented as being irresponsible, inadequate and anti-social, rather than vulnerable, marginalized or disadvantaged. In both periods, it has been anti-social to be in need or different, which has led to further marginalization and stigmatization. Many contributors to this book discuss the legitimacy of governments and other forms of governance to judge, censure and control certain behaviours. They question whether it is morally, socially, and politically 'right' for powers to impose restrictions on and prosecute life-styles, tastes and opinions in the neoliberal twenty-first century, as was the case in the Victorian nineteenth century. In contemporary Britain, it really would be better to have a less repressive, more constructive approach to difficult or challenging behaviour, along with more tolerance of potentially anti-social behaviour.

References

Ackroyd, Peter (2000). *London: The Biography.* London: Chatto & Windus.

Acton, Thomas (1974). *Gypsy Politics and Social Change: The Development of Ethnic Ideology and Pressure Politics among British Gypsies from Victorian Reformism to Romani Nationalism.* London: Routledge & Kegan Paul.

Adler, Jeffrey S. (1989). 'A Historical Analysis of the Laws of Vagrancy'. *Criminology*, 27: 209–29.

Aitchison, Guy and Peters, Aaron (2011). 'The Open-Sourcing of Political Activism: How the Internet and Networks Help Build Resistance'. In Dan Hancox (ed.). *Fight Back! A Reader on the Winter of Protest.* London: OpenDemocracy, 44–61.

Alcohol Concern (2001). *Alcopops: Factsheet.* London: Alcohol Concern.

Alcohol Concern (2004). *Alcohol and Crime: Factsheet 10.* London: Alcohol Concern.

Allegretti, Bree (2013). 'Occupy Sussex Comes to an End as Police Move in'. *The Independent.* 2 April (http://www.independent.co.uk/student/news/occupy-sussex-comes-to-an-end-as-police-move-in-8556987.html).

Anderson, Isobel (1993). 'Housing Policy and Street Homelessness in Britain'. *Housing Studies*, 8(1): 17–28.

Anon (1871). 'Drawing Room Alcoholism'. *Saturday Review*, 21 January: 75–6.

Anon (1871). 'Women and Alcohol'. *The Spectator*, 18 February: 11–12.

Anon (1872). 'Editorial'. *The Times*, 27 June: 11.

Anon (1875). 'Drink: The Vice and the Disease'. *Quarterly Review*, July 1875: 396–434.

Arms, Robert L. and Russell, Gordon W. (1997). 'Impulsivity, Fight History, and Camaraderie as Predictors of a Willingness to Escalate a Disturbance'. *Current Psychology*, 15(4): 279–85.

Arnett Melchiori, Barbara (1985). *Terrorism in the Late-Victorian Novel.* London: Croom Helm.

Ashworth, Andrew; Gardner, John; Morgan, Rod; Smith, A.H.T; von Hirsch, Andrew and Wasik, Martin (1998). 'Neighbouring on the Oppressive: The Government's "Anti-Social Behaviour Order" Proposals'. *Criminal Justice*, 16(1): 7–14.

Audit Commission (2010). *Against the Odds. Re-engaging Young People in Education, Employment or Training.* London: Audit Commission.

Austin, James and Krisberg, Barry (1981). 'Wider, Stronger and Different Nets'. *Journal of Research in Crime and Delinquency*, 18(1): 165–96.

Bacon, Matthew (2013). 'Dancing around Drugs: Policing the Illegal Drug Markets of the Night-Time Economy in England and Wales'. In Saitta Pieto, Joanne Shapland and Antoinette Verhage (eds). *Getting by or Getting Rich? The Formal, Informal and Criminal Economy in a Globalised World.* The Hague: Eleven International Publishing.

Baggott, Rob (1990). *Alcohol, Politics and Social Policy.* Aldershot: Avebury.

Bagnoli, Carla (2007). 'Respect and Membership in the Moral Community'. *Ethical Theory and Moral Practice*, 10(2): 113–28.

Bailey, Michael and Freedman, Des (2011). *The Assault on Universities. A Manifesto for Resistance.* London: Pluto Press.

Bailey, Peter (1978). *Leisure and Class in Victorian England: Rational Recreation and the Contest for Control, 1830–1885.* London: Routledge.

Bailey, Peter (ed.) (1986). *Music Hall: The Business of Pleasure.* Milton Keynes: Open University Press.

Bailey, Peter (1987). *Leisure and Class in Victorian England: Rational Recreation and the Contest for Control 1830–1885*. London: Methuen.

Bailey, Peter (1998). *Popular Culture and Performance in the Victorian City*. Cambridge: Cambridge University Press.

Bailey, Victor (1993). 'The Fabrication of Deviance: "Dangerous Classes" and "Criminal Classes" in Victorian England'. In John Rule and Robert Malcolmson (eds). *Protest and Survival: The Historical Experience*. London: Merlin Press, 221–56.

Baker, Richard Anthony (1990). *Marie Lloyd, Queen of the Music Halls*. London: Robert Hale.

Bakhtin, Mikhail M. (1993). *Rabelais and his World*. Bloomington: Indiana University Press.

Banks, Cyndi (2013). *Youth, Crime and Justice*. London: Routledge.

Banksy (2006). *Wall and Piece*. London: Century.

Bannister, Jon and Kearns, Ade (2009). 'Tolerance, Respect and Civility amid Changing Cities'. In Andrew Millie (ed.). *Securing Respect: Behavioural Expectations and Antisocial Behaviour in the UK*. Bristol: Policy Press, 171–92.

Bannister, Jon and Kearns, Ade (2012). 'Overcoming Intolerance to Young People's Conduct: Implications from the Unintended Consequences of Policy in the UK'. *Criminology and Criminal Justice*, 13(3): 380–97.

Bannister, Jon; Fyfe, Nick and Kearns, Ade (2006). 'Respectable or Respectful? (In)civility and the City'. *Urban Studies*, 43(5/6): 919–37.

Bantman, Constance (2013). *The French Anarchists in London, 1880–1914. Exile and Transnationalism in the First Globalisation*. Liverpool: Liverpool University Press.

Barkham, Patrick (2005). 'Council Must Find Land for Gypsies'. *The Guardian*, 9 March, (http://www.theguardian.com/uk/2005/mar/09/localgovernment.immigration policy).

Barnardo's (2011). 'ASB Plans Could Put Vulnerable Children at Risk', (http://www.barnardos.org.uk/news/media_centre/press_releases.htm?ref=69050).

Barr, Andrew (1998). *Drink: A Social History*. London: Pimlico.

Barrie, David (2010). 'Police in Civil Society: Police, Enlightenment and Civic Virtue in Urban Scotland, c. 1870–1833'. *Urban History*, 1(1): 45–65.

Barthes, Roland (1972). *Mythologies*. [Translated by A. Lavers.] New York: Hill & Wang.

Bartlett, David (2011). 'Liverpool Will Not Be Beaten by Mindless Thugs After Riots, Says Liverpool Council Leader Joe Anderson (VIDEO)'. *The Liverpool Echo*, 10 August (http://www.liverpoolecho.co.uk/liverpool-news/local-news/2011/08/10/liverpool-will-not-be-beaten-by-mindless-thugs-after-riots-says-liverpool-council-leader-joe-anderson-video-100252-29209478/#ixzz1YEXy3Cus).

Bass, Michael T. (1864). *Street Music in the Metropolis*. London: John Murray.

Batty, David (2010). 'Royal Attack: Police Say Radio Link was Not to Blame'. *The Guardian*, 11 December (http://www.theguardian.com/education/2010/dec/11/met-police-criticism-tuition-fees-protest-attack-royals).

Bauman, Zygmunt (2000). *Liquid Modernity*. Cambridge: Polity Press.

BBC (2005). 'Romany Roots: Making a Living'. BBC Kent (http://www.bbc.co.uk/kent/voices/living.shtml).

BBC (2006). 'Rise in Asbos Prompts Criticism'. 30 March (http://news.bbc.co.uk/2/hi/4860384.stm).

BBC (2009). 'Truancy Timeline 1997–2009'. 11 February (http://news.bbc.co.uk/2/hi/uk_news/education/7851787.stm).

BBC (2012). 'Londonderry Shooting: "My Son had to be Shot" ', 15 May (http://www.bbc.co.uk/news/uk-18068691).

BBC (2014). 'More under 18s are Taking Risks with Illegal Tattoos', 3 February (www.bbc.co.uk/news/uk-26013128).

Bean, J.P. (1981). *The Sheffield Gang Wars*. Sheffield: D&D Publications.

Beaumont, Matthew (2006). 'Cacotopianism, the Paris Commune, and England's Anti-Communist Imaginary, 1870–1900'. *English Literary History*, 73(2): 465–87.

Beckett, Katherine and Herbert, Steve (2010). *Banished: The New Social Control in Urban America*. New York: Oxford University Press.

Beddoe, John (1885). *The Races of Britain. A Contribution to the Anthropology of Western Europe*. Bristol: Arrowsmith/London: Trübner & Co.

Behlmer, George K. (1985). 'The Gypsy Problem in Victorian England'. *Victorian Studies*, 28(2) (Winter): 231–53.

Beier, Anthony Lee (1985). *Masterless Men: The Vagrancy Problem in England 1560–1640*. London: Methuen & Co. Ltd.

Beier, Anthony Lee (1986). *Masterless Men: The Vagrancy Problem in England 1560–1640*, New York: Methuen.

Bell, Emma (2007). Interviews with Male and Female Prisoners at HMP East Sutton Park and HMP Lewes (unpublished field research).

Bellis, Mark; Hughes, Karen; Wood, Sara; Wyke, Sacha and Perkins, Clare (2011). 'National Five-Year Examination of Inequalities and Trends in Emergency Hospital Admission for Violence across England'. *Injury Prevention*, 17(5): 319–25.

Bennett, Shea (2011). 'Twitter Sees All-time Record Traffic Spike during London Riots'. *All Twitter: The Unofficial Twitter Resource* (http://www.mediabistro.com/alltwitter/twitter-record-london-riots_b12430).

Benyon, John (2012). 'England's Urban Disorder: The 2011 Riots'. *Political Insight*, 2(1): 12–17.

Berman, Marshall (1982). *All that is Solid Melts into Air: The Experience of Modernity*. New York, NY: Penguin Books.

Best, Joel (1999). *Random Violence: How We Talk About New Crimes and New Victims*. Berkley: University of California Press.

Better Regulation Task Force (1998). *Licensing Legislation*. Great Britain: Cabinet Office.

Blackman, Shane (2004). *Chilling Out: The Cultural Politics of Substance Consumption, Youth and Drug Policy*. Maidenhead: McGraw Hill–Open University Press.

Blackman, Shane (2014). 'Subculture Theory: An Historical and Contemporary Assessment of the Concept for Understanding Deviance'. *Deviant Behavior*, 35(6): 496–512.

Blair, Tony (1993). 'Why Crime is a Socialist Issue'. *New Statesman and Society*, 29 January: 27–8.

Blair, Tony (1996). *New Britain: My Vision of a Young Country*. London: Fourth Estate.

Blair, Tony (1997). 'Welfare Reform: Giving People the Will to Win'. Speech delivered at Aylesbury Estate, Southwark, 2 June (http://www.bbc.co.uk/news/special/politics97/news/06/0602/blair.shtml).

Blair, Tony (2004a). Speech on the Launch of the Five-year Strategy for Crime. 19 July.

Blair, Tony (2004b). Speech on Anti-social Behaviour. 28 October.

Blair, Tony (2010). *A Journey*. London: Hutchinson.

Bloom, Clive (2012). *Riot City. Protest and Rebellion in the Capital*. Basingstoke: Palgrave Macmillan.

Blunkett, David (2008). *The Inclusive Society? Social Mobility in 21st Century Britain*. London: Progress.

Bohstedt, John (1994). 'The Dynamics of Riots: Escalation and Diffusion/Contagion'. In Michael Potegal and John F. Knutson (eds). *The Dynamics of Aggression: Biological and Social Processes in Dyads and Groups*. Hillsdale: Erlbaum: 257–306.

Bond-Taylor, Sue and Somerville, Peter (2013). *Evaluation of Families Working Together: Final Report*, Lincoln: University of Lincoln.

Booth, Charles (1889). *Life and Labour of the People*. 2 Volumes. London: Macmillan & Co.

Booth, William (1890). *In Darkest England and the Way Out*. London: Funk & Wagnal.

Borsay, Peter (2007). *Binge Drinking and Moral Panics: Historical Parallels?* (http://www.historyandpolicy.org/papers/policy-paper-62.html).

Böse, Martina (2005). 'Difference and Exclusion at Work in the Club Culture Economy'. *International Journal of Cultural Studies*, 8(4): 427–44.

Bottoms, Anthony (2006). 'Incivilities, Offence and Social Order in Residential Communities'. In Andrew von Hirsch and A.P. Simester (eds). *Incivilities: Regulating Offensive Behaviour*. Oxford: Hart Publishing.

Bottoms, Anthony (2009). 'Disorder, Order and Control Signals'. *British Journal of Sociology*, I.60(1): 49–55.

Bourdieu, Pierre (1979/2010). *Distinction: A Social Critique of the Judgement of Taste*. London: Routledge.

Bourdieu, Pierre (1990). *Homo Academicus*. [Translated by Peter Collier.] Cambridge: Polity Press.

Bourdieu, Pierre (1996). *The Rules of Art*. Stanford: Stanford University Press.

Bowers, Jake (2011). 'Why Big Fat Gypsy Weddings Betrays us Real Romanies'. *The Sun*, 10 February (http://www.thesun.co.uk/sol/homepage/features/3402592/Gypsy-Weddings-is-a-TV-ratings-smash-but-its-left-British-gipsies-crying-discrimination.html).

Bowling, Benjamin (1999). 'The Rise and Fall of New York Murder: Zero Tolerance or Crack's Decline?' *British Journal of Criminology*, 39(4): 531–54.

Bowman, Helen (2001). 'Talking to Families in Leeds and Sheffield: A Report on the First Stage of the Research'. CASE Report. London: London School of Economics.

Boyson, Rhodes (1975). *The Crisis in Education*. London: Woburn Press.

Boyson, Rhodes and Brian Cox (eds) (1975). *Black Paper. The Fight for Education*. London: Dent.

Braid, Mary (1993). 'Return of the Bogywoman: The Single Mother, Stigmatized and Penalized for Centuries until the Sixties, is back in the Firing line'. *The Independent*, 10 October: 24.

Branigan, Tania (2007). 'Every Asbo a Failure, says Balls, in Break with Blair Era on Crime'. *The Guardian*, 28 July: 13.

Brantlinger, Patrick (1994). 'The Case of the Poisonous Book: Mass Literacy as Threat in Nineteenth-Century British Fiction'. *Victorian Review*, 20(2) (Winter): 117–33.

Brewer, John. D; Lockhart, Bill and Rodgers, Paula (1998). 'Informal Social Control and Crime Management in Belfast'. *British Journal of Sociology*, 49(4): 570–85.

Bridge, A. (1898). 'Manners in our Elementary Schools'. *New Century Review*, 4(22): 313–16. October.

Briggs, Asa (1963). *Victorian Cities*. London: Odhams Press.

Briggs, Asa (1968). *Victorian Cities*. London: Pelican Books.

Briggs, Daniel (ed.) (2012a). *The English Riots of 2011: A Summer of Discontent*. Hampshire: Waterside Press.

Briggs, Daniel (2012b). 'Frustrations, Urban Relations and Temptations: Contextualising the English Riots'. In Daniel Briggs (ed.). *The English Riots of 2011. A Summer of Discontent*. Hampshire: Waterside Press, 27–41.

British Crime Survey (2013). *Crime in England and Wales, Year Ending March 2013*. Office for National Statistics (ONS) (www.ons.gov.uk/ ... /crime ... /crime ... 2013/stb-crime–period-ending-march-2013.html).

British Institute for Brain-Injured Children (BIBIC) (2005). *Ain't Misbehavin': Young People with Learning and Communication Difficulties and Anti-Social Behaviour.* London: BIBIC.

Brontë, Anne (2008). *The Tenant of Wildfell Hall* (1848). Oxford: Oxford University Press.

Brotherton Special Collection (1907). Leeds, DUR Cuttings, Volume 1, 65: 'KM', 'A Romany Chal', 9 August.

Brown, Alison P. (2004). 'Anti-Social Behaviour, Crime Control and Social Control'. *Howard Journal of Criminal Justice*, 43(2): 203–11.

Brown, Alison (2008). 'The War on "Neds": Media Reports as Evidence Base'. *Criminal Justice Matters*, 59(1): 16–17.

Brown, Donna Marie (2013). 'Young People, Anti-Social Behaviour and Public Space: The Role of Community Wardens in Policing the ASBO Generation'. *Urban Studies*, 50(3): 538–55.

Brown, Edward M. (1985). ' "What Shall we do with the Inebriate?": Asylum Treatment and the Disease Concept of Alcoholism in the Late Nineteenth Century'. *Journal of the History of the Behavioral Sciences*, 21(1): 48–59.

Browne, John (2010). *Securing a Sustainable Future for Higher Education. An Independent Review of Higher Education Funding and Student Finance (The Browne Review).* Department for Business, Innovation and Skills (BIS).

Bucknill, John C. (1878). 'Habitual Drunkards Bill'. Letter to the Editor of *The Times*, 9 July: 12.

Burgess, Simon; Gardiner, Karen and Propper, Carol (2002). *The Economic Determinants of Truancy*. Centre for Analysis of Social Exclusion. CASE paper 61.

Burn, William Laurence (1964). *The Age of Equipoise. A Study of the Mid-Victorian Generation.* London: Allen & Unwin.

Burney, Elisabeth (2009). *Making People Behave. Anti-Social Behaviour, Politics and Policy.* Cullompton: Willan Publishing.

Burney, Elizabeth (2009). 'Respect and the Politics of Behaviour'. In Andrew Millie (ed.). *Securing Respect: Behavioural Expectations and Anti-Social Behaviour in the UK.* Bristol: Policy Press, 23–40.

Burn-Murdoch, John; Lewis, Paul; Ball, James; Oliver, Christine; Robinson, Michael and Blight, Garry (2011). 'Twitter Traffic during the Riots'. *The Guardian*, 24 August (http://www.guardian.co.uk/uk/interactive/2011/aug/24/riots-twitter-traffic-interactive).

Butler, Sophie (1998). *Access Denied.* London: Shelter.

Caine, Thomas Henry Hall (1897). *The Christian. A Story.* London: William Heinemann

Callinicos, Alex (1996). 'Betrayal and Discontent: Labour under Blair'. *International Socialism*, 72.

Cameron, David (2007). 'Crime and our Broken Society'. 24 August.

Cameron, David (2010). Speech on 'Big Society'. Liverpool, 19 July (https://www.gov.uk/government/speeches/big-society-speech).

Cameron, David (2011a). Cited in 'Vox Pop: the Riots'. *The Guardian*, 12 August (http://www.guardian.co.uk/uk/2011/aug/12/vox-pop-riots).

Cameron, David (2011b). Speech on the 'Fight Back After the Riots'. Oxfordshire, 15 August (http://www.number10.gov.uk/news/pms-speech-on-the-fightback-after-the-riots).

Cameron, David (2011c). Speech on 'Troubled Families'. 15 December (http://www.number10.gov.uk/news/troubled-families-speech).

Cameron, S. (1974). 'Truancy Survey Wide Open to Rigging By Heads'. *Times Educational Supplement.* 2 August.

Campbell, Siobhan (2002). *Implementing Anti-Social Behaviour Orders: Messages for Practitioners*, Findings 160. London: Home Office.

Cantlie, James (1885). *Degeneration Amongst Londoners.* London: Field & Tuer, Leadenhall Press.

Carlen, Pat; Gleeson, Denis and Wardhaugh, Julia (1992). *Truancy. The Politics of Compulsory Schooling.* Buckingham: Open University Press.

Carlile, Jane; Carlile, Richard and Holmes, William (1825). *The Trials with the Defences at Large of Mrs. Jane Carlile, Mary Ann Carlile, William Holmes etc.*, London.

Carlyle, Thomas (1998). 'Chartism'. Extract reprinted in J.M. Guy (ed.) (1840). *The Victorian Age: An Anthology of Sources and Documents.* London: Routledge. Originally published London: James Fraser, 155–66.

Carpenter, Joseph E. (1879). *The Life and Work of Mary Carpenter.* London: Macmillan.

Carpenter, Mary (1851). *Reformatory Schools for the Children of the Perishing and the Dangerous Classes and for Juvenile Offenders.* London: C. Gilpin.

Carpenter, Mary (1852). *Juvenile Delinquents: Their Condition and Treatment.* London: W. & F.G. Cash.

Carpenter, William B. (1877). *Sketch of the Life and Work of Mary Carpenter*, Bristol: Arrowsmith.

Carter, Alexandra (2005). *Dance and Dancers in the Victorian and Edwardian Music Hall Ballet.* Aldershot: Ashgate.

Cartwright-Reed, S. (1872). 'Alcohol as a Medicine'. Letter to the editor of *The Times*, 12 January: 5.

Carvel, John (2007). 'Fivefold Rise in Rows over Noise Marks less Tolerant Society'. *The Guardian*, 11 April.

Casey, Louise (2012). *Listening to Troubled Families: A Report by Louise Casey CB.* London: Department for Communities and Local Government (DCLG).

Casserly, Jo (2011). 'The Art of Occupation'. In Clare Solomon and Tania Palmieri (eds). *Springtime. The New Student Rebellions.* London: Verso, 71–5.

Caulfield, Sophia F.A. (1884). 'Etiquette in Walking, Riding and Driving'. *Girl's Own Paper*, 26 April.

Centre for Social Justice (CSJ) (2006). *Breakdown Britain: Interim Report on the State of the Nation.* London: Centre for Social Justice (CSJ).

Centre for Social Justice (CSJ) (2009). *Dying to Belong: An In-Depth Review of Street Gangs in Britain.* London: Centre for Social Justice (CSJ).

Centre for Social Justice (CSJ) (2012). *Time to Wake Up: Tackling Gangs one Year after the Riots.* London: Centre for Social Justice (CSJ).

Chambliss, William J. (1964). 'A Sociological Analysis of the Laws of Vagrancy'. *Social Problems*, 12 (1): 67–77.

Chatterton, Paul and Hollands, Robert (2002). 'Theorising Urban Playscapes: Producing, Regulating and Consuming Youthful Nightlife City Spaces'. *Urban Studies*, 1(Jan): 95–116.

Chatterton, Paul and Hollands, Robert (2003). *Urban Nightscapes: Youth Cultures, Pleasure Spaces and Corporate Power.* London: Routledge.

Cheshire Police (2014). *Anti-social Behaviour* (https://www.cheshire.police.uk/advice–information/anti-social-behaviour.aspx).

Chinn, Carl (1991). *Better Betting with a Decent Feller. Bookmakers, Betting and the British Working Class, 1750–1990.* Hemel Hempstead: Harvester Wheatsheaf.

Clapson, Mark (1992). *A Bit of a Flutter: Popular Gambling in England c. 1820–1961.* Manchester: Manchester University Press.

Clark, Colin (1997). 'New Age Travellers: Identity, Sedentarism and Social Security'. In Thomas Acton (ed.). *Gypsy Politics and Traveller Identity*. Hatfield: University of Hertfordshire Press: 125–41.

Clark, Colin (2002). 'Not Just Lucky White Heather and Clothes Pegs: Putting European Gypsy and Traveller Economic Niches in Context'. In Steve Fenton and Harriet Bradley (eds). *Ethnicity and Economy: Race and Class Revisited*. Basingstoke: Palgrave Macmillan, 183–98.

Clark, Colin and Cemlyn, Sarah (2005). 'The Social Exclusion of Gypsy and Traveller Children'. In Gabrielle Preston (ed.). *At Greatest Risk: The Children Most Likely to be Poor*. London: Child Poverty Action Group, 150–65.

Clark, Colin and Greenfields, Margaret (2006). *Here to Stay: The Gypsies and Travellers of Britain*. Hatfield: University of Hertfordshire Press.

Clarke, Alan; Williams, Kate and Wydall, Sarah (2011). *Describing and Assessing Interventions to Address Anti-Social Behaviour*. Research Report 51. London: Home Office.

Cloke, Paul; May, Jon and Johnsen, Sarah (2010). *'Swept up Lives? Re-envisioning the Homeless City'*. Chichester: Wiley-Blackwell.

Close, Francis (1827). *The Evil Consequences of Attending the Racecourse Exposed in a Sermon*. London: Hatchard.

Cockayne, Emily (2007). *Hubbub: Filth, Noise and Stench in England*. New Haven and London: Yale University Press.

Cockayne, Emily (2012). *Cheek by Jowl: A History of Neighbours*. London: Bodley Head.

Cohen, Antony P. (1993). *The Symbolic Construction of Community*. London: Tavistock.

Cohen, Nick (2012). 'We only Pretend to Defend Free Speech'. *Standpoint*, January/February edition.

Cohen, Phil (1979). 'Policing the Working-Class City'. In National Deviancy Conference. *Capitalism and the Rule of Law*. London: Hutchinson & Co, 118–36.

Cohen, Stanley (1972 1st edition and 2002 3rd edition). *Folk Devils and Moral Panics*. London: Routledge.

Cohen, Stanley (2005). *Visions of Social Control*. Cambridge: Polity Press.

Coleman, Roy (2004). *Reclaiming the Streets: Surveillance, Social Control and the City*. Cullompton: Willan Publishing.

Coleman, Roy; Tombs, Steve and Whyte, David (2005). 'Capital, Crime Control and Statecraft in the Entrepreneurial City'. *Urban Studies*, 42(13): 2511–30.

Collin, Matthew (1997). *Altered State: The Story of Ecstasy Culture and Acid House*. London: Serpent's Tail.

Communities and Local Government (2011). *A New Mandatory Power of Possession for Anti-social Behaviour: Consultation*. London: Department for Communities and Local Government (DCLG).

Communities and Local Government (2012). *The Troubled Families Programme: Financial Framework for the Troubled Families Programme's Payment-by-Results Scheme for Local Authorities*. London: Communities and Local Government.

Community Care (2006). 'Punish and be Damned'. 4 April (http://www.communitycare.co.uk/articles/01/04/2006/101748/punish-and-be-damned.htm).

Conan Doyle, Sir Arthur (1887). *A Study in Scarlet*. London: Ward Lock and Co.

Conservative Party (2010). *Invitation to Join the Government of Britain, Conservative Manifesto 2010*. Uckfield: Pureprint.

Coomber, Ross (2006). *Pusher Myths: Re-Situating the Drug Dealer*. London: Free Association Books.

Cooter, Roger (1984). *The Cultural Meaning of Popular Science: Phrenology and the Organization of Consent in Nineteenth Century Britain*. Cambridge: Cambridge University Press.

Cops off Campus Now! (2013) (http://www.dazeddigital.com/artsandculture/article/18110/1/cops-off-campus-university-of-london-protest-ban).

Coughlan, Sean (2010). 'Student Tuition Fee Protest Ends with 153 Arrests'. *BBC News Online*. 1 December (http://www.bbc.com/news/education-11877034).

Coughlan, Sean and Westhead, James (2009). 'Truancy Jailing Every Two Weeks'. *BBC News Online*. 12 February (http://news.bbc.co.uk/2/hi/uk_news/education/7868061.stm).

Council of the European Union (2010). 'Council Resolution 165'. *Official Journal of the European* Union, 24 June: 1–21.

Crawford, Adam (1998). 'Community Safety and the Quest for Security: Holding Back the Dynamics of Social Exclusion'. *Policy Studies*, 19(3/4): 237–53.

Crawford, Adam (2003). ' "Contractual Governance" of Deviant Behaviour'. *Journal of Law and Society*, 30(4): 479–505.

Crawford, Adam (2009a). 'Governing Through Anti-Social Behaviour: Regulatory Challenges to Criminal Justice'. *British Journal of Criminology*, 49(6): 810–31.

Crawford, Adam (2009b). 'Criminalizing Sociability through Anti-Social Behaviour Legislation: Dispersal Powers, Young People and the Police'. *Youth Justice*, 9(1): 5–26.

Crawford, Adam and Lister, Stuart (2007). *The Use and Impact of Dispersal Orders: Sticking Plasters and Wake-up Calls*. Bristol: Policy Press.

Crisis (2013). ' "Priority need" definitions' (http://www.crisis.org.uk/pages/priority-need-definitions.html).

Croall, Hazel (2009). 'Community Safety and Economic Crime'. *Criminology and Criminal Justice* 9: 169–85.

Croll, Andy and Martin Johnes (2004). In 'A Heart of Darkness? Leisure, Respectability and the Aesthetics of Vice'. In Mike Huggins and James Anthony Mangan (eds). *Disreputable Pleasures: Less Virtuous Victorians at Play*. Abingdon: Frank Cass, 153–71.

Croll, Andy (1997). ' "Naming and Shaming" in late-Victorian and Edwardian Britain'. *History Today*, 47(5): 3–6.

Croll, Andy (1999). 'Street Disorder, Surveillance and Shame: Regulating Behaviour in the Public Spaces of the Late Victorian British Town'. *Social History*, 24(3): 250–68.

Crone, Rosalind (2012). *Violent Victorians: Popular Entertainment in Nineteenth-Century London*. Manchester: Manchester University Press.

Crook, Tom (2008). 'Accommodating the Outcast: Common Lodging Houses and the Limits of Urban Governance in Victorian and Edwardian London'. *Urban History*, 35(3): 416–36.

Crowley John W. and White, William L. (2004). *Drunkard's Refuge The Lessons of the New York State Inebriate Asylum*. Amherst: University of Massachusetts Press.

Cruickshank, Dan (2009). *The Secret History of Georgian London: How the Wages of Sin Shaped the Capital*. London: Random House.

Cullen, Jane (1996). 'The Return of the Residuum'. In Lynn Revell and James Heartfield (eds), *A Moral Impasse: The End of Capitalist Triumphalism*. London: Junius.

Cummings, Dolan (2005). In Craig O'Malley and Stuart Waiton. *Who's Anti-social: The Politics of Anti-social Behaviour*. London: Academy of Ideas.

Curtis, Polly (2003). 'Truancy Strategy a Success, Say Ministers'. *The Guardian*, 2 July (http://www.theguardian.com/education/2003/jul/02/schools.uk1).

Daly, Frederick H. (1879). 'Overstimulation in Women'. *The Gentleman's Magazine*, 22: 111–20.

Darwar, Anil and Wintour, Patrick (2008). 'Tories and Lib Dems Praise Smith's Anti-social Behaviour Plans'. *The Guardian*, 8 May (http://www.guardian.co.uk/politics/2008/may/08/police.justice1).

Davetian, Benet (2009). *Civility: A Cultural History*. Toronto: University of Toronto Press.

Davie, Neil (2005). *Tracing the Criminal: The Rise of Scientific Criminology in Britain, 1860–1918*. Oxford: Bardwell Press.

Davie, Neil (2006). 'Corps et Délinquance Juvénile en Angleterre dans les Années 1830–1865: Le Milieu Remis en Question?' *Revue d'Histoire de l'Enfance 'Irrégulière'*, 8: 49–62.

Davies, Andrew (1998). 'Youth Gangs, Masculinity and Violence in Late Victorian Manchester and Salford'. *Journal of Social History*, 32(2): 349–69.

Davies, Andrew (2008). *The Gangs of Manchester. The Story of the Scuttlers, Britain's First Youth Cult*. Preston: Milo Books.

Davies, John Dwyfor and Lee, John (2006). 'To Attend or Not to Attend? Why Some Students Chose School and Others Reject it'. *Support for Learning: Journal of the National Association for Remedial Education*, 21(4): 204–9.

Davis, Bruce (2011). *The Need for a New Approach: Developing an Ethnographic Understanding of Families with Complex Needs*. A Report for Leicestershire Together, 18 October (http://www.leicestershiretogether.org/211111_ethographer_report.pdf).

Davis, Mike (1990/1998). *City of Quartz: Excavating the Future in Los Angeles*. London: Pimlico.

Davis, Petra (2013). 'Alfie Meadows and Zak King are not Guilty: Now it's Time for Police Behaviour to be Scrutinised'. *New Statesman*, 9 March (http://www.newstatesman.com/austerity-and-its-discontents/2013/03/alfie-meadows-and-zak-king-are-not-guilty-now-its-time-police-).

Day, William (1880). *The Racehorse in Training, With Hints on Racing and Racing Reforms*. London: Chapman & Hall.

Dayan, Daniel and Katz, Elihu (1998). 'Articulating Consensus: The Ritual and Rhetoric of Media Events'. In Jeffrey Alexander (ed.). *Durkheimian Sociology: Cultural Studies*. Cambridge: Cambridge University Press, 161–86.

De la Roche, Roberta Senechal (2001). 'Why is Collective Violence Collective?' *Sociological Theory*, 19(2): 126–44.

De Venanzi, Augusto (2008). 'Social Representations and the Labelling of Non-compliant Youths: The Case of Victorian and Edwardian Hooligans'. *Deviant Behaviour*, 29(3): 193–224.

Deacon, Alan (2003). 'Social Security Policy'. In Nick Ellison and Chris Pierson (eds). *Developments in British Social Policy 2*. Basingstoke: Palgrave Macmillan, 129–42.

Deacon, Alan; Vincent, Jill and Walker, Robert (1995). 'Whose Choice, Hostels or Homes? Policies for Single Homeless People'. *Housing Studies*, 10(3): 345–63.

Deadly Knitshade (2011). *Knit the City: A Whodunnknit set in London*. Chichester: Summersdale.

Dearing, Ronald (1997). *Higher Education in the Learning Society. National Committee of Inquiry into Higher Education (The Dearing Report)*. London: Department for Education and Employment (DfEE).

Defend the Right to Protest (2013). 'Victory for Alfie Meadows and Zak King' (http://www.defendtherighttoprotest.org).

Denham, Jess (2013). 'Police Accused of Disproportionate Force at ULU Chalking Arrest'. *The Independent*. 17 July (http://www.independent.co.uk/student/news/police-accused-of-disproportionate-force-at-ulu-chalking-arrest-8713380.html).

Department for Communities and Local Government (DCLG) (2006). *'Places of Change: Tackling Homelessness through the Hostels Capital Improvement Programme'* (http://webarchive.nationalarchives.gov.uk/20120919132719/http://www.communities.gov.uk/documents/housing/pdf/152564.pdf).

Department for Communities and Local Government (DCLG) (2010). *16 Areas get 'Community Budgets' to Help the Vulnerable.* DCLG Announcement. 22 October (https://www.gov.uk/government/news/16-areas-get-community-budgets-to-help -the-vulnerable).

Department for Communities and Local Government (DCLG) (2010). *Guidance on Managing Anti-social Behaviour Related to Gypsies and Travellers.* London: DCLG.

Department for Communities and Local Government (DCLG) (2011). *Community Budgets Prospectus.* London: DCLG.

Department for Communities and Local Government (DCLG) (2012a). *Dealing with Rogue Landlords: A Guide for Local Authorities.* London: DCLG.

Department for Communities and Local Government (DCLG) (2012b). *Listening to Troubled Families.* London: DCLG.

Department for Communities and Local Government (DCLG) (2012c). *The Troubled Families Programme: Financial Framework for the Troubled Families Programme's Payment-by-results Scheme for Local Authorities.* London: DCLG.

Department for Communities and Local Government (DCLG) (2012d). *Working with Troubled Families: A Guide to the Evidence and Good Practice.* London: DCLG.

Department for Education and Employment (DfEE) (1998). *Pupil Absence and Truancy from Schools in England: 1993/94–1997/98.* Statistical Bulletin Number 14/98.

Department of Culture, Media and Sport (DCMS), Home Office, Office of the Deputy Prime Minister (ODPM) (2005). *Drinking Responsibly: The Government's Proposals.* London: ODPM.

Department of Culture, Media and Sport (DCMS) (2002). *Licensing Bill Launched.* Department for Culture, Media and Sport press release, 15 November 2002.

Department of Culture, Media and Sport (DCMS) (2004). *DCMS Statistical Bulletin – Liquor Licensing England and Wales July 2003–June 2004.* London: Office for National Statistic (ONS).

Department of the Environment (DofE) (1982). *The Accommodation Needs of Long-distance and Regional Travellers: A Consultation Paper.* London: DOE.

Department of the Environment (DofE) (1993). *Planning Policy and Guidance Note 6.* Great Britain: DoE.

Department of the Environment (DofE) (1995). *Anti-Social Behaviour on Council Estates: A Consultation Paper on Probationary Tenancies.* London: HMSO.

DeScioli, Pete; Gilbert, Sarah and Kurzban, Robert (2012). 'Indelible Victims and Persistent Punishers in Moral Cognition'. *Psychological Inquiry,* 23: 143–9.

DeVerteuil, Geoffrey; May, Jon and von Mahs, Jürgen (2009). 'Complexity not Collapse: Recasting the Geographies of Homelessness in a 'Punitive' Age'. *Progress in Human Geography,* 33(5): 646–66.

Dickens, Charles (2009). *Uncollected Writings from Household Words Volume 1.* Newcastle-upon-Tyne: Cambridge Scholars Publishing.

Dillane, Jennifer; Bannister, Jon and Scott, Suzie (2001). *Evaluation of the Dundee Families Project–Final Report.* Edinburgh: Scottish Executive.

Dingle, Anthony Edward (1980). *The Campaign for Prohibition in Victorian England: The UK Alliance 1872–1895.* London: Croom Helm.

Dixon, David (1991). *From Prohibition to Regulation. Bookmaking. Anti-gambling and the Law.* Oxford: Clarendon Press.

Donajgrodzki, A.P. (1977). ' "Social Police" and the Bureaucratic Elite: a Vision of Order in the Age of Reform'. In A.P. Donajgrodzki (ed.). *Social Control in Nineteenth Century Britain*. London: Croom Helm, 51–76.

Donzelot, Jacques (1979). *The Policing of Families*. London: Hutchinson University Press.

Doolin, Katherine; Child, John; Raine, John and Beech, Anthony (2011). *Whose Criminal Justice? State or Community?* Hook: Waterside Press.

Dorn, Nicolas (1983). *Alcohol, Youth and the State: Drinking Practices, Controls and Health Education*. London: Croom Helm.

Douglas, Mary (1987). 'A Distinctive Anthropological Perspective'. In Mary Douglas (ed.). *Constructive Drinking: Perspectives on Drink from Anthropology*. Cambridge: Cambridge University Press, 3–15.

Downes, David (1993). *Contrasts in Tolerance: Post-war Penal Policy in the Netherlands and England and Wales*. Oxford: Oxford University Press.

Duckworth, Jeannie (2002). *Fagin's Children. Criminal Children in Victorian England*. London: Hambledon.

Dugan, Emily and Paige, Jonathan (2010). 'Riots and Recriminations'. *The Independent*, 12 December (http://www.independent.co.uk/news/uk/politics/riots-and-recriminations-2158113.html).

Duncan, Alan (2007). Speech at the Centre for Policy Studies, 16 February (http://conservativehome.blogs.com/torydiary/files/alan_duncan_speech.pdf).

Duncan, Simon (2007). 'What's the Problem with Teenage Parents? And What's the Problem with Policy?' *Critical Social Policy*, 27(3): 307–34.

Dunning, Eric; Murphy, Pat and Williams, John (1988). *The Roots of Football Hooliganism*. London: Routledge.

Dynes, Russell R. and Quarantelli, Enrico L. (1968). 'What Looting in Civil Disturbances Really Means'. *Trans-Action*, 5(6): 9–14.

Easton, Mark (2008). 'Cameron's Britain: Social Policy'. *BBC News*, 26 June (http://news.bbc.co.uk/2/hi/uk_news/politics/7471370.stm).

Eco, Umberto (1979). *A Theory of Semiotics*. Bloomington, IN: Indiana University Press.

Ehrlich, Cyril (1985). *The Music Profession in Britain since the Eighteenth Century. A Social History*. Oxford: Clarendon.

Elias, Norbert (1978). *What is Sociology?* [Translated by Stephen Mennell and Grace Morrissey.] London: Hutchinson.

Elias, Norbert (1996). *The Germans: Power Struggles and the Development of Habitus in the Nineteenth and Twentieth Centuries*. [Translated by Eric Dunnell and Stephen Mennell.] New York: Columbia University Press.

Elias, Norbert (2000 [1939]). *The Civilizing Process*. [Translated by Edmund Jephcott.] Oxford: Blackwell.

Emsley, Clive (1996). *The English Police: A Political and Social History*. 2nd edn. Harlow and London: Longman.

Engels, Friedrich (1889). *Letter to Friedrich Adolph Sorge in Hoboken* (www.marxists.org/archive/marx/works/1889/letters/89_12_07.htm).

Engels, Friedrich (1999). *The Condition of the Working Class in England*. Oxford: Oxford University Press.

Engels, Friedrich (2009). *Socialism, Utopian and Scientific*. Gloucester: Dodo Press.

Erenburg, Lewis A. (1981). *Steppin' Out: New York Nightlife and the Transformation of American culture 1890–1930*. London: Greenwood.

Eriksson, Anna (2009). *Justice in Transition: Community Restorative Justice in Ireland*. Portland: Willan Publishing.

Etzioni, Amitai (1993). *The Spirit of Community: The Reinvention of American Society*. New York: Simon & Schuster.

Farrall, Stephen and Hay, Colin (2010). 'Not So Tough On Crime? Why Weren't the Thatcher Governments More Radical in Reforming the Criminal Justice System?' *British Journal of Criminology*, 50(3): 550–69.

Farson, Daniel (1972). *Marie Lloyd and Music Hall*. London: Tom Stacey.

Faulk, Barry J. (2004). *Music Hall and Modernity. The Late-Victorian Discovery of Popular Culture*. Athens OH: Ohio University Press.

Fedotov, Yury (2014). Speaking on BBC Radio 4, *Today Programme*, 13 March.

Feenan, Dermot (2002). 'Justice in Conflict: Paramilitary Punishment in Ireland (North)'. *International Journal of the Sociology of Law*, 30(2): 151–72.

Feinberg, Joel (1984). *Harm to Others: The Moral Limits of the Criminal Law Volume 1*. New York: Oxford University Press.

Feinberg, Joel (1985). *Offence to Others: The Moral Limits of the Criminal Law Volume 2*. New York: Oxford University Press.

Ferrell, Jeff (1996). *Crimes of Style: Urban Graffiti and the Politics of Criminality*. Boston: Northeastern University Press.

Ferrell, Jeff (2001). *Tearing Down the Streets: Adventures in Urban Anarchy*. Basingstoke: Palgrave Macmillan.

Ferrell, Jeff (2006). 'The Aesthetics of Cultural Criminology'. In Bruce A. Arrigo and Christopher R. Williams (eds). *Philosophy, Crime, and Criminology*. Urbana and Chicago: University of Illinois Press, 257–78.

Field, Frank (2010). *The Foundation Years: Preventing Poor Children Becoming Poor Adults. The Report of the Independent Review on Poverty and Life Chances*. London: HM Government.

Field, Frank (1989). *Losing Out: The Emergence of Britain's Underclass*. London: Blackwell.

Field, Frank (1996). 'Britain's Underclass: Countering the Growth'. In Ruth Lister (1996). *Charles Murray and the Underclass*. London: Institute of Economic Affairs (IEA) Health and Welfare Unit.

Field, Frank (2003). *Neighbours from Hell: The Politics of Behaviour*. London: Politico's.

Fielding, Henry (1751). *An Enquiry into the Causes of the Late Increase in Robberies with some Proposals for Remedying this Growing Evil*. London: A. Miller.

Finnegan, Frances (1979). *Poverty and Prostitution: A Study of Victorian Prostitutes in York*. Cambridge: Cambridge University Press.

Finney, Andrea (2004). *Violence in the Night-time Economy: Key Findings from the Research*. London: Home Office.

Fishman, William (2004). *East End Jewish Radicals 1875–1914*. Nottingham: Five Leaves Publications.

Fitzpatrick, Suzanne; Pawson, Hal; Bramley, Glen and Wilcox, Steve (2011). *The Homelessness Monitor* (http://www.crisis.org.uk/data/files/publications/TheHomelessnessMonitor_141011.pdf).

Flint, John (2006). *Housing, Urban Governance and Anti-social Behaviour: Perspectives, Policies and Practice*. Bristol: Policy Press.

Flint, John (2012). 'The Inspection House and Neglected Dynamics of Governance: The Case of Domestic Visits in Family Intervention Projects'. *Housing Studies*, 27(7): 822–39.

Flint, John and Powell, Ryan (2012). 'The English City Riots, 'Broken Britain' and the Retreat into the Present'. *Sociological Research On-line*, 17(3) (http://www.socresonline.org.uk/17/3/20.html).

Forsythe, Bill (1995). 'The Garland Thesis and the Origins of Modern English Prison Discipline: 1835 to 1939'. *Howard Journal of Criminal Justice*, 34(3): 259–73.

Foucault, Michel (1977). *Discipline and Punish: The Birth of the Prison*. London: Allen Lane.

Foucault, Michel (1980). 'The Eye of Power'. In Colin Gordon (ed.). *Power / Knowledge: Selected Interviews and Other Writings, 1972–1977*. Brighton: Harvester, 145–65.

France, Alan (2009). 'Young People and Anti-social Behaviour'. In Andy Furlong (ed.). *Handbook of Youth and Young Adults. New Perspectives and Agendas*. London: Routledge, 430–5.

Frankel, Hannah (2007). 'Absent Without Leave'. *Times Education Supplement*. 25 May (http://www.tes.co.uk/article.aspx?storycode=2391718).

Fraser, Derek (1984). *The Evolution of the British Welfare State: A History of Social Policy Since the Industrial Revolution*. Second edition. Basingstoke: Palgrave Macmillan.

Frosdick, Steve and Marsh, Peter (2005). *Football Hooliganism*. London: Willan Publishing.

Furedi, Frank (1997). *Culture of Fear: Risk-Taking and the Morality of Low Expectations*. London: Cassell.

Furedi, Frank (2004). *Therapy Culture: Cultivating Vulnerability in an Uncertain Age*. London: Routledge.

Furedi, Frank (2005). *The Politics of Fear: Beyond Left and Right*. London: Continuum.

Furlong, Andy (2013). *Youth Studies. An Introduction*. London: Routledge.

Gabb, Sean (1994). *Truancy: Its Measurement and Causation: A Brief Review of the Literature* (http://www.seangabb.co.uk/?q=node/109).

Gabbatt, Adam and Lewis, Paul (2010). 'Student Protests: Video Shows Mounted Police Charging London Crowd'. *The Guardian*, 26 November (http://www.guardian.co.uk/uk/2010/nov/26/police-student-protests-horses-charge).

Gainer, Bernard (1972). *The Alien Invasion. The Origins of the Aliens Act 1905*. London: Heinemann Educational Books.

Galton, Sir Francis (1883). *Inquiries into Human Faculty and its Development*. London: Macmillan and Co.

Garland, David (1985). *Punishment and Welfare*. Aldershot: Gower Publishing.

Garland, David (1996). 'The Limits of the Sovereign State: Strategies of Crime Control in Contemporary Society'. *British Journal of Criminology*, 36(4): 445–71.

Garland, David (2002). *The Culture of Control: Crime and Disorder in Contemporary Society*. Oxford: Oxford University Press.

Garratt, Sheryl (1998). *Adventures in Wonderland: A Decade of Club Culture*. London: Headline Publishing Group.

Garrett, Paul Michael (2009). *'Transforming' Children's Services?: Social Work, Neoliberalism and the 'Modern' World*. Maidenhead: Open University Press.

Garrett, Paul M. (2007a). ' "Sinbin" Solutions: The "Pioneer" Projects for "Problem Families" and the Forgetfulness of Social Policy Research'. *Critical Social Policy*, 27(2): 203–30.

Garrett, Paul. M. (2007b). ' "Sinbin" Research and the "Lives of Others": A Rejoinder in an Emerging and Necessary Debate'. *Critical Social Policy*, 27(4): 560–64.

Garside, Patricia L. (1993). 'Housing Needs, Family Values and Single Homeless People'. *Policy and Politics*, 21(4): 319–28.

Gatrell, V[ictor] A.C. (1994). *The Hanging Tree: Execution and the English People 1770–1868*. Oxford: Oxford University Press.

Gatrell, V[ictor] A.C. (1990). 'Crime, Authority and the Policeman-State'. In F[rancis] M.L. Thompson (ed.). *The Cambridge Social History of Britain, 1750–1950, Volume 3: Social Agencies and Institutions*, Cambridge: Cambridge University Press, 243–310.

Gillies, Val (2005). 'Meeting Parents' Needs? Discourses of "Support" and "Inclusion" in Family Policy'. *Critical Social Policy*, 25(1): 70–90.

Gillis, John (1975). 'The Evolution of Juvenile Delinquency in England 1890–1914'. *Past and Present*, 67(1): 96–126.

Gilpin, William (1786). *Observations, Relative Chiefly to Picturesque Beauty, Made in the Year 1772, On Several Parts of England; Particularly the Mountains and Lakes of Cumberland and Westmoreland, Volume 1*. London: R. Blamire.

Gil-Robles, Alvaro (2005). *Report by the Commissioner for Human Rights on his Visit to the United Kingdom, 4th–12th November, 2004*, CommDH(2005)6. Strasbourg: Council of Europe.

Girardet, Raoul (1986). *Mythes et Mythologies Politiques*. Paris: Seuil.

Girling, Evi; Loader, Ian and Sparks, Richard (2000). *Crime and Social Change in Middle England: Questions of Order in an English Town*. London: Routledge.

Glass, Norman (1999). 'Sure Start: The Development of an Early Intervention Programme for Young Children in the United Kingdom'. *Children & Society*, 13(4): 257–64.

Gofton, Les (1990). 'On the Town: Drink and the New Lawlessness'. *Youth and Policy*, 29(April): 33–9.

Goode, Erich and Ben-Yehuda, Nachman (1994). *Moral Panics: The Social Construction of Deviance*. Oxford: Wiley-Blackwell.

Gornall, Jonathan (2014). 'Under the Influence'. *British Medical Journal*, (348): f7646 (http://www.bmj.com/content/348/bmj.f7646?tab=citation).

Gorringe, Hugo and Rosie, Michael (2011). 'King Mob: Perceptions, Prescriptions and Presumptions about the Policing of England's Riots'. *Sociological Research Online*, 16(4) (http://www.socresonline.org.uk/16/4/17.html).

Gove, Michael (2011). Speech. Durand Academy. London. 1 September (www.education.gov.uk/inthenews/speeches/a00197684/michael-gove-to-the-durand-academy).

Graham, John (2000). 'Drug Markets and Neighbourhood Regeneration'. London: London School of Economics (LSE unpublished paper).

Greenaway, John (2003). *Drink and British Politics since 1830. A Study in Policy Making*. Basingstoke: Palgrave Macmillan.

Greenslade, Roy (2011a). 'London Riots Attract International Coverage'. *The Guardian*, 9 August (http://www.guardian.co.uk/media/greenslade/2011/aug/09/london-riots-newspapers).

Greenslade, Roy (2011b). 'How the Newspapers Headlined the London Riots'. *The Guardian*, 9 August (http://www.guardian.co.uk/media/greenslade/2011/aug/09/national-newspapers-london-riots).

Greenwood, James (1869). *The Seven Curses of London*. London: Stanley Rivers.

Greer, Germain (2007). 'What Should We Do About Graffiti?: Instead of spending a fortune getting rid of it, why don't we just give it marks out of 10?' *The Guardian*, 24 September (www.theguardian.com/artanddesign/artblog/2007/sep/24/whatshouldwedoaboutgraffiti).

Gregg, David (2010). *Family Intervention Projects: A Classic Case of Policy-based Evidence*. London: Centre for Crime and Justice Studies (CCJS) (http://www.crimeandjustice.org.uk/opus1786/Family_intervention_projects.pdf).

Gregson, Keith (1983) 'Songs of Horseracing on Tyneside'. *North East Labour History*, 17: 13.

Groome, Francis H. (1881). *In Gypsy Tents*. London: W.P. Nimmo & Company.

Guardian (The) / London School of Economics (LSE) (2011). *Reading the Riots. Investigating England's Summer of Disorder*. London: Guardian Shorts.

Gullickson, Gay, L. (1996). *Unruly Women of Paris: Images of the Commune.* Ithaca: Cornell University Press.

Guy, Josephine (ed.) (1998). *The Victorian Age: An Anthology of Sources and Documents.* London: Routledge.

Hacking, Ian (1986). 'Making up People'. In Thomas Heller, Morton Sosna and David Wellbery (eds). *Reconstructing Individualism: Autonomy, Individuality, and the Self in Western Thought.* Stanford: Stanford University Press, 222–36.

Hacking, Ian (1996). 'The Looping Effects of Human Kinds'. In Dan Sperber, David Premack and Anne Premack (eds). *Causal Cognition: A Multidisciplinary Approach.* Oxford: Oxford University Press, 351–83.

Hacking, Ian (2007). 'Kinds of People: Moving Targets'. *Proceedings-British Academy.* 151: 285–31.

Hadfield, Phil (2006). *Bar Wars: Contesting the Night in Contemporary British Cities.* Oxford: Oxford University Press.

Halfacree, Keith (1996). 'Out of Place in the Country: Travellers and the "Rural Idyll" '. *Antipode,* 28(1): 42–72.

Hall, Nicholas (2013). *Strategic Assessment 2013.* Richmond upon Thames, Community Safety Partnership (www.richmond.gov.uk/strategic_assessment_2013.pdf).

Hall, Peter (1998). *Cities in Civilization.* London: Weidenfeld & Nicolson.

Hall, Stuart; Critcher, Chas; Jefferson, Tony; Clarke, John and Roberts, Brian (1978). *Policing the Crisis. Mugging, the State and Law and Order.* Basingstoke: Palgrave Macmillan.

Hall, Wayne and Lynskey, Michael (2005). 'Is Cannabis a Gateway Drug? Testing Hypotheses about the Relationship between Cannabis Use and the Use of other Illicit Drugs'. *Drug and Alcohol Review,* 24(1): 39–48.

Hancock, Lynn and Mooney, Gerry (2012). 'Beyond the Penal State: Advanced Marginality, Social Policy and Anti-welfarism'. In Peter Squires and John Lea (eds). *Criminalisation and Advanced Marginality.* Bristol: Policy Press.

Hancox, Dan (2011a). *Fight Back! A Reader on the Winter of Protest.* London: OpenDemocracy.

Hancox, Dan (2011b). *Kettled Youth. The Battle Against the Neoliberal Endgame.* Summer of Unrest series. Vintage Digital.

Hancox, Dan (2011c). 'Kettling has Radicalised Britain's Youth'. *The Guardian,* 15 April (http://www.theguardian.com/commentisfree/2011/apr/15/kettling-radicalises-youth).

Hansard (http://hansard.millbanksystems.com).

Harcourt, Bernard E. (2001). *Illusion of Order: The False Promise of Broken Windows Policing.* Cambridge MA: Harvard University Press.

Harding, Allison and Harding, Jamie (2006). 'Inclusion and Exclusion in the Re-housing of Former Prisoners'. *Probation Journal,* 53(2): 139–53.

Harding, Jamie; Irving, Adele; Fitzpatrick, Suzanne and Pawson, Hal (2013). *Evaluation of Newcastle's 'Co-operative' Approach to the Prevention and Management of Homelessness in the Light of Changing Government Policy* (https://docs.google.com/file/d/0B-LgwFproy7odHhZQ0ZSWUVMS1U/edit?usp=sharing&pli=1).

Harding, Simon (2012). 'A Reputational Extravaganza? The Role of the Urban Street Gang in the Riots in London'. *Criminal Justice Matters,* 87(1): 22–3.

Harling, Philip (2001). 'The Law of Libel and the Limits of Repression, 1790–1832'. *Historical Journal,* 44(1): 107–34.

Harrison, Brian (1965). 'The Sunday Trading Riots of 1855'. *Historical Journal,* 8(2): 219–45.

Harrison, Brian (1971/1994). *Drink and the Victorians: The Temperance Question in England 1815–1872*. Keele: Keele University Press. 2nd edition.

Harrison, J[ohn] F.C. (1971). *The Early Victorians 1832–1851*. London: Weidenfeld & Nicolson.

Hartless, Julie; Ditton, Jason; Nair, Gwyneth and Phillips, Samuel (1995). 'More Sinned Against than Sinned'. *British Journal of Criminology*, 35(1): 114–33.

Hay, Colin (2007). *Why We Hate Politics*. Cambridge: Polity Press.

Hayden, Carole and Martin, Denis (eds) (2011). *Crime, Anti-Social Behaviour and Schools*. Basingstoke: Palgrave Macmillan.

Hayton, Richard (2012). 'Fixing Broken Britain'. In Timothy Hepple and David Seawright (eds). *Cameron and the Conservatives: The Transition to Coalition Government*. Basingstoke: Palgrave Macmillan.

Hayward, Keith and Yar, Majid (2006). 'The "Chav" Phenomenon: Consumption, Media and the Construction of a New Underclass'. *Crime, Media, Culture*, 2(1): 9–28.

Haywood, James (2011). 'The Significance of Millbank'. In Clare Solomon and Tania Palmieri (eds). *Springtime. The New Student Rebellions*. London: Verso, 69–70.

Healy, William (1915). *The Individual Delinquent. A Text-book of Diagnosis and Prognosis for all Concerned in Understanding Offenders*. Boston: Little, Brown and Co.

Heartfield, James (2002). *The 'Death of the Subject' Explained*. Sheffield: Sheffield Hallam University Press.

Heath, Deana (2010). *Purifying Empire: Obscenity and the Politics of Moral Regulation in Britain, India and Australia*. New York: Cambridge University Press.

Heins, Marjorie (1993). *Sex, Sin and Blasphemy: A Guide to America's Censorship Wars*. New York: Norton.

Helm, Toby (2013). 'New Asbos Will Punish Children for Being Children'. *The Observer*, 13 October (http://www.theguardian.com/society/2013/oct/13/asbo-ipna-punish-children).

Helm, Toby; Townsend, Mark and Asthana, Anushka (2010). 'Student Protests Set Stage for Winter Wave of Unrest'. *The Observer*, 14 November (http://www.theguardian.com/society/2010/nov/14/millbank-student-protests-analysis).

Henley, John (2011). 'The UK Riots and Language: "Rioter", "Protester" or "Scum"?' *The Guardian*, 10 August (http://www.guardian.co.uk/uk/2011/aug/10/uk-riots-language).

Her Majesty's Inspectorate of Constabulary (HMIC) (2009). *Adapting to Protest. Nurturing the British Model of Policing*. London: HMIC.

Hillyard, Paddy and Tombs, Steve (2008). 'Beyond Criminology'. In Danny Dorling, David Gordon, Paddy Hillyard, Christina Pantazis, Simon Pemberton and Steve Tombs (eds). *Criminal Obsessions: Why Harm Matters more than Crime*. 2nd edn. London: Centre for Crime and Justice Studies (CCJS).

Hillyard, Paddy; Pantazis, Christina; Tombs, Steve and Gordon, Dave (eds) (2004). *Beyond Criminology: Taking Harm Seriously*. London: Pluto Press.

Himmelfarb, Gertrude (1989). *Marriage and Morals among the Victorians*. London: I.B. Tauris and Co. Ltd.

Himmelfarb, Gertrude (1991). *Poverty and Compassion: The Moral Imagination of the Late Victorians*. New York: Alfred Knopf.

HM Government (2011a). *Vision to end Rough Sleeping: No Second Night out Nationwide*. London: The Stationery Office (TSO) (https://www.gov.uk/government/uploads/system/uploads/attachment_data/file/6261/1939099.pdf).

HM Government (2011b). *Ending Gang and Youth Violence: A Cross-Government Report.* London: The Stationery Office.

HM Revenue and Customs (2012). *A General Anti-Abuse Rule: Consultation Document* (http://customs.hmrc.gov.uk/channelsPortalWebApp/downloadFile?contentID=HMCE_PROD1_032113)

Hobbs, Dick; Hadfield, Philip; Lister, Stuart and Winlow, Simon (2003). *Bouncers: Violence and Governance in the Night-time Economy.* Oxford: Oxford University Press.

Hogg, Michael A. and Mullin, Barbara A. (1999). 'Joining Groups to Reduce Uncertainty: Subjective Uncertainty Reduction and Group Identification'. In Dominic Abrams and Michael Hogg (eds). *Social Identity and Social Cognition.* Oxford: Blackwell, 249–79.

Holloway, Sarah (2005). 'Articulating Otherness? White Rural Residents Talk about Gypsy-Travellers'. *Transactions*, 30(3): 351–67.

Holmwood, John (ed.) (2011). *A Manifesto for the Public University.* London: Bloomsbury Academic.

Holt, Richard (1992). *Sport and the British: A Modern History.* Oxford: Clarendon Press.

Home Affairs Select Committee House of Commons (2005). *Anti-Social Behaviour,* fifth Report of Session 2004–05. HC 80–1. London: The Stationery Office.

Home Office (1998). *Tackling Drugs to Build a Better Britain: The Government's 10-year Strategy for Tackling Drug Misuse.* London: The Stationery Office.

Home Office (2002a). *Liquor Licensing England and Wales July 2000–June 2001.* London: The Stationery Office.

Home Office (2002b). *Truancy and Crime: Tackling it Together.* Video listed on the British Institute of Films website (http://ftvdb.bfi.org.uk/sift/title/845760).

Home Office (2003). *Respect and Responsibility – Taking a Stand Against Anti-Social Behaviour.* London: The Stationery Office.

Home Office (2004). *Defining and Measuring Anti-Social Behaviour.* London: The Stationery Office.

Home Office (2006). *Guide to Anti-social Behaviour Orders.* London: The Stationery Office.

Home Office (2010a). *Crime in England and Wales, 2009–10.* London: The Stationery Office (http://www.homeoffice.gov.uk/publications/science-research-statistics/research-statistics/crime-research/hosb1210/hosb1210?view=Binary).

Home Office (2010b). *More Effective Responses to Antisocial Behaviour.* London: The Stationery Office (http://www.homeoffice.gov.uk/publications/consultations/cons-2010-antisocial-behaviour/asb-consultation-document?view=Binary).

Home Office (2011a). *National Standard for Incident Recording 2011.* London: The Stationery Office.

Home Office (2011b). *An Overview of Recorded Crimes and Arrests Resulting from Disorder Events in August 2011.* London: The Stationery Office (https://www.gov.uk/government/uploads/system/uploads/attachment_data/file/116257/overview-disorder-aug2011.pdf).

Home Office (2012a). *Alcohol and Late Night Refreshment Licensing England and Wales.* London: The Stationery Office.

Home Office (2012b). *Putting Victims First: More Effective Responses to Anti-Social Behaviour,* CM 8367. London: The Stationery Office.

Home Office (2012c). *The Government's Alcohol Strategy.* London. The Stationery Office.

Home Office (2013). *Alcohol and Late Night Refreshment Licensing in England and Wales 31st March 2013.* London: The Stationery Office.

Home, Robert (2006). 'The Planning System and the Accommodation Needs of Gypsies'. In Colin Clark and Margaret Greenfields (eds). *Here to Stay: The Gypsies and Travellers of Britain*. Hatfield: University of Hertfordshire Press, 90–107.

Hooper, J.F. (1890). 'A Word on Etiquette'. *Royal Cornwall Gazette*, 6 March.

Hopkins, Matt (2013). 'Ten Seasons of the Football Banning Order: Police Officer Narratives on the Operation of Banning Orders and the Impact on the Behaviour of "Risk Supporters" '. *Policing and Society*, 24(3): 285–301.

Hoppen, Karl T. (1998). *The Mid-Victorian Generation 1856–1886*. Oxford: Oxford University Press.

Horn, Pamela (1980). *The Rural World (1780–1850): Social Change in the English Countryside*. London: Hutchinson University Press.

Horn, Pamela (2010). *The Victorian and Edwardian Schoolchild*. Stroud: Amberley.

Hostettler, John (2009). *A History of Criminal Justice in England and Wales*. Hook: Waterside Press.

Hotaling, Gerald T. (1980). 'Attribution Processes in Husband–Wife Violence'. In Murray Arnold Strauss and Gerald T. Hotaling (eds). *The Social Causes of Husband–Wife Violence*. Minneapolis: University of Minneapolis Press, 136–54.

House of Commons Library (2013a). *Anti-social Behaviour, Crime and Policing Bill. Research Paper 13/34*. London: House of Commons Library.

House of Commons Library (2013b). *Anti-social Neighbours in Private Housing*. London: House of Commons Library.

House of Lords Select Committee on Religious Offences in England and Wales (2003). *Report*.

Hudson, John and Kühner, Stefan (2009). 'Towards Productive Welfare'. *Journal of European Social Policy*, 19(1): 34–46.

Huggins, Mike (2000). *Flat Racing and British Society 1790–1914: A Social and Economic History*. London: Frank Cass.

Hughes, Nathan (2010). 'An Alternative Approach to Tackling "Anti-social" Youth: The Case of Victoria, Australia'. *ECAN Bulletin*, 4(6): 9–12.

Hughes, Nathan (2011). 'Young People "as Risk" or Young People "at Risk": Comparing Discourses of Anti-social Behaviour in England and Victoria'. *Critical Social Policy*, 31(3): 388–409.

Humphreys, Robert (1999). *No Fixed Abode: A History of Responses to the Roofless and the Rootless in Britain*. Basingstoke: Palgrave Macmillan.

Hunt, Alan (1999). *Governing Morals: A Social History of Moral Regulation*. Cambridge: Cambridge University Press.

Hunt, Geoffrey; Mellor, Jenny and Turner, Janet (1989). 'Wretched, Hatless and Miserably Clad: Women and the Inebriate Reformatories from 1900–1913'. *British Journal of Sociology*, 40(2): 244–70.

Hunt, Tristram (2004). *Building Jerusalem: The Rise and Fall of the Victorian City*. Harmondsworth: Penguin.

Hyman, Gwen (2008) ' "An Infernal Fire in My Veins": Gentlemanly Drinking in The Tenant of Wildfell Hall'. *Victorian Literature and Culture*, 36(2): 451–70.

Independent Commission on Youth Crime and Anti-social Behaviour (2010). *Time for a Fresh Start: The Report of the London Independent Commission on Youth Crime and Anti-social Behaviour*. London: The Police Foundation.

Independent Police Complaints Commission (IPPC) (2011). 'IPCC Partially Upholds Appeal by Jody McIntyre'. 24 August (http://www.ipcc.gov.uk/news/ipcc-partially-upholds-appeal-jody-mcintyre).

Innes, Martin (2004). 'Crime as a Signal, Crime as a Memory'. *Journal for Crime, Conflict and the Media*, 1(2): 15–22.

Innes, Martin and Fielding, Nigel (2002). 'From Community to Communicative Policing: "Signal Crimes" and the Problem of Public Reassurance'. *Sociological Research Online*, 7(2) (www.socresonline.org.uk/7/2/innes.html).

INQUEST (2012). 'Deaths in Police Custody or Otherwise Following Contact with the Police, England & Wales 1990–date' (http://www.inquest.org.uk).

Inwood, Stephen (1990). 'Policing London's Morals: The Metropolitan Police and Popular Culture, 1829–1850'. *London Journal*, 15(2): 129–46.

Irish Traveller Movement in Britain (ITMB) (2012). *Gypsies and Travellers in the Press*, Submission by the Irish Traveller Movement in Britain to the Leveson Inquiry. April 2012 (http://www.levesoninquiry.org.uk/wp-content/uploads/2012/07/Submission-from-The-Irish-Traveller-Movement-March-2012.pdf).

Irvine, Chris (2010). 'Government Announces Crackdown on Anti-social Behaviour by Gypsies', *The Telegraph*, 23 March (http://www.telegraph.co.uk/news/politics/6758043/Government-announces-crackdown-on-anti-social-behaviour-by-gypsies.html).

Isal, Sarah (2006). *Equal Respect. ASBOs and Race Equality*. London: The Runnymede Trust.

Ismail, Feyzi (2011). 'The Politics of Occupation'. In Michael Bailey and Des Freedman. *The Assault on Universities. A Manifesto for Resistance*. London: Pluto Press, 123–31.

Jacobson, Jessica; Millie, Andrew and Hough, Mike (2008). 'Why Tackle Anti-social Behaviour?' In Peter Squires (ed.). *ASBO Nation: The Criminalisation of Nuisance*. Bristol: Policy Press, 37–56.

James, Mark (2013). *Sports Law*. Basingstoke: Palgrave Macmillan.

James, Mark and Pearson, Geoff (2006). 'Football Banning Orders: Analysing their Use in Court'. *Journal of Criminal Law*, 70(6): 509–30.

James, Zoe (2007). 'Policing Marginal Spaces: Controlling Gypsies and Travellers'. *Criminology and Criminal Justice*, 7(4): 367–89.

Jamieson, Janet (2012). 'Bleak Times for Children? The Anti-social Behaviour Agenda and the Criminalization of Social Policy'. *Social Policy and Administration*, 46(4): 448–64.

Jarman, Neil (2004). 'From War to Peace? Changing Patterns of Violence in Northern Ireland 1990–2003'. *Terrorism and Political Violence*, 16(3): 420–38.

Jenkins, Philip (1992). *Intimate Enemies: Moral Panics in Contemporary Great Britain*. New York: Walter de Gruyter.

Jerram, Leif (2011). *Streetlife. The Untold History of Europe's Twentieth Century*. Oxford: Oxford University Press.

Jeyes, S.H. (1892). 'Foreign Pauper Immigration'. In Arnold White (ed.). *The Destitute Alien in Great Britain*. London: Swan Sonnenschein & Co Ltd, 189–91.

Johnstone, Gerry (1996). 'From Vice to Disease? The Concepts of Dipsomania and Inebriety, 1860, 1908'. *Social and Legal Studies*, 5(1): 37–56.

Jones, Trevor; Maclean, Brian and Young, Jock (1986). *The Islington Crime Survey*. Aldershot: Gower.

Jones, David (1982). *Crime, Protest, Community and Police in Nineteenth-Century Britain*. London: Routledge & Kegan Paul.

Jones, Owen (2011). *CHAVS: The Demonization of the Working Class*. London: Verso.

Jordon, Bill (1974). *Poor Parents: Social Policy and the 'Cycle of Deprivation'*. London: Routledge.

Kabachnik, Peter and Ryder, Andrew (2013). 'Nomadism and the 2003 Anti-Social Behaviour Act: Constraining Gypsy and Traveller Mobilities in Britain'. *Romani Studies*, 23(1): 83–106.

Kant, Immanuel (1790/2011). 'Extracts from "Analytic of Aesthetic Judgment" and "Dialectic of Aesthetic Judgment", Critique of Judgment'. In Clive Cazeaux (ed.). *The Continental Aesthetics Reader*. Second edition, Abingdon: Routledge, 3–39.

Kasson, John F. (1990). *Rudeness and Civility: Manners in Nineteenth-Century Urban America*. New York: Hill & Wang.

Kavanagh, Dennis (1989). *Consensus Politics from Attlee to Thatcher*. Oxford: Wiley-Blackwell.

Kean, Arnold W.G. (1937). 'The History of the Criminal Liability of Children'. *Law Quarterly Review*, liii: 364–70.

Kelling, George and Wilson, James (1982). 'Broken Windows: The Police and Neighbourhood Safety'. *The Atlantic*, 1 March (http://www.theatlantic.com/magazine/archive/1982/03/broken-windows/304465).

Kelling, George L. (2001). ' "Broken Windows" and the Culture Wars: A Response to Selected Critiques'. In Roger Matthews and John Pitts (eds). *Crime, Disorder and Community Safety: A New Agenda?* London: Routledge, 120–44.

Kendall, Sally; Kinder, Kay and White, Richard (2003). *School Attendance and the Prosecution of Parents: Perspectives from Education Welfare Service Management: First Report*. Slough: National Foundation for Educational Research.

Kilminster, Richard (1998). *The Sociological Revolution: From the Enlightenment to the Global Age*. London: Routledge.

Kilminster, Richard (2008). 'Narcissism or Informalization? Christopher Lasch, Norbert Elias and Social Diagnosis'. *Theory, Culture and Society*, 25(3): 131–51.

Kilminster, Richard (2014). 'The Dawn of Detachment: Norbert Elias and Sociology's Two Tracks', *History of the Human Sciences* (http://hhs.sagepub.com).

King, Anthony (2001). *The End of the Terraces: The Transformation of English Football in the 1990s*. Leicester: Leicester University Press.

King, Laura J. (1993). 'Matrons, Maidens and Magdalenes, Women's Patronage of Nineteenth Century London Music Halls'. Master's dissertation, Simon Fraser University, Vancouver, 1993.

King, Peter (1999). 'The Rise of Delinquency in England, 1780–1840'. *Past and Present*, clx: 116–66.

Kirbee, Terry (1993). 'Police Welcome Support for Moves to Curb Youth Crime'. *The Independent*, 5 February: 18.

Kirkup, James (2007). 'Ministers Abandon Truancy Targets'. *Daily Telegraph*. 25 October (http://www.telegraph.co.uk/news/uknews/1567240/Ministers-abandon-truancy-targets.html).

Kisby, Ben (2010). 'The Big Society: Power to the People?' *Political Quarterly*, 81(4): 484–91.

Klein, Axel (2012). 'Policing as a Causal Factor: A Fresh View on Riots and Social Unrest'. *Safer Communities*, 11(1): 17–23.

Knell, B.E.F. (1965). 'Capital Punishment: Its Administration in Relation to Juvenile Offenders in the Nineteenth Century and its Possible Administration in the Eighteenth'. *British Journal of Criminology, Delinquency and Deviant Social Behaviour*, 5(2): 198–207.

Knelman, Judith (1998). *Twisting in the Wind: The Murderess and the English Press*. Toronto: Toronto University Press.

Knepper, Paul (2009). *The Invention of International Crime. A Global Issue in the Making, 1881–1914*. Basingstoke: Palgrave Macmillan.

Knox, Colin (2001). 'Establishing Research Legitimacy in the Contested Political Ground of Contemporary Northern Ireland'. *Qualitative Research*, 1(2): 205–22.

Knox, Colin (2002). ' "See No Evil Hear No Evil": Insidious Paramilitary Violence in Northern Ireland'. *British Journal of Criminology*, 42(1): 164–85.

Knox, Colin (2003). ' "Joined-up" Government: An Integrated Response to Communal Violence in Northern Ireland?' *Policy & Politics*, 3(1): 19–35.

Kohn, Marek (1992). *Dope Girls: The Birth of the British Underground*. London: Granta Books.

Korsmeyer, Carolyn (2005). 'Taste'. In Berys Gaut and Dominic McIver Lopes (eds). *The Routledge Companion to Aesthetics*. 2nd Edition, London: Routledge, 267–79.

Kubiak, Chris and Hester, Richard (2009). 'Just Deserts? Developing Practice in Youth Justice'. *Learning in Health and Social Care*, 8(1): 47–57.

Kumar, Ashok (2011). 'Achievements and Limitations of the UK Student Movement'. In Michael Bailey and Des Freedman. *The Assault on Universities. A Manifesto for Resistance*. London: Pluto Press: 132–42.

Labour Party (1997). Labour Party Manifesto. *New Labour: Because Britain Deserves Better*.

Labour Party (1997, 2010). Election manifestoes, London: Labour Party (http://www.labour-party.org.uk/manifestos).

Laïdi, Zaki (1998). *A World without Meaning*. London: Routledge.

Lasch, Christopher (1977). *Haven in a Heartless World*. New York: Basic Books.

Law, Alex and Gerry Mooney (2005). 'Urban Landscapes'. *International Socialism*, 106 (http://www.isj.org.uk/index.php4?id=95&issue=106).

Lawless, Paul and Brown, Frank (1986). *Urban Growth and Change in Britain: An Introduction*. London: Harper & Row.

Lawrence, Paul (2004). 'Policing the Poor in England and France, 1850–1900'. In Clive Emsley, Eric Johnson and Pieter Spierenburg (eds). *Social Control in Europe. v.2: 1800–2000*. Columbus: Ohio State University Press, 210–25.

Lee, Catherine (2013). *Policing Prostitution, 1856–1886*. London: Chatto and Pickering.

Lee, Christopher Paul (1995). 'And Then there Were None: Government Legislation and Manchester Beat Clubs 1965'. Critical Musicology Conference. Salford.

Lee, Murray (2007). *Inventing Fear of Crime: Criminology and the Politics of Fear*. Cullompton: Willan Publishing.

Lefebvre, Henri (1961/2008). *Critique of Everyday Life, Introduction. Volume 1.* [Translated by John Moore.] London: Verso.

Lessing, Doris (1969/1972). *The Four-Gated City*. London: Granada Publishing.

Levine, Mark; Cassidy, Clare; Brazier, Gemma and Reicher, Stephen (2002). 'Self-Categorization and Bystander Non-intervention: Two Experimental Studies'. *Journal of Applied Social Psychology*, 32(7): 1452–63.

Levitas, Ruth (1996). 'The Concept of Social Exclusion and the New Durkheimian Hegemony'. *Critical Social Policy*, 16(46): 5–20.

Levitas, Ruth (1999). 'New Labour and Social Exclusion'. Citizenship and Social Exclusion Panel (http://www.psa.ac.uk/cps/1999/levitas.pdf).

Levitas, Ruth (2012). *There may be 'Trouble' Ahead: What we Know about Those 120,000 'Troubled' Families'*, Poverty and Social Exclusion (PSE) in the UK Policy Working Paper No.3, 21 February (http://www.poverty.ac.uk/policy-response-working-paper-families-social-justice-life-chances-children-parenting-uk-government).

Lewis, E.O. (1933). 'Types of Mental Deficiency and Their Social Significance', *Journal of Mental Science*, 79: 298–304.

Lewis, Paul; Taylor, Matthew and Ball, James (2011). 'Kenneth Clarke blames English Riots on a "Broken Penal System"'. *The Guardian*, 5 September (http://www.guardian.co.uk/uk/2011/sep/05/kenneth-clarke-riots-penal-system).

Liberal Democrats (The) (2010). *Liberal Democrat General Election Manifesto 2010. Change That Works for You: Building a Fairer Britain*. Liberal Democrat publications.

Linebaugh, Peter (1991). *The London Hanged: Crime and Civil Society in the 18th Century*. London: Allen Lane.

Lipsett, Anthea (2008). 'Truancy Rate Rises to 63,000 Pupils a Day'. *The Guardian*. 27 February (http://www.theguardian.com/education/2008/feb/27/schools.uk1).

Lister, Ruth (1996). *Charles Murray and the Underclass*. London: Institute of Economic Affairs, Health and Welfare Unit.

Lister, Ruth (2006). 'Children (but not women) First: New Labour, Child Welfare and Gender'. *Critical Social Policy*, 26(2): 315–35.

Lloyd, Cheryl; Wollny, Ivonne; White, Clarissa; Gowland, Sally and Purdon, Susan (2012). *Monitoring and Evaluation of Family Intervention Services and Projects Between February 2007 and March 2011*. London: Department for Education.

Lombroso, Cesare (1896). *Les Anarchistes*. Paris: Flammarion.

Lovatt, Andy (1996). 'The Ecstasy of Urban Regeneration: Regulation of the Night-time Economy in the Transition to a Post-Fordist City'. In Justin O'Connor and Derek Wynne (eds). *From the Margins to the Centre: Cultural Production and Consumption in the Post-Industrial City*. Aldershot: Arena, 141–68.

Luhmann, Niklas (1995). *Social Systems*. Stanford: Stanford University Press.

Lund, Brian (1996). *Housing Problems and Housing Policy*. Harlow: Longman.

Lundie, H. (1844). *The Phrenological Mirror; or, Delineation Book*. Leeds: C. Croshaw.

Lupton, Ruth; Wilson, Andrew; May, Tiggey; Warburton, Hamish and Turnbull, Paul (2002). '*A Rock and a Hard Place: Drug Markets in Deprived Neighbourhoods*'. London: Home Office Research Study 240.

Lycett, Andrew (2013). *Wilkie Collins: A Life of Sensation*. London: Random House.

Lyman, J.L. (1964). 'The Metropolitan Police Act of 1829'. *Journal of Criminal Law and Criminology*, LV: 141–54.

Mac Ginty, Roger (2004). 'Looting in the Context of Violent Conflict: A Conceptualisation and Typology'. *Third World Quarterly*, 25(5): 857–70.

MacDonald, Robert (ed.) (1997). *Youth, the Underclass and Social Exclusion*. London: Routledge.

MacDonald, Robert; Shildrick, Tracy and Blackman, Shane (eds) (2010). *Young People, Class and Place*. London: Routledge.

Macdonald, Stuart (2006). 'A Suicidal Woman, Roaming Pigs and a Noisy Trampolinist: Refining the ASBO's Definition of "Anti-social Behaviour"'. *Modern Law Review*, 69(2): 183–213.

Macintyre, Donald (1997). 'Labour Taskforce to Help Underclass'. *The Independent*, 14 August (http://www.independent.co.uk/news/labour-taskforce-to-help-underclass-1245298.html).

Mackenzie, Simon; Bannister, Jon; Flint, John; Parr, Sadie; Millie, Andrew and Fleetwood, Jennifer (2010). *The Drivers of Perceptions of Anti-Social Behaviour*. Home Office Research Report 34. London: Home Office.

Macleod, Roy (1967). 'The Edge of Hope: Social Policy and Chronic Alcoholism. 1870–1900'. *Journal of the History of Medicine*, 22(3): 215–45.

Macnicol, John (1999). 'From "Problem Family" to "Underclass", 1945–1995'. In Helen Fawcett and Rodney Law (eds). *Welfare Policy in Britain: The Road from 1945*. Basingstoke: Macmillan.

Magarey, Susan (1978). 'The Invention of Juvenile Delinquency in Early Nineteenth-Century England'. *Labour History*, xxxiv: 11–27.

Major, John (1993). Interview in the *Mail on Sunday*, 21 February.

Malcolmson, Robert W. (1973). *Popular Recreations in English Society 1700–1850*. Cambridge: Cambridge University Press.

Maloney, Paul (2003). *Scotland and the Music Hall 1850 to 1914*. Manchester: Manchester University Press.

Manders, Gary (2009). 'The Use of Anti-social Behaviour Powers with Vulnerable Groups: Some Recent Research'. *Social Policy & Society*, 9(1): 145–53.

Mandler, Peter (2000). ' "Race" and "nation" in mid-Victorian Thought'. In *History, Religion and Culture: British Intellectual History, 1750–1950*. Stefan Collini, Richard Whatmore and Brian Young (eds). Cambridge: Cambridge University Press, 224–44.

Mannheim, Hermann (1946). *Criminal Justice and Social Reconstruction*. London: Routledge & Kegan Paul.

Manning, Peter K. (1980). 'Violence and the Police Role'. *The Annals of the American Academy of Political and Social Science*, 452(1): 135–44.

Marne, Pauline (2001). 'Whose Public Space Was It Anyway? Class, Gender and Ethnicity in the Creation of the Sefton and Stanley Parks, Liverpool'. *Social and Cultural Geography*, 2(4): 421–43.

Marx, Roland (1987). *Jack l'Eventreur et les Fantasmes Victoriens*. Paris: Complexe.

Mason, Paul (2010). 'Dubstep Rebellion. The British Banlieue Comes to Millbank'. *BBC, Newsnight, Paul Mason's Blog*. 9 December (http://www.bbc.co.uk/blogs/newsnight/paulmason/2010/12/9122010_dubstep_rebellion_-_br.html).

Mason, Paul (2013). *Why it's Still Kicking off Everywhere: The New Global Revolutions*. Updated edition. London: Verso.

Mass Observation (1943). *The Pub and the People: A Worktown Study*. London: Victor Gollancz Ltd.

Matthews, Glen (1986). 'The Search for a Cure for Vagrancy in Worcestershire, 1870–1920'. *Midland History*, 11: 100–16.

Matthews, Roger and Young, Jock (1986). *Confronting Crime*. London: Sage.

May, Margaret (1973). 'Innocence and Experience: The Evolution of the Concept of Juvenile Delinquency in the Mid-nineteenth Century'. *Victorian Studies*, xvii: 7–29.

May, Theresa (2012). 'Home Secretary Foreword'. In Home Office (2012). *Putting Victims First: More Effective Responses to Anti-Social Behaviour*. Cm 8367. London: The Stationery Office.

Mayall, David (2004). *Gypsy Identities 1500–2000: From Egipcyans and Moon-men to the Ethnic Romany*. London: Routledge.

Mayhew, Henry (1861). *London Labour and the London Poor*. London: Griffin, Bohn & Company.

Mayhew, Henry (1864). *German Life and Manners as seen in Saxony at the Present Day*. London: W.H. Allen and Co.

McAra, Lesley and McVie, Susan (2010). 'The Usual Suspects? Street-Life, Young People and the Police'. *Criminology and Criminal Justice*, 5(1): 5–36.

McEvoy, Kieran and Mika, Harry (2002). 'Restorative Justice and the Critique of Informalism in Northern Ireland'. *British Journal of Criminology*, 42(3): 534–62.

McGowen, Randall (2007). 'Cruel Inflictions and the Claims of Humanity in Early Nineteenth-Century England'. In Katherine D. Watson (ed.). *Assaulting the Past: Violence and Civilization in Historical Context*. Cambridge: Cambridge Scholars Publishing, 38–57.

McGrattan, Cillian (2010). 'Community-Based Restorative Justice in Northern Ireland: A Neo-Traditionalist Paradigm?' *British Journal of Politics and International Relations*, 12(3): 408–24.

McIntyre, Andrew (2012). 'Ofcom Dismisses Big Fat Gypsy Wedding Complaints'. *New Statesman*, 20 March (http://www.newstatesman.com/broadcast/2012/03/gypsier-gypsy-code-ofcom).

McIntyre, Jody (2011). 'My Wheelchair is the Beginning'. In Clare Solomon and Tania Palmieri (eds). *Springtime. The New Student Rebellions*. London: Verso, 76–9.

McLaughlin, Patrick M. (1991). 'Inebriate Reformatories in Scotland: An Institutional History'. In Susanna Barrows and Robin Room. *Drinking. Behavior and Belief in Modern History*. Berkeley: University of California Press, 287–314.

McPhail, Clark (1971). 'Civil Disorder Participation'. *American Sociological Review*, 36(6): 1058–72.

McVeigh, Robbie (1997). 'Theorising Sedentarism: The Roots of Anti-nomadism'. In Thomas Acton (ed.). *Gypsy Politics and Traveller Identity*. Hatfield: University of Hertfordshire Press, 7–25.

Mearns, Rev. Andrew (1883). *The Bitter Cry of Outcast London: An Inquiry into the Condition of the Abject Poor*. London: James Clarke & Co.

Mennell, Stephen and Goudsblom, Joop (1998). *Norbert Elias: On Civilization, Power and Knowledge*. London: University of Chicago Press.

Metropolitan Police Service (2010). 'Protestors Urged to Think Carefully'. London: London Metropolitan Police, 29 November (http://content.met.police.uk/News/Protestors-urged-to-think-carefully/1260267890470/1257246745756).

Metropolitan Police Service (2011). 'MPS Response to G20 Judgement', London: London Metropolitan Police Service, 14 April (http://content.met.police.uk/News/MPS-response-to-G20-judgement/1260268832924/1257246741786).

Mika, Harry and McEvoy, Kieran (2001). 'Restorative Justice in Conflict: Paramilitarism, Community, and the Construction of Legitimacy in Northern Ireland'. *Contemporary Justice Review*, 4(3, 4): 291–319.

Mill, John Stuart (1856/1999). *On Liberty*. Oxford: Oxford University Press.

Mill, John Stuart (1869/2006). *The Subjection of Women*. Harmondsworth: Penguin.

Millie, Andrew (2008). 'Anti-social Behaviour, Behavioural Expectations and an Urban Aesthetic'. *British Journal of Criminology*, 48(3): 379–94.

Millie, Andrew (2009a). *Anti-Social Behaviour*. Maidenhead: Open University Press.

Millie, Andrew (ed.) (2009b). *Securing Respect: Behavioural Expectations and Anti-social Behaviour in the UK*. Bristol: Policy Press.

Millie, Andrew (2011). 'Value Judgments and Criminalization'. *British Journal of Criminology*, 51(2): 278–95.

Millie, Andrew (2012). 'Police Stations, Architecture and Public Reassurance'. *British Journal of Criminology*, 52(6): 1092–112.

Millie, Andrew (2013). 'Replacing the ASBO: An Opportunity to Stem the Flow into the Criminal Justice System'. In Anita Dockley and Ian Loader (ed.) *The Penal Landscape: The Howard League Guide to Criminal Justice in England and Wales*. London: Routledge, 64–88.

Mills, Charles Wright (1959). *The Sociological Imagination*. Oxford: Oxford University Press.

Mills, Charles Wright (1968). *Power Politics and People*. New York: Ballantine.

Mills, Heather (1995). 'Straw Sets Agenda for Reclaiming the Streets'. *The Independent*, 5 September (http://www.independent.co.uk/news/straw-sets-agenda-for-reclaiming-the-streets-1599506.html).

Ministry of Justice (MJ) (2010). 'Table 2.1: Number of Penalty Notices for Disorder, 2005–2009'. *Criminal Statistics: England and Wales 2009 Statistics Bulletin*. London: Ministry of Justice.

Ministry of Justice (MJ) (2011). *Statistical Notice: Anti-Social Behaviour Order (ASBO) Statistics England and Wales 2010*. London: Ministry of Justice.

Ministry of Justice (MJ) (2012). *Statistical Notice: Anti-Social Behaviour Order (ASBO) Statistics England and Wales 2011*. London: Ministry of Justice.

Ministry of Justice (MJ) (2013). *Statistical Notice: Anti-Social Behaviour Order (ASBO) Statistics: England and Wales 2012*. London: Ministry of Justice.

Minton, Anna (2006). *The Privatisation of Public Space*. London: Royal Institution of Chartered Surveyors.

Minton, Anna (2012). *Ground Control: Fear and Happiness in the Twenty-first-century City*. Harmondsworth: Penguin.

Mitchell, Don (2001). 'Postmodern Geographical Praxis? Postmodern Impulse and the War Against Homeless People in the "Post-Justice" City'. In Claudio Minca (ed.). *Postmodern Geography: Theory and Praxis*. Oxford: Blackwell, 57–92.

Mitchell, Gaye and Campbell, Lynda (2011). 'The Social Economy of Excluded Families'. *Child and Family Social Work*, 16(4): 422–33.

Monaghan, Rachel (2002). 'The Return of "Captain Moonlight": Informal Justice in Northern Ireland'. *Studies in Conflict & Terrorism*, 25(1): 41–56.

Monbiot, George (2000). *Captive State: The Corporate Takeover of Britain*. Basingstoke and New York: Palgrave Macmillan.

Moore, Stephen (2008). 'Street Life, Neighbourhood Policing and "The Community" '. In Peter Squires (ed.). *ASBO Nation: The Criminalisation of Nuisance*. Bristol: Policy Press, 179–202.

Morgan, Marjorie (1994). *Manners, Morals and Class in England, 1774–1858*. Basingstoke: Palgrave Macmillan.

Morgner, Christian (2010). 'The Public of Media Events'. MedieKultur. *Journal of Media and Communication Research*, 27(50): 143–59.

Morrell, Gareth; Scott, Sara; McNeish, Di and Webster, Stephen (2011). 'The August Riots in England: Understanding the Involvement of Young People. National Centre for Social Research (https://www.gov.uk/government/uploads/system/uploads/attachment_data/file/60531/The_20August_20Riots_20in_20England_20_pdf__201mb_.pdf).

Morris, Kate (2013). 'Troubled Families: Vulnerable Families Experiences of Multiple Service Use'. *Child and Family Social Work*, 18(2): 198–206.

Morris, Lydia (1994). *Dangerous Classes: The Underclass and Social Citizenship*. London: Routledge.

Morris, Rachel (1999). 'The Invisibility of Gypsies and other Travellers'. *Journal of Social Welfare and Family Law*, 21(4): 399–404.

Morris, Steven and Smithers, Rebecca (2002). 'Minister Hails Jailing of Mother whose Daughters Played Truant'. *The Guardian*. 14 May (http://www.theguardian.com/uk/2002/may/14/schools.publicservices).

Mortimer, Raymond (1958). *The Jockey Club*. London: Cassell.

Mulholland, Hélène (2011). 'Duncan Smith Blames Riots on Family Breakdown and Benefits system'. *The Guardian*, 3 October (http://www.guardian.co.uk/politics/2011/oct/03/duncan-smith-riots-benefits-system).

Mullen, John (2012). *'The Show Must Go On'. La Chanson Populaire en Grande-Bretagne Pendant la Grande Guerre 1914–1918*. Paris: L'Harmattan.

Mumford, Katharine (2001). 'Talking to Families in East London'. CASE Brief: London School of Economics (LSE) (http://eprints.lse.ac.uk/28302/1/CASEreport9.pdf).

Murray, Charles (1990). 'Underclass'. In Ruth Lister (ed.). *Charles Murray and the Underclass*. London: Institute of Economic Affairs Health and Welfare Unit, 23–53.

Murray, Charles (1990). *The Emerging British Underclass*. London: Institute of Economic Affairs.

Murray, Charles (2001). *Underclass + 10: Charles Murray and the British Underclass 1990–2000*. London: CIVITAS and *The Sunday Times*.

Myers, Daniel J. (2000). 'The Diffusion of Collective Violence: Infectiousness, Susceptibility, and the Mass Media Networks'. *American Journal of Sociology*, 106(1): 173–208.

Nash, David (1999). *Blasphemy in Modern Britain: 1789 to the Present*. Aldershot: Ashgate.

Nash, David (2010). *Blasphemy in the Christian World: A History*. Oxford: Oxford University Press.

National Archives of Scotland (1883). *Letters from Donald Grant to Alan MacDonald*. 20 June and 10 August. Edinburgh, GD176/2629 and /2631.

National Audit Office (NAO) (2003). *Making a Difference: Performance of Maintained Secondary Schools in England*. London: The Stationery Office (TSO).

National Audit Office (NAO) (2005). *Improving School Attendance in England*. London: The Stationery Office (TSO).

National Policing Improvement Agency (2010). *Guidance on Football Policing* (http://www.acpo.police.uk/documents/uniformed/2010/201008UNGPF01.pdf).

Nead, Lynda (2000). *Victorian Babylon: People, Streets and Images in Nineteenth-Century London*. New Haven and London: Yale University Press.

Nead, Lynda (2005). *People, Streets and Images in Nineteenth-Century London*. New Haven: Yale University Press.

Neocleous, Mark (2000). *The Fabrication of Social Order: A Critical Theory of Police Power*. London: Pluto Press.

Netpol (2012). *Report into the Policing of Protest 2010–2011* (http://netpol.files.wordpress.com/2012/07/wainwright-report-final1.pdf).

Netpol (2013). 'Protest Treated as Anti-social Behaviour'. 6 May (http://netpol.org/2013/05/01/protest-treated-as-anti-social-behaviour).

Newburn, Tim (2011). 'Policing Youth Anti-social Behaviour and Crime: Time for Reform'. *Journal of Children's Services*. 6(2): 96–105.

Nicholls, James (2009). *The Politics of Alcohol: A History of the Drinks Question in England*. Manchester: Manchester University Press.

Nicholls, James (2011). *Wine, Supermarkets and British Alcohol Policy* (http://www.historyandpolicy.org/papers/policy-paper-110.html).

Nichols, Thomas Low (1873). *How to Behave: A Manual of Manners and Morals*. London: Longman Green.

Nixon, Judy; Blandy, Sarah; Hunter, Caroline and Reeve, Kesia (2003). *Developing Good Practice in Tackling Anti-Social Behaviour in Mixed Tenure Areas*. Sheffield: Sheffield Hallam University.

Nixon, Judy; Hunter, Caroline; Parr, Sadie; Myers, Stephen; Whittle, Sue and Sanderson, Diana (2006). *Anti-social Behaviour Intensive Family Support Projects: An Evaluation of Six Pioneering Projects*. London: Office of the Deputy Prime Minister (ODPM).

Nolan, James (1998). *The Therapeutic State: Justifying Government at Century's End*. New York: New York University Press.

Nordau, Max (1892). *Entartung*. [Translated as *Degeneration*.] Berlin: Berlag von Carl Duncker. [London: William Heinemann, 1895].

O'Connor, Justin and Wynne, Derek (eds) (1996). *From the Margins to the Centre: Cultural Production and Consumption in the Post-Industrial City*. Aldershot: Arena.

Office for Standards in Education (Ofsted) (2007). *Attendance in Secondary Schools, Briefing Note*. London: Ofsted.

Ogborn, Miles (1993). 'Ordering the City: Surveillance, Public Space and the Reform of Urban Policing in England 1835–1856'. *Political Geography*, 12(6): 505–21.

Okely, Judith (1983). *The Traveller-Gypsies*. Cambridge: Cambridge University Press.

Olcese, Cristiana and Saunders, Claire (2014). 'Students in the Winter Protests: Still a New Social Movement?' In Sarah Pickard (ed.), *Higher Education in the UK and the US: Converging University Models in a Global Academic World?* Leiden/Boston: Brill, 250–73.

Orr, Deborah (2011). 'The Judge was Wrong in his Sentencing of Edward Woollard'. *The Guardian*, 13 January (http://www.theguardian.com/commentisfree/2011/jan/13/judge-wrong-in-sentencing-edward-woollard).

Orwell, George (1940/2000). *The Lion and the Unicorn*. Harmondsworth: Penguin.

Orwell, George (1970). 'Such, Such Were the Joys', *The Collected Essays, Journalism and Letters of George Orwell*, Volume IV. Harmondsworth: Penguin, 379–422.

Osvaldsson, Karin (2004). ' "I Don't Have No Damn Cultures": Doing "Normality" in a "Deviant" Setting'. *Qualitative Research in Psychology*, 1(3): 239–64.

Oswald, Janet (2012). 'The Spinning House Girls: Cambridge University's Distinctive Policing of Prostitution, 1823–1894'. *Urban History*, 39(3): 453–70.

Owen, Jeanette (2006). 'Heads Should have More say on Absences'. *The Guardian*. 21 March (http://www.theguardian.com/education/2006/mar/21/schoolgovernors.teaching).

Pain, Rachel (1995). 'Elderly Women and Fear of Violent Crime: The Least Likely Victims? *British Journal of Criminology*, 35(4): 584–98.

Paine, Thomas (2004). *The Age of Reason*. Mineola: Dover Publications.

Parker, Howard; Aldridge, Judith and Egginton, Roy (2001). *UK Drugs Unlimited: New Research and Policy Lessons on Illicit Drug Use*. Basingstoke: Palgrave Macmillan.

Parker, Howard; Williams, Lisa and Judith Aldridge (2002). 'The Normalization of "Sensible" Recreational Drug Use. Further Evidence from the North West England Longitudinal Study'. *Sociology*, 36(4): 941–64.

Parr, Sadie (2009). 'Confronting the Reality of Anti-Social Behaviour'. *Theoretical Criminology*, 13(3): 363–81.

Parr, Sadie (2009). 'Family Intervention Projects: A Site of Social Work Practice'. *British Journal of Social Work*, 39: 1256–73.

Parr, Sadie and Nixon, Judy (2008). 'Rationalising Family Intervention Projects'. In Peter Squires (ed.). *ASBO Nation: The Criminalisation of Nuisance*. Bristol: Policy Press, 161–78.

Parr, Sadie and Nixon, Judy (2009). 'Family Intervention Projects: Sites of Subversion and Resilience'. In Marian Barnes and David Prior (eds). *Subversive Citizens: Power, Agency and Resistance in Public Services*. Bristol: Policy Press, 101–18.

Parry, Glenys; van Cleemput, Patricia; Peters, Jean; Moore, Julia; Walters, Stephen; Thomas, Kate and Cindy Cooper (2004). *The Health Status of Gypsies and Travellers in England*. A Report for the Department of Health. The School of Health and Related Research (ScHARR): Sheffield: University of Sheffield.

Parsons, John Frederick and Young, John Anthony (1992). *Bournemouth's Victorian Schools. Forerunners of Education for All*. Bournemouth: Bournemouth Local Studies Publications.

Paterson, Alexander (1915). *Across the Bridges: Or Life by the South London River-side.* 2nd edition. London: Edwin Arnold.

Paterson, Craig and Allyson MacVean (2006). 'Understanding Deviant Lifestyles: Critically Evaluating Anti-social Behaviour and Problem Drug Use'. *Police Research and Management,* 6(3): 33–42.

Payne, Malcolm (2005). *The Origins of Social Work.* Basingstoke: Palgrave Macmillan.

Pearson, Carl (1892). *The Grammar of Science.* London: Walter Scott.

Pearson, Geoff (1998). 'The English Disease? The Socio-Legal Construction of Football Hooliganism'. *Youth and Policy,* 60: 1–15.

Pearson, Geoff (2012). *An Ethnography of English Football Fans.* Manchester: Manchester University Press.

Pearson, Geoff and James, Mark (2009). 'The Legality and Effectiveness of Using Football Banning Orders in the Fight against Racism and Violence at Sports Events'. In Simon Gardiner, Richard Parrish and Robert Siekmann. *EU, Sport, Law and Policy.* Basingstoke: Palgrave Macmillan, ch.28.

Pearson, Geoff and Sale, Arianna (2011). 'On the Lash: Revisiting the Effectiveness of Alcohol Controls at Football Matches'. *Policing and Society,* 21(2): 150–66.

Pearson, Geoffrey (1983). *Hooligan: A History of Respectable Fears.* Basingstoke: Palgrave Macmillan.

Pearson, Geoffrey (2006). 'Disturbing Continuities: "Peaky Blinders" to "Hoodies"'. *Criminal Justice Matters,* 65(1): 6–7.

Pearson, Geoffrey (2009). '"A Jekyll in the Classroom, a Hyde in the Street": Queen Victoria's Hooligans'. In Andrew Millie (ed.) *Securing Respect: Behavioural Expectations and Anti-social Behaviour in the UK.* Bristol: Policy Press: 41–73.

Pedley, Catherine (2004). 'Maria Marten, or the Murder in the Red Barn: The Theatricality of Provincial Life'. *Nineteenth Century Theatre & Film,* 31(1): 26–38.

Penny, Laurie (2010). 'It was no Cup of Tea Inside the Whitehall Police Kettle'. *New Statesman,* 25 November (http://www.newstatesman.com/blogs/laurie-penny/2010/11/children-police-kettle-protest).

Penny, Laurie (2013). 'Police Violence Won't Stop this New Alliance of Students and Workers'. *The Guardian,* 10 December (http://www.theguardian.com/commentisfree/2013/dec/10/police-violence-students-workers-protests).

Philips, David and Storch, Robert D. (1999). *Policing Provincial England 1829–1856. The Politics of Reform.* London and New York: Leicester University Press.

Phoenix, Jo (2008). 'ASBOs and Working Women: A New Revolving Door'. In Peter Squires (ed.). *ASBO Nation: The Criminalisation of Nuisance.* Bristol: Policy Press, 289–303.

Phoenix, Jo (2009). 'Beyond Risk Assessment: The Return of Repressive Welfarism'. In Fergus McNeil and Monica Barry (eds). *Youth Offending and Youth Justice: Research Highlights in Social Work.* London: Jessica Kingsley.

Pickard, Sarah (2012). Interviews with protestors before and during demonstration, 21 November.

Pickard, Sarah (2014a). 'Productive Protest? The Contested Higher Education Reforms in England under the Coalition Government'. In Emmanuelle Avril and Johann Neem (eds). *Democracy, Participation and Contestation: Civil Society, Governance and the Future of Liberal Democracy.* London and New York: Routledge, 93–106.

Pickard, Sarah (2014b). 'Widening Participation in English Universities: Accessing Social Justice?'. In Sarah Pickard (ed.). *Higher Education in the UK and the US: Converging University Models in a Global Academic World?* Leiden/Boston: Brill, 113–39.

Pickard, Sarah (ed.) (2014c). 'Les Mouvements Sociaux en Mutation'. In Emmanuelle Avril and Pauline Schnapper (eds). *Le Royaume-Uni au XXIe Siècle: Mutation d'un Modèle*. Paris: Ophrys, ch 5.6.

Pickard, Sarah (2014d). '"The Trouble with Young People These Days": "Deviant" Youth, the Popular Press and Politics in Contemporary Britain'. In Emma Bell and Gilles Christoph (eds). 'Labelling the Deviant. Othering and Exclusion in Britain from Past to Present', *Revue Française de Civilisation Britannique (RFCB)* – French Journal of British Studies online (http://www.cercles.com/rfcb).

Pinfold, John (2004). 'Dandy Rats at Play: The Liverpudlian Middle Classes and Horse-Racing in the Nineteenth Century'. In Mike Huggins and James Anthony Mangan (eds). *Disreputable Pleasures: Less Virtuous Victorians at Play*. Abingdon: Frank Cass, 57–82.

Pinker, Steven (2011). *The Better Angels of Our Nature. A History of Violence and Humanity*. Harmondsworth: Penguin.

Piven, Frances and Cloward, Richard (1972). *Regulating the Poor*. London: Tavistock.

Police Service of Northern Ireland (2012). *Anti-Social Behaviour Incidents Recorded by the Police in Northern Ireland: Monthly Update to 31 March 2012*. Northern Ireland Statistics and Research Agency.

Police Service of Northern Ireland (2013). *Police Recorded Security Situation Statistics: Annual Report covering the period 1 April 2012–31 March 2013*. Northern Ireland Statistics and Research Agency.

Poovey, Mary (1995). *Making a Social Body: British Cultural Formation: 1830–1864*. Chicago: University of Chicago Press.

Popplewell, Mr Justice (1986). *Committee of Inquiry into Crowd Safety and Control at Sports Grounds (Final Report)*. London: HMSO.

Porter, Aaron (2010). 'An Inspiring Student Protest that We Won't Let the Violent Undermine'. *The Guardian*, 11 November (http://www.theguardian.com/commentisfree/2010/nov/11/student-protest-violence-political-message).

Porter, Bernard (1987). *The Origins of the Vigilant State*. London: Weidenfeld & Nicolson.

Powell, Ryan (2007). 'Civilising Offensives and Ambivalence: The Case of British Gypsies'. *People, Place and Policy Online*, 1(3): 112–23.

Powell, Ryan and Flint, John (2009). '(In)Formalisation and the Civilising Process: Applying the Work of Norbert Elias to Housing-Based Anti-social Behaviour Interventions in the UK'. *Housing, Theory and Society*, 26(3): 159–78.

Pratt, John; Brown, Mark and Hallsworth, Simon (eds) (2005). *The New Punitiveness: Trends, Theories, Perspectives*. Cullompton: Willan Publishing.

Prison Reform Trust (2011). *Bromley Briefings Prison Factfile: December 2011* (http://www.prisonreformtrust.org.uk/Portals/0/Documents/Bromley%20Briefing%20December%202011.pdf).

Pryce, Ken (1976). *Endless Pressure: A Study of West Indian Life-styles in Bristol*. Harmondsworth: Penguin.

Public Records (1964). *Licensing of Unregistered Clubs for Young People: Working Party Chaired by the Home Secretary to Discuss Provision for New Legislation HO300/24*. London: Public Records Office.

Raban, Jonathan (1974). *Soft City*. London: Hamilton.

Radzinowicz, Leon (1948). *A History of English Criminal Law and its Administration from 1750*. Vol II. London: Stevens.

Ramsay, Peter (2004). 'What is Anti-social Behaviour?' *Criminal Law Review*, November: 908–25.

Ramsay, Peter (2012). *The Insecurity State: Vulnerable Autonomy and the Right to Security in the Criminal Law*. Oxford: Oxford University Press.

Randall, Geoff and Brown, Susan (2002). *Helping Rough Sleepers off the Street: A Report to the Homelessness Directorate*. Wetherby: Office of the Deputy Prime Minister Publications.

Rappaport, Erika Diane (2001). *Shopping for Pleasure: Women in the Making of London's West End*. Princeton: Princeton University Press.

Reay, Diane (2010). 'Tony Blair, the Promotion of the "Active" Educational Citizen, and Middle-Class Hegemony'. In Geoffrey Walford (ed.). *Blair's Educational Legacy?* London: Routledge, 2–13.

Rees, John (2011). 'Student Revolts Then and Now'. In Michael Bailey and Des Freedman. *The Assault on Universities. A Manifesto for Resistance*. London: Pluto Press, 113–22.

Reeves, John (1915). *Recollections of a School Attendance Officer*. London: Stockwell.

Reicher, Steve and Cliff Stott (2011). *Mobs and Englishmen? Myths and Realities of the 2011 Riots*. London: Constable & Robinson Ltd.

Reid, Kiron (2003). 'Law and Disorder: Victorian Restraint and Modern Panic'. In Judith Rowbotham and Kim Stevenson (eds). *Behaving Badly, Social Panic and Moral Outrage – Victorian and Modern Parallels*. Aldershot: Ashgate, 77–96.

Reiner, Robert (2010). *The Politics of the Police*, 4th edition. Oxford: Oxford University Press.

Respect Taskforce (2006). *Respect Action Plan*. London: Home Office.

Richardson, Jo (2006). *The Gypsy Debate: Can Discourse Control?* Exeter: Imprint.

Riley, Dan (2007). 'Anti-social Behaviour: Children, Schools and Parents'. *Education and the Law*. 19(3–4): 221–36.

Riots Communities and Victims Panel (2012). *After the Riots: The Final Report of the Riots Communities and Victims Panel*. London: Ministry of Justice (MJ).

Roberts, Elizabeth (1984). *A Woman's Place: An Oral History of Working-Class Women 1890–1940*. Oxford: Blackwell.

Roberts, Michael (2004). *Making English Morals: Voluntary Association and Moral Reform in England, 1787–1886*. Cambridge: Cambridge University Press.

Roberts, Robert (1990). *The Classic Slum: Salford Life in the First Quarter of the Century*. Harmondsworth: Penguin.

Robinson, Cara (2010). 'Nightscapes and Leisure Spaces: An Ethnography of Young People's use of Free Space'. In Robert MacDonald, Tracy Shildrick and Shane Blackman (eds). *Young People, Class and Place*. London: Routledge, 44–57.

Rodger, John (2006). 'Anti-social Families and Withholding Welfare Support'. *Critical Social Policy*, 26(1): 121–43.

Rodger, John (2008). *Criminalising Social Policy: Anti-Social Behaviour and Welfare in a De-civilised Society*. Cullompton: Willan Publishing.

Rose, Nikolas (1985). *The Psychological Complex: Psychology, Politics and Society in England 1869–1939*. London: Routledge.

Rose, Nikolas (1999). *Powers of Freedom: Reframing Political Thought*. Cambridge: Cambridge University Press.

Rosenfeld, Michael J (1997). 'Celebration, Politics, Selective Looting and Riots: A Micro Level Study of the Bulls Riot of 1992 in Chicago'. *Social Problems*, 44(4): 483–502.

Rough Sleepers Unit (1999). *Coming in From the Cold: The Government's Strategy on Rough Sleeping* (http://webarchive.nationalarchives.gov.uk/20120919132719/http:/www.communities.gov.uk/documents/housing/pdf/roughsleepersstrategy.pdf).

344 *References*

Ruggiero, Vincenzo (1999). 'Drugs as a Password and the Law as a Drug: Discussing the Legalisation of Illicit Substances'. In Nigel South (ed.). *Drugs: Cultures, Controls and Everyday Life*. London: Sage, 123–39.

Russell, Adrienne (2007). 'Digital Communication Networks and the Journalistic Field: The 2005 French Riots'. *Critical Studies in Media Communication*, 24(4): 285–302.

Russell, Bertrand (1916). *Principles of Social Reconstruction*. London: Allen & Unwin.

Ryan, Frances (2012). 'Five Reasons Why "Smart cards" for Benefits Claimants are a Bad Idea'. *New Statesman*, 19 October (http://www.newstatesman.com/politics/2012/10/five-reasons-why-smart-cards-benefits-claimants-are-a-bad-idea).

Ryder, Andrew; Cemlyn, Sarah; Greenfields, Margaret; Richardson, Joanna and Van Cleemput, Patrice. (2012). *Report on Coalition Government Gypsies, Roma and Travellers Policy*. Unpublished Report (http://www.edf.org.uk/blog/?p=19051).

Sacks, Harvey (1992). *Lectures on Conversation*, Volumes I and II, edited by Gail Jefferson with introductions by Emanuel A. Schegloff. Oxford: Blackwell.

Saito, Yuriko (2007). *Everyday Aesthetics*. Oxford: Oxford University Press.

Salter, Michael (1985). 'The Judges v the Football Fan: A Sporting Contest?' *Northern Ireland Law Quarterly*, 36(4): 351–64.

Sampson, Robert J. and Raudenbush, Stephen W. (1999). 'Systematic Social Observation of Public Spaces: A New Look at Disorder in Urban Neighbourhoods'. *American Journal of Sociology*, 105(3): 603–51.

Samuel, Raphael (1981). *East End Underworld: Chapters in the Life of Arthur Harding*. London: Routledge & Kegan Paul.

Sartre, Jean-Paul (1947). *Huis Clos*. Paris: Gallimard.

Saywell, Ruby (2001). *Mary Carpenter of Bristol*. Bristol: Bristol Branch of the Historical Association.

Scanlon, Christopher and Adlam, John (2008). 'Refusal, Social Exclusion and the Cycle of Rejection: A Cynical Analysis?' *Critical Social Policy*, 28(4): 529–49.

Schlör, Joachim (1998). *Nights in the Big City: Paris, Berlin, London, 1840–1930*. London: Reaktion Books Ltd.

Scott, Francis (1879). 'English County Asylums'. *Fortnightly Review*, 26: 114–43.

Scottish Government (2009). *Promoting Positive Outcomes*. Edinburgh: Scottish Government.

Scraton, Phil (2007). *Power, Conflict and Criminalisation*. London: Routledge.

Scruton, Roger (2009). *Beauty*. Oxford: Oxford University Press.

Seddon, Toby (2011). 'What is a Problem Drug User?' *Addiction Research & Theory*, 19(4): 334–43.

Sennett, Richard (1970). *The Uses of Disorder: Personal Identity and City Life*. New York: W.W. Norton and Company, Inc.

Sennett, Richard (1977). *The Fall of Public Man*. New York: Alfred A. Knopf.

Sennett, Richard (2003). *Respect: The Formation of Character in an Age of Inequality*. London: Penguin/Allen Lane.

Sharp, Paul and Peter H. Gosden (1978). *The Development of an Education Service: The West Riding, 1889–1974*. Oxford: Martin Robertson.

Sharpe, J.A. (2000). 'Civility, Civilizing Processes, and the End of Public Punishment in England'. In Peter Burke, Brian Harrison and Paul Slack (eds). *Civil Histories: Essays Presented to Sir Keith Thomas*. Oxford: Oxford University Press, 215–30.

Sheffield Star, The (2010). 'Gypsy Site Race Fear,' *The Sheffield Star*, 28 May (http://www.thestar.co.uk/what-s-on/out-about/gypsy-site-race-fear-1-855451).

Sheldon, Nicola (2009). 'Tackling Truancy: Why Have the Millions Invested not Paid Off?' *History and Policy* (http://www.historyandpolicy.org/papers/policy-paper-84.html).

Sheron, Nick; Hawkey, Chris and Gilmore, Ian (2011). 'Projection of Alcohol Deaths – a Wake Up Call'. *The Lancet*, 377(April 16): 297–9.

Shiman, Lilian Lewis (1988). *Crusade against Drink in Victorian England*. Basingstoke: Macmillan.

Shore, Heather (1999). *Artful Dodgers*. Woodbridge: Boydell Press.

Shore, Heather (2002). *Artful Dodgers: Youth and Crime in Early Nineteenth-Century London*. Woodbridge: Boydell Press.

Shore, Heather (2011). 'Criminality and Englishness in the Aftermath: The Racecourse Wars of the 1920s'. *Twentieth Century British History*, 22(4): 474–97.

Shpayer, Haia (1981). *'British Anarchism 1881–1914: Appearance and Reality'*. PhD dissertation, University College London (UCL).

Shpayer-Makov, Haia (1988). 'Anarchism in British Public Opinion, 1880–1914'. *Victorian Studies*, 31(4): 487–516.

Shubin, Sergei and Swanson, Kate (2010). ' "I'm an Imaginary Figure": Unravelling the Mobility and Marginalisation of Scottish Gypsy Travellers'. *Geoforum*, 41(6): 919–29.

Sibley, David (1981). *Outsiders in Urban Society*. Basingstoke: Palgrave Macmillan.

Silke, Andrew (1998). 'The Lords of Discipline: The Methods and Motives of Paramilitary Vigilantism in Northern Ireland'. *Low Intensity Conflict and Law Enforcement*, 7(2): 121–56.

Silke, Andrew (1999). 'Rebel's Dilemma: The Changing Relationship between the IRA, Sinn Féin and Paramilitary Vigilantism in Northern Ireland'. *Terrorism and Political Violence*, 11(1): 55–93.

Silke, Andrew and Taylor, Max (2000). 'War without End: Comparing IRA and Loyalist Vigilantism in Northern Ireland'. *Howard Journal of Criminal Justice*, 39(3): 249–66.

Simmel, Georg (1964). *Conflict and the Web of Group Affiliations*. [Translated and edited by Kurt Wolff.] Glencoe, IL: Free Press.

Simon, Jonathan (2007). *Governing Through Crime: How the War on Crime Transformed American Democracy and Created a Culture of Fear*. Oxford: Oxford University Press.

Sindall, Rob (1990). *Street Violence in the Nineteenth Century: Media Panic or Real Danger?* Leicester: Leicester University Press.

Singer, Benjamin D. (1970). 'Mass Media and Communication Processes in the Detroit Riot of 1967'. *Public Opinion Quarterly*, 34(2): 236–45.

Skeggs, Beverley and Helen Wood (eds) (2012). *Reacting to Reality Television: Performance, Audience and Value*. London and New York: Routledge.

Slack, James and James Chapman (2010). 'Victims of Anti-social Behaviour Can Name and Shame Police who Don't Help Them, Says Theresa May in Crackdown on Louts'. *Daily Mail*, 5 October (http://www.dailymail.co.uk/news/article-1317757/Theresa-May-Victims-anti-social-behaviour-police-dont-help.html#axzz2K7Zq1IRm).

Slater, Philip E. (1963). 'On Social Regression'. *American Sociological Review*, 28(3): 339–64.

Smith, George (1883). *I've Been a Gipsying, or Rambles Among Gypsies and their Children in their Tents and Vans*. London: T. Fisher Unwin.

Smith, Neil (1996). *The New Urban Frontier: Gentrification and the Revanchist City*. London: Routledge.

Smith, Neil (2001). 'Global Social Cleansing: Postliberal Revanchism and the Export of Zero Tolerance'. *Social Justice*, 28(3): 68–74.

Smith, Olivia (1984). *The Politics of Language, 1791–1819*. Oxford: Oxford University Press.

Smith, Peter J. (1980). 'Planning as Environmental Improvement: Slum Clearance in Victorian Edinburgh'. In Anthony Sutcliffe (ed.). *Planning and the Environment in the*

Modern World: vol 1, The Rise of Modern Urban Planning 1800–1914. London: Mansell, 99–133.

Snow, David A; Burke Rochford, Jr, E.; Worden, Steven K and Benford, Robert D. (1986). 'Frame Alignment Processes, Micromobilization, and Movement Participation'. *American Sociological Review*, 51(4): 464–81.

Social Exclusion Task Force (2007). *Families at Risk: Background on Families with Multiple Disadvantages*. London: Cabinet Office.

Social Exclusion Unit (SEU) (1998). *Truancy and School Exclusion Report* (http://dera.ioe.ac.uk/5074/2/D5074New.pdf).

Society for the Suppression of Vice (1818). *Being a Compendium of the Duties and Powers of Constables and Other Peace Officers; Chiefly as the they relate to the Apprehending of Offenders, and the Laying of Informations before Magistrates* (Third Edition with additions). London.

Society for the Suppression of Vice (1818). *The Constable's Assistant. Being a Compendium of the Duties and Powers of Constables and Other Peace Officers*. London.

Solomon, Clare (2011). 'We Felt Liberated'. In Clare Solomon and Tania Palmieri (eds). *Springtime. The New Student Rebellions*. London: Verso, 11–16.

Solomon, Clare and Palmieri, Tania (eds) (2011). *Springtime. The New Student Rebellions*. London: Verso.

Soloway, Richard (1982). 'Counting the Degenerates: The Statistics of Race Deterioration in Edwardian England'. *Journal of Contemporary History*, 17(1): 137–64.

Sournia, Jean-Charles (1990). *A History of Alcoholism*. Oxford: Basil Blackwell.

South Kesteven District Council (2013). 'What is Anti-social Behaviour?' (http://www.southkesteven.gov.uk/index.aspx?articleid=2137).

Speaight, George (1975). *Bawdy Songs of the Early Music Hall*. London: David & Charles.

Speed, Peter Frederick (1983). *Learning and Teaching in Victorian Times: An Elementary School in 1888*. Harlow: Longman.

Spierenburg, Pieter (2004/2013). *Violence and Punishment: Civilizing the Body through Time*. Cambridge: Polity Press.

Spierenburg, Pieter (2004). 'Social Control and History: An Introduction'. In Clive Emsley, Eric Johnson and Pieter Spierenburg (eds). *Social Control in Europe. v.2: 1800–2000*. Columbus: Ohio State University Press, 1–21.

Springhall, John (1994, Winter). ' "Pernicious Reading"? The "Penny Dreadful" as Scapegoat for Late-Victorian Juvenile Crime'. *Victorian Periodicals Review*, 27(4): 326–49.

Squires, Peter (1990). *Anti-Social Policy: Welfare, Ideology and the Disciplinary State*. Hemel Hempstead: Harvester/Wheatsheaf Books.

Squires, Peter (2006). 'New Labour and the Politics of Anti-Social Behaviour'. *Critical Social Policy*, 26(1): 144–68.

Squires, Peter (ed.) (2008a). *ASBO Nation: The Criminalisation of Nuisance*. Bristol: Policy Press.

Squires, Peter (2008b). 'Why ASB?' In Peter Squires (ed.) *ASBO Nation: The Criminalisation of Nuisance*. Bristol: Policy Press.

Squires, Peter (2008c). 'The Politics of Anti-Social Behaviour'. *British Politics*, 3(3): 300–23.

Squires, Peter and Lea, John (eds) (2012). *Criminalisation and Advanced Marginality: Critically Exploring the Work of Loïc Wacquant*. Bristol: Policy Press.

Squires, Peter and Stephen, Dawn (2005). *Rougher Justice: Anti-Social Behaviour and Young People*. Cullompton: Willan Publishing.

Squires, Peter and Stephen, Dawn (2010). 'Pre-Crime and Precautionary Criminalisation'. *Criminal Justice Matters*, (81): 28–9.

Staab, Joachim Friedrich (1990). 'The Role of News Factors in News Selection: A Theoretical Reconsideration'. *European Journal of Communication*, 5: 423–43.

Standing, Guy (2011). *The Precariat: The New Dangerous Class*. London: Bloomsbury.

Statewatch (2012a). 'Cases of ASBOs used for General Public Order Issues' (http://www.statewatch.org/asbo/asbowatch-puborder.htm).

Statewatch (2012b). 'Cases of ASBOs used Against Protesters' (http://www.statewatch.org/asbo/asbowatch-protesters.htm).

Stedman-Jones, Gareth (1971). *Outcast London: A Study in the Relationship between Classes in Victorian Society*. Oxford: Clarendon Press.

Steedman, Caroline (1984). *Policing the Victorian Community: The Formation of English Provincial Police Forces, 1856–80*. London: Routledge & Kegan Paul.

Stenson, Kevin (2005). 'Sovereignty, Bio-politics and the Local Government of Crime in Britain'. *Theoretical Criminology*, 9(3): 265–87.

Storch, Robert D. (1975). ' "The Plague of Blue Locusts": Police Reform and Popular Resistance in Northern England, 1840–57'. *International Review of Social History*, 20(1): 61–90.

Storch, Robert D. (1976). 'The Policeman as Domestic Missionary: Urban Discipline and Popular Culture in Northern England, 1850–1880'. *Journal of Social History*, 9(4): 481–509.

Storch, Robert D. (1977). 'The Problem of Working-Class Leisure: Some Roots of Middle-Class Moral Reform in the Industrial North: 1825–50'. In A.P. Donajgrodzki (ed.). *Social Control in Nineteenth Century Britain*. London: Croom Helm, 138–62.

Storch, Robert D. (1993). 'The Policeman as Domestic Missionary: Urban Discipline and Popular Culture in Northern England, 1850–80'. In R.J. Morris and Richard Rodger (eds). *The Victorian City: A Reader in British Urban History, 1820–1914*. London: Longman, 281–306.

Stott, Clifford and Pearson, Geoff (2007). *Football Hooliganism: Policing and the War on the English Disease*. London: Pennant Books.

Stott, Clifford; Hoggett, James and Pearson, Geoff (2012). 'Keeping the Peace: Social identity, Procedural Justice and the Policing of Football Crowds'. *British Journal of Criminology*, 52(2): 381–99.

Strange, Julie-Marie (2011). 'Tramp: Sentiment and the Homeless Man in the Late-Victorian and Edwardian City'. *Journal of Victorian Culture*, 16(2): 242–58.

Stratton, Allegra (2013). 'Plan to Divert Benefits of Troubled Families Scrapped'. *BBC News*. 26 September (http://www.bbc.co.uk/news/uk-politics-24286726).

Straus, Murray; Strauss, Arnold and Hotaling, Gerald T. (eds) (1980). *The Social Causes of Husband–Wife Violence*. Minneapolis: University of Minneapolis Press.

Straw, Jack (1995a). 'On the Record. Interviews'. *BBC Online*, 29 October (http://www.bbc.co.uk/otr/intext95-96/Straw29.10.95.html).

Straw, Jack (1995b). *A Quiet Life. Tough Action on Criminal Neighbours*. Labour Party.

Straw, Jack (1996). *Speech by Shadow Home Secretary, Jack Straw, Speech to the NACRO AGM* (www.prnewswire.co.uk/cgi/news/release?id=19432).

Strickland, Pat (2012). *Anti-social Behaviour. The Government's Proposals*. House of Commons Library, SN/HA/6344, 20 August.

Stuart-Smith, Lord Justice (1998). *Scrutiny of Evidence Relating to the Hillsborough Football Stadium Disaster*. London: HMSO.

Sweet, Roey (2002). 'Topographies of Politeness'. *Transactions of the Royal Historical Society*, 6th series, 12: 355–74.

Talbot, Deborah (2004). 'Regulation and Racial Differentiation in the Construction of Night-time Economies: A London Case Study'. *Urban Studies*, 41(4): 887–901.

Talbot, Deborah (2006). 'The Licensing Act 2003 and the Problematisation of the Night-time Economy: Planning, Licensing and Subcultural Closure'. *International Journal of Urban and Regional Research*, 30(1): 159–71.

Talbot, Deborah (2007). *Regulating the Night: Race, Culture and Exclusion in the Making of the Night-time Economy*. Aldershot: Ashgate.

Taylor, David (1997). *The New Police in Nineteenth Century England: Crime, Conflict and Control*. Manchester: Manchester University Press.

Taylor, David (2002). *Policing the Victorian Town: The Development of the Police in Middlesbrough c. 1840–1914*. Basingstoke: Palgrave Macmillan.

Taylor, Lord Justice (1990). *Hillsborough Stadium Disaster (Final Report)*. London: HMSO.

Taylor, Rebecca (2008). *A Minority and the State: Travellers in Britain in the Twentieth Century*. Manchester: Manchester University Press.

Taylor, Rebecca (2011). 'Britain's Gypsy Travellers: A People on the Outside'. *History Today*, 61(6) (http://www.historytoday.com/becky-taylor/britains-gypsy-travellers-people-outside).

Taylor, Rebecca (2014). *Another Darkness, Another Dawn: A History of Gypsies, Roma and Travellers*. London: Reaktion Press.

Thane, Pat (1996). *Foundations of the Welfare State*. Second edition. London: Routledge.

Thomas, Terry (2005). 'The Continuing Story of the ASBO'. *Youth and Policy*, 87(Spring): 5–14.

Thompson, Edward (1991). *Customs in Common*. Harmondsworth: Penguin.

Thompson, F[rancis] M[ichael] L. (1988). *The Rise of Respectable Society: A Social History of Victorian Britain, 1830–1900*. London: Fontana Press.

Thompson, F[rancis] M[ichael] L. (ed.) (1990). *The Cambridge Social History of Britain, 1750–1950, Volume 3: Social Agencies and Institutions*. Cambridge: Cambridge University Press.

Thompson, Ken (1998). *Moral Panics*. London: Routledge.

Thorp, Arabella and Kennedy, Steven (2010). 'The Problems of British Society: Is Britain Broken? What are the Policy Implications?' *Key Issues for the New Parliament 2010*. House of Commons Library Research Paper: 68 (http://www.parliament.uk/documents/commons/lib/research/key_issues/Full-doc.pdf).

Till, Jeremy (2012). 'The Broken Middle: The Space of the London Riots'. *Cities: The International Journal of Urban Policy and Planning*, 34: 71–4.

Tisdall, Kay (2006). 'Anti-social Behaviour Legislation Meets Children's Services: Challenging Perspectives on Children, Families and the State'. *Critical Social Policy*, 26(1): 101–20.

Tonkin, Emma; Pfeiffer, Heather D. and Tourte, Greg (2012). 'Twitter, Information Sharing and the London Riots?' *Bulletin of the American Society for Information Science and Technology*, 38(2): 49–57.

Tonry, Michael (2004). *Punishment and Politics: Evidence and Emulation in the Making of English Crime Control Policy*. Cullompton: Willan Publishing.

Tonry, Michael (2010). 'The Costly Consequences of Populist Posturing: ASBOs, Victims, "Rebalancing" and Diminution in Support for Civil Liberties'. *Punishment & Society*, 12(4): 387–413.

Topping, Alexandra and Bawdon, Fiona (2011). ' "It Was Like Christmas": A Consumerist Feast Amid the Summer Riots'. *The Guardian*, 5 December (http://www.guardian.co.uk/uk/2011/dec/05/summer-riots-consumerist-feast-looters).

Travis, Alan (2006). 'Sinbins for Problem Families as Blair Attacks Yob Culture'. *The Guardian*, 11 January.

Travis, Alan (2010). 'Theresa May to Scrap ASBOs'. *The Guardian*. 28 July (http://www.theguardian.com/society/2010/jul/28/theresa-may-scraps-asbos).

Travis, Alan (2011). 'Youth Justice Board Saved before Expected Lords Defeat'. *The Guardian*, 23 November (http://www.guardian.co.uk/society/2011/nov/23/youth-justice-board-saved).

Treadwell, James (2008). ' "Call the (Fashion) Police": How Fashion Becomes Criminalised'. *Papers from the British Criminology Conference*, (8): 117–33.

Tremlett, Annabel (2013). 'Demotic or Demonic? Race, Class and Gender in "Gypsy" Reality TV'. *Sociological Review*. DOI: 10.1111/1467-954X.12134.

Turner, Royce (2002). 'Gypsies and British Parliamentary Language: An Analysis'. *Romani Studies*, 12(1): 1–34.

UK Drug Policy Commission (UKDPC) (2010). 'Representations of Drug use and Drug Users in the British Press'. London: UK Drug Policy Commission.

United Nations (UN) (2009). *United Nations Drug Report* (http://www.unodc.org/unodc/en/data-and-analysis/WDR-2009.html).

Valentine, Gill and McDonald, Ian (2004). *Understanding Prejudice, Attitudes towards Minorities*. London: Stonewall.

Valverde, Mariana (1997). ' "Slavery from Within": The Invention of Alcoholism and the Question of Free Will'. *Social History*, 22(3): 251–68.

Vamplew, Wray (1976). *The Turf: A Social and Economic History of Horse Racing*. London: Allen Lane.

Vamplew, Wray (1988). *Pay Up and Play the Game: Professional Sport in Britain 1875–1914*, Cambridge: Cambridge University Press.

van Cleemput, Patricia and Parry, Glenys (2001). 'Health Status of Gypsy Travellers'. *Journal of Public Health Medicine*, 23(2): 129–34.

Van Dijk, Jan; Tseloni, Andromachi and Farrell, Graham (2012). *The International Crime Drop: New Directions in Research*. Basingstoke: Palgrave Macmillan.

Van Wel, Fritz (1992). 'A Century of Families under Supervision in the Netherlands'. *British Journal of Social Work*, 22(2): 147–66.

Varul, Matthias Zick (2011). 'Veblen in the (Inner) City: On the Normality of Looting'. *Sociological Research Online*, 16(4) (http://www.socresonline.org.uk/16/4/22.html).

Virilio, Paul (2004). *Ville Panique*. Paris: Éditions Galilée. [Translated by Rose, Julie. *City of Panic*. Oxford, New York: Berg, 2005].

von Hirsch, Andrew and Simester, Andrew (ed.) (2006). *Incivilities: Regulating Offensive Behaviour*. Oxford: Hart Publishing.

Vowles, Gordon (2003). *A Century of Achievement: A History of Local Education Authorities in Bedfordshire 1903–2003*. Bedford: Bedfordshire County Council.

Wacquant, Loïc (2001). 'The Penalisation of Poverty and the Rise of Neo-Liberalism'. *European Journal of Criminal Policy and Research*, 9(4): 401–12.

Wacquant, Loïc (2009). *Punishing the Poor: The Neo-liberal Government of Social Insecurity*. Durham, NC: Duke University Press.

Wacquant, Loïc (2013). Class, Ethnicity and the State in the Making of Marginality. Revisiting Urban Outcasts: http://loicwacquant.net/assets/Papers/REVISITINGURBANOUTCASTS-Danish-article-version.pdf

Waddington, David (2012). 'The Law of Moments: Understanding the Flashpoint that Ignited the Riots'. *Criminal Justice Matters*, 87(1): 6–7.

Waiton, Stuart (2008). *The Politics of Anti-social Behaviour. Amoral Panics*. London: Routledge.

Walker, Samuel (1984). ' "Broken Windows" and Fractured History: The Use and Misuse of History in Recent Patrol Analysis'. *Justice Quarterly*, 1(1): 75–90.

Walkowitz, Judith (1980). *Prostitution and Victorian Society. Women, Class and the State.* Cambridge: Cambridge University Press.

Walkowitz, Judith (1992). *City of Dreadful Delight: Narratives of Sexual Danger in Late-Victorian London.* London: Virago.

Walters, Reece (2009). *Crime is in the Air: Air Pollution and Regulation in the UK.* London: Centre for Crime and Justice Studies (CCJS).

Walton, John K. and Wilcox, Alastair (1991). *Low Life and Moral Improvement in Mid-Victorian England: Liverpool through the Journalism of Hugh Shimmin.* Leicester: Leicester University Press.

War on Want (2012). *Avoiding Avoidance* (http://www.waronwant.org/attachments/Avoiding%20Avoidance.pdf).

Ward, Colin (ed.) (1973). *Vandalism.* London: Architectural Press.

Warner John, H. (1980) 'Physiological Theory and Therapeutic Explanation in the 1860s: The British Debate on the Medical Use of Alcohol'. *Bulletin of the History of Medicine*, 54(2): 235–57.

Warner, Jessica (2003). *Craze: Gin and Debauchery in an Age of Reason.* London: Profile Books.

Waters, Christopher (1990). *British Socialists and the Politics of Popular Culture 1884 to 1914.* Manchester: Manchester University Press.

Watson, Sophie and Austerberry, Helen (1986). *Housing and Homelessness: A Feminist Perspective.* London: Routledge & Kegan Paul.

Webb, Sydney and Webb, Beatrice (1903). *The History of Liquor Licensing in England, Principally from 1700–1830.* London: Longmans and Co.

Weinberger, Barbara (1981). 'The Police and the Public in Mid-Nineteenth Century Warwickshire'. In Victor Bailey (ed.). *Policing and Punishment in Nineteenth Century Britain.* London: Croom Helm.

Weiner, Martin (1990). *Reconstructing the Criminal: Culture, Law and Politics in England, 1830–1914.* Cambridge: Cambridge University Press.

Welshman, John (2012). *From Transmitted Deprivation to Social Exclusion: Policy, Poverty and Parenting.* Bristol: Policy Press.

White, Arnold (1886). *The Problems of a Great City.* London: Remington and Co.

White, Arnold (1909, July). 'Eugenics and National Efficiency'. *Eugenics Review*, 1(2): 105–11.

White, Rob and Cunneen, Chris (2006). 'Social Class, Youth Crime and Justice'. in Barry Goldson and John Muncie. *Youth Crime and Justice: Critical Issues.* London: Sage, 17–29.

Whiteford, Martin (2013). 'New Labour, Street Homelessness and Social Exclusion: A Defaulted Promissory Note?' *Housing Studies*, 28(1): 10–32.

Whyte, David (2004). 'Punishing Anti-social Business'. *New Law Journal*: 1293.

Whyte, David (2007). 'Gordon Brown's Charter for Corporate Criminals'. *Criminal Justice Matters*, 70: 32.

Wiener, Martin J. (1990). *Reconstructing the Criminal: Culture, Law and Policy in England, 1830–1914.* Cambridge: Cambridge University Press.

Williams, Chris A. (2003). 'Catégorisation et Stigmatisation Policières à Sheffield au Milieu du XIXe Siècle'. *Revue d'Histoire Moderne et Contemporaine*, 1(50): 104–25.

Williams, Karel (1981). *From Pauperism to Poverty.* London: Routledge.

Willis, Paul (1978). *Profane Culture.* London: Routledge & Kegan Paul.

Wilson, Andrew (2007). *Northern Soul: Music, Drugs and Subcultural Identity.* Cullompton: Willan Publishing.

Wilson, Andrew; May, Tiggey; Warburton, Hamish; Lupton, Ruth and Turnbull, Paul (2002). 'Heroin and Crack Cocaine Markets in Deprived Areas: Seven Local Case Studies'. CASE Report 19. London: London School of Economics (LSE).

Wilson, Graeme (2011). ' "Feral Underclass" to Blame for Riots'. *The Sun*, 6 September (http://www.thesun.co.uk/sol/homepage/news/3797021/Feral-underclass-to-blame -for-riots.html).

Wilson, James (1985). *Thinking about Crime*. New York: Vintage Books.

Wilson, James and Kelling, George L. (1982) 'Broken Windows: The Police and Neighbourhood Safety'. *Atlantic Monthly*, 249(3): 29–38.

Winston, Tom (1997). 'Alternatives to Punishment Beatings and Shootings in a Loyalist Community in Belfast'. *Critical Criminology*, 8(1): 122–8.

Winter, Andrew (1879). *The Borderlands of Insanity and Other Papers*: London: Henry Renshow.

Winter, James (1993). *London's Teeming Streets 1830–1914*. London: Routledge.

Wintour, Patrick (2007). 'Blair's Respect Agenda Ditched, Claim Tories'. *The Guardian*, 24 December (http://www.guardian.co.uk/politics/2007/dec/24/uk.publicservices1).

Wintour, Patrick (2011a). 'David Cameron Unveils £448m Plan to Help "Problem Families" '. *The Guardian*, 15 December (http://www.guardian.co.uk/politics/2011/dec/ 15/david-cameron-plan-problem-families).

Wintour, Patrick (2011b). 'David Cameron Appoints Louise Casey to Lead Government Response to Riots'. *The Guardian*, 12 October (http://www.guardian.co.uk/ society/2011/oct/12/david-cameron-louise-casey-riots).

Wise, Sarah (2008). *The Blackest Streets: The Life and Death of a Victorian Slum*. London: Bodley Head.

Wise, Sarah (2009). *The Blackest Streets. The Life and Death of a Victorian Slum*. London: Vintage.

Wise, Sarah (2012). *Inconvenient People: Lunacy, Liberty and the Mad Doctors in Victorian England*. London: Bodley Head.

Wohl, Anthony, S. (1977). *The Eternal Slum: Housing and Social Policy in Victorian London*. London: Edward Arnold.

Wollaston, Sam (2012). 'TV review – "Gypsy Blood: True Stories" '. *The Guardian*, 19 January (http://www.theguardian.com/tv-and-radio/2012/jan/19/gypsy-blood-true-stories-review).

Wood Report (1929). 'Report of the Mental Deficiency Committee being a Joint Committee of the Board of Education and Board of Control'. London: HMSO.

Wood, J. Carter (2004). *Violence and Crime in Nineteenth-Century England: The Shadow of our Refinement*. London: Routledge.

Wood, J. Carter (2007). 'Locating Violence: The Spatial Production and Construction of Physical Aggression'. In Katherine D. Watson (ed.). *Assaulting the Past: Violence and Civilization in Historical Context*. Newcastle: Cambridge Scholars Publishing, 20–37.

Wouters, Cas (1986). 'Formalization and Informalization: Changing Tension Balances in Civilizing Processes'. *Theory, Culture & Society*, 3(2): 1–18.

Wouters, Cas (2007). *Informalization: Manners and Emotions Since 1890*. London: Sage.

Wynn Davies, Patricia (1993). 'Ministers Keep up Campaign against Single Mothers'. *The Independent*, 8 July.

Wynn-Jones, Michael (1979). *The Derby: A Celebration of the World's Most Famous Horse Race*. London: Croom Helm.

Young, Alison (2014). *Street Art, Public City: Law, Crime and the Urban Imagination*. Abingdon: Routledge.

Young, Jock (1971). *The Drugtakers: The Social Meaning of Drug Use*. London: Paladin.

Young, Jock (1988). 'Radical Criminology in Britain: The Emergence of a Competing Paradigm'. *British Journal of Criminology*, 28(2): 159–83.

Young, John H. (1881). *Our Deportment, or the Manners, Conduct and Dress of the Most Refined Society*. Chicago: Union Publishing House (http://www.gutenberg.org/files/17609/17609.txt).

Youth Justice Board (YJB) (2006). *A Summary of Research into Anti-Social Behaviour Orders Given to Young People between January 2004 and January 2005* (http://www.yjb.gov.uk/Publications/Resources/Downloads/ASBO%20Summary.pdf).

Youth Justice Board (YJB) (2006). *Anti-Social Behaviour Orders*. London: Youth Justice Team (YJT).

Youth Justice Board (YJB) (2012). *Youth Justice Statistics 2010/2011. England & Wales*.

Youth Justice Board (YJB) (2013). *Youth Justice Statistics 2011/2012. England & Wales* (https://www.gov.uk/government/uploads/system/uploads/attachment_data/file/218552/yjb-stats-2011-12.pdf).

Zedner, Lucia (1991). *Women, Crime and Custody*. Oxford: Clarendon Press.

Zemon Davis, Natalie (1971). 'The Reasons of Misrule: Youth Groups and Charivaris in Sixteenth-Century France'. *Past & Present*, 50(1): 41–75.

Zhang, Ming (2004). 'Time to Change the Truancy Laws? Compulsory Education: Its Origin and Modern Dilemma'. *Pastoral Care in Education*, 22(2): 27–33.

Zimbardo, Philip G. (1973). 'A Field Experiment in Auto Shaping'. In Colin Ward (ed.). *Vandalism*, London: Architectural Press.

Zinberg, Norman (1984). *Drug, Set, and Setting: The Basis for Controlled Intoxicant Use*. New Haven: Yale University Press.

Žižek, Slavoj (2009). *Violence*. London: Profile Books.

Zukin, Sharon (1989). *Loft Living: Culture and Capital in Urban Change*. New Brunswick: Rutgers University Press.

Zukin, Sharon (1991). *Landscapes of Power: from Detroit to Disney World*. California: University of California Press.

Zukin, Sharon (1995). *The Cultures of Cities*. Oxford: Blackwell Publishers Inc.

Government Bills, Acts, Legislation, Statutes, Select Committees

Alcohol etc. (Scotland) Act 2010.
Aliens Act 1905.
Anti-social Behaviour Act 2003.
Anti-social Behaviour (Northern Ireland) Order 2004.
Anti-social Behaviour, Crime and Policing Act 2014.
Anti-social Behaviour, Crime and Policing Bill 2013–14.
Beerhouse Act 1830.
Beerhouse Act 1834.
Beerhouse Act 1840.
Black Act 1723.
Borough Police Act 1844.
Caravan Sites Act 1968 (c. 52).
Casual Poor Law Act 1882.
Children and Young Persons Act 1908 (8 Edw. 7, c. 67).
Clean Neighbourhoods and Environment Act 2005.
Common Lodging Houses Act 1853.
Crime and Disorder Act 1998.
Criminal Justice and Court Services Act 2000.

Criminal Justice and Immigration Bill 2007–08.
Criminal Justice and Police Act 2001.
Criminal Justice and Public Order Act 1994 (c. 33).
Cruelty to Animals Act 1835 (5 & 6 Will. 4, c. 59).
Disorderly Houses Act 1752.
Education Act 1902.
Education Act 1994.
Education Act 1996.
Elementary Education Act 1870 (33 & 34 Vict. c. 75).
Elementary Education Act 1876.
Elementary Education Act 1880.
Equality Act 2010, C. 15.
European Convention on Human Rights 1950.
Factory and Workshop Acts 1878.
Factory and Workshop Acts 1901.
Football (Disorder) Act 2000.
Football (Offences and Disorder) Act 1999.
Football (Offences) Act 1991.
Football Spectators Act 1989.
Geneva Conventions 1949.
Higher Education Act 2004.
Homelessness (Priority Need for Accommodation) (England) Order 2002.
Homelessness Act 2002.
Housing (Homeless Persons) Act 1977.
Housing Act 1996.
Housing of the Working Classes Act 1885 (c. 72).
Housing of the Working Classes Act 1890 (29 & 30 Vict. c. 90).
Licensing Act 2003.
Local Government Act 1888 (51 & 52 Vict. c.41).
Metropolitan Police Act 1839.
Metropolitan Police Act 1929.
National Assistance Act 1948.
Nuisance Removal Act 1855.
Police and Justice Act 2006.
Police Reform Act 2002.
Police Reform and Social Responsibility Act 2011.
Prevention of Cruelty to, and Better Protection of, Children Act 1889 (52 & 53 Vict. c.44).
Prisons Act 1865.
Prisons Act 1877.
Public Decency Act 1986.
Public Health Act 1875.
Public Order Act 1986.
Racecourse Licensing Act 1879 (43 Vict. c. 18).
Sanitary Improvement Act 1845.
Sporting Events (Control of Alcohol) Act 1985.
Teaching and Higher Education Act 1998.
Town Police Clauses Act 1847 (51 & 52 Vict. c. 47).
Vagrancy Act 1349.
Vagrancy Act 1824.

Violent Crime Reduction Act 2006.

11 Henry VII.c.2 (1495).
19 Henry VII.c.12 (1504).
5&6 Edward VI.c.25 (1552).

HO 144 871 160552
HO45 10406 A46794
HO45 3017
HO45 3537
HO45 9613A9
HO45 9645A3

'Aliens Bill', Second Reading. House of Lords Sitting, 1894.
'Anarchist meeting in Trafalgar Square'. House of Commons Sitting, 1893.
'Anarchist Meetings in Trafalgar Square'. House of Commons Sitting, 1893.
'The Anarchist Bourdin'. House of Commons Sitting, 1894.
'The Anarchists in Trafalgar Square'. House of Commons Reading, 1893.
'The Anarchists'. House of Commons Sitting, 1893.
'Foreign Anarchists in London'. House of Commons Sitting, 1894.
'The Greenwich Explosion'. House of Commons Sitting. 1894.
'Public meetings in Trafalgar Square'. House of Commons Sitting, 1893.
'Trafalgar Square Meetings'. House of Commons Sitting, 1898.

Hansard's Parliamentary Debates: Habitual Drunkards Bill. HC Deb, 12 July 1871, Volume 207 cc.1501–25.
Hansard's Parliamentary Debates: Habitual Drunkards Bill. HC Deb, 3 July 1878, Volume 241 cc. 688–724.
Hansard's Parliamentary Debates: Habitual Drunkards-Resolution. HC Deb, 4 March 1870, Volume 199 cc. 1241–8.
House of Commons (HC) (1844). *Minutes of Evidence Taken Before the Select Committee on Gaming*. H. C. 297.
House of Commons (HC) (2014). Deb 4 February, Volume 575, Column 1WH (http://www.publications.parliament.uk/pa/cm201314/cmhansrd/cm140204/halltext/140204h0001.htm#14020454000001).

Parliamentary papers

PP 1852, vol VII. Select Committee on Criminal and Destitute Juveniles.
PP 1852 (6), vol XLI. Abstract of Return of Number of Juvenile Offenders Committed to Prison in England and Wales.
PP 1852–53, vol XXIII. Select Committee on the Treatment of Criminal and Destitute Children, together with proceedings of the Committee and minutes of evidence.
PP 1854, vol VI. Youthful Offenders Act.
PP 1906, *Report of the Departmental Committee on Vagrancy, 1906*. PP 103: II, Cmd 2891. London: Stationery Office.
Select Committee of the House of Lords. Session, 1878–79. Report from the Select Committee of the House of Lords on Intemperance together with the Proceedings of the Committee, and an Appendix.
Select Committee on Habitual Drunkards. 1872. Report from the Select Committee on Habitual Drunkards with proceedings, minutes of evidence, appendix and index.

Archives

Archives de la Préfecture de Police de Paris (APP). BA1508, BA1509, BA435.

Bristol Record Office collections

BRO 40556. Volume of extracts from the Western Daily Press regarding 53 Bristol schools, hospitals and benevolent institutions, 1883.
BRO 12693/3. Rules and Regulations of the Red Lodge Girls' Reformatory School
BRO 12693/7. Records of Mary Carpenter and the Red Lodge Reformatory, Minute Book 1; 1878–89.
BRO12693/1. Red Lodge Journal, 1855–57.
BRO 12693/13. Red Lodge Certificate.

Periodicals

Blackwood's (1861). 'On Manners'. *Blackwood's Edinburgh Magazine*, 90(550): 154–65. August.
Bow Bells (1866). 'Etiquette for Gentlemen'. *Bow Bells*, 5(118): 330. 31 October.
Bradford Observer (1871). 'Rowdyism'. *Bradford Observer*, 28 June.
Chambers' (1853). 'The Dignity of Non-Complaint'. *Chambers' Edinburgh Journal*, N.S. 149: 289–90. 7 November.
Chelmsford Chronicle.
Cheshire Observer (1860). 'Street Nuisances'. *Cheshire Observer*, 27 October.
Daily News (1887). 'Aristocratic Rowdyism'. *Daily News*, 1 October.
Eclectic Review (1860). 'The Amenities of Social Life'. *Eclectic Review*, 4: 292–8. September.
Edinburgh Evening News.
Hearth and Home (1897). 'Manners for Women'. *Hearth and Home*, 23 December.
Household Words (1851). 7 June.
Huddersfield Chronicle (1890). 'Youthful Ruffianism'. *Huddersfield Chronicle*, 23 August.
John Bull (1870). 'Accidents and Offences'. *John Bull*, 12 November.
Le Gaulois.
Leicester Chronicle (1852). 'Ritual Treatment of Women'. *Leicester Chronicle*, 21 August.
Liverpool Mercury (1843). 'Civilizing Amusements'. *Liverpool Mercury*, 7 July.
Liverpool Mercury (1869). 'Grievous Public Nuisances'. *Liverpool Mercury*, 8 February.
London Society (1864). 'Politeness, Insular and Continental'. *London Society*, 6(36): 396–404. November.
Manchester Courier.
Manchester Evening News.
Manchester Times (1893). 'Civility'. *Manchester Times*, 14 July.
Morning Post (1856). 'Street Nuisances'. *Morning Post*, 30 September.
Morning Post (1870). 'A Lady's Plaint'. *Morning Post*, 18 March.
Nottingham Evening Post.
Otautau Standard and Wallace County Chronicle.
Pall Mall Gazette (London).
Pall Mall Gazette (1882). Untitled. *Pall Mall Gazette*, 21 March.
Punch (1870). 'Our Roughs and Rulers'. *Punch*, 19 November.
Reynold's Miscellany (1855). 'Civility'. *Reynold's Miscellany*, 14(364): 359.
Reynold's Newspaper (1851a). 'Police Ruffianism and its Results'. *Reynold's Newspaper*, 11 May.

Reynold's Newspaper (1851b). 'Aristocratic Ruffianism'. *Reynold's Newspaper*, 10 August.

Reynold's Newspaper (1859). 'Ruffianism in Broadcloth'. *Reynold's Newspaper*, 24 July.

Reynold's Newspaper (1869). 'Aristocratic Rowdyism'. *Reynold's Newspaper*, 11 July.

Reynold's Newspaper (1900). 'Rejoicings versus Rowdyism'. *Reynold's Newspaper*, 27 May.

Saturday Review (1870). 'Inefficiency of the London Police'. *Saturday Review*, 29(757): 574–5. 30 April.

Saturday Review (1877). 'Social Rowdyism'. *Saturday Review*, 44(1141): 301–2. 8 September.

Saturday Review (1880). 'Street Nuisances'. Saturday Review, 49(1286): 786–7. 19 June.

Sheffield & Rotherham Independent (1843). 'Street Nuisances'. *Sheffield and Rotherham Independent*, 28 October.

Sheffield & Rotherham Independent (1878). 'Ruffianism Rampant'. *Sheffield and Rotherham Independent*, 5 November.

Sheffield Evening Telegraph.

The Bristol Mercury and Daily Post.

The Daily Express (2013). 'Giggling Toddler Warned of Asbo,' 14 May.

The Daily Express (2013). 'Pet owner Threatened with Asbo Because Parrot won't Stop Singing Old MacDonald', 23 August.

The Daily Mail (2012). 'Is this Britain's meanest moggy? Oscar the "ASBO cat"'. 7 November (www.dailymail.co.uk/ . . . /Is-Britains-meanest-moggy-Oscar-ASBO-cat-terrorises-village-retired-colonel-hospital-days.html).

The Daily Mirror (2011). 'UK Riots: Mindless Rioting Highlights Folly of Firing Police'. 10 August (http://www.mirror.co.uk/news/uk-news/uk-riots-mindless-rioting-highlights-146714#ixzz2rauA8YyX).

The Daily News.

The Encore.

The Era.

The Era (1884). 'Officers and Gentlemen'. *The Era*, 21 June.

The Examiner (1858). 'The Street Nuisances'. *The Examiner*, 2622: 275–6. 1 May.

The Examiner (1863). 'The Great Street Nuisance'. *The Examiner*, 2895: 466–7. 25 January.

The Performer.

The Spectator (http://archive.spectator.co.uk).

The Sunday Express (2005). 'Cut Council Tax bill if Gypsies Can Live Near our Houses'. 23 January: 50.

The Times.

The Times (1857). 'Street Nuisances'. *The Times*, 25 November.

The Times (1877). 'Seaside Manners'. *The Times*, 4 September.

The Yorkshire Herald.

Western Mail.

Western Times.

Case list

Austin v Commissioner of Police of the Metropolis (2009). 1 AC 564.

Barnfather v Islington London Borough Council (2003). EWHC 418 (Admin).

Chief Constable of Avon and Somerset v Bargh (2011). Bristol Magistrates' Court, 27 January.

Chief Constable of Greater Manchester v Clarke (2006). Trafford Magistrates' Court, 14 February.

Chief Constable of Greater Manchester v Messer (2012). Manchester City Magistrates' Court, 16 December.
Chief Constable of Greater Manchester v Reilly (2006). Trafford Magistrates' Court, 16 February.
Chief Constable of Greater Manchester v Sutton (2006). Trafford Magistrates' Court, 13 February.
Gough and Smith v Chief Constable of Derbyshire (2002). EWCA Civ 351.
Leeds United Football Club Ltd v Chief Constable of West Yorkshire (2013). EWCA Civ 115.
Mengesha v Commissioner of Police for the Metropolis (2013). EWHC 1695 (Admin).
R (Laporte) v Chief Constable of Gloucestershire Constabulary (2007). 2 All ER 529.

Songs

Plan B (2012). *Ill Manors*. London: Atlantic Records (title track).
Skinnyman (2004). *Council Estate of Mind*. London: Low Life Records.
U2 (1981). *October*. London: Island Records.

Television programmes

Little Britain (2003–06). BBC (www.bbc.co.uk/comedy/littlebritain).
My Big Fat Gypsy Wedding (2010). Channel 4, 18 February.
Newsnight (2010). BBC. 'Hijacked Protest or True Student Feeling?' 10 November (http://news.bbc.co.uk/2/hi/programmes/newsnight/9180613.stm).
Maguire, Leo (2012). 'Gypsy Blood'. Channel 4 TV documentary.

Index